South Vietnam

U.S.-Communist
Confrontation in
Southeast Asia

Volume 6

1971

South Vietnam

U.S.-Communist Confrontation in Southeast Asia

Volume 6
1971

Edited by Lester A. Sobel
Contributing editor: Hal Kosut

FACTS ON FILE, INC.   NEW YORK, N.Y.

South Vietnam

U.S.-Communist Confrontation in Southeast Asia

Volume 6

1971

Library of Congress Card Catalog No. 66-23943
ISBN 0-87196-238-1
9 8 7 6 5 4 3 2 1
PRINTED IN
THE UNITED STATES OF AMERICA

Contents

	Page
Foreword	1
U.S. Policy	3
The Fighting	13
South Vietnamese Offensive in Laos	25
Paris Talks & POWs	47
Fighting Continues	59
U.S. Policy Debate	99
The Pentagon Papers	121
The Substance of the Pentagon Papers	136
U.S. Dissent	173
Atrocities & War Crimes	199
Politics, Drugs & Other Developments	211
Index	235

Foreword

THIS CHRONICLE OF THE U.S. involvement in Vietnam during 1971 is the sixth volume in the FACTS ON FILE record of the conflict in Indochina.

1971 was a year in which many Americans began to have fresh hope that their country would finally extricate itself from the war in Southeast Asia. U.S. troops continued to leave Vietnam for home under the Vietnamization policy, and the number of U.S. servicemen in Vietnam declined from about 280,000 at the beginning of 1971 to some 159,000 as the year ended. President Richard M. Nixon's announcement of his plan to visit mainland China in 1972 produced a short-lived wave of euphoria as even some of his most bitter critics lauded him for what they described as a bold stroke in the direction of resolving the Vietnam dilemma. The Paris talks began to show signs of agonizingly slow progress during 1971, and Communist negotiators suggested that all prisoners would be freed if the U.S. troop withdrawal were hastened and completed. Antiwar Congress members in the U.S., however, failed in efforts to enforce a deadline for the departure of the American soldiers.

Meanwhile, the fighting continued. As the U.S. combat role diminished in Indochina, the number of Americans being killed in action there dropped—from 4,204 in 1970 to 1,386 in 1971. The total number of Americans killed in the more than a decade of U.S. involvement in Indochina, however, rose to

more than 45,600 by the end of 1971. South Vietnam lost
about 21,500 servicemen killed in 1971, and Viet Cong/North
Vietnamese combat deaths were estimated at 97,000. South
Vietnamese and Cambodian troops continued operations
against Communist forces in Cambodia during 1971. The U.S.
provided air support for a South Vietnamese drive to smash
North Vietnamese supply bases along the Ho Chi Minh Trail
in Laos. Control of the Boloven Plateau in southern Laos and
of Laos' strategic Plaine des Jarres shifted hands at least twice.
Much of 1971's fighting took place in northern South Vietnam
and along the demilitarized zone between North and South
Vietnam.

Controversy flared during 1971 with the publication of the
"Pentagon papers," which cast light on U.S. government de-
liberations over Vietnam. U.S. antiwar protests were generally
at a more moderate level than in previous years. The radical
Mayday Tribe's efforts to "close down" Washington resulted
in mass arrests. Lt. William Calley was convicted of the
murder of South Vietnamese civilians in Mylai.

In South Vietnam, Nguyen Van Thieu was reelected
president in an election in which he was the sole candidate. And
the U.S. acted against an "epidemic" of drug addiction among
GIs in Vietnam.

This book consists almost exclusively of the printed record
from the weekly issues of FACTS ON FILE. Any editorial
changes, generally minor, were usually made to eliminate
repetition, correct errors or add facts that might not have been
available when the original record was being compiled. As in
all FACTS ON FILE books, great pains were taken to make this
volume a balanced and accurate reference work and to keep it
free of bias.

U.S. Policy

Nixon claims progress. President Nixon claimed Jan. 4 that the primary achievement of the first two years of his Administration was that "we can now see the end of Americans' combat role in Vietnam in sight." In an hour-long, televised conversation with four network correspondents, Nixon admitted that while the U.S. had not yet ended the war in Vietnam, "we are on the way out and we're on the way out in a way that will bring a just peace, the kind of peace that will discourage that kind of aggression in the future and will build, I hope, the foundation for a generation of peace."

When a reporter asked the President to disclose the reasons for the U.S.' bombing raids on North Vietnam during December 1970, Nixon said: "There was an understanding that after the bombing halt [in 1968], that unarmed reconnaissance planes could fly over North Vietnam with impunity. We had to insist on that because otherwise we would have no intelligence with regard to what they were planning on an attack. So when they fire on those planes, I've given instructions that we will take out the SAM site or whatever it is that has fired upon them. We will continue to do so. And if they say there is no understanding in that respect, then there are no restraints whatever on us."

"Now the other understanding is one that I have laid down. . . . It is a new one which goes along with our Vietnamization program and our withdrawal program. Now the President of the United States as commander in chief owes a responsibility to those men [the 280,000 U.S. troops currently remaining in South Vietnam] to see that they are not subjected to an overwhelming attack from the North. That's why we must continue reconnaissance. And that is why, also, if the enemy at a time we are trying to deescalate, at a time we are withdrawing, starts to build up its infiltration, starts moving troops and supplies through the Mugia Pass and other passes, then I as commander in chief will have to order bombing strikes on those key areas."

Asked how the U.S. would respond if there were a massive North Vietnamese attack on South Vietnam in 1972 after most American troops had been withdrawn, Nixon said: ". . . our Vietnamization policy has been very carefully drawn up, and we are withdrawing in a measured way on the basis that the South Vietnamese will be able to defend themselves as we withdraw." ". . . it is possible, of course, that at that time [after the U.S. has withdrawn] North Vietnam might launch an attack. But I am convinced that at that time, based on the training program of the South Vietnamese . . . that they will be able to hold their own and defend themselves in 1972."

Laird on Indochina situation. U.S. Defense Secretary Melvin R. Laird visited Thailand Jan. 7 and South Vietnam Jan. 8–11 to assess the military situation in Indochina. Adm. Thomas H. Moorer, chairman of the U.S. Joint Chiefs of Staff, who accompanied Laird, flew to Pnompenh Jan. 12 to appraise the military situation in Cambodia.

During a stopover in Paris Jan. 6, Laird told a news conference at the U.S. embassy that the U.S. would terminate its "combat responsibility" in South Vietnam by mid-summer 1971. The American mission thereafter would be confined to logistical and air support, he said. "The combat forces which will be assigned to the logistic support and artillery roles," Laird said, "will not be a combat mission but will be a security mission. They will be there to protect and to secure the forces that are assigned these roles."

During a meeting with Thai officials in Bangkok Jan. 7, Laird said the U.S. would increase military aid to Thailand over the next 10 years.

Laird's visit to South Vietnam Jan. 8–11 was devoted to meetings with Ambassador Ellsworth Bunker, Gen. Creighton Abrams, military commander, and other American officials, to discuss the Vietnamization program and American troop withdrawals. He also visited U.S. and South Vietnamese bases in the field. Before departing for Washington Jan. 11, Laird told an airport news conference that the Vietnamization program had improved to the point where it was possible that "additional thousands" of Americans would be withdrawn in 1971. But he emphasized that any further troop pullout beyond May 1, when the current withdrawal phase was completed, would depend on the pace of Vietnamization, progress at the Paris peace talks and the extent of the Communist military threat. President Nixon would announce in April the extent of the withdrawal rate after May 1, Laird said.

Laird was reported Feb. 16 to have advised the President and cabinet to expect "some tough days ahead" in the southern Laos operation. His concern was apparently based on intelligence reports of enemy troop buildups north of Route 9.

Clarifying his Jan. 6 statement on the end of the American combat role, Laird made clear that the remaining security forces in South Vietnam would engage in at least minor operations and searches around American installations. "I don't want to give the impression here that the security forces . . . will not be used to protect the lives of Americans stationed here."

Adm. Moorer conferred with U.S. and Cambodian officials in Pnompenh Jan. 12. After the meeting, he conceded the military situation in Cambodia was deteriorating "but I don't think it is deteriorating as much as has been reported."

McGovern begins presidential bid. Sen. George S. McGovern (D, S.D.) opened his campaign for the 1972 Democratic presidential nomination Jan. 18. In a televised speech in South Dakota, McGovern pledged to withdraw every American soldier from Vietnam and to shift resources from the war to the rebuilding of America.

Calling the war a "dreadful mistake," McGovern said "there is now no way to end it and to free our prisoners except to announce a definite, early date for the withdrawal of every American soldier. I make that pledge without reservation."

He said "the kind of campaign I intend to run will rest on candor and reason" and "will be rooted not in the manipulation of our fears and divisions but in a national dialogue based on mutual respect and common hope." The central issue, he said, would be to delineate a choice—"whether our civilization can serve the freedom and happiness of every citizen or whether we will become the ever more helpless servants of a society we have raised up to rule our lives."

In campaign letters sent to about 2,500 newspaper editors and 275,000 potential contributors across the country, McGovern criticized the Nixon Administration for having "deepened the sense of depression and despair throughout our land."

Invasion by Saigon not barred. President Nixon Feb. 17 refused to rule out a possible unilateral South Vietnamese military move into North Vietnam, or any South Vietnamese operation which did not require U.S. cooperation.

The President also declined to set any limits on the use of U.S. air power in the Indochina war except to bar the use of tactical nuclear weapons. But he reiterated that the U.S. would not use ground forces or advisers in Laos or Cambodia.

At a 40-minute news conference held in the White House and without television cameras present, Nixon refused to speculate on any South Vietnam decision on a possible incursion into North Vietnam, and he reiterated his frequently asserted policy to "take strong action," specifically including the use of air power, against any enemy action that would threaten U.S. troops remaining in Indochina.

Nixon added that South Vietnam "has an ever-increasing responsibility to defend itself" and would "have to make decisions with regard to its ability to defend itself." Although decisions on American participation "will be made here," Nixon said, "when you put it in terms of what would happen in the event the South Vietnamese went into North Vietnam, I am not going to speculate on what they will or will not do."

As for U.S. response to any incursion across the DMZ by North Vietnam, Nixon said, "I think the very fact that the North Vietnamese know that I intend to take strong action to deal with that incursion means that they are not going to take it. If they do, . . . I would not be bound . . . by any so-called understandings which they have already violated at the time of the bombing halt."

Nixon also discussed a heavy U.S.-supported drive by South Vietnam into Laos that began Feb. 8 in an effort to destroy North Vietnamese supply bases along the Ho Chi Minh Trail. He said the Paris negotiations would be pursued for "the primary reason" of attaining settlement of the POW issue. He added that politically time was "running out" for North Vietnam to negotiate with the U.S. "because, as our forces come out of South Vietnam, it means that the responsibility for the negotiations increasingly, then, becomes that of South Vietnam."

The President indicated that the American presence in South Vietnam would be continued, and with "enough Americans," as long as North Vietnam held American POWs.

The current Laotian operation, he said, had "gone according to plan" and

the South Vietnamese had cut three major trails on the enemy's Ho Chi Minh supply artery. The South Vietnamese troops, he said, also had been accorded a "superior" rating from the U.S. commander, General Creighton Abrams, for their performance there as well as an "excellent" rating for their separate operation in the Chup plantation area in Cambodia.

He suggested that the decision to mount an operation in Laos had not been made before, perhaps, because neither the U.S. nor South Vietnam felt that the South Vietnamese had the capability for it and that it was undertaken now "because of the confidence, the training they gained as the result of their actions in Cambodia" and agreement by the U.S. and South Vietnamese commanders that the operation could be mounted now.

Nixon said the operation in southern Laos would continue as long as it took to accomplish its objective, which was to disrupt enemy communications, supply and infiltration lines along the "three or four trails" utilized by the enemy.

Nixon said the southern Laos operation presented "no threat" to Communist China and "should not be interpreted by Communist Chinese as being a threat against them." Although Communist Chinese had been "operating in northern Laos for some time," he said, the South Vietnamese thrust in southern Laos was "not directed against Communist China" but against North Vietnamese "who are pointed towards" South Vietnam and Cambodia.

The President cautioned that the South Vietnamese had "run into very heavy resistance on the road into Tchepone" in the southern Laos action. The stiff resistance was "expected," he said, since the North Vietnamese "have to fight here or give up the struggle to conquer South Vietnam, Cambodia and [give up] their influence extending through other parts of Southeast Asia."

The war situation also was reviewed by Secretary of State William P. Rogers in a news conference Feb. 10. He assured reporters that no assault of any kind was contemplated against North Vietnam.

He also denied a report from Saigon that more than 100 American soldiers had entered Laos and joined the fighting there. (A national telephone poll, conducted by Opinion Research Corp. Feb. 6–7, indicated that 46% of 1,031 people contacted believed American ground troops had entered Laos.)

President Nixon's communications adviser Herb Klein said Feb. 13 there were between 500 and 600 Americans in Laos acting as advisers to the Laotian government. They were "not involved in the current situation," he said, and had "been there for years."

(Klein reportedly circulated to U.S. newspaper editors a column by Joseph Alsop published in the Washington Post and other newspapers Feb. 8 defending the Laos operation and charging that Sen. J. W. Fulbright [D, Ark], persistent critic of Administration war policy in Indochina, was "eager to be proved right by an American defeat.")

Rogers also said Feb. 10 the U.S. forces in South Vietnam would be "outside the combat role" after May 1. "I don't want to say that they will be totally out of the combat role," he said, "but for all major combat assignments, they will be out."

The President Feb. 17 rejected discussion of a time factor of an end to the U.S. ground combat role in South Vietnam because negotiations were still going on at Paris, even though they were "negotiations with no progress." "We are not going to remove any incentive for possible negotiations by announcing what our plans are further down the road," he said.

U.S. vs. invasion of North Vietnam. U.S. Presidential adviser Henry A. Kissinger said Feb. 26 that the U.S. had no plans to invade North Vietnam, but he refrained from categorically denying that South Vietnamese forces would do so. The statement by Kissinger and remarks by other Administration officials aimed at discounting the possibility of extending the war into the North followed a reported remark by President Nguyen Van Thieu that an invasion was only a matter of time and a charge by Hanoi that the U.S. was planning a ground attack on North Vietnam.

In a television interview on the "CBS Morning News," Kissinger said: "We are not threatening the national existence of North Vietnam by anything we are doing now or for that matter by any-

thing that we are intending to do." As for a possible South Vietnamese ground strike into North Vietnam, Kissinger would only say it was "not a dominant probability."

The South Vietnamese news service had reported Feb. 25 that President Thieu told a rally in Pleiku that day that the question of an invasion of North Vietnam "only depended on a time factor." Thieu was quoted as predicting "a march to the north in order to attack the lair of aggressive Communists directly. This will occur in the near future." (Thieu had told an audience in Vungtau Feb. 22 "If we dare launch operations into neutral Laos and Cambodia, why shouldn't we dare to attack the very origin of aggression.")

A spokesman for Thieu, press secretary Hoang Duc Nha, explained Feb. 26 that Thieu's statement at Pleiku as reported by the press was "inaccurate and out of context." Nha stated that Thieu had said "that South Vietnamese forces have taken the initiative and are now capable of fighting the Communists any time, any place, on any battlefield."

Hanoi's chief delegate to the Paris peace talks, Xuan Thuy, asserted Feb. 25 at another negotiating session that "while sustaining heavy losses in Laos, the Nixon Administration is feverishly preparing for attacks against North Vietnam." Nixon, Thuy charged, "is playing a dangerous game, leading to a major war in Southeast Asia."

Thieu repeated the threat of a possible invasion of North Vietnam in another statement March 3. According to an official version of his remarks released by his press secretary, Thieu said ". . . although we have to think about attacking the Communists in North Vietnam, then it will just be because they themselves have put us in a situation which forces us to think about that option in order to defend ourselves." To forestall an attack "right in their own territory," Thieu called on the North Vietnamese to "immediately stop their aggression in the South and withdraw their troops back to the North."

Indochina legislation. Legislation was introduced in both houses of Congress Feb. 25 to bar U.S. participation or support of any South Vietnamese ground invasion of North Vietnam without explicit approval of Congress. The Senate bill was backed by 19 senators. Chief sponsors were Sens. Walter Mondale (D, Minn.) and William Saxbe (R, Ohio). In the House, the bill was introduced by Rep. Michael J. Harrington (D, Mass.). The same day, Senate Foreign Relations Committee Chairman J. W. Fulbright (D, Ark.) contended on the floor that the Laos incursion was illegal in light of Congress' repeal in the previous session of the Gulf of Tonkin Resolution, which left the President, according to Fulbright, with legal authority only to wind down the war and withdraw U.S. troops. President Nixon "says," Fulbright remarked, "though I do not know how any reasonable person can believe, that invading Laos is protecting our troops."

New proposals were introduced in the Senate March 1. One by Sen. Thomas F. Eagleton (D, Mo.) called for a prohibition against presidential commitment of troops to military action, even in compliance with a treaty, without specific declaration of war or Congressional statute, except in certain exceptional circumstances and then only for 30 days. A second proposal by Sen. Edward W. Brooke (R, Mass.) would have authorized three-month studies of the problems and consequences of an "orderly withdrawal" of all U.S. armed forces from South Vietnam.

Sen. Edmund S. Muskie (D, Me.) Feb. 23 denounced President Nixon's Vietnamization policy as a plan that "perpetuates the illusion of ultimate military victory." Speaking at an antiwar teach-in at the University of Pennsylvania, Muskie indicated his support for a resolution sponsored by Sen. George McGovern (D, S.D.) and Sen. Mark Hatfield (R, Ore.) to require withdrawal of all American troops from Indochina by Dec. 31.

Muskie said the Administration policy could only lead to "the continuation of a war which must come to an end" and ran the risk of the "incalculable dangers" of broadened conflict in Indochina. He said the U.S. could not "dictate"the terms of a political settlement in Vietnam. But he said that once a U.S. withdrawal date was set, "I have no doubt we could then negotiate the release of our American prisoners . . . the safe withdrawal of all our troops . . . and a cease-fire between our troops and theirs which could be the first step toward a complete stand-still cease-fire among all the parties."

Risk of under-involvement stressed. President Nixon in his annual State of the World message stressed the necessity for the U.S. to steer "a steady course between the past danger of over-involvement and the new temptation of under-involvement." The phrase was used in a radio speech by the President Feb. 25 on the major themes of his 180-page, 65,000-word message sent to Congress that day.

In his speech, Nixon warned that the "deceptively smooth road of the new isolationism is surely the road to war." While reaffirming the Nixon Doctrine— the U.S. would maintain its treaty commitments but help allies assume primary responsibility for their own defense— Nixon emphasized "that we cannot transfer burdens too swiftly. We must strike a balance between doing too much and preventing self-reliance and suddenly doing too little and undermining self-confidence. We intend to give our friends the time and the means to adjust, materially and psychologically, to a new form of American participation in the world."

The Nixon Doctrine was a basic theme of his first State of the World message as well as his second, but the emphasis had shifted from the 1970 message's insistence on disengagement with honor to the "grave risk" of under-involvement. A corollary theme was that the process of implementing the Nixon Doctrine might be lengthy and arduous, especially in Indochina.

While he saw there "aggression turned back, a war ending," Nixon said the key point was "the way in which we end this conflict." "The right way out of Vietnam," he said, "is crucial to our changing role in the world and to peace in the world."

Nixon said in his message: "If winding down the war is my greatest satisfaction in foreign policy, the failure to end it is my deepest disappointment." "From the outset our constant primary goal has been a negotiated end to the war for all participants. We would take no satisfaction in the fact that after U.S. involvement and casualties were ended, Vietnamese continued to fight Vietnamese."

He said, however that the enemy's constant response had been "to demand that we unconditionally withdraw all U.S. forces and replace the leaders of the Republic of Vietnam with a coalition government" and "their position is unacceptable...."

The "alternative, and hopefully the spur, to negotiations," was Vietnamization, which fulfilled the objective of reducing U.S. involvement. But Nixon conceded Vietnamization "cannot, except over a long period, end the war altogether," adding that: "Still, if Vietnamization leads to perpetuating the war, it is not by our design but because the other side refuses to settle for anything less than a guaranteed takeover."

He claimed concrete results for his Vietnamization program. U.S. withdrawals were proceeding "on schedule." South Vietnamese forces showed increasing capability, "self-confidence and initiative." And the program for pacification of the countryside had proceeded to the point where "roughly 80%" of the total population of South Vietnam was controlled by the government. But pacification progress had "been slower" in certain key northern provinces and Nixon said the South Vietnamese government must increase its efforts there to develop capable forces and gain the support of the rural population.

Much of the accelerated progress in Vietnamization, he said, "was due to the now-indisputable military success of the allied operations against the enemy sanctuaries in Cambodia last spring."

"Substantial problems remain, however," in the way of the Vietnamization process. He cited the negotiating stalemate as one problem, with the concomitant problem that "as our forces decline, the role we can play on many aspects of a settlement is also bound to decline."

He cited "very serious problems" facing U.S. policy in Laos and Cambodia: *At the conference table,* since "even if Hanoi were to negotiate genuinely about Vietnam, difficult issues remain concerning its neighbors." *On the battlefield,* where "enemy intentions and ca-

pabilities in Indochina will pose some hard choices about the deployment of allied troops as we pursue our own withdrawals"—"some of the 60,000 [enemy] troops massed in southern Laos could move into South Vietnam or into Cambodia or against northern Laos," and "in Cambodia we can expect sustained enemy thrusts against the government." *In the U.S.,* where the President had the responsibility "of explaining the purpose and extent of our activities in Laos and Cambodia," and "North Vietnamese actions could require high levels of American assistance and air operations in order to further Vietnamization and our withdrawals."

The President conceded that one of the "realities" upon which Indochina policy was based was that "the support of the American people during the remainder of the conflict required a diminishing U.S. involvement." Another was that "the health of the American society after the conflict called for a solution that would not mock the sacrifices that had been made."

The one "irreducible objective," Nixon said, was that the South Vietnamese people gain the opportunity to determine their own political future without outside interference.

Democrats see 'endless war.' A Democratic analysis Feb. 26 of President Nixon's State of the World message described it as "uninformative rhetoric" and condemned the Administration's Vietnamization policy, which it said offered the "prospect of endless war." "Generalities and well-meaning declarations," it said, "attempt to conceal the failure to formulate definite policies or to take effective action."

Regarding the Indochina war, the Democrats advocated "a firm, unequivocal declaration that all American forces will be withdrawn by the end of this year." Such a stand, they said, rather than Vietnamization, would lead to release of prisoners of war.

The analysis said the Administration claimed credit for reducing American troop strength and casualties through its Vietnamization program but provided "no assurance of the withdrawal of all American forces." Furthermore, it said, "South Vietnamese are dying in larger number and civilian casualties continue to mount" and "it is callous to assume that only American deaths are important."

The Democratic statement, issued by the party's national committee, was prepared by former diplomat W. Averell Harriman and former Assistant Defense Secretary Paul C. Warnke.

Dispute over Vietnamization. Senate Republican leader Hugh Scott (Pa.) charged Feb. 26 that the Democrats had "hitchhiked" on the withdrawal program originated by President Nixon by urging a pullout by 1973, the date called for by the Senate Democratic caucus. Senate Democratic whip Robert C. Byrd (W. Va.) responded that the Democrats were ready to support troop withdrawals but feared that the Administration's program meant the forces would not be withdrawn for some time.

Nixon rating slips. President Nixon's popularity fell in February to the lowest point of his presidency, with 51% of those polled approving of the way he was handling the job, according to a Gallup poll released March 3. The survey was conducted Feb. 19-21, after the Feb. 8 Laos invasion, which was cited as a possible factor in the decline from a 56% approval rating recorded in January. His previous Gallup poll low point was 52% in December 1970.

In response to a question about the Laos invasion, 40% of those surveyed who had heard or read about it (87% of the sampling) thought the invasion would lengthen the war; 19% thought it would shorten it.

In a February survey attempting to gauge the depth of popularity for the President, Gallup reported that 14% expressed strong approval of Nixon, a fall from 23% in September 1969, when the question on intensity had last been asked, and 16% expressed strong disapproval, a rise from 8% from the previous survey.

In other surveys, Gallup reported March 6 that 69% of those polled (Feb. 19-21) thought the Nixon Administration was not telling the public the facts about the Vietnam war. For the first time since he assumed the office, more people disapproved (46%) than approved (41%) of the way Nixon was handling the war situation.

A Louis Harris survey March 8 reported that more people disapproved (42%) than approved (39%) of the Laos invasion and a plurality (46%) of those polled felt that the pace of withdrawal of U.S. troops from Vietnam was too slow.

Foreign affairs news conference. President Nixon held an evening news conference that was telecast from the White House March 4. By Presidential request, the questioning was restricted to foreign affairs, in light of Nixon's recent State of the World message. Nine of 16 questions concerned the Indochina war. Two others were on the related matter of a possible foreign policy information gap between the Administration and Congress.

Most of the questions on Indochina related to the troop withdrawals. Several were asked about the U.S. position concerning a possible South Vietnamese invasion of North Vietnam. Nixon repeated that he would not speculate about South Vietnam's course but the U.S. would have "no ground forces in North Vietnam, in Cambodia or in Laos" except for teams to rescue downed fliers or POWs. Air power would be used against North Vietnam, he said, in retaliation against missile attacks aimed at U.S. planes or against increased infiltration that endangered U.S. forces in South Vietnam during the withdrawal program.

Regarding "protective reaction" measures against enemy missile defenses, the President asserted, they would "not be tit for tat."

As for an invasion of the north, Nixon said "no such plan has ever been suggested by [South Vietnamese] President Thieu to us, none has been considered and none is under consideration." The test as to what the U.S. would do in North Vietnam was "not what happens to forces of South Vietnam but . . . whether . . . the President . . . considers that North Vietnamese activities are endangering, or may endanger, the American forces as we continue to withdraw. It is then, and only then, that I will use air power against military complexes on the borders of North Vietnam." Regarding the rate of troop withdrawals and the effect of the Laos invasion on the rate, Nixon promised that the withdrawals would continue "at least at the present rate" and said the Laos action assured "even more the success of our troop withdrawal program." Further plans on the withdrawal program were to be announced in April.

Contrary to what he called "a drumbeat of suggestion" from "some" television commentators that the Laos invasion would not work, the President declared it was the right decision and would "reduce American casualties" and insure the pullout program.

It had disrupted enemy supply lines and "very seriously damaged the enemy's ability to wage effective action against our remaining forces in Vietnam," he said. Much enemy equipment had been captured and destroyed, including 67 tanks, and the flow of supply trucks down the Ho Chi Minh trails, according to the U.S. commander in South Vietnam, Gen. Creighton Abrams, was down 55%.

Abrams also reported, Nixon said, that the South Vietnamese soldiers proved in both the Laos and Cambodia operations that they "can hack it" and "give a better account of themselves even than the North Vietnamese units."

As for eventual total withdrawal, Nixon insisted that as long as American POWs were held in North Vietnam "we will have to maintain a residual force in South Vietnam." He affirmed that the U.S. negotiating proposal for withdrawal was "for a Southeast Asia settlement," a "one-package situation" calling for North Vietnamese troop withdrawal from that area.

Nixon says war 'probably last one.' President Nixon told an interviewer March 8 the Vietnam war was ending and he "seriously doubt[ed] if we will ever have another war. This is probably the very last one." The interviewer was C. L. Sulzberger, foreign affairs columnist of The New York Times, which published Sulzberger's account of the interview March 10.

According to the account, Nixon repeatedly referred to the Vietnam war as "ending" and expressed concern that the nation would "retreat into isolationism" or "recede . . . from its efforts to maintain an adequate defense force."

At this point in our history, he said, "no one who is really for peace in this country can reject an American role in the rest of the world."

"Our responsibilities are not limited to this great continent," he said, "but include Europe, the Middle East, Southeast Asia, East Asia, many areas whose fate affects the peace of the world. We must above all tend to our national obligations. We must not forget our alliances or our interests. Other nations must know that the United States has both the capability and the will to defend these allies and protect their interests. Unless people understand this and understand it well, the United States will simply retreat into isolationism, both politically and diplomatically."

The President said he was "caught up in a vicious cross fire" between "superdoves" and "superhawks" with both sides tending toward isolationism. The superhawks wanted "to develop a Fortress America at home and cram it full of missiles while the superdoves want us to pull out of the world also, but reducing our strength at home."

He warned, "we can't heed either our superhawks whose policy would ultimately lead to war or to our superdoves. . . . The trouble is that their policy of weakness would also quickly lead to war."

"I'd like to see us not end the Vietnamese war foolishly and find ourselves all alone in the world," the President said. "I could have chosen that course my very first day in office. But I want the American people to be able to be led by me, or by my successor, along a course that allows us to do what is needed to help keep the peace in this world."

"If America winds up the war in Vietnam in failure and an image is developed that the war was fought only by stupid scoundrels, there would be a wave of isolationism. . . . What we now have to do is end the war—as we are doing—in a way that gives South Vietnam a reasonable chance to survive without our help. But this doesn't mean we would withdraw all our responsibilities everywhere."

People, he said, "should be under no illusion that you can play a role in one area but wholly ignore another. Of course, we're not going to get into every little firefight everywhere. The Nixon

Doctrine says only that we will help those who help themselves."

Historian warns vs. war power. Historian Henry Steele Commager urged curbs on the president's war-making power in testimony March 8 before the Fulbright committee, which had before it several bills to limit such power. Commager said the nation had misused its "prodigious" power for decades and was "even now engaged in a monstrous misuse of power in waging war on a distant people that does not accept our ideology or our determination of its future." The problem he said, stemmed from "the psychology of cold war, our obsession with power, our assumption that the great problems that glare upon us so hideously from every corner of the horizon can be solved by force." With the exception of the Civil War, and possibly, the Korean War, Commager said there were "no instances in our history where the use of war-making powers by the executive without authority of Congress was clearly and incontrovertibly required by the nature of the emergency which the nation faced." In almost every instance, he said, the nation would have been better served by "consultation and delay."

The Fighting

Communist truce ends. The Viet Cong's three-day New Year's cease-fire ended at 1 a.m. Jan. 3 amid reports that fighting had continued through most of the period. By contrast, the allied 24-hour truce begun at 6 p.m. Dec. 31, 1970 had been the quietest of the holiday fighting pauses reported since their inception in 1967. The U.S. command reported one American killed and 10 wounded and South Vietnam reported its forces had suffered nine killed and 52 wounded during the 24-hour period. Casualties for the three-day truce were listed as 12 Americans killed and 49 wounded and 32 South Vietnamese slain and 93 wounded. Communist deaths totaled 53, according to allied estimates.

The heaviest fighting of the three-day cease-fire had occurred Jan. 2 when South Vietnamese forces swept into the southern half of the demilitarized zone to pursue North Vietnamese troops that had attacked a Saigon unit patrolling just below the DMZ. The South Vietnamese rushed reinforcements into the buffer area, including armored personnel carriers. One of the vehicles was reported to have struck a mine, wounding five soldiers. The South Vietnamese withdrew from the zone after engaging the North Vietnamese for 10 hours.

U.S. raids enemy supply routes—A large force of U.S. B-52 bombers accompanied by 300 fighter-bombers flying support missions carried out widespread raids Jan. 3 against Communist supply routes in Cambodia, Laos and South Vietnam. One fighter-bomber was shot down near the Plaine des Jarres in Laos. The raids reportedly were aimed at interdicting the flow of North Vietnamese war supplies through Laos and Cambodia to South Vietnam and to provide air support for Cambodian and Laotian troops.

North Vietnamese supply depots along the Ho Chi Minh trail in Laos were reported to have been heavily pounded during American bombing raids Dec. 19–28, 1970, the U.S. command reported Dec. 31. Pilots reported more than 7,000 secondary explosions, causing about 225 sustained fires, and claimed 40 trucks had been destroyed or damaged. The command said the air strikes had disrupted North Vietnamese plans for an early spring offensive.

Hanoi charges U.S. raids. North Vietnam charged Jan. 20 that American planes had carried out almost daily raids on North Vietnam between Jan. 4 and 17, bombing targets between the 17th Parallel (that divided North and South Vietnam) and the Mugia Pass on the Laotian border. A communique published a detailed list of the alleged strikes and claimed that U.S. planes had flown defoliation missions, spraying

North Vietnamese forests in an attempt to cut their use as refugee and supply dumps.

The North Vietnamese statement said the raids were "very grave acts of aggression and are part of [U.S. President] Nixon's plans to get out of a critical situation in South Vietnam, Cambodia and Laos." The communiqué added that since Jan. 1 U.S. planes had flown reconnaissance missions over nearly all North Vietnamese provinces and towns and that U.S. warships had violated North Vietnamese waters several times.

The U.S. Defense Department Jan. 20 denied the North Vietnamese charges. It said the only U.S. strikes on North Vietnamese territory between Jan. 4–17 cited by the Hanoi communique were "protective reaction" strikes by escort planes flying cover for bombing operations against the Ho Chi Minh trail in Laos. The department denied American defoliation raids on the North.

North Vietnam missile bases hit. U.S. jets bombed two missile bases in North Vietnam Jan. 8 after their radar equipment had indicated they were about to be fired upon. It was the first such "protective reaction" attacks on the North since Nov. 30, 1970.

The first raid was reported by the U.S. command in Saigon Jan. 9 and the second Jan. 12. In the first reported incident, an F-105 fighter-bomber attacked a Communist missile site 75 miles north of the demilitarized zone near the Mugia Pass after the pilot found his plane "locked in" by enemy radar. The jet was flying escort for B-52 bombers raiding the Ho Chi Minh supply trail in Laos. It was not known whether the two Shrike missiles dropped by the F-105 destroyed the target.

In the second reported attack, a Navy A-4 jet dropped bombs on a coastal missile base at Hatinh, 110 miles north of the demilitarized zone, but missed the target. The A-4 was returning from a mission of escorting reconnaissance planes over North Vietnam when its sensing devices signaled that the missile site was tracking it preparatory to firing.

North Vietnam did not mention the raid near the Mugia Pass, but a Foreign Ministry protest against the Hatinh attack was made public Jan. 12.

U.S. jets attacked missile bases in North Vietnam Jan. 15–17 while escorting B-52s on raids along the Laotian-North Vietnamese frontier. The attacks were described as "protective reaction" strikes against enemy installations whose radar were reported locked onto the aircraft preparatory to firing.

The U.S. command said three missile sites were hit Jan. 15 about 80 miles north of the demilitarized zone, one was struck Jan. 16 10 miles north of the DMZ and two more were pounded Jan. 17 46 miles above the buffer area.

The Communist radar-controlled antiaircraft installations were struck at positions 19 miles southwest of Donghoi Feb. 14, 21 miles west of that city Feb. 15 and six miles north of Vinh Feb. 16. No missiles had been fired at any of the jets, but the planes detected radar tracking apparently preparatory to firing, the command said.

Fresh "protective reaction strikes" against missile and antiaircraft artillery positions in North Vietnam were carried out by U.S. jets Feb. 20–23, the U.S. command announced Feb. 23. A spokesman said that the aerial attacks had been ordered "after repeated hostile acts and recent SAM [Soviet-built surface-to-air missile] firings by anti-aircraft positions against United States craft involved in interdictions of North Vietnamese supplies along the Ho Chi Minh Trail in Laos."

According to the announcement: Twenty planes carried out an hour-long strike Feb. 20 and 30 planes the following day conducted another hour-long attack; both raids were targeted "near the Laotian border" below the 19th Parallel, 120 miles south of Hanoi. Two F-105 fighter-bombers flying on a mission the night of Feb. 22 over the Ho Chi Minh Trail fired three missiles at radar-controlled antiaircraft positions 28 miles southeast of the Ban Karai Pass on the Laotian-North Vietnamese border. Another F-105 Feb. 23 fired a single missile against a similar position 25 miles southeast of the pass.

The four-day raid was the heaviest over North Vietnam since attacks by 250 planes Nov. 21, 1970.

U.S. planes attacked missile sites in North Vietnam March 21–22. The raids, the heaviest since November 1970, ranged up to 120 miles north of the DMZ. The U.S. command said the "limited-duration protective reaction" strikes were in response to North Vietnamese antiaircraft attacks against American planes bombing supply lines in Laos.

A command report March 24 on the results of the raids said three surface-to-air missile sites had been destroyed— one just east of the Mugia Pass on the Laotian border, about 50 miles north of the DMZ; another about 15 miles east of the pass; and a third near the Laotian frontier 16 miles north of the buffer zone.

The command acknowledged that North Vietnamese gunners had shot down an Air Force F-4 plane near the coastal city of Donghoi, 35 miles inside North Vietnam, but said the two crewmen had been rescued on the ground March 23. It was the first American aircraft brought down by a North Vietnamese missile since February 1969, a military spokesman said.

South Vietnam Tet truce. Sporadic fighting continued in South Vietnam during separate truces declared by allied forces Jan. 26–27 and by Communist troops Jan. 26–30 in observance of Tet, the lunar new year.

The U.S. and South Vietnamese commands reported Jan. 27 at least 53 enemy troops violations during the allied truce, but called it the quietest in recent years. The U.S. command reported no American deaths, but South Vietnam said seven of its soldiers had been killed and 28 wounded. The enemy death toll was listed at 22.

The allied command said the Viet Cong and North Vietnamese had committed a number of violations during their own cease-fire, directing attacks against civilians. In Binhdinh Province, a Communist grenade ripped through a theater, killing 10 South Vietnamese. About 80 miles north, nine civilians were reported killed when a bomb exploded in a market place.

Among other military developments prior to and following the truces:

Twenty-seven Americans were killed and 83 were wounded in action in Indochina Jan. 3–9. The U.S. command re-

ported Jan. 14 that the casualties were the lowest weekly combined toll since the week ended Oct. 23, 1965, when 14 U.S. servicemen were killed and 70 were wounded.

American losses increased sharply the following two weeks. A total of 37 were killed and 211 wounded Jan. 10–16, while 50 were slain and 295 wounded Jan. 17–23. The Jan. 17–23 increase was attributed largely to two plane crashes that killed 14 servicemen.

An upsurge of Communist attacks on American positions was reported by the U.S. command Feb. 1. Six Americans were killed and at least 26 were wounded in six Communist shelling attacks against large bases at Danang, Camranh Bay and Tuyhoa and against two U.S. troop positions in Binhdinh and Pleiku Provinces. Five of the American fatalities resulted from the ambush of an Americal Division patrol four miles west of Chulai in the northern part of the country. Five Communists were slain in the same engagement.

Cambodian drive to clear Route 4. Cambodian and South Vietnamese troops continued a drive in January to clear Communist forces from Route 4, linking Pnompenh with the country's only port, Kompong Som. The soldiers were attacking from north and south to break the road blockade that had been in force since Nov. 20, 1970. The offensive was pressed as the gasoline shortage in Pnompen, which received the fuel from Kompong Som, grew more acute.

In a move to ease the blockade, the South Vietnamese government announced Jan. 2 that it would provide armed escorts for tanker ships and trucks carrying petroleum supplies to Pnompenh. Three such boats heading for the capital were shelled on the Mekong River by the Communists Jan. 5 and 6. In the first attack, two small tankers and their gunboat escorts were struck by Viet Cong and North Vietnamese recoilless rifle fire near Neak Luong, about 38 miles southeast of Pnompenh. The two supply vessels arrived in Pnompenh the following day. In the Jan. 6 incident, a South Vietnamese landing boat carrying gasoline and other fuel was shelled by the Communists from a Mekong River island 25 miles from Pnompenh. The boat, heading for the capital from Neak Luong, exploded. Casualties were not known.

Electricity rationing was imposed in downtown Pnompenh Jan. 8 as diesel fuel to operate the city's generators continued to run low.

A force of 3,500 Cambodian troops moving southward Jan. 4, attacked the heights of Pich Nil, commanding the highway about 60 miles southwest of the capital. At first, little enemy resistance was encountered, but Communist assaults later stalled the Cambodian push. More than 1,000 South Vietnamese troops pushed out of Pnompenh Jan. 12 in an attempt to join up with the Cambodians at Pich Nil. 5,000 South Vietnamese and 8,000 Cambodians were committed to the battle along the 115-mile road.

A Saigon armored force moving up from the south was reported Jan. 19 to be only 10–15 miles from linking up with Cambodian units stalled at the northern entrance to Pich Nil pass,

More than 1,000 South Vietnamese troops and artillery were helicoptered Jan. 19 to the Cambodian garrison at Kompong Seila, about 75 miles southwest of the capital and just below the southern approaches to Pich Nil. The Cambodian command had reported Jan. 18 that a South Vietnamese force had reached Kompong Seila and relieved heavy enemy pressure on the garrison.

In their northward push, the South Vietnamese reported the capture Jan. 16 of another strategic point, Stung Chhay pass, 95 miles southwest of Pnomphenh, after two days of fighting three North Vietnamese battalions and a battalion of Khmer Rouge soldiers, the Cambodian insurgents. The two allied columns were reported Jan. 22 to have linked up at Pich Nil Pass on Route 4, wresting the strategic road from Communist control. The main Saigon force, moving up from the south, and the Cambodians pushing through the pass from the north, had met three miles from the northern end of the mountain gateway. Advance elements of the South Vietnamese force reportedly had reached the Cambodians Jan. 20.

A South Vietnamese spokesman said Jan. 23 that about 1,800 enemy troops remained in the Pich Nil Pass area, raising the possibility that the Saigon forces might have to be recommitted to the sector. But "for now the route has been cleared," he said. Although the road was in allied hands, it remained unusuable because it was scarred by bomb craters and many of its bridges were damaged.

In simultaneous but separate announcements Jan. 25, the U.S. command disclosed the withdrawal that day of two American helicopter carriers stationed off the Cambodian coast since Jan. 13 and South Vietnam said 1,500 of its troops involved in the Route 4 operations had been pulled out. A Saigon spokesman said an additional 3,800 troops returned to South Vietnam that day. The American war vessels had taken up stations in the Gulf of Siam when the South Vietnamese began their operations on Route 4.

The ships had supplied and fueled U.S. helicopter gunships supporting South Vietnamese troops. Although the carriers rejoined the 7th Fleet, American air strikes against Communist forces and supply lines in Cambodia continued.

In a clash near the South Vietnamese frontier Jan. 20, Saigon troops had killed 56 Communist soldiers in the Route 7 area at Khet Kandol in repelling an enemy attack on their positions. The enemy ground assault followed the firing of 300 mortar shells.

U.S. air role in Cambodia, Laos. The U.S. was reported Jan. 18 and 19 to have significantly stepped up its air operations against Communist forces in Cambodia and Laos. The latter missions were said to be in direct support of Laotian ground troops. The White House Jan. 19 acknowledged the widening of American air operations in Cambodia, but insisted that the U.S. was not embarking on a "full-time expanded war over Indochina."

The increasing American involvement in Cambodia coincided with a sharp rise in combat there, particularly along Route 4. A combined Cambodian-South Vietnamese force was battling to clear Viet Cong and North Vietnamese from the vital highway link between Pnompenh and the port of Kompong Som. U.S. helicopter gunships were said to have flown at least three strikes Jan. 18 in direct support of the operation. The aircraft were believed to have flown from two American helicopter carriers stationed off the Cambodian coast in the Gulf of Siam. The U.S. command Jan. 18 confirmed the presence of the two helicopter carriers and said they were part of the 7th Fleet "amphibious readiness group" used for the "interdiction" of enemy lines and the supplying of allied forces fighting in Cambodia.

The reports of the enlarged American combat role in Cambodia were preceded and followed by Defense Department warnings of the possible further use of American air power to strengthen the allied position in Cambodia. Department spokesman Jerry Friedheim said Jan. 14 that Defense Secretary Melvin R. Laird "has not foreclosed and will not foreclose the possibility" of providing American logistic and air-lift support for allied troops "seeking to prevent the re-establishment of enemy sanctuaries in Cambodia."

Friedheim said Jan. 18 that the U.S. intended to use all necessary air power against Communist forces in Cambodia which "ultimately" might threaten American troops in South Vietnam. He said this would include the use of helicopters to fly South Vietnamese combat troops into the country. Friedheim conceded that American crews might sometimes leave their craft while on the ground in the course of these operations. But he said President Nixon's pledge not to employ American ground forces in Cambodia would be strictly observed.

Friedheim denied an Associated Press report from Saigon Jan. 17 that U.S. air liaison officers might have operated from Cambodian soil. An accompanying AP photograph showed what appeared to be an American in camouflage uniform running toward a helicopter during fighting along Route 4. Friedheim said a few American troop ferrying missions might have been conducted in Cambodia over the weekend, but he retracted this statement the following day. The U.S. command in Saigon Jan. 19 also denied the report, saying "This has not been done, although it is within the guidelines laid down for United States air power to prevent the re-establishment of enemy sanctuaries in Cambodia."

Another Defense Department official Jan. 18 confirmed a report that Secretary Laird had rejected a Joint Chiefs of Staff suggestion that U.S. transport planes and helicopters be permitted to fly ammunition and South Vietnamese troops into Cambodia. Laird was said to have been opposed because it would have violated Nixon's pledge not to use American combat soldiers. (Laird, returning to Washington from a Southeast Asia trip Jan. 15, said the Cambodian situation would be critical in the next few months. However, he said he foresaw no obstacles to the continued withdrawal of American troops from South Vietnam.)

The Defense and State Departments Jan. 19 issued conflicting assessments of the AP newsphoto showing an American racing for a helicopter during combat. Friedheim said the American might be assigned to the U.S. embassy in Pnompenh. But State Department spokesman Robert J. McCloskey said "to my knowledge" embassy personnel were "not authorized" to leave Pnompenh to take part in combat operations.

McCloskey acknowledged for the first time that American helicopter gunships had been conducting combat air support for Laotian troops. But he insisted that it was "within the scope of our air operations in Laos."

A Jan. 19 report from Saigon said U.S. Air Force, Army and Marine helicopter gunships had been flying support missions for Laotian troops for some time, striking at enemy troops and supplies along the Ho Chi Minh trail in southeastern Laos. The report also told of one of the largest American aerial offensives of the war in Laos, with B-52 bombers, fighter-bombers and gunships attempting to stem the flow of North Vietnamese troops and equipment into Laos, Cambodia and South Vietnam.

Prisoner camp raided in Cambodia. A force of about 300 South Vietnamese paratroopers with U.S. air support Jan. 17 raided a Communist prisoner of war camp in Cambodia believed to hold 20 American captives but found it empty. South Vietnamese sources disclosed the attack Jan. 19 but U.S. officials refused comment.

The South Vietnamese were airlifted by helicopter to the site of the camp, in an area west of the Cambodian town of Mimot, 75 miles northwest of Saigon and five miles inside Cambodia. U.S. helicopter gunships flew escort and American advisers accompanied the landing party. Commenting on the three-hour raid, a South Vietnamese officer said "It worked perfectly. We suffered no casualties." Thirty enemy soldiers were captured in the operation, led by Lt. Gen. Do Cao Tri, commander of South Vietnamese forces in the Parrot's Beak. The raid was part of a 6,000-man South Vietnamese operation under way in an area extending from South Vietnam's Tayninh Province to Mimot, across the border.

Communists attack Pnompenh. Striking at Pnompenh for the first time in the Indochina war, Communist forces Jan. 22 carried out a devastating shelling attack on the city's Pochentong international airport and nearby installations, virtually wiping out Cambodia's tiny air force and causing widespread damage. The raid was followed by a series of smaller enemy assaults on the capital the following two days,

The Communist infiltrators were reported to have entered the airport behind a mortar barrage. They ran from plane to plane attaching explosive charges. Three of the attackers were reported killed.

Other guerrillas fired 30 rocket and mortar shells at the Chran Changvar Naval Base across the Tonle Sap River from Pnompenh, wounding four persons. Some enemy shells also landed in the center of the city.

U.S. officials were said to have expressed dismay that tighter security measures were not taken despite Cambodian government acknowledgment that Communist plans to strike at Pnompenh were known eight days in advance.

The Pnompenh airport came under fresh harassment attacks Jan. 24 as the Communists fired mortars and anti-tank rockets.

In the other incidents in Pnompenh, an explosion shattered the Cambodian immigration office Jan. 23 and South Vietnamese Ambassador Tran Van Phuoc was slightly injured when a blast rocked his home. A Communist bomb destroyed the headquarters of the city's power utility Jan. 24, wounding 10

government employes. Electricity was cut off in parts of the city.

Meanwhile, sharp clashes between Cambodian and Communist forces occurred near the outskirts of Pnompenh. A major army fuel storage depot at Prek Phoneu, 14 miles north of the city, came under sharp enemy attack Jan. 24. Government forces Jan. 25 beat off three enemy attacks at Prey Khiev, 24 miles north of the capital, at Saang, 18 miles southeast of the city, and at Lovea Sar Kandal, 28 miles southeast.

More than 20 Cambodian battalions launched a major drive Jan. 27 to wipe out Communist troop concentrations west and northwest of Pnompenh. A Cambodian military spokesman said Jan. 29 that "the sweeps are designed primarily to cut off infiltrations. There is no longer any danger of an attack force." The drive followed heavy enemy assaults against the capital and surrounding sectors Jan. 22–25. Such raids continued on a small scale.

Cambodian-South Vietnamese clashes —Cambodian forces and their South Vietnamese allies fought two separate clashes Jan. 30, but reasons for them could not be determined. In the first engagement, South Vietnamese sailors and Cambodian soldiers exchanged mortar and machine gun fire for 15 minutes in the center of Pnompenh. Cambodian tanks and troop reinforcements broke up the melee. A civilian bystander was killed and 14 others were wounded.

In the second incident, South Vietnamese marines attacked a Cambodian outpost at Vealthhom, seven miles east of Pnompenh, and the outpost later came under attack by Viet Cong forces. Three Cambodians were killed and seven wounded at the base, but it was not known whether the casualties were inflicted by the South Vietnamese or Viet Cong.

U.S. role in Cambodia opposed. Congressional displeasure with the expanded U.S. military role in Cambodia was expressed in both houses. In the House, 64 Democratic representatives joined to introduce legislation Jan. 21 to ban the use of funds to "provide United States air or sea combat support for any military operations in Cambodia." Another resolution was presented by 13

Democrats urging an "immediate halt of all offensive actions by the United States in Southeast Asia" and a withdrawal of all U.S. troops by June.

In the Senate, Sens. Frank Church (D, Idaho) and John Sherman Cooper (R, Ky.), co-sponsors of the 1970 legislation banning funds for U.S. ground forces or advisers in Cambodia, charged Jan. 21 that the Administration had violated the restriction "in spirit" by ferrying South Vietnamese troops into battle and providing other support for them in Cambodia by air. They urged prompt hearings by the Senate Foreign Relations Committee on the issue. Chairman J. W. Fulbright (D, Ark.), charging that "the spirit of the amendment is quite inconsistent with our greatly enlarged role in Cambodia," announced Jan. 25 that the Foreign Relations Committee would probe the issue. He said Secretary of State William P. Rogers had been requested to testify.

Rogers had conferred with Cooper on the issue Jan. 22.

Senate Democratic Leader Mike Mansfield (Mont.) joined the protest over Cambodia, warning a Democratic caucus Jan. 21 that "even greater vigilance" by Congress was necessary as "the sounds of war in Indochina again grow ominous." On the CBS "Face the Nation" broadcast Jan. 24, Mansfield called the U.S. air role in Cambodia "contrary to the intent and spirit" of Congressional restrictions.

U.S. Secretary of State Rogers reportedly assured members of the Senate Foreign Relations Committee Jan. 28 that the Administration had no intention of expanding the U.S. military role in Cambodia. Rogers also was reported to have assured the committee the Administration did not plan to seek a softening of the Congressional prohibition embodied in the Cooper-Church amendment against the introduction of U.S. ground combat troops and military advisers into Cambodia.

(The final version of the Cooper-Church curb on the President's warmaking powers was incorporated in the defense appropriations bill, which the President signed Jan. 11.)

Such a relaxation of the Congressional restriction had been broached by Sen. John C. Stennis (D, Miss.), chairman of the Senate Armed Services Committee, after Defense Secretary Melvin R. Laird had briefed his panel Jan. 27 on the same topic. The committee hearings with Rogers and Laird were closed sessions.

Stennis said the Cooper-Church provision might have to be revised, possibly to allow ground controllers to direct U.S. planes providing air support for Cambodian and South Vietnam troops, if the military situation worsened in Cambodia. In that event, Stennis said, "we may have to re-examine our policy and restrictions."

Laird and Stennis agreed after the closed briefing that up to that point the Administration had not violated the Cooper-Church provision. Stennis also described Laird's testimony before his panel as a "strongly confident" report that the military situation was "improving" in Cambodia and "fair progress" was being made through the use of U.S. air support.

A concurrent view that the Cooper-Church restriction had not been violated also was expressed Jan. 28 after the Rogers' hearing by the authors of the amendment, Sens. John Sherman Cooper (R, Ky.) and Frank Church (D, Idaho) and Foreign Relations Committee Chairman J. W. Fulbright (D, Ark.) and other members of the panel, including Sen. Edmund S. Muskie (D, Me.).

Although Rogers' assurances apparently mollified the committee members on the issue (public hearings, which had been tentatively planned, were not announced), the larger problem of Congressional curbs on presidential warmaking power remained an issue. Cooper emerged from the session showing concern and remarking he was going "to see the President." Church told reporters "that our helicopters are hovering above the ground like hummingbirds, firing at every target of opportunity."

Rogers, in his remarks to newsmen, upheld the use of air power "in the way the President feels is necessary to protect American lives." But, in attempting to define the issue further, he aroused Church and Fulbright. "We are not going to use close air support," Rogers said, "in the exact definition of that term because close air support means we would have to have coordinators and communicators on the ground in Cambodia."

Church's comment was that "if you get so technical that everything is redefined each time the policy changes, then I do think the committee has a basis for legitimate and genuine concern" about adherence to the amendment. Fulbright doubted that Congress, faced with such an "endless kind of maze" of semantics, could write legislative provisions that would cover all possible military actions in Cambodia. "If they do not choose to follow Congressional advice," he observed, "there is no practical way to make them follow it."

The controversy was renewed in a Rogers' news conference Jan. 29 when the secretary, ruling out the use of U.S. ground combat troops in Cambodia or Laos, refused, in reply to a question, to rule out the possibility that U.S. air power might be used to support a South Vietnamese expedition against Communist supply bases in southern Laos.

"We do not rule out the use of air power to support Asians in any effort they make to fight the common enemy," he declared. "There is one enemy: it is North Vietnam." He stressed that the period "between now and May 1" was critical in the war situation because of the continuing U.S. troop withdrawals and the probability of increased enemy action in the dry season. So, he said, the President "intends to use the air power as he sees fit against enemy forces, enemy supplies, enemy communications and to prevent the enemy from re-establishing base areas."

At a news conference Jan. 20, Laird said U.S. air power in Cambodia was "crucial to the success" of the U.S. troop withdrawals from South Vietnam. In justifying the action, Laird cited the Nixon Doctrine emphasis upon U.S. readiness to provide "material assistance and air and sea assistance" to Asian allies while encouraging them to assume greater responsibility for their own defense.

"That is precisely what is happening today in Cambodia," he declared. He also cited the Congressional proscription adopted in December 1970 against the use of U.S. ground combat troops and military advisers in Cambodia. The

Administration, he said, was within the "letter and spirit" of the restriction.

Laird added that the U.S. would use air power and he would recommend its use "to supplement the South Vietnamese forces, as far as the air campaign in South Vietnam, Laos and Cambodia" was concerned. He stressed that there were no plans to return U.S. troops to Cambodia. "We will not," he said, "and I repeat it again, not—commit United States ground combat forces to Cambodia directly or indirectly."

Asked if he was justifying the expanded U.S. air role under the Nixon Doctrine and because of the lack of a specific prohibition by Congress, Laird replied, "You are correct in both cases."

Meanwhile, the U.S. supportive air role in Cambodia continued on a large scale. About six C-130 cargo planes, carrying ammunition, fuel and other supplies, arrived in Pnompenh from South Vietnam Jan. 27. The American airlift to Cambodia, in operation since Nov. 12, 1970, had brought in 1,400 tons of ammunition, 22,000 gallons of fuel and 60 tons of equipment, according to Saigon reports. In another action involving the American military aid program in Cambodia, the U.S. command announced Jan. 27 that it had turned over eight armed river patrol boats to the Cambodian navy.

In a report on the American air involvement in the Route 4 operation Jan. 13–25, the U.S. command said Jan. 28 that U.S. Army planes from a carrier stationed off the coast had flown "less than 25 sorties a day" and that U.S. Air Force jets, including B-52 bombers, had flown "less than 15 sorties a day." About 60 fliers were involved in the operation, in addition to 40 Army communication workers aboard the carrier, the command said. No pilots had been injured and no aircraft had been lost to enemy fire during the Route 4 battle, the command said. It reported that 34 American airmen had been killed during the U.S. ground operations in Cambodia May 1-June 30, 1970 and another five had been lost in daily missions over Cambodia since then. In the latest incident, a U.S. Air Force F-100 fighter-bomber had crashed from "unknown causes" and its pilot was killed Jan. 27 while on an apparent mission near Route 4.

American officials disclosed Jan. 22 that the Defense Department had issued new instructions to forbid the landing of U.S. military personnel in Cambodian combat. Responding to the controversy arising from the AP photo of an American racing to a helicopter in Cambodia near heavy fighting, the officials conceded that some American personnel had been on the ground in Cambodia but termed the instances "mistakes" involving landings of no more than 10 minutes for emergency repairs.

"Military delivery teams." A group of 15–20 Americans, in civilian clothes but wearing sidearms, landed at Pnompenh airport Jan. 25 and retrieved two U.S. helicopters, damaged in an enemy raid on the airport Jan. 22, and returned them to South Vietnam for repairs. The Defense Department acknowledged the action Jan. 26 but identified the men involved only as "U.S. personnel." They were identified by a CBS radio report as members of the 520th Transportation Battalion, Phuloi, South Vietnam.

Defense Secretary Laird, in a meeting with newsmen Jan. 27, explained that the soldiers had worn civilian clothes during the incident at the suggestion of U.S. Ambassador Emory C. Swank because he felt, Laird said, the U.S. should "keep its profile as low as possible." Laird disagreed about the uniforms, upholding the assignment of military men on such missions as part of the military assistance program to Cambodia.

The use of "military delivery teams" or "military equipment teams"—to monitor or "audit" the military hardware purchased with the $100 million allocated by the U.S. for that purpose— had been disclosed by Laird Jan. 20. American officials in Pnompenh also talked about it Jan. 25 (the day of the Pnompenh landing), but with the indication it was still under discussion by authorities.

Indicating concern for the Congressional restriction against U.S. ground combat troops or military advisers in Cambodia, the officials said the teams, under the jurisdiction of the ambassador, would be barred from acting in an advisory capacity, even from showing Cambodians how to use the equipment. Defense Department spokesman Jerry Friedheim, however, said Jan. 25 the American military men operating out of the embassy would be permitted from time to time to show the Cambodians how the equipment worked.

Both sides start new drives in Laos. Unconfirmed accounts of a large-scale South Vietnamese incursion into southern Laos aided by U.S. air power and a major allied buildup in the northwestern section of South Vietnam were reported by foreign and U.S. sources Jan. 30– Feb. 2. Exact accounts were obscured by an embargo imposed by the U.S. command in Saigon Jan. 29 on all news reports from the northern part of South Vietnam.

Meanwhile, the Laotian government announced Feb. 3 that the North Vietnamese had launched a major drive against its positions in northern Laos.

The purported new allied operation was preceded by the disclosure Jan. 29 that U.S. B-52 bombers had intensified saturation raids against North Vietnam's Ho Chi Minh Trail and supply bases in southern Laos. The sustained strikes were concentrated in an area immediately west of the former U.S. Marine base at Khesanh. It was known to be a principal staging point and supply base for the 35,000–40,000 North Vietnamese troops estimated to be operating in southern Laos. American pilots were reported Jan. 31 to have said they had destroyed or damaged 2,000 enemy trucks on the Ho Chi Minh Trail in January.

Among reports and statements on the operations:—Japan's Kyodo news agency, quoting "reliable sources," said in a dispatch from Saigon Feb. 2 that "before daybreak Feb. 1, 4,000–5,000 South Vietnamese troops spearheaded by paratroopers" had launched a thrust into the Boloven Plateau of southern Laos. This was considerably south of the Khesanh area where other reports placed a heavy concentration of U.S. and South Vietnamese forces. Kyodo said U.S. planes and helicopters were aiding the operation but no U.S. ground troops were involved. The news agency added "there is also a report here in Saigon that 1,000 Thai troops have been sent to the Boloven area."

In Washington, Senate Republican leader Hugh Scott (Pa.) said Feb. 2 that a major allied offensive had been launched in northwestern South Vietnam. Other Congressional sources said about 25,000 South Vietnamese and 9,000 Americans were committed to the operation. Scott said "the operation will run from seven to 10 days from the time it started, which was a couple of days ago." Scott's statement confirmed a report by Washington officials Feb. 1 that thousands of U.S. and South Vietnamese troops had launched a major drive against a concentration of Communist soldiers west of Khesanh.

The Soviet Union charged Feb. 1 that an invasion of Laos had begun. Tass quoted Premier Aleksei N. Kosygin as saying that the U.S.S.R. "cannot help giving serious attention to the further aggravation of the situation in Indochina where an outrageous invasion of the southern provinces of Laos is under way."

The North Vietnamese Communist party newspaper Nhan Dan said Feb. 1 that the U.S. and South Vietnam were "feverishly preparing further steps of war expansion and escalation" in southern Laos, but did not mention an actual invasion. The newspaper said that since the beginning of January "several thousand Thais" and South Vietnamese commandos had been training for a push into Laos. Hanoi sources contended that the U.S. had increased air strikes on both sides of the demilitarized zone, including the entire North Vietnamese province just north of the DMZ. The purpose of the intensified raids, it was said, was to "widen the demilitarized zone" and to cut off the North from the South by an impassable area.

Laotian officials Jan. 31 reported receiving no official word about the reputed incursion by South Vietnamese troops into southern Laos. Laotian Premier Souvanna Phouma was said to have made a direct inquiry at the U.S. embassy in Vientiane, but was told that nothing was known at the moment. The premier said: "It is difficult to know what is happening in the Ho Chi Minh Trail sector where the Royal Laotian army

exercises no control. . . It is not impossible that the North Vietnamese—who really should withdraw from Laos—might one day draw in the South Vietnamese. If that happens, I shall make a statement."

A warning that Laos would oppose any South Vietnamese military move into Laos was voiced Feb. 1 by Laotian Gen. Thongphanh Knoksy. Knoksy, however, indicated that Laos would be in no military position to successfully counter such a thrust. He said "the area in question is one over which we have no control. It is under the control of the North Vietnamese."

The latest military developments in Indochina was the apparent topic of a White House meeting Feb. 2 of President Nixon and his leading military and diplomatic advisers. A White House spokesman would only confirm that a long meeting had taken place and that its participants included Defense Secretary Melvin R. Laird, Secretary of State William P. Rogers, Presidential adviser Henry Kissinger and Adm. Thomas Moorer, chairman of the Joint Chiefs of Staff.

Communists start drive in Laos—Laotian Defense Minister Sissouk Na Champassak announced Feb. 3 that North Vietnamese troops had captured key towns in northern Laos in what appeared to be the start of a major offensive. The strategic towns of Muong Soui and Phou So had been seized Feb. 2 and two adjacent government positions on the western edge of the Plaine des Jarres had fallen into Communist hands, the minister said.

Enemy forces had also overrun four small positions guarding the royal capital of Luang Prabang, he said. Muong Soui, 100 miles north of Vientiane, had been abandoned by government defenders after it came under enemy shelling. Contact with the 5,000 government troops there had been lost. Government forces had occupied Muong Soui since its recapture from the North Vietnamese in October 1970. In another successful foray, North Vietnamese troops Jan. 27 had captured the town of Phalane, 54 miles from Savannakhet, a strategic village on the Mekong River border between Thailand and Laos.

Premier Souvanna Phouma had warned Jan. 30 that North Vietnam was beginning to start a general offensive in his country because it faced "stronger opposition" in South Vietnam. Souvanna speculated that it was possible that Hanoi first planned to conquer Cambodia and Laos and then deal with South Vietnam later.

Commenting on Laos' unsuccessful attempts to start peace negotiations with the Pathet Lao rebel forces, Souvanna charged that "all the propositions they [the Pathet Lao] made represent only propaganda meant to conceal the preparations they are making for a general offensive against us." Pathet Lao representative Souk Vongsak had completed another in a series of contacts with government officials in Vientiane and had returned the previous week to the Lao Patriotic Front headquarters in Sam Neua. A Pathet Lao statement Jan. 30 accused the Laotian government and the U.S. of "deliberately delaying" talks to end the civil war in Laos.

Laotian government officials had claimed Jan. 11 that their forces had dealt a sharp setback to North Vietnamese troops on the Boloven Plateau the previous week. They said 250 North Vietnamese had been slain Jan. 8 in an unsuccessful attack against a Laotian government outpost at Ban Houei Sai in the northern part of the plateau. Government losses totaled two killed and 10 wounded in the battle against 1,500 North Vietnamese soldiers. Government sources described the battle as the fiercest in Laos in 18 months.

Laos refugee aid diverted. Sen. Edward M. Kennedy (D, Mass.) charged Feb. 6 that American aid for war refugees in Laos was being supplied to guerrilla forces directed by the Central Intelligence Agency. "Until recent times," he said, "the U.S. AID [Agency for International Development] refugee program was simply a euphemism to cover American assistance to persons who agreed to take up arms against the [Communist] Pathet Lao."

"A very significant measure of this assistance apparently continues," Kennedy said. Such activity had been disclosed in 1970.

The information was based on reports from the General Accounting Office which were released by Kennedy's Senate Refugees and Escapees Subcommittee. The reports said "substantial amounts" of medical supplies were being furnished "Lao military" by AID.

South Vietnamese Offensive in Laos

Drive against Communist supply lines. Sweeping across the border from the northwestern corner of South Vietnam, an estimated 5,000 South Vietnamese troops invaded southern Laos Feb. 8 in a drive aimed at smashing North Vietnamese supply bases along the Ho Chi Minh Trail. American forces were committed to provide air, artillery and logistical support for the South Vietnamese drive, code-named Operation Lam Son 719, but were providing this assistance from inside South Vietnam's Quangtri Province.

Communist resistance to the initial incursion was said to be light. In one of the few reported engagements, 14 North Vietnamese and three South Vietnamese were killed in a clash southwest of Langvei, South Vietnam. In the first few hours of the drive, a regiment of 3,000 troops was airlifted 20 miles south of Tchepone, a key Communist supply center 20 miles west of the South Vietnamese frontier. Another Saigon force set up a fire base 10 miles inside Laos on Route 9, one-third the way to Tchepone. The remaining 2,000 troops were said to have moved into Laos in armored personnel carriers along Route 9.

About 200 American fighter-bombers and helicopter gunships were said to have flown tactical support missions for this force. Six of the helicopters were reported lost in the early hours of the invasion—four to enemy fire and two

because of mechanical problems. An initial airborne force of 500 South Vietnamese Rangers was said to have been sent into Laos Feb. 7 to secure a landing.

The first stage of the drive had started Jan. 30 when 20,000 South Vietnamese and 9,000 American soldiers reactivated the former American base at Khesanh and pushed west to the frontier preparatory to the actual crossing. Reports of the operation were not officially disclosed until Feb. 4 when the U.S. command in Saigon lifted a six-day news blackout with an announcement that the drive was under way.

The command said the mission, code-named Dewey Canyon II, had been ordered because of a "North Vietnamese buildup threatening the western regions of Military Region I" which covered the five northern provinces of South Vietnam. The American role in the first stage of the assault consisted of clearing the roads leading to the frontier, repairing abandoned air strips, providing air cover and highway security, and airlifting South Vietnamese troops to the area. At the start of the operation Jan. 30, elements of the American 1st Brigade of the 5th Infantry Division Mechanized left Quangtri combat base, briefly moving north on Route 1 and then turning west on Route 9 toward the Laotian frontier.

A Congressional ban against the use of American ground forces in Laos prevented the U.S. troops from crossing the frontier. A sign posted 100 yards from the Laotian line read: "Warning, no U.S. personnel beyond this point."

(The U.S. command had reported Feb. 7 that South Vietnamese planes had accidentally dropped bombs on Saigon troops massing near the Laotian frontier, killing six and wounding 51. The mishap occurred within six miles of Khesanh.)

The invasion of Laos had been reported earlier by the pro-Communist Pathet Lao rebels Feb. 6. The Japanese Kyodo news agency quoted Col. Soth Phethrasy, a representative of the Pathet Lao mission in Vientiane, as saying that South Vietnamese troops had reached Tchepone, and with the aid of American troops were advancing toward Muong Phine, 15 miles to the southwest. The colonel said Pathet Lao troops in the Boloven Plateau in the south had killed at least 20 South Vietnamese troops and shot down four helicopters.

Allies explain incursion. The South Vietnamese incursion into Laos was explained in official statements by President Nguyen Van Thieu Feb. 7 and by the U.S. State Department Feb. 8 as a move aimed at depriving the Communists of sanctuaries close to the South Vietnamese borders.

Thieu described the drive "as an operation limited in time as well as in space." Asserting that Saigon had no territorial ambitions and did not seek to interfere in the "internal politics of Laos," Thieu pledged that his country's forces would withdraw as soon as they accomplished their objectives. He said their purpose was to disrupt "the supply and infiltration network of the Communist North Vietnamese in Laos, which territory has for many years been occupied by North Vietnamese Communists and used as a base to launch attacks on our country."

Thieu justified the move as a "necessary act of legitimate self-defense of South Vietnam against the Communist North Vietnamese aggressors."

Thieu insisted that the operation was "not an expansion of the war" but "an action taken to help end soon the war

in Vietnam and restore peace in this part of the world."

The State Department expressed similar views in an eight-point statement Feb. 8. It called the incursion limited in scope aimed at protecting "the security and safety of American forces in South Vietnam" and to "make the enemy less able to mount offensives and strengthen South Vietnam's ability to defend itself as U.S. forces are withdrawn from South Vietnam." "The limited operation is not an enlargement of the war" and was "fully consistent with international law," the statement said.

The State Department acknowledged that the Laotian government that day was "critical of the current military action," but noted that Vientiane had held North Vietnam primarily responsible for the continued violation of Laos' neutrality.

The Laotian protest, expressed by Premier Souvanna Phouma, said that although North Vietnam had used southeastern Laos as a supply network for years, there was "no justification" for the South Vietnamese thrust into his country. Appealing for withdrawal of all non-Laotian forces, Souvanna deplored "once again that foreign troops belonging to countries and governments that have pledged to guarantee and defend the sovereignty, neutrality and inviolability of Laos have chosen to deliberately use our territory as a field of battle."

Action to shorten war, Senate told. The Nixon Administration informed Congress Feb. 9 that the allied thrust into Laos would insure the U.S. troop withdrawal program from South Vietnam and shorten the war. The spokesmen were Secretary of State William P. Rogers, who briefed the Senate Foreign Relations Committee, and Defense Secretary Melvin R. Laird, who appeared before the Senate and House Armed Services Committees.

Both gave assurance that the Administration did not intend to send American ground combat troops into Laos if the South Vietnamese encountered difficulties.

"We have not widened the war," Laird said afterwards. "To the contrary, we have shortened it." The "success of Viet-namization" would be insured and the withdrawal of "additional" American troops made possible, he said.

Senate reaction to the briefings Feb. 9 was muted, with some members of the Armed Services Committee, notably Sens. John Stennis (D, Miss.), the Senate panel's chairman, and Henry M. Jackson (D, Wash.), expressing approval of the operation in Laos and Sen. J. W. Fulbright (D, Ark.), chairman of the Foreign Relations Committee, confining himself to "very grave reservations" about the action.

Earlier reaction from Senate war critics was similarly muted, although Sen. Edmund S. Muskie (D, Me.) expressed the view, over the ABC "Issues and Answers" broadcast Feb. 7, that use of combat air support in the drive went "beyond the spirit of any policies" endorsed by Congress. The same day Sen. Stuart Symington (D, Mo.) expressed concern "that we're expanding the war." Sen. Frank Church (D, Idaho), sponsor with Sen. John Sherman Cooper (R, Ky.) of the Congressional proscription against use of U.S. ground combat troops in Laos, while viewing the incursion as "a further widening" of the war, expressed hope Feb. 7 that it would prove "to be one of the last rear-guard actions."

U.S. denies ground forces role—Reports of American ground troops operating in Laos came from some U.S. soldiers and American newsmen. Some members of Troop D, 7th Battalion, 17th Air Cavalry were quoted as saying Feb. 10 that 100 or more Americans had been fighting the Communists inside Laos the last three days. These troops belonged to a unit that was rushed by helicopter into areas where ground forces were needed on short notice, according to the soldiers' account.

American Broadcasting Co. correspondent Howard Tuckner reported Feb. 11 that he had observed what appeared to be an American swimming with two South Vietnamese soldiers 25 miles inside Laos. Tuckner said South Vietnamese riding with him in a truck said the man was a "GI adviser." The newsman also said he had witnessed an American helicopter pick up the bodies

of four U.S. helicopter crewmen killed in a crash and the body of a fifth American wearing the uniform of a South Vietnamese paratrooper. The U.S. command in Saigon Feb. 12 refuted the claim, insisting that the body of the fifth man was a South Vietnamese paratrooper.

The Columbia Broadcasting System reported Feb. 11 that American Special Forces men, some in South Vietnamese uniform, were accompanying South Vietnamese troops flown into Laos in American helicopters.

(American correspondents were forbidden to fly in American helicopters supplying the South Vietnamese in the Laos operations. Some newsmen, however, were permitted to ride in South Vietnamese aircraft and thus were able to obtain brief, first-hand assessments of the military situation.)

The White House Feb. 11 denied the ABC and CBS reports of American troop involvement in Laos. A statement said: "Our policy is and will continue to be that there will be no United States combat troops or advisers in Laos." A similar denial was issued by the White House Feb. 12.

(Four news photographers were missing and presumed dead after the helicopter in which they were riding crashed Feb. 10 11 miles inside Laos. The men were Larry Burrows of Life, Henri Huet of the Associated Press, Kent Potter of United Press International and Keisaburo Shimamoto of the Pan-Asia Newspaper Alliance.)

Laos declares emergency—Mounting North Vietnamese military pressure in northern Laos prompted the Laotian government to declare a state of emergency Feb. 12. The decision, adopted by the cabinet the previous day, gave armed forces commander Gen. Ouane Rathikoune power to take measures for general security throughout the country. The cabinet also adopted a communique calling the South Vietnamese incursion and the continued presence of North Vietnamese troops in Laos a violation of the 1962 Geneva convention, which guaranteed Laos' neutrality.

The North Vietnamese and rebel Pathet Lao forces posed a military threat to Sam Thong and Long Tieng, the two government positions southwest of the Plaine des Jarres. Long Tieng was a U.S. Central Intelligence Agency base manned by 6,000 Meo tribesmen under the command of Maj. Gen. Vang Pao. Communist forces were reported Feb. 10 to have taken several hilltop positions flanking the two strongholds, which were 15 miles apart. Rocket fire also blasted the air strips at Sam Thong and at the nearby post of Bhan Na. North Vietnamese commandos penetrated Long Tieng's defense perimeter Feb. 14 but withdrew after coming under attack by U.S. and Laotian planes. The American aircraft accidentally dropped bombs on a friendly position, killing 30 Meo tribesmen and wounding 200, according to Laotian sources. Troop reinforcement and supplies were rushed into Long Tieng Feb. 15.

The heightened fighting around Sam Thong and Long Tieng prompted the start of the evacuation of 20,000–30,000 civilians, it had been reported Feb. 11. The refugees were moving to new home sites in the mountains 15–25 southwest. They were receiving relief supplies dropped by American planes.

Ho Chi Minh Trail cut. Saigon military officials claimed Feb. 15 that South Vietnamese forces, continuing their thrust into southern Laos, had severed all but two key sections of North Vietnam's Ho Chi Minh Trail, cutting off the movement of Communist supplies and troops into the northernmost province of South Vietnam.

The commander of the South Vietnamese operation, Lt. Gen. Hoang Xuan Lam, said Feb. 15 that his forces had cut the main part of the Ho Chi Minh Trail. "We hold the part they need to resupply their troops to the south," he said. Since the start of the incursion Feb. 8, the South Vietnamese claimed to have killed 449 enemy soldiers, destroyed about 30 tanks, and captured large quantities of Communist supplies. South Vietnamese losses through Feb. 13 were listed as 35 killed and 124 wounded.

The South Vietnamese also attributed the slowness of their drive to "the discovery of so many supply caches we have to have time to search."

Some reports placed the South Vietnamese penetration at 15 miles inside Laos. Other accounts put Saigon's advance units around the abandoned enemy base of Tchepone, which was more than 25 miles inside Laos. Additional South Vietnamese troops poured across the border into Laos, raising the total force there to about 12,000 men.

Among other major military and political developments relating to the fighting in Laos:

■ Inclement weather and U.S. bomb-craters on Highway 9, the invasion route, slowed down the westward drive that continued to meet little enemy ground resistance.

■ U.S. helicopters, flying combat and logistic missions, suffered heavy losses with an estimated 15 downed, mostly by enemy ground fire, through Feb. 17.

■ Reports that some American combat troops were participating in ground operations in Laos were denied by the Nixon Administration.

■ The upsurge of fighting in the north prompted the Laotian government Feb. 12 to declare a state of emergency.

■ Communist China Feb. 12 issued a stern warning against the South Vietnamese incursion, but U.S. officials discounted the possibility of Chinese military intervention.

Allied spokesmen Feb. 17 estimated American losses thus far at 31 killed and 65 wounded. The losses included airmen killed over Laos and ground troops slain in the South Vietnamese phase of the operation.

Of the 15 downed American helicopters, eight were lost over Laos Feb. 12, while some of the others were downed around Khesanh, the South Vietnamese jumping off point for the incursion.

International reaction. Among the major international reaction Feb. 8 to the South Vietnamese incursion into Laos:

The Pathet Lao charged that U.S. and South Vietnamese troops were "carrying out a new and extremely dangerous venture by invading Laos." The statement was contained in a protest sent to Britain and the Soviet Union, as co-chairmen of the 1962 convention on Laos. It urged them to take steps to have the U.S. halt its "aggressive operation in Laos."

The British Foreign Office called the South Vietnamese move "fully understandable" in view of North Vietnam's continued violation of Laos' neutrality in defiance of the 1962 Geneva agreement. Britain, the statement said, supported Washington's "Vietnamization policy and American troop withdrawals and this operation seems likely to ensure its continued progress."

The Soviet Union charged that the U.S. had escalated the Indochina conflict to "a dangerous new stage by opening a new front of war." Assailing the action as "a further dangerous expansion of aggression," the statement warned that the U.S. had "assumed heavy responsibility to world and American public opinion for its aftermath."

North Vietnam asserted that "the aggression in Laos under the direction of the U.S. imperialists is a real sabotage of the 1962 Geneva agreement and the violation of Laotian sovereignty." Hanoi pledged that "with the assistance of the Khmer people and army," the Vietnamese people "will fight and defeat the U.S. aggressors."

Peking, noting that Laos was a "close neighbor" of Communist China, described the South Vietnamese incursion as a "grave provocation" against the Chinese people. A Foreign Ministry statement accused the U.S. of "wildly plotting to launch a sudden attack on North Vietnam." (In a previous statement scoring the allied buildup near the Laotian border, the Foreign Ministry had warned Feb. 4 that China would not permit the U.S. to "do what it pleases in Indochina.")

Communist China warned Feb. 12 that it "will not remain indifferent" to the movement into Laos of any "large numbers of U.S. puppet forces." Peking assailed the U.S. for "savage crimes of aggression against Laos" and declared that the Chinese people would "take all effective measures" to assist Communist forces in Laos, Cambodia and Vietnam.

A White House statement Feb. 12 expressed the belief that South Vietnamese efforts to cut the Ho Chi Minh Trail in Laos would not precipitate Chinese Communist military intervention in Laos. "These operations pose absolutely no threat to Communist China, and we can therefore see no reason for them to be interpreted as such."

The U.S. State Department Feb. 12 discounted concern expressed by Laotian Premier Souvanna Phouma that Communist China might intervene. In a report published that day by the Washington Post, Souvanna was quoted as telling foreign diplomats in Vientiane that it was highly likely that Chinese "volunteers" would push into Laos if South Vietnamese forces appeared to be about to cut off the Ho Chi Minh Trail in Laos.

Thousands of Chinese rallied in Peking Feb. 14 to denounce the allied action in Laos and pledge support for Communists in Indochina. An editorial appearing the same day in the Chinese Communist party newspaper Jenmin Jih Pao scoffed at U.S. government assertions that the invasion of Laos did not pose a threat to Communist China. The editorial said: "China and Laos are next-door neighbors linked by the same mountains and rivers and as close to one another as lips to teeth. The new war venture of U.S. imperialism in Laos definitely poses a grave threat to China."

Other Communist nations continued to assail the incursion into Laos. Among the reactions and related diplomatic developments:

The Soviet Union Feb. 9 scored "the stepped-up imperialist aggression" in Indochina. An editorial appearing in the Communist party newspaper Pravda contended that U.S. planes had dropped bombs on densely populated civilian areas in an action that "can only be called genocide."

North Vietnam Feb. 9 warned the U.S. and South Vietnam that "the liberated zone of Laos" would be "the tomb of the Americans and their agents." Hanoi charged that the operation in Laos had been directed by President Nixon with the "cooperation of the general staffs of Saigon and Vientiane."

Soviet Premier Aleksei N. Kosygin Feb. 10 denounced U.S. "aggression" in Indochina and particularly in Laos. The Soviet news agency Tass said that in a meeting with Kosygin, North Vietnamese Deputy Prime Minister Le Than Nghi had told him of "the aggravation of the situation in Indochina," including "expansion of the aggression in Laos and Cambodia and the staging of new provocations" against North Vietnam. Nghi, accompanied by members of North Vietnam's politburo, had signed an agreement in Moscow for more Soviet technical assistance to North Vietnam.

As a member of the International Control Commission for Laos, Poland Feb. 12 called on Britain and the Soviet Union, co-chairmen of the Geneva Conference on Laos, "to use their utmost influence" to prevent a further U.S. military expansion in Indochina, particularly in Laos. Warsaw's memorandum charged that the invasion of Laos had "pushed Laos into the tragedy of civil war." A Foreign Ministry spokesman said Polish diplomats had been instructed "to discuss the issue at foreign ministries in Peking, New Delhi, Ottawa and other capitals." (Canada and India were the other two members of the ICC for Laos.) The Polish ambassador to the U.S. was said to have taken up the matter with American officials in Washington.

Britain and the Soviet Union were reported Feb. 12 to have received a protest from Prince Souphanouvong, head of the Pathet Lao. The prince charged that 50 battalions, including more than 10 American battalions, had "massacred the civilian population in an utterly savage manner throughout their journey" into Laos.

Ky sees protracted Laos drive. Vice President Nguyen Cao Ky predicted Feb. 10 that South Vietnamese forces would continue their operations in Laos until the dry season ended in May. The ensuing monsoon weather would make it difficult for the troops to operate along the Communists' supply network, Ky said. But he foresaw the possibility of another thrust into Laos in 1971, asserting there might be a need for "continuous actions" against the Ho Chi Minh Trail to insure the safety of South Vietnamese troops.

Ky recalled that he had long advocated the current drive into Laos, partly to attempt "to force North Vietnam to reconsider its policy" and begin meaningful peace negotiations in Paris. "Since the goal is so important, we have to achieve it by any means," Ky said.

He said it was vital not only to strike at Communist bases in Laos "but also their rear bases in North Vietnam."

Communists slow Laos drive. Mounting North Vietnamese ground resistance Feb. 18–22 stalled the South Vietnamese drive into southern Laos. The South Vietnamese penetration remained blocked about 17 miles inside the country. At the same time, intense Communist antiaircraft fire continued to take a heavy toll of U.S. helicopters. Despite the apparent slowdown of the incursion, U.S. officials asserted Feb. 22 that the operation was going well.

Saigon's forces suffered their first serious setback in the fighting Feb. 20 when a 450-man battalion of rangers was driven by the North Vietnamese from a hilltop patrol and artillery base a few miles west of Phu Loc, six miles inside Laos and nine miles north of Route 9, the east-west axis of the drive against the Ho Chi Minh Trail. It was reported that 298 South Vietnamese were killed or wounded in a siege that had started Feb. 18. The survivors were said to have brought out 108 wounded, but left 60 others behind with the bodies of 130. North Vietnamese losses were put at 639 killed. The North Vietnamese overran the base despite large-scale U.S. air strikes. Heavy antiaircraft fire prevented U.S. helicopters from bringing in men and supplies to the beleaguered stronghold. Another South Vietnamese ranger base, one mile away, was reported Feb. 22 to be holding out under enemy fire.

North Vietnamese representatives at the Paris peace talks said Feb. 22 that the troops that had attacked the rangers at Phu Loc were Pathet Lao guerrillas, not North Vietnamese.

An American helicopter crew chief, Spec. 5 Dennis Fujii, had taken virtual command of the Phu Loc defense. He was wounded and airlifted to safety Feb. 23, the U.S. command reported. Fujii had been participating in a medical-evacuation mission at Phu Loc and remained after giving up his seat to a wounded South Vietnamese. Since then, the command said, he had been directing air and artillery strikes against the Communist attackers.

The fighting at Phu Loc followed reports Feb. 17 that two additional North Vietnamese regiments totaling about 4,000 troops had moved into positions just north of Route 9, in the vicinity of Phu Loc.

A South Vietnamese communique Feb. 22 on the incursion since Feb. 8 said 1,960 North Vietnamese had been killed, including about 500 by American air strikes. (U.S. officials called these figures exaggerated.) South Vietnamese losses were put at 168 killed and 661 wounded. This did not include losses suffered in the Phu Loc engagement. The communique said ground attacks and U.S. air strikes had accounted for destruction of 12,603 tons of Communist ammunition, 12 tanks, 65 trucks, 400 bicycles and 125,000 gallons of fuel.

The U.S. command reported Feb. 22 that 26 American helicopters had been lost since the start of the invasion Feb. 8. Of these, 17 had been shot down in Laos and nine in northern South Vietnam. Total casualties in these crashes were 29 killed, 26 wounded and 15 missing. Five of the aircraft were shot down over Laos Feb. 18.

South Vietnamese forces operating in Laos totaled 16,000 men. A South Vietnamese spokesman conceded Feb. 19 that although some branches of the Ho Chi Minh Trail had been cut, others remained open. He said it was possible the North Vietnamese had shifted their supply movements further west to avoid the attackers.

In other fighting connected with the Laos operation, an American artillery base 10 miles northwest of Khesanh, South Vietnam came under North Vietnamese siege Feb. 16. Eight Americans were wounded in the initial six-hour Communist attack. Bad weather prevented helicopters from landing reinforcements at the base, six miles from the demilitarized zone.

(American support of the South Vietnamese drive into Laos resulted in a sharp increase in U.S. casualty figures in the Feb. 7–13 period. Fifty-one were killed, compared with 24 slain Jan. 31–Feb. 6. GIs wounded Feb. 7–13 totaled 217, a drop from the 367 listed the previous week. South Vietnamese losses also increased considerably, with 478 killed and 1,159 wounded, compared with 345 killed and 805 wounded the previous week.)

The main allied rear base for the drive into Laos—Quangtri, South Vietnam—was struck by 17 Communist shells Feb. 24 for the first time.

The South Vietnamese command reported Feb. 25 that helicopter gunships Feb. 18–19 had destroyed four fuel pipelines running parallel to the Ho Chi Minh Trail.

Brig. Gen. Pham Van Phu, commander of the South Vietnamese 1st Infantry Division, said Feb. 24 that North Vietnamese ambushes along Route 9 had made it impossible to move supplies along that east-west invasion route into Laos.

Hanoi claims successes—The North Vietnamese army newspaper Quan Doi Nhan Dan reported Feb. 23 that Hanoi's forces had made Route 9 "the cemetery of helicopters and armored vehicles." Providing North Vietnam's own detailed version of the fighting for the first time, the newspaper said 170 U.S. and South Vietnamese aircraft and 210 vehicles had been destroyed, and 4,000 allied troops had been put out of action since the start of the incursion into Laos Feb. 8.

President Nixon's Vietnamization plan had been dealt "a hard blow" in Laos, the newspaper said. The Communist party newspaper Nhan Dan discounted allied explanations that their drive had been slowed by bad weather and by the removal of Communist arms and supply depots. "The real reason for the slowness of the operation is the resolute riposte of the liberation armies of southern Laos and northern Quangtri Province which coordinated their actions very well," the newspaper said.

Allies provide battle figures—A U.S. command spokesman reported Feb. 24 that 500 North Vietnamese had been killed by American planes and helicopter gunships since the start of the Laotian campaign. The air action also had destroyed 120 supply and weapons caches, 330 vehicles, 115 bunkers, 420 structures and 35 gun positions.

The U.S. command acknowledged Feb. 28 that a total of 35 American helicopters and two fighter-bombers had been destroyed in the Laotian drive on both sides of the border. Field reports had listed many more helicopters shot down or damaged, but the command reported only those cases in which aircraft were considered a total loss. American air casualties totaled 40 dead, 18 missing and 34 wounded.

In its cumulative report on the Laos operation, the Saigon command reported Feb. 27 that 2,416 Communists had been killed as of Feb. 26. Government losses for the same period were 310 killed, 971 wounded and 99 missing.

South Vietnamese ground forces and artillery and air strikes had destroyed 12 Soviet-built tanks, 87 trucks, 400 bicycles, 550 houses, 132,000 gallons of fuel, 12,703 tons of ammunition and large quantities of food, the Saigon command had reported Feb. 24.

U.S., Saigon optimistic on Laos. The U.S. and South Vietnam Feb. 22 and 23 continued to express optimism on the progress of the allied operation in Laos despite the reversals suffered by South Vietnamese forces at Phu Loc and a slowdown of the offensive.

White House Press Secretary Ronald Ziegler said President Nixon felt the operation was "going well." Ziegler denied reports that the North Vietnamese had stepped up the movement of supplies down the Ho Chi Minh Trail since Feb. 8. The average flow of about 1,000 North Vietnamese trucks north and south of the supply network had increased to 2,000 a day in the last two weeks, according to press reports from South Vietnam and Laos that quoted American pilots.

Ziegler said: "There is no question that the enemy continues to make substantial attempts to force supplies down the Ho Chi Minh Trail complex. But I have no information that they have doubled their flow of supplies." Ziegler insisted that the main objective of the operation, disruption of enemy infiltration and supplies, "is being met."

U.S. Defense Department spokesman Jerry Friedheim minimized the importance of the major Communist supply base at Tchepone, which the South Vietnamese thus far had failed to reach. He said "I realize that that particular city gets written about because it sits in the middle of Route 9, but this is an airmobile operation with a great deal of

flexibility permitted and it would be incorrect to pick out a specific single geographic point and call it the objective." The capture of Tchepone had been regarded by many officials as a prime target of the invasion of Laos, although this had never been publicly stated.

President Nguyen Van Thieu asserted that the South Vietnamese thrust into Laos had upset a North Vietnamese plan to seize the five northernmost provinces of South Vietnam to improve the Communists' bargaining position at the Paris peace talks. In first announcing the invasion Feb. 8, Thieu had said its objective was "disrupting the supply and infiltration network" of the North Vietnamese.

Successes in the Laos operation also were reported by Presidential adviser Henry Kissinger in a White House briefing given to a group of Congressmen Feb. 23. One of those attending the session, Rep. Gerald R. Ford (R, Mich.), later quoted Kissinger as saying that Saigon's forces had cut several North Vietnamese supply routes in Laos. Ford identified the blocked roads as Route 9, the principal east-west road on which South Vietnamese troops were attempting to push westward, and Routes 92 and 914, running roughly north and south across Route 9.

Defense Secretary Melvin R. Laird told newsmen Feb. 23 that the Laos operation was "proceeding on schedule" and that its purpose of cutting off Communist supply lines was "being achieved." He warned, however, that South Vietnamese forces in Laos and Cambodia faced "tougher, difficult fighting."

Laird said Feb. 24 that the drive "is going according to plan." South Vietnamese forces had deliberately paused in their offensive to "assess the enemy reactions" and they did not slow down as a result of North Vietnamese attacks, he asserted. His remarks, at a Pentagon news conference, were made before big battles fought around Hills 30 and 31.

Laird's optimism on the progress of the fighting was shared by Lt. Gen. John W. Vogt Jr., director of the Joint Staff of the Joint Chiefs of Staff, who appeared at the news conference with him. Vogt said: "The enemy has not stopped the

[South Vietnamese] movement along Highway 9. There are no major engagements in the area stopping our forces." Vogt said Saigon's troops had accomplished "the first portion" of their objectives, severing Route 92, which he described as the main north-south road in the Ho Chi Minh Trail complex, and blocking the intersection of Routes 914, 99 and 92, which he said the North Vietnamese had attempted to use to evade the South Vietnamese attacks. Vogt said since the start of the drive Feb. 8, North Vietnam had reinforced its 15,000 combat troops and 10,000 logistic soldiers in Laos with six regiments.

Laird reiterated the view that cutting off the Communists' supply routes remained the prime objective of the invasion of Laos. He said: "The key thing is to disrupt the logistic supply routes. I believe that this operation, even if it were to terminate—and there is no fixed time limit on it—now has been successful in disrupting the logistic supplies." Laird downgraded the importance of the principal Communist supply base at Tchepone, reportedly the principal target of the offensive. "Tchepone, as such, has never been an objective," he said.

In a reversal of American policy, Laird announced in a separate statement Feb. 24 that newsmen would be permitted to fly in a specially designated American helicopter to cover the operations in Laos. The correspondents had previously been barred from U.S. helicopters since the start of the incursion, but were permitted to fly in South Vietnamese 'copters, which were relatively scarce. The original ban resulted from invoking a Defense Department edict against using military aircraft to carry civilians across international borders.

U.S. troop use in Laos planned. U.S. officials announced Feb. 26 that small groups of American infantry could be sent into Laos to help rescue downed American airmen despite the ban on the use of U.S. "ground troops" in that country. Defense Department spokesman Jerry Friedheim said this would represent "no change in policy" since the soldiers assigned would be regarded as "rescue forces, not combat troops." Some American officials termed the projected missions "protective encirclement."

Commenting on the possible rescue missions in Laos, a U.S. military spokesman in Saigon said, "If the need arose and an American life was at stake, we would do it" or "anything we felt necessary to rescue downed crew members."

The Viet Cong delegation at the Paris peace talks Feb. 27 denounced the American plan to rescue downed airmen in Laos. A statement said: "This is a perfidious maneuver of the Nixon Administration to make public and to legalize the presence of American combat troops that have already been sent and will be increased to expand aggression in Laos and other places." The statement repeated the Communist charge that American infantry and motorized troops had taken part in the South Vietnamese drive into Laos.

Saigon bases attacked in Laos. South Vietnamese and North Vietnamese soldiers fought one of the fiercest battles of the Indochina war Feb. 25–27 around two South Vietnamese artillery support bases six miles inside Laos. Although an official casualty toll was not released, South Vietnamese losses were said to be the heaviest since the Communists' 1968 Tet offensive in South Vietnam. The fighting tapered off Feb. 28–March 1, but the two strongholds were reported still under enemy siege.

The heaviest action took place at Hill 31 north of Route 9, about six miles west of the Laotian border where the Saigon troops had first come under enemy attack Feb. 22. The second stronghold was the artillery base on Hill 30, four miles away and just south of Route 9.

Using tanks for the first time in the Laotian fighting, North Vietnamese forces were reported to have driven the South Vietnamese troops from their defensive positions on Hill 31 Feb. 25. The 500 defenders withdrew with heavy losses after coming under attack by 20 light Soviet-made tanks.

Following intensive American air strikes on the 2,000 attackers and the moving in of troop reinforcements, South Vietnamese military authorities reported Feb. 27 that the Saigon soldiers had regained control of Hill 31. Heavy Communist antiaircraft fire around the base prevented American helicopters from flying in supplies during the height of the fighting. But as the firing eased off Feb. 28, the 'copters were able to bring in matériel and reinforcements.

U.S. helicopter pilots reported March 1 that both sides occupied opposite slopes of Hill 31 with the top of the hill a no-man's-land.

Maj. Gen. Du Quoc Dong, commander of the South Vietnamese paratroopers in Laos, claimed Feb. 27 that "we killed at least 1,000" of the enemy in the battle for the hill. Other South Vietnamese sources said 15 of the 20 Soviet-made tanks involved in the fighting had been destroyed, five of them by American air strikes. More North Vietnamese tanks were spotted by helicopter pilots around Hill 30, posing a threat to that South Vietnamese support base.

Another South Vietnamese artillery base south of Route 9 at Hong Ha Ha, southeast of Tchepone, was reported March 1 to have been evacuated because of heavy North Vietnamese pressure.

Eight North Vietnamese tanks were reported destroyed March 1 by U.S. jet fighters near the town of Bandong on Route 9. A South Vietnamese spokesman in Saigon said the tanks were closing in on a position established by South Vietnam's 1st Infantry Division.

The North Vietnamese were reported March 2 to have moved heavy Soviet-made T-54 tanks into Laos for the first time.

In preparation for a possible new North Vietnamese attack, a force of 10,-000 South Vietnamese troops in the northeastern corner of South Vietnam were reported March 1 moving westward toward the Laotian frontier. The reinforcements were described as prepared to assist in the blocking of a possible push toward South Vietnam or to cross into Laos to bolster the 16,000 Saigon troops already there.

An estimated 600 men crossed into Laos March 2. A U.S. Army spokesman reported March 1 that more American planes had been flown to the allied re-supply and staging base at Khesanh. The air reinforcements were said to include 30 Cobra attack helicopters.

There were indications that the North Vietnamese were pushing their supply trails westward in the face of the South Vietnamese advance. A Laotian military spokesman reported March 2 that North Vietnamese engineers were building a major road in Laos west of the Ho Chi Minh Trail. He said the engineers had first been observed March 1 on the road starting from Highway 9 west of Tchepone and running northwest toward the Mekong River.

In ground fighting around Hill 30, eight miles northwest of Lao Bao, Saigon military authorities claimed that South Vietnamese forces March 3 killed 98 North Vietnamese soldiers, while the attackers suffered only one killed and three wounded. The South Vietnamese were supported by air and artillery strikes, which were said to have accounted for 60 of the enemy dead.

In another action near Lao Bao, five miles west, Saigon claimed its troops March 4 killed 325 enemy soldiers, while suffering only 20 wounded.

South Vietnamese troops engaged North Vietnamese soldiers six miles east of Tchepone March 5-6 and killed 152 of the enemy, according to South Vietnamese military authorities. South Vietnam said its losses were two killed and 38 wounded.

Seven American helicopters flying in support of South Vietnamese troops were shot down by enemy ground fire and destroyed March 3, making it the highest toll for one day since the start of the operation. The command said one crewman was killed, 10 were wounded and six were listed as missing. Another four 'copters were downed March 4, three over Laos and one over South Vietnam. In a revised report issued March 9, the U.S. command said 58 American helicopters had been downed since the start of the Laos campaign. The air losses resulted in 50 Americans killed, 50 wounded and 16 missing. U.S. pilots estimated that as many as 140 'copters had been shot down or badly damaged.

Antiaircraft gunners in North Vietnam March 2 fired three missiles across the demilitarized zone against American planes flying missions near Khesanh over South Vietnam. A fourth American plane was fired at over Laos by a North Vietnam-based missile installation. This incident occurred 12 miles north-northwest of Lao Bao, a border crossing point. None of the planes were hit.

The following day, March 3, a U.S. fighter-bomber operating in Laos crossed the border into North Vietnam to fire a missile at a radar-controlled SAM anti-aircraft position 10 miles northeast of Bheban Raving Pass.

South Vietnamese capture Tchepone. After being stalled 16 miles inside southern Laos for nearly two weeks, reinforced South Vietnamese troops pushed westward and March 6 captured Tchepone, the main North Vietnamese supply base on the Ho Chi Minh Trail, about 25 miles inside the country. Meanwhile, fierce fighting erupted closer to the South Vietnamese border with the North Vietnamese reportedly taking heavy casualties. At the same time, U.S. planes and helicopters continued their supportive attacks on a massive scale. Particularly heavy raids were carried out March 7–8 over Laos as well as Cambodia and involved 2,000 planes.

More than 2,000 Saigon troops pushed into Tchepone which was found almost destroyed, having come under American air attack for days before the assault. About 200 enemy bodies were discovered in the town; a few Laotian civilians were found living amid the rubble. A South Vietnamese spokesman said the troops had found large quantities of ammunition and food and 15 antiaircraft guns and other weapons.

After taking Tchepone, South Vietnamese troops began setting up a ring of helicopter-landing zones and at least two artillery bases two and a half miles south and west of the town to prepare for a possible North Vietnamese counterstrike.

The first counterattacks against the new South Vietnamese forward positions came March 7 at an artillery base called Lolo, about six miles southeast of Tchepone. A South Vietnamese spokesman said 31 of the enemy and four of the Saigon soldiers had been killed.

The renewed push westward had been preceded by the movement of South Vietnamese reinforcements into Laos starting March 2. Fresh soldiers were ferried in by U.S. helicopters March 3–4 to a forward position east of Tchepone, the jumping-off point for the attack on the base itself. The additional troops totaled 2,000, raising the South Vietnamese strength in Laos to 18,000 men.

The 2,000 South Vietnamese reinforcements flown into Laos March 2–5 fought their first major engagement March 8, 12 miles southwest of the South Vietnamese border outpost at Langvei. Supported by American air and artillery strikes, they claimed to have killed 250 of the enemy, while losing 12 men. In an encounter 19 miles northeast of Tchepone, South Vietnamese paratroopers March 8 reported the slaying of 78 of the enemy, 55 by air strikes.

Reporting on the progress of the operation, Lt. Gen. Hoang Xuan Lam, commander of South Vietnamese forces in Laos, said March 9 that his troops now held three main junctions of the North Vietnamese supply trails. They were at Tchepone, Ban Dong, about halfway between Tchepone and the South Vietnamese border on Route 9, and Muong Nong, 20 miles south of Ban Dong.

While fighting raged in Laos, North Vietnamese forces carried out harassing attacks against the South Vietnamese rear bases serving the Laotian drive. The Communists March 2 fired 1,000 artillery and rocket shells at Dongha, causing some damage. Quangtri and Khesanh were shelled March 6–7 and at least seven Americans were killed.

Secret Laos operation disclosed. A clandestine South Vietnamese operation in Laos prior to the Feb. 8 incursion into that country was confirmed by U.S. Defense Department officials for the first time March 8.

The disclosure was made after newsmen had questioned the authenticity of a three-foot length of North Vietnamese pipeline that had been displayed at a department news conference Feb. 24 by Lt. Gen. John W. Vogt Jr., director of the Joint Staff of the Joint Chiefs of Staff. Vogt had said the pipe was a sample of a longer section, "some 300 meters," torn up by South Vietnamese ground forces "in the last two days." Although Vogt did not specifically say that the pipeline he was showing had been obtained during the current incursion, reporters were left with that impression.

Questioned further by reporters March 3, Defense Department spokesman Jerry Friedheim refused to say when and where the pipeline sample had been obtained. But he conceded it had been around "for more than a year." Department officials later conceded that the pipeline had been retrieved from an earlier South Vietnamese operation in Laos.

Defense Secretary Melvin R. Laird, asked whether the department had been "completely candid" about the matter, acknowledged March 4 that "it probably would have been better to make it clear" that the sample had not been captured during the current fighting in Laos.

Laotians under heavy attack. Laotian government forces came under heavy attack by North Vietnamese and Pathet Lao forces in the southern and northern parts of the country March 8–10, losing a vital base used to harass the Ho Chi Minh Trail near the Boloven Plateau in the south.

Describing the military situation as grave, the Defense Ministry announced March 9 that the northern army base at Long Tieng had been struck by Communist rocket fire March 8–9. The residence of King Savang Vathana, who was away at the time, was reported damaged. At least four Thai battalions and three battalions from the northern panhandle were said to have reinforced the Meo and Lao Theung tribesmen defending the Long Tieng base. The Thai troops, whose presence in Laos was officially denied, had taken up strong positions around Long Tieng, at Ban Na and Sam Thong to the northeast.

In the fighting to the south, government troops were driven from Position 22 March 9 and three smaller strongholds on the eastern edge of the Boloven Plateau following two days of Communist rocket, mortar and ground attacks. Three government battalions defending the positions were said to have retreated in good order, removing about 50 wounded.

The loss of Position 22 deprived the government of its strongest base in the area and threatened its hold over the plateau. The position had been used for government surveillance and raids against Route 16, the principal western branch of the Ho Chi Minh Trail.

U.S. and Laotian planes were reported to have participated during the last action in the Boloven fighting. Gen. Thongphanh Knoksy, a Defense Ministry spokesman, had said March 9 that in two days of fighting near the plateau, Laotian troops had killed 200 enemy soldiers while losing only one killed and 10 wounded

Saigon troops pull back in Laos. In the face of mounting North Vietnamese counterattacks, about 6,000 of South Vietnam's 21,000 troops in Laos began pulling back to the Vietnamese border March 12. The withdrawing forces abandoned several fixed positions, including their bases in and around the principal Communist supply center at Tchepone, which they had captured March 6.

The U.S. State Department March 17 denied Saigon's forces were in retreat. The department said the South Vietnamese were engaged in "mobile maneuvering" and were "proceeding according to plan."

A Saigon spokesman March 14 had denied press reports that government forces had pulled out of Tchepone to avoid a fight with the North Vietnamese. He said the South Vietnamese withdrew to avoid being hemmed in by superior Communist forces and to remove themselves as "a fixed target for the enemy."

Communist successes in the fighting were claimed in communiques and statements issued March 16 by North Vietnam, the Viet Cong and the rebel Pathet Lao in Laos. A North Vietnamese high command statement said Communist forces that day had captured Hill 723, six miles southwest of Ban Dong, east of Tchepone, following three days of artillery fire. A mobilization order to the troops said: "The enemy is in complete disarray, and is seeking to withdraw. Let all comrades . . . annihilate the enemy completely. Encircle him, prevent his withdrawal."

The South Vietnamese National Liberation Front radio claimed that the U.S.-South Vietnamese incursion into Laos "has failed" and that the South Vietnamese were "in full retreat." It appealed to the Saigon troops to put down "your weapons, and join your compatriots."

The Pathet Lao command issued an order to its troops to "completely annihilate" and "prevent the withdrawal" of South Vietnamese troops, who it said were fleeing "in disorder."

After capturing Tchepone, a force of about 2,500 South Vietnamese troops had established positions in the surrounding hills March 8–9 because the valley town was vulnerable to enemy attacks. The launching of the North Vietnamese drive March 12 forced the South Vietnamese to pull out of those positions, including Fire Base Sophia, three miles east of Tchepone. The South Vietnamese then established five or six new combat bases on a mountain ridge 5–15 miles southeast of Tchepone.

Another base, Lolo, six miles southeast of Sophia, was evacuated by the South Vietnamese March 15–16 under a Communist tank and artillery assault launched March 14. Bad weather and intense Communist antiaircraft fire had prevented U.S. helicopters from bringing supplies into the base. Official Saigon reports said 1,100 Communists had been killed in the fighting for Lolo while the South Vietnamese lost 16 killed and 190 wounded. Field accounts said the South Vietnamese casualties were higher than the official reports. Before pulling out of Lolo, the Saigon troops had destroyed six howitzers to make them useless to the North Vietnamese. Other South Vietnamese equipment left at the base was bombed by U.S. aircraft.

About 1,500 South Vietnamese, retreating five miles eastward, established positions March 16 at Landing Zone Brown, an artillery base three miles south of the principal invasion highway, Route 9, and came under North Vietnamese assault the following day. Pounded by mortar, artillery and rocket fire, the South Vietnamese retreated from the base and 100–150 North Vietnamese moved in. Assisted by heavy American air strikes, the Saigon troops pushed back into Landing Zone Brown March 17 and found the bodies of 80 enemy soldiers.

In a clash closer to the Vietnamese border, South Veitnamese troops March 12 killed 18 Communists nine miles northwest of the frontier town of Laobao. Government losses were put at three dead and two wounded.

In an air action three miles inside Laos, an American fighter-bomber March 14 accidentally attacked South Vietnamese ground troops, killing 10 and wounding 12. It was the fifth mistaken U.S. air strike on South Vietnamese forces since the start of the Laos operation Feb. 8 and raised the toll in such mishaps to 28 killed and 150 wounded. In two previous accidental air strikes, eight South Vietnamese soldiers had been killed and 54 injured by U.S. planes east of Tchepone March 5.

The allied rear support base at Khesanh, a frequent target of the North Vietnamese, came under the heaviest attack of the Laos operation March 15. The base was struck by 150 mortar and rocket shells. Damage was reported light and there were no fatalities. Most of the helicopters at Khesanh had taken off for other areas at the start of the two-hour assault.

In one of the largest air strikes since the start of the incursion, American pilots reported setting off 1,600 explosions of Communist fuel and ammunition supplies in Laos March 9. The targets were pounded in the same area where South Vietnamese troops had observed 500 secondary explosions set off by B–52 strikes March 7 about one mile northeast of Tchepone.

In a cumulative report on the ground fighting since Feb. 8, the South Vietnamese army said March 14 that 8,208 Communist troops had been killed, while its own losses were 726 killed, 2,700 wounded and 165 missing in action.

The Saigon command disclosed March 16 that its forces had been conducting an operation since Feb. 14 against elements of three North Vietnamese regiments in South Vietnam's Kontum Province, adjacent to the southern Laotian border. Although there had been little significant fighting, the command said 563 enemy had been killed, mostly by air strikes.

Battle near Luang Prabang. Heavy fighting erupted around Luang Prabang March 22 with a force of 3,000 North Vietnamese and Pathet Lao troops attacking in an area between one and five and a half miles north of the royal Laotian capital.

The Communist ground attack was preceded by extensive shelling of the city's airport March 20–22. The 150 rocket and mortar shells fired reportedly killed at least six persons, destroyed or damaged five planes and caused widespread damage to airport structures. Defense Ministry spokesman Gen. Thongphanh Knoksy said March 23 that six Communist battalions followed up the shelling with assaults on six government positions between Luang Prabang and Pak Ou, a town 22 miles to the northeast.

The threat to Luang Prabang was eased March 24 when government reinforcements, totaling three battalions, pushed the Communist forces from the edge of the city.

A Pathet Lao broadcast March 24 said the rebels had no intention of capturing Luang Prabang. The statement explained that the attacks were aimed at warning Premier Souvanna Phouma not to abandon his neutrality. This was regarded as a warning to rightists not to attempt a coup.

During the fighting, about 120 dependents of American embassy employes were evacuated from Luang Prabang and flown to Vientiane, 133 miles south. The State Department said the removal of the women and children was a "short-term measure."

Nixon lauds operation. President Nixon's interim assessment March 22 of the allied invasion of Laos was that it assured the next phase of U.S. withdrawal from South Vietnam, which would be "at least" at the current withdrawal pace of 12,500 men monthly. The President discussed the invasion during an hour-long interview, televised live from the White House library, with Howard K. Smith of the American Broadcasting Co. The war was the dominant topic.

The President cautioned that the success or failure of the operation could not be judged before or even after it was concluded since "its goals were long range." He said those goals were to insure the continuation of the American withdrawal, to "reduce the risk to the remaining Americans as we withdraw" and to "ensure the ability of the South Vietnamese to defend themselves after we have left."

There had been "considerable progress" toward these goals, he said. In addition to the assured continuance of the U.S. pullout, the danger to the U.S. forces remaining "has been substantially

reduced" and 18 of 22 South Vietnamese battalions involved had performed creditably.

Thus far in the six-week invasion, Nixon said, the South Vietnamese forces had "developed a considerable capability on their own, and considerable confidence on their own—their better units—to handle the situation as we withdraw."

Nixon also stressed that the purpose of the invasion was to disrupt supply lines and "defend South Vietnam." On that score, he said, the enemy "can never gain back the time," the six weeks when their "supplies to the south have been drastically cut" and "great amounts" of ammunition and material "chewed up."

The President criticized U.S. news coverage of the Laotian invasion as incomplete and distorted. Citing Gen. Creighton W. Abrams, commander of U.S. forces in Vietnam, Nixon said 18 of 22 South Vietnamese battalions were doing "extremely well" in the operation while television films had shown only the four battalions "that were in trouble."

Nixon said the overall newspaper and television coverage of the 1970 Cambodia invasion had been similarly remiss in stressing the possibility of Chinese intervention, high casualties, expansion of the war and risk to the pullout program. But none of these things happened, he said. On the contrary, American prospects in Indochina had been improved.

South Vietnamese quit Laos. The Saigon operation against North Vietnamese supply lines in southern Laos came to an end March 24 as the last of the invading force fought its way back across the border into South Vietnam with Communist soldiers and tanks in hot pursuit.

It had been predicted Feb. 8, at the start of the incursion, that the operation would end shortly before the start of the rainy season, which normally began 10 days to two weeks before or after May 1. This timetable apparently was upset by the fierce North Vietnamese assaults which forced the South Vietnamese to start pulling back March 12. Saigon's troops began leaving Laos March 18, and virtually the entire 21,000-man invading army completed the pullback March 24.

Despite the premature termination of the operation, U.S. and South Vietnamese authorities said the objective of disrupting enemy supply lines on the Ho Chi Minh Trail network had been accomplished. U.S. intelligence sources in Saigon, however, said March 24 that the North Vietnamese had begun to repair parts of the trail cut by the South Vietnamese and were rebuilding their major supply base at Tchepone.

U.S. Defense Department sources were reported to have said March 24 that President Nguyen Van Thieu had decided to end the Laos operation to cut his army's losses. Thieu was said to have rejected American military suggestions to send in replacements and continue the operation in Laos for a few more weeks.

Defense Secretary Melvin R. Laird said March 24 that the Laos mission had been brought to a halt because of the "tremendously vicious and violent reaction on the part of the North Vietnamese and also the fact that the South Vietnamese feel that they have carried out a primary objective of the operation— that is, to disrupt the logistic supply routes."

A Defense Department statement on the fighting March 23 had confirmed that the operation was coming to a close. It conceded that some South Vietnamese units "did not perform as they should," but said the Saigon forces as a whole had given a good account of themselves and had "won the overall battle."

About 500 South Vietnamese marines remained behind in Laos on Co Roc Mountain, two miles from the border just south of Route 9. Their mission was to defend the rear allied support base at nearby Khesanh, South Vietnam, which had been under almost constant North Vietnamese attack for the past two weeks.

The South Vietnamese command reported March 25 that 1,146 South Vietnamese were killed in the Laos campaign, 245 were missing and 4,235 were wounded. The command listed North Vietnamese deaths at 13,668, many of them slain by American air strikes. U.S. military authorities believed that South Vietnamese losses were higher than reported and that Saigon had exaggerated the Communist casualty figures.

The first strongpoint abandoned by the South Vietnamese as they started their pullout from Laos March 18 was Fire Base Lolo, about 21 miles from the South Vietnamese border, where fighting had raged for four days. The men retreated to Landing Zone Brown, five miles away, but by March 20 were forced to leave this base and their main base of Aloui, just to the north on Route 9.

About 300 American jets had pounded enemy targets in Laos March 20 in a futile attempt to stem the North Vietnamese advance. In another air strike connected with the Laos operation, American planes carried out heavy raids on missile sites in North Vietnam March 21–22. In providing air cover for the fleeing South Vietnamese troops on the final day of the withdrawal March 24, American fighter-bombers attacked 21 Soviet-made PT-76 tanks and destroyed seven of them. The attack occurred on a trail only a mile southwest of the border crossing point of Laobao. Three other North Vietnamese tanks were attacked by helicopter gunships half a mile closer to the border, and one was reported destroyed and two damaged.

Almost all available American helicopters were utilized in rescuing the battered Saigon troops from the battle zone and transferring them to the staging base at Khesanh. There were reports of desperate South Vietnamese soldiers, unable to board overcrowded helicopters, clinging to the aircrafts' landing skids as the 'copters took off. Some of the soldiers managed to hold on during the flights to safety, but many were said to have fallen to their deaths. Other fleeing South Vietnamese troops made their way out of Laos in armored personnel carriers.

Khesanh March 23 came under the first Communist ground assault since North Vietnamese shelling of the base started March 14. About 40 sappers broke into the base under cover of a heavy artillery barrage, but were driven off with the loss of 20 men killed. Less than a dozen Americans were reported killed or wounded. Several helicopters were destroyed by the artillery shells, fired from inside Laos, and by satchel charges planted by the sappers.

Khesanh appeared to be under a further threat following a report March 24 that the North Vietnamese had begun to move long-range artillery into their side of the demilitarized zone, directly north of the allied base.

North Vietnam had claimed March 22 that the South Vietnamese were being routed in Laos. An article in the army paper Quan Doi Nhan Dan said Saigon's units "are now in a dead end, and cannot either advance or retreat." The newspaper said that faced with these setbacks, the U.S. may be tempted to "go all the way" by attacking North Vietnam and using atomic weapons.

The Pathet Lao rebels, fighting alongside the North Vietnamese, reported March 22 that their forces March 19 had dealt a sharp blow to two South Vietnamese brigades in the Ban Dong area near the Vietnamese frontier. The report said the Pathet Lao had "wiped out 500 enemy troops, shot down 30 helicopters and one enemy jet fighter coming to the rescue of the battered troops." About 250 South Vietnamese were taken prisoner, the statement said.

U.S. troops defy orders—During the South Vietnamese withdrawal from Laos, 53 soldiers of two platoons of Troop B, First Squadron, First Cavalry, Americal Division, refused an order March 20 to move forward to retrieve a damaged helicopter and their commanding officer's armored vehicle from a battle zone between Langvei, South Vietnam and the Laotian border five miles to the west. The commanding officer, Capt. Carlos A. Poveda, was relieved of his command, and the recalcitrant troops were reassigned; no disciplinary action was planned against the GIs.

Three times the two platoons had tried to dislodge an enemy ambush on Route 9 near the Laos border but were stopped by heavy Communist fire. On the third attempt, the commander's armored vehicle hit a mine as the unit was pulling back. Two other armored personnel carriers later rescued the commander and his crew. Shortly afterwards, a helicopter made a forced landing behind the damaged vehicle, but its crew escaped to safety. Troop B was then ordered to return to the area to bring back

the helicopter and the armored vehicle, but the men refused. Another armored unit was sent in March 21 and retrieved the equipment.

One of the men who defied the order to move forward, Spec. 4 Randy Thompson, said "the reason given wasn't a very good one. It was after a piece of machinery that could have been replaced. I didn't see any sense in risking more lives."

Action after withdrawal—At the end of the major operations of Saigon's forces in Laos, allied troops began to withdraw from bases on the South Vietnamese border that had supported the incursion. The pullback was carried out amid growing concern over a possible major North Vietnamese attack on allied installations in the area. The Communists had begun a series of harassing raids against allied positions in the Khesanh area March 25-30 and struck further south near Danang March 28, killing 33 Americans.

Meanwhile, several hundred South Vietnamese marines were sent to patrol the Laotian frontier while a small force of other marines moved back into Laos to reoccupy a hill position two miles across the border just south of Route 9. Their mission was to protect the continuing withdrawal of the allied forces from the northernmost part of South Vietnam.

In the allied troop withdrawal March 26, the South Vietnamese pulled out of their westernmost base at Langvei, four miles from the Laotian frontier, and moved to Hamnghi, which had been the forward command post for the drive into Laos. American soldiers began dismantling equipment at Khesanh preparatory to leaving that base.

In the Khesanh area clashes, the U.S. command reported nine Americans had been killed and 11 wounded in skirmishes with Communist infiltrators March 25. One American died and three were wounded in the shelling of the Langvei base that day. A South Vietnamese convoy was ambushed on Route 9 in South Vietnam and at least two soldiers were killed. Three more Americans were slain in a clash with enemy troops 14 miles northeast of Khesanh March 27. American helicopter gunships were reported to have killed 14 Communists nine miles northeast of Khesanh the same day.

Despite the end of operations in Laos, American planes continued to bomb the Ho Chi Minh Trail complex in that country. In one raid 13 B-52s took part in a total of 330 sorties carried out March 25. Meanwhile, five American helicopters were shot down over the Khesanh area inside South Vietnam the same day while supporting the withdrawal of Saigon forces from Laos. This brought to 94 the number of 'copters lost since the start of the Laos operations Feb. 8. Casualties in the crashes totaled 66 killed, 79 wounded and 28 listed as missing.

In a slightly revised count of total South Vietnamese losses in the entire Laos operations, a Saigon command spokesman reported March 29 that 1,160 government troops were killed, 4,271 wounded and 240 missing. The spokesman denied reports that half of the government's 20,000-man force had been killed, wounded and missing.

An Associated Press dispatch from Saigon March 25, quoting sources with access to battle figures, had said South Vietnamese forces suffered casualties of nearly 50% in the 45-day campaign—3,800 killed, 5,200 wounded and 775 missing.

Hanoi newspapers March 25 claimed North Vietnamese forces had scored a "complete victory" in Laos. An editorial in the Communist party newspaper Nhan Dan said: "The Highway 9 victory is a major milestone in the history of the coordinated fight by the Indochinese peoples...."

The Saigon government asserted March 26, however, that Operation Lam Som 719, the campaign in Laos, had not officially terminated, although all government troops had been pulled out. A spokesman said: "We could not tell you the new area of operations in case the operations could be continuing."

The commander of the South Vietnamese operations in Laos, Lt. Gen. Hoang Xuan Lam, said that during the six-week operation enemy gunners had damaged 608 U.S. helicopters, shooting down 104, according to a report made available April 4. The report, submitted by Lam to the South Vietnamese Senate Defense Committee, said of the 104 'copters downed, "about half were abandoned in southern Laos." Lam said 450 Americans had been killed supporting the Laos incursion.

Thieu hails Laos operation. President Nguyen Van Thieu March 31 hailed the recently-completed South Vietnamese incursion into Laos as "the biggest victory ever" and not a defeat as claimed by some press publications.

Addressing a news conference at an army base cemetery at Dongha, Thieu insisted that the operation had achieved its objectives of disrupting Communist supply lines and of preventing any future Communist attacks on South Vietnam's northern provinces during the remainder of 1971.

Thieu denied the operation was cut short and dismissed the alleged differences between Saigon and U.S. military officials over the timing of the withdrawal of Saigon's forces from Laos. The decision to terminate the operation, Thieu said, was "a decision of the Vietnamese and we ended it because we judged the objectives of the operations to have been achieved."

Operation officially over. A Saigon military official April 9 announced the official conclusion of the South Vietnamese operation in Laos. Meanwhile U.S. pilots had reported April 7 that North Vietnamese supplies along the Ho Chi Minh Trail in Laos were moving freely once again, despite allied claims that this traffic had been disrupted by the South Vietnamese February-March campaign in the country.

According to the reports: North Vietnamese trucks were driving north and south along the supply trails supposedly cut by the South Vietnamese. Communist antiaircraft fire which had been diverted against troop-carrying helicopters taking part in the Laos operation was "right back to where it was before" and was now directed at U.S. planes attempting to interdict the trail.

Among other developments in Laos:

Laotian and North Vietnamese troops continued fighting around the royal capital of Luang Prabang March 26–April 6.

The Laotian government forces finally abandoned several strategic hill positions near the city as the attackers drove to within four to five miles of the capital. The Laotians used air and artillery strikes in an effort to stem the Communist advance. By April 5 the North Vietnamese were reported by the Laotian Defense Ministry to be reinforcing their positions and bringing in antiaircraft guns. The North Vietnamese and Pathet Lao soldiers widened their attacks in northern Laos April 6, overrunning seven government positions. Six of the outposts were seized on a 15-mile stretch of Route 13 between Vientiane and Luang Prabang, 135 miles north. Another government position was evacuated 10 miles northeast of Luang Prabang in the face of heavy North Vietnamese mortar fire.

The U.S. Defense Department reported April 5 that Communist China had moved an additional 4,000–6,000 troops into northern Laos, bringing its total strength there to 18,000–20,000 men. The force was being used largely to protect the Chinese crews constructing a major road linking Yunan Province in southern China with the Mekong River in Laos.

Another raid into Laos—A force of 200 South Vietnamese commandos carried out a 10-hour attack against enemy positions inside Laos April 6. The raiders were brought in by U.S. helicopters to a point just south of Khesanh. This was the same area that had been struck by South Vietnamese commandos in a raid March 31–April 1. In the latest attack, the raiders reported finding the bodies of 15 North Vietnamese soldiers, apparently killed by American air strikes. They reported destroying 20 weapons, 10 tons of rice and other food and 10 storage huts.

In a report on the commando strike into Laos March 31, a Saigon spokesman reported April 2 that the bodies of 85 North Vietnamese, victims of U.S. air strikes, had been found in the area and that the raiders destroyed 12 huts and 1,000 gallons of petroleum products.

Laos drive protested in U.S. Antiwar activists in the U.S. Feb. 10 protested the operation in Laos with nationwide demonstrations described as the most widespread since the reaction to the campaign in Cambodia in May 1970.

Despite predictions, however, that the Laos invasion and other recent developments in Southeast Asia had reactivated the antiwar movement, the initial protests did not reach the level of dissent in past years.

About 2,000 protesters demonstrated peacefully in New York City Feb. 10, but a protest and march by 4,000 demonstrators in Boston led to 14 arrests as windows were broken and two policemen were injured. Violence also broke out in Baltimore where a protest by more than 300 demonstrators ended in rock and bottle throwing during which six policemen were injured, windows were broken and 23 persons were arrested.

About 1,500 demonstrators protested Feb. 10 near the Berkeley campus of the University of California. Two persons were arrested as some protesters clashed with police. Several hundred protesters occupied the Social Science Building for several hours at the University of Wisconsin. There were six arrests and some window breaking in Washington, D.C. as 1,000 protesters marched from George Washington University to the White House.

At Stanford University, where protests and window breaking that began Feb. 7 caused $13,500 in damage, 70 demonstrators occupied the computer center Feb. 10. As protests continued at Stanford the next day, two persons were shot by an unknown assailant as they stood near the office of the Free Campus Movement, a conservative group. (Stanford professor Howard Bruce Franklin, 37, was suspended Feb. 13 due to his alleged "important role" in the antiwar demonstrations.)

Several thousand demonstrated near the University of Michigan Feb. 10 and 11, and the marchers were joined by Ann Arbor Mayor Robert Harris. Among other actions Feb. 10 were peaceful protests in San Francisco, Chicago and Des Moines, Iowa. A University of Washington (Seattle) protest Feb. 11 drew 1,500 participants.

Student antiwar spokesmen had called Feb. 7 for May demonstrations in Washington to disrupt the federal government and for local demonstrations Feb. 10 to protest what they called the invasion of Laos. The statement came at the end of a national student conference attended by 2,000 youths in Ann Arbor, Mich.

The conference had been called to discuss plans to implement a "people's peace treaty," negotiated by 15 student body leaders during a December 1970 trip to Hanoi sponsored by the National Student Association (NSA). The U.S. students, including NSA President David Ifshin, drafted the "people's" treaty in Hanoi with South Vietnamese student leaders and professors and journalists of North Vietnam.

The treaty, which the students planned to circulate for signatures in U.S. cities and on campuses, stated: "Be it known that the American and Vietnamese people are not enemies. . . . The war is carried out in the names of the people of the United States and South Vietnam but without our consent." The treaty, similar to an eight-point proposal presented by Vietcong delegates to the Paris talks, called for an immediate U.S. withdrawal from Vietnam, the release of all political and war prisoners and self-determination for the people of South Vietnam.

Among other developments:

■ The National Peace Action Coalition, described as a successor of groups that coordinated past peace demonstrations, called Feb. 3 for spring antiwar demonstrations to culminate in marches and rallies in Washington and San Francisco April 24. Jerry Gordon, speaking in Washington, said President Nixon had temporarily defused the peace movement by ordering troop withdrawals. "Now he had re-fused it," Gordon said, by what he described as the "U.S.-sponsored invasion of Laos" and the "violation of the Cooper-Church amendment by sending United States troops into Cambodia dressed in civilian clothes."

■ An explosion at the Armed Forces Induction Center in Oakland, Calif. Feb. 4 broke 200 windows and tore doors off their hinges. A message received by the Oakland Tribune and signed "the Bay Bombers" read: "This is our reply to the invasion of Laos, in Cambodia, in Thailand, in Vietnam, and to the Pentagon's

'protective retaliation' policies." The Atlanta induction office was bombed Feb. 13, and Bucks County, Pa. draft files were burned Feb. 15 in Bristol.

■ A Reserve Officers Training Corps building was damaged by fire Feb. 5 following an antiwar rally at the University of California at Santa Barbara. On the same day, 300 protesters demonstrated at Kent State University in Ohio against the Laos invasion.

■ Fourteen young people, identified as members of the Philadelphia Resistance, broke into the South Vietnamese embassy in Washington Feb. 8. There was no damage and the protesters left after arrests were made.

■ "Chicago 7" defendants Rennie Davis and David Dellinger joined other antiwar leaders and Rep. Bella Abzug (D, N.Y.) Feb. 8 in Washington to call for protests Feb. 10. Sponsoring the news conference in Lafayette Square across the street from the White House were the Student and Youth Conference on a People's Peace and the People's Coalition for Peace and Justice, which was described by Dr. Sidney Peck as the "direct successor to the New Mobe" (the New Mobilization Committee to end the War in Vietnam). Peck said the coalition was the result of a "developing unity between the peace and antipoverty movements."

■ In Cambridge, Mass. Feb. 11, a group of student and labor leaders and noted professors announced formation of an antiwar Labor-University Alliance and released a statement condemning a "widening of the war into Laos." The statement said: "The Administration tries to obscure the fact that still it seeks the vain goal of military victory in Vietnam." Signing the statement as individuals were United Auto Workers President Leonard Woodcock and Teamsters International Vice President Harold Gibbons. Professors who signed included Noam Chomsky of the Massachusetts Institute of Technology, Seymour Melman of Columbia University and George Wald of Harvard University. A number of student body presidents and National Student Association President David Ifshin also signed.

■ Three offices in the Columbia University School in International Affairs were wrecked by antiwar protesters Feb. 12. A student and three policemen were injured slightly and one student was arrested. Dr. William J. McGill, Columbia president, Feb. 15 condemned the attempt by the protesters to disrupt a political science class. He said: "I did not spend the last three years in bitter public struggle defending the teaching rights of Linus Pauling, Herbert Marcuse and Angela Davis, only to watch such rights trampled at Columbia." McGill was chancellor of the University of California at San Diego before coming to Columbia.

Antiwar teach-ins begin. A speech by former Sen. Eugene J. McCarthy Feb. 22 in Boston launched a new effort to mobilize antiwar sentiment on the campuses. McCarthy spoke at a preliminary session before an antiwar teach-in began at Harvard University.

At the Harvard meeting, attended by 1,500 students, speakers urged the students to avoid violence and to organize political pressure campaigns against the war.

(McCarthy, at a Boston news conference, said the incursion into Laos "raises the possibility of a Red Chinese counter-invasion." He added: "In the same light, a significant invasion of North Vietnam would also put the pressure on Red China to come in.")

At a teach-in at Yale Feb. 22, W. Averill Harriman, former chief negotiator for the U.S. at the Paris peace talks, said the best way to influence U.S. policy in Indochina was to "elect a new president."

Operation Spurs Congress. Debate over Nixon Administration policy in Indochina was renewed in the wake of the Loatian operation. The debate, highlighted by action by the House Democratic caucus March 31 calling for an end to U.S. involvement in Indochina by the end of 1972, focused on criticism of the drive in Laos and calls for deadlines on withdrawal of U.S. troops.

The issues were being raised in the Democratic party and in Congress, where House antiwar sentiment was making its first firm appearance and forcing consideration by House leaders.

The Democratic party's Policy Council, appointed to draft proposals for the party's platform committee prior to the 1972 convention, voted unanimously March 24 in favor of a Congressional cutoff of all funds for U.S. military operations in Indochina after Dec. 31. The council said, "The choice does not lie, as the President asserts, between 'neo-isolation' or 'bugging out' as the one alternative and Vietnamization of the war as the other. A decision should be made now for responsible withdrawal."

The council declared its opposition to "any expansion of the war by American or South Vietnamese forces in Cambodia, Laos or North Vietnam or by the bombing of North Vietnam."

Sen. Hubert H. Humphrey, the party's presidential candidate in 1968, presided at the meeting and voted for the fund cutoff.

Doubts about the Laotian invasion were expressed by leading senators March 21. Senate Democratic Leader Mike Mansfield (Mont.), while unsure "whether you can call it a failure or not," said it appeared that the withdrawal "has been hastened." He said the operation seemed to have brought the Communist forces closer to the South without gaining a military cushion for continuing U.S. troop withdrawals.

Sen. George Aiken (R, Vt.) said it took the South Vietnamese "several days longer to get in there than they'd planned on and they're coming out rather faster than they'd planned to do, with the enemy in hot pursuit." Sen. George McGovern (D, S.D.) said the invasion seemed to cast doubt on "the whole credibility of the South Vietnam force" and "the reliability of the predictions of our own leaders." McGovern expressed assurance that he could attain a negotiated settlement of the war within weeks if he assumed the presidency in 1973. It could be accomplished, he said, by setting a date for total U.S. withdrawal and telling the Saigon regime "that we're not going to stay there indefinitely."

Other prominent Democratic spokesmen attacked the Laos invasion during a meeting in Washington March 25–26 of Democratic state chairmen. At the opening session, Sen. Edward M. Kennedy (Mass.) described the invasion as "a nightmare" that "was carried out in flagrant violation of the spirit of legislation passed by Congress" and ended in "humiliating retreat" effected "so obviously in panic." America, he said "is coming out of Laos on the skids." Denouncing the Administration's "cruel and inhuman policy of . . . indiscriminate bombing," Kennedy asked: "Can America ever wash its hands of the innocent Asian blood it has spilled?"

Sen. Harold E. Hughes (D, Iowa) told the Democratic state chairmen March 25 the Laos operation left "a real question about the viability" of the South Vietnamese army. Like Humphrey, Hughes criticized Nixon for "unleashing" Agnew—Hughes called him "the most divisive man I've heard in my lifetime in politics"—against critics and the news media.

Sen. Edmund S. Muskie (D, Me.) told the state chairmen March 26 the Laos venture was "a serious military defeat which . . . can mean nothing but prolongation of the war."

Chairman J. W. Fulbright of the Senate Foreign Relations Committee accused the Nixon Administration March 30 of either "massive deception" in its handling of the Laotian campaign or of "massive misjudgment" and perhaps both. He could not remain silent any longer about it, he said, "when we are being told that the Laos operation went according to plan when I know it did not go according to plan."

Mansfield, in a speech March 29, charged that the Nixon Administration was failing to "follow through" with the Nixon Doctrine of reducing U.S. military commitments abroad. Instead, he said, the pattern was increased violence in Indochina and resistance to troop withdrawals from Western Europe.

Antiwar sentiment grows in House—House Democratic Whip Thomas P. O'Neill Jr. (Mass.) March 29 became the first House leader to publicly endorse a deadline for a U.S. pullout. Joined by Reps. Dan Rostenkowski (D, Ill.), Hugh L. Carey (D, N.Y.) and James C. Corman (D, Calif.), O'Neill issued a "statement of purpose" calling for withdrawal of U.S. military forces from Indochina by Dec. 31. Other House leaders opposed setting a deadline, but a group of House Democrats mounted an effort to bring before a caucus of House Democrats an "end-the-war" resolution sponsored by Rep. Spark Matsunaga (D, Hawaii), which would put the Democrats on record to "work to end involvement in Indochina and to bring about withdrawal of all U.S. forces and the release of all prisoners by Dec. 31, 1971." It also urged action on a bill to bar war funds after May 1 except for withdrawal, prisoner release or asylum for the Vietnamese.

Prior to the caucus, the "end-the-war" proponents gained conferences with Chairman Thomas Morgan (D, Pa.) of the House Foreign Affairs Committee, who up to that time had refused to countenance antiwar proposals in his committee. Morgan told an interviewer March 22 he was "trying to establish an entire new image for the Foreign Affairs Committee" toward a more aggressive, independent foreign policy role.

In the House Democratic caucus March 31, the Matsunaga resolution was replaced, by a 101–100 vote, by one calling for an end to the U.S. involvement in Indochina by the end of the 92nd Congress (the start of 1973). The final version, approved by 138–63 vote, was the same position approved by Senate Democrats in February.

House Speaker Carl Albert also expressed satisfaction with the caucus action and viewed the resolution as neither "a slap at President Nixon" nor "a vote of confidence in his conduct of the war."

Republican reaction leaned toward the vote of confidence side. House GOP Leader Gerald R. Ford (Mich.) said it strengthened the President "in the courageous course he is pursuing." White House Press Secretary Ronald L. Ziegler thought, too, the resolution seemed "to be directed towards support of the President and his Vietnam policy."

Evidence of GOP split—Some evidence of a split among Republicans over the war issue and its effect on Nixon's future was apparent during a Minnesota GOP party meeting in St. Paul March 27.

An invitation as guest speaker to Gov. Ronald Reagan (Calif.) led to a competing rally addressed by former New York Sen. Charles E. Goodell.

Reagan lauded Nixon for "winding down the war" and termed the Laos invasion successful. Goodell said "Laos is a disaster" and warned that, without a change in policy, "this war will be the rock upon which he [Nixon] and the Republican party founders."

Vice President Agnew March 19 had described the South Vietnamese pullout from Laos as "an orderly retreat" and the operation as "successful" in barring an enemy buildup that could impede Vietnamization.

Ratings show dissatisfaction—The President's poll ratings also reflected public dissatisfaction attributed to the war issue and Laos. The Gallup poll reported March 31 public confidence in the way Nixon was handling the presidency had fallen to 50% in mid-March, the lowest figure of his term.

A Harris poll March 12 reported a 10-point drop since January in the President's war-handling rating, only 34% considering it good to excellent in a survey conducted Feb. 22–27. In a companion survey, 51% considered it morally wrong for the U.S. to be fighting in Vietnam.

Bomb explodes in Capitol. A powerful bomb exploded in the Senate wing of the Capitol at 1:32 a.m. March 1, 33 minutes after a telephone warning that the blast would occur as a protest against the U.S.-supported Laos invasion. The explosion, in an unmarked, out-of-the way men's lavatory, damaged seven rooms. There was some damage as far as 250 feet away. No one was injured.

The telephone message to a Capitol operator warned: "This building will blow up in 30 minutes. You will get many calls like this, but this one is real. Evacu-ate the building. This is in protest of the Nixon involvement in Laos."

President Nixon March 1 issued a statement calling the bombing a "shock-ing act of violence which will outrage all Americans."

Members of Congress also expressed shock, coupled with concern over the security of the Capitol. Senate Majority Leader Mike Mansfield (D, Mont.) said the bombing was an "outrageous and sacrilegious" action against a "public shrine."

Sen. George S. McGovern (D, S.D.), in one of the few statements to connect the bombing with the U.S. Indochina policy, blamed "our Vietnam madness" for the "barbaric" action. He said, "The massive bombardment we are continuing year after year against the peoples of Indochina has its counterpart in the mounting destruction of humane values in our own land. . . . It is not possible to teach an entire generation to bomb and destroy others in an undeclared, unjustified, unending war without paying a terrible price in the derangement of our society."

A conspiracy theory developed early, supported by a report from Leonard H. Ballard of the Capitol police force that two telephone callers from Chicago and Spokane, Wash., within an hour of the explosion, asked about damage. "That was almost before it was on the air and before it was known nationally," Ballard contented.

In letters postmarked March 1 after the bombing and sent to the New York Times, the New York Post and the Associated Press, a group calling itself the Weather Underground claimed responsibility for the bombing. The letters, mailed from Elizabeth, N.J., said: "We have attacked the Capitol because it is, along with the White House and the Pentagon, the worldwide symbol of the government which is now attacking Indochina."

Paris Talks & POWs

Deadlock in January. The peace negotiations in Paris continued in a state of deadlock during January.

North Vietnamese chief delegate Xuan Thuy charged at the Jan. 7 session that assertions by President Nixon that the end of the American combat role in Vietnam was in sight was "only propaganda." He said the U.S. was actually stepping up its military activities. North Vietnamese press spokesman Nguyen Thanh Le said after the meeting that U.S. Defense Secretary Melvin R. Laird was bringing new war plans with him on his visit to Saigon.

At the Jan. 14 meeting, U.S. chief delegate David K. E. Bruce sought to hand the Viet Cong and North Vietnamese delegates a list of 1,534 missing American servicemen and urged that they "provide any information on them." It covered the period to Dec. 30, 1970. The Communist refused to accept the document, insisting that the list of 339 American prisoners released by Hanoi Dec. 22, 1970 was "complete and definitive."

U.S. press spokesman Stephen Ledogar said the American roster included about 780 airmen missing over North Vietnam.

The Jan. 21 session marked the 100th time the allies and Communists met since the start of the peace talks Jan. 25, 1969. Both sides acknowledged the talks were a failure and blamed each other for it.

The Communist delegates charged at the Feb. 11 meeting that 10 American battalions, including elements from the 5th Mechanized, the 101st Airborne and Americal Divisions, were fighting in Laos. U.S. press spokesman Stephen Ledogar called the charge "heaping exaggeration upon lies."

Communist prisoners freed. South Vietnam released 37 ill and disabled North Vietnamese prisoners of war Jan. 24. The captives rowed themselves across the Benhai River in the demilitarized zone that divided North and South Vietnam. The men were greeted by North Vietnamese troops on the opposite shore.

South Vietnamese officials said 40 North Vietnamese prisoners had been chosen to be freed but three of them "changed their mind at the last minute" and decided not to return.

This was the fifth time South Vietnam had released Communist prisoners of war and brought to 231 the number of North Vietnamese set free since January 1966.

Communist China move again hinted. North Vietnam charged at the Paris peace talks Feb. 18 that the U.S. was threatening to extend the war to North Vietnam and thus posed a threat to Communist China. A spokesman for Hanoi's chief delegate Xuan Thuy warned after the meeting that Peking would not "remain with folded arms and watch her neighbors being attacked by the United States."

Thuy took particular issue with President Nixon's Feb. 17 news conference statement refusing to rule out a possible unilateral South Vietnamese military move into North Vietnam. Nixon's remark, Thuy said, showed that the U.S. "does not want to settle the Vietnam problem peacefully."

U.S. chief negotiator David K. E. Bruce told Thuy that "it is you, and no one else, who is responsible for the continued fighting and killing in Indochina."

Pacifists meet with Paris delegates. A group of 171 American pacifists departed for the U.S. March 10 after spending a week in Paris in what they said was an effort to discover the "requisites for peace" in Indochina. The group spoke with all the delegations represented at the Paris peace talks.

The pacifists, from 41 states, were sponsored by three antiwar organizations —the American Friends Service Committee, the Fellowship of Reconciliation and Clergy and Laymen Concerned about Vietnam. The group spoke with Mrs. Nguyen Thi Bihn, head of the Viet Cong delegation, March 6 and met with David K. E. Bruce, chief U.S. negotiator, March 9.

Spokesmen for the group charged "rigidity" on the part of the U.S. negotiators and argued that the key to peace was U.S. withdrawal from Vietnam. Folk singer Judy Collins led the pacifists and U.S. representatives in singing "Give Peace a Chance" during a final meeting March 9.

Communists boycott Paris talks. The American bombing of North Vietnam March 21–22 prompted the North Vietnamese and Viet Cong delegates to cancel the March 25 session of the Paris peace talks in protest.

Hanoi's decision, announced March 24, asserted that "these acts of war of the American imperialists constitute a wholesale violation of the sovereignty and security of North Vietnam, a violation of the commitments made by the

American government to cease completely the bombings over all of the territory [of North Vietnam] and a serious threat to the work of the Paris conference."

The Communist delegations, however, indicated their willingness to attend the next plenary session April 1.

Meanwhile, the chief delegates of the North Vietnamese and Viet Cong negotiating teams, Xuan Thuy and Mrs. Nguyen Thi Binh, boycotted the meeting for the fourth successive week in protest against earlier American air attacks on North Vietnam. The March 11 and 18 sessions were brief and no progress was reported.

Paris talks resume. The Paris peace talks, in suspension since the March 18 meeting, resumed April 8.

The April 8 meeting was dominated by a debate over President Nixon's announcement the previous day of an increase in American troop withdrawal and a new South Vietnamese offer for a prisoner exchange. The Communist representative called the pullout decision "a maneuver aimed at disguising the prolongation and widening of the war." Saigon representative Pham Dang Lam proposed the repatriation or internment in a neutral country of "able-bodied prisoners of war who have undergone a long period of captivity." U.S. chief delegate David K. E. Bruce supported the proposal, but the Communists rejected it.

Thuy ends Paris boycott. North Vietnamese chief delegate Xuan Thuy returned to the Paris peace talks April 15, ending a seven-week boycott of the conference. He had remained away since the March 4 session.

Thuy presented previous Communist demands: American agreement to withdraw from Vietnam by a "reasonable" date, a halt to all further attacks on North Vietnam and acceptance of a new peace government in Saigon.

U.S. chief delegate David K. E. Bruce called Thuy's proposals "absolutely nothing new."

A spokesman for the North Vietnamese delegation, Nguyen Thanh Le, said April 16 that despite the apparent thaw in U.S.-Communist Chinese relations, Peking's support of Hanoi remained "invariable" and "without limit."

Hanoi asks U.S. pullout talks. North Vietnam April 29 proposed negotiating a date for the total withdrawal of U.S. troops from South Vietnam. President Nixon in effect rejected the offer the same day by reiterating his insistence that he would not set a definite date for a complete pullout until Hanoi made "a commitment to release our prisoners."

The Communist plan was advanced at the Paris peace talks by Xuan Thuy, North Vietnam's chief delegate. Addressing the American representatives, Thuy said the proposed talks could be held "this very day, or tomorrow, or another day of your choice" on "the question of fixing a date for the withdrawal from South Vietnam of United States forces" and allied troops, "so as to be able then to take up the question of the guarantee of the security of the United States soldiers during their withdrawal, and the question of the release" of American prisoners of war.

North Vietnamese press spokesman Nguyen Thanh Le explained at a later news conference that the negotiations on the withdrawals could be held within the framework of the Paris conference or in private talks. He said it would not be necessary for the U.S. to publicly announce the withdrawal date, "they can tell us privately."

Mrs. Nguyen Thi Binh, chief delegate of the Viet Cong's Provisional Revolutionary Government, renewed a Communist proposal "to cease fire on American soldiers who do not undertake hostile action toward" the Viet Cong. A spokesman later reported that this statement was a shorter version of the Viet Cong's April 26 "Order of the Day" appealing to American troops opposed to the war to stop fighting or desert.

The two Communist proposals were dismissed by U.S. chief delegate David K. E. Bruce, who said they were nothing new. Bruce proposed instead that North Vietnam name a neutral country or some international group that would assure "the humane treatment" of prisoners of both sides. Bruce complained that "there has, so far as we know, been no inspection of conditions of internment

of prisoners-of-war held by your side by any respected body of international stature."

South Vietnamese negotiator Pham Dang Lam proposed transfer of 1,200 North Vietnamese prisoners to "temporary detention" in a neutral country named by Hanoi.

At the April 22 session of the Paris talks, Xuan Thuy had assailed President Nixon's April 16 news conference statement in which he conditioned total American withdrawal upon release of U.S. prisoners and South Vietnam's capacity to defend itself [see p. 291B2]. Thuy interpreted Nixon's remarks as "a cynical pretext for not pulling out all American forces from South Vietnam."

The proposals by Bruce and Pham Dang Lam for a neutral role on the prisoner issue were followed by a published report April 30 that Sweden had offered the use of its ships to transfer American captives from North Vietnam to internment facilities in Sweden.

A statement issued on behalf of President Nixon May 3 expressed "great satisfaction" with Stockholm's proposal. Nixon urged Hanoi to "move promptly to negotiate an agreement on this issue to take advantage of this humanitarian offer on the part of the Swedish government."

A spokesman for the North Vietnamese delegation in Paris May 4 responded to the latest American suggestion by reiterating its latest positions on the prisoner issue as advanced at the April 29 session.

Peace talks enter fourth year. The Paris peace talks entered their fourth year May 13 in a continued deadlock.

Speaking to newsmen before the start of the 113th session, Xuan Thuy, North Vietnam's chief delegate, said: "We came here three years ago, exactly on the same day and the same month, to settle the Vietnam problem . . . but unfortunately all our efforts have been combatted by President Nixon."

Thuy praised Averell Harriman, first U.S. chief negotiator, for having negotiated with him the bombing halt of North Vietnam, an agreement "unfortunately, fought by Mr. Nixon. President Nixon has violated this agreement and continued to send U.S. warplanes to bomb our cities and population."

In the talks, the Communist delegations endorsed and clarified new peace proposals advanced by the Pathet Lao the previous day for ending the fighting in Laos. They said the Pathet Lao cease-fire bid applied to "all forces," apparently meaning the North Vietnamese as well. Unlike previous Pathet Lao offers, the latest proposal provided for an immediate end to the fighting and immediate discussions on restoration of a coalition government in Laos, the North Vietnamese and Viet Cong representatives explained.

At the May 6 meeting, U.S. chief delegate David K. E. Bruce said the U.S. would not consider negotiating the withdrawal of its troops unless North Vietnamese forces were included. The Hanoi delegation denounced the proposal as "absurd."

Bruce asked Thuy for a clarification of his statement made at the April 29 meeting in which he had said his side was ready to "discuss today, tomorrow or any other day" a date for complete American withdrawal, the security of the withdrawing troops and the release of prisoners. In direct reply to this statement, Bruce said: "If this means that you are now prepared to withdraw North Vietnamese forces from South Vietnam, Laos and Cambodia, then I believe we can make serious progress here toward an honorable and lasting negotiated settlement."

Thuy links pullout to POWs. In a statement May 21, Xuan Thuy reiterated Hanoi's position that the question of releasing U.S. war prisoners could be settled quickly if President Nixon set a date for total withdrawal of U.S. troops from South Vietnam.

In an interview with the New York Times, Thuy asserted that Nixon's reasons for refusing to announce a specific timetable of total U.S. pullout was a pretext for keeping the troops in the country. Conceding that "prisoners are a question for the aftermath of a war," Thuy said North Vietnam nevertheless was prepared to make an "appropriate response" before the end of hostilities if Nixon set a withdrawal date.

Thuy claimed Nixon had made three mistakes in his Indochina policy since assuming office in 1969: Vietnamization, the ouster of Cambodian Chief of State Prince Norodom Sihanouk in 1970 and the February-March incursion into Laos.

He said the Vietnamization policy had failed because instead of "ending the war" as it was acclaimed to do, it was prolonging it. The allied objective to "destroy the political base of the National Liberation Front and the guerrilla fighters" in South Vietnam was self-defeating because it provoked internal opposition in the country, Thuy said.

Thuy accused Nixon of staging the coup that deposed Sihanouk in order to "draw Cambodia onto the American side and isolate the revolutionary forces in South Vietnam. But on the contrary, he has made Cambodia another battlefield. Now a part of the Saigon army is pinned down in Cambodia, and the U.S. has to send advisers and aid there."

Thuy said the allied drive into Laos had met "bitter defeat" despite "great determination."

Thuy concluded: "These three errors prove that Mr. Nixon does not want to engage in genuine negotiations. He only wants to settle the problem by military victory."

Hanoi to accept prisoners. A South Vietnamese offer to free 570 ill North Vietnamese prisoners of war was accepted by Hanoi May 14. The Saigon proposal had been confirmed April 30. The North Vietnamese agreement, contained in a four-point statement of conditions, said the captives would be accepted June 4. The Hanoi announcement did not mention Saigon's April 29 offer to transfer 1,200 other North Vietnamese prisoners held in South Vietnam to a neutral country.

Text of North Vietnam's agreement on acceptance of its prisoners:

1. Those persons must be transported by unarmed U.S.-puppet civil ships flying Red Cross flags to a spot three to five kilometers southeast of Cuatung at the 17th parallel at . . . 10:30 o'clock on June 4, 1971. Those persons will be transferred to unarmed civil ships of the Democratic Republic of Vietnam flying Red Cross flags.

2. In an area with a 30-kilometer radius around the spot for release and reception, every military activity in the air, at sea, and on the mainland must be ceased on June 4, 1971.

3. The U.S. and the Saigon administrations must announce in advance the number and characteristics of the ships transporting the patriots to be released this time.

4. If the weather is bad, the release and reception will be postponed until a further time and will still follow the procedures of release and reception as mentioned in provisions 1, 2 and 3.

POWs refuse to return. After arranging to return 570 sick and wounded prisoners to North Vietnam, Saigon authorities announced May 31 that only 13 of 660 POWs (prisoners of war) screened by International Red Cross officials wished to be repatriated. South Vietnam said it had added another 90 North Vietnamese to the list of potential returnees.

But Hanoi June 3 refused to accept only the 13 who were willing to go. The North Vietnamese decision was announced as a U.S. Navy transport ship was on its way to a prearranged rendezvous with a North Vietnamese barge off the coast of the demilitarized zone to transfer the captives. The American vessel returned to Danang, South Vietnam June 4 with the prisoners.

Hanoi's June 3 statement announcing cancellation of the prisoner transfer accord said: North Vietnam's May 14 agreement "was intended for the reception of 570 persons. Now, because the U.S. and puppets have treacherously gone back on the decision to send 570 persons to the North, the stipulations for the scheduled June 4 reception are considered annulled."

Nguyen Thanh Le, press spokesman for North Vietnam's delegation to the Paris peace talks, insisted that the U.S. and South Vietnam "must release all patriots [war prisoners] who are being illegally held in South Vietnam and permit them to go free in South Vietnam or North Vietnam."

Nguyen Trieu Dan, spokesman for South Vietnam's delegation to the Paris peace talks, June 3 speculated that Communist agents may have pressured the North Vietnamese prisoners to refuse repatriation.

South Vietnamese Foreign Minister Tran Van Lam had said June 2 that most of the North Vietnamese prisoners who had refused to be freed fear "dread reprisals" and "violence against them" if they returned home. "They seem to have enjoyed better treatment in South Vietnam."

Nguyen Thanh Le June 2 had said the U.S. and South Vietnam were engaging in "a vile and cynical maneuver" by pretending that only 13 prisoners wanted to go home. Both countries, Le said, "have never been sincere in freeing captive patriots." Le also charged that President Nixon June 1 had "given new evidence of the U.S.-puppet deliberate detention of Vietnamese patriots and laid bare the fallacy and hypocrisy in allegedly proposing the release of a number of Vietnamese patriots."

South Vietnam had formally submitted the prisoner release plan to the May 27 session of the Paris peace talks. North Vietnamese chief delegate Xuan Thuy reiterated at the meeting that "only after the Nixon Administration had set a date for the rapid and total withdrawal from South Vietnam of U.S. forces and those of the other foreign countries in the U.S. camp, can other questions, including the question of captured military personnel, be easily and rapidly settled."

More than 100 American women relatives of men missing in Indochina waited outside the building where the peace talks were being held May 27 in an unsuccessful effort to meet with the Communist delegations. A Viet Cong spokesman said such a meeting would be "useless" since his delegation's views were well known. The North Vietnamese referred the women to Hanoi's permanent representative in France. The women were members of the National League of Families of American Prisoners and Missing in Southeast Asia. Their national coordinator, Mrs. Joan Vinson, said: "We would like to get a guarantee that if a withdrawal date is set by the United States all the prisoners of war held by North Vietnam, the Viet Cong and the Pathet Lao and their allies would be released prior to that date."

Viet Cong offers peace plan. A new seven-point peace plan advanced by the Viet Cong July 1 proposed the release of all American and allied prisoners of war in North and South Vietnam by the end of 1971 if all U.S. troops were withdrawn by that date. Both procedures were to start and end simultaneously.

The Nixon Administration reacted cautiously to the formula, saying it contained "positive as well as unacceptable elements."

The Communist proposal was presented to the 119th session of the Paris peace talks by Mrs. Nguyen Thi Binh, head of the Viet Cong delegation, and was endorsed by North Vietnam. It contained two basic Communist demands repeatedly rejected by the U.S.: total American withdrawal and removal of the present South Vietnamese government.

The latest plan contrasted with the previous Communist proposal that merely called for the start of immediate discussion of the prisoner issue as soon as Washington set what the Communists regarded as a reasonable date for a pullout.

The troop withdrawal-captive issue appeared in the first of the seven points of the Viet Cong plan. It also said the U.S. "must put an end to its war of aggression, stop the policy of 'Vietnamization' of the war" and that all American and other non-Vietnamese troops be pulled out of South Vietnam and that their bases in the country be dismantled "without posing any condition whatever." The statement said "a cease-fire will be observed" between the Viet Cong and U.S. forces "as soon as the parties reach agreement" on the withdrawal proposal.

The remaining six points dealt with the political aspects of the problem:

2. The U.S. must "put an end to its interference in the internal affairs of South Vietnam, cease backing the bellicose group headed by [President] Nguyen Van Thieu, . . . and stop all maneuvers, including tricks on elections, aimed at maintaining" Thieu in power. Viet Cong and Thieu administration officials would hold immediate talks on forming "a broad three-segment government of national concord that will assume its functions during the restoration of peace and the holding of general elections. . . ." A truce was to be observed as soon as the new government was formed.

3. The Vietnamese themselves would "settle the question of Vietnamese armed forces in South Vietnam . . . without foreign interference. . . ."

4. The reunification of Vietnam was "to be achieved step by step by peaceful means, on the basis of discussions and agreements between the two zones, without constraint and annexation from either party, without foreign interference."

"Pending the reunification of the country, the North and the South zones will re-establish normal relations, guarantee free movement, free correspondence, free choice of residence, and maintain economic and cultural relations on the principle of mutual interests and mutual assistance.

"All questions concerning the two zones will be settled by qualified representatives of the Vietnamese people in the two zones on the basis of negotiations, without foreign interference.

"In keeping with the provisions of the 1954 Geneva agreements on Vietnam, in the present temporary partition of the country into two zones, the North and the South zones of Vietnam will refrain from joining any military alliance with foreign countries, from allowing any foreign country to have military bases, troops, and military personnel on their soil, and from recognizing the protection of any country, of any military alliance or bloc."

5. South Vietnam must "pursue a foreign policy of peace and neutrality."

6. The U.S. "must bear full responsibility for the losses and the destruction it has caused to the Vietnamese people in the two zones."

7. The "parties will find agreement on the forms of respect and international guarantees of the accords that will be concluded."

Nguyen Trieu Dan, the South Vietnamese spokesman at the talks, objected to the plan's proposed replacement of the Thieu regime. "We cannot compromise on the right of self-determination of the South Vietnamese people," he said.

(The submission of the new Communist proposal followed the return to Paris June 24 of Le Duc Tho, "special adviser" to the North Vietnamese delegation, following his absence from the talks since Feb. 10, 1969. On his arrival Tho said in an airport statement that he had brought no new peace proposals.)

South Vietnam as well as the U.S. remained noncommital about the Viet Cong's seven-point plan. Vice President Nguyen Cao Ky said July 3 that he could "see no obstacle on the South Vietnamese side" to an American troop withdrawal by the end of 1971. Thieu said the suggested U.S. pullout was something the U.S. and South Vietnam "must discuss together."

Communist China July 4 expressed "firm support for the just stand and reasonable proposal" of the Viet Cong. The government newspaper Jenminh Jih Pao said if President Nixon "wants to end the war of aggression in Vietnam, he has no reason whatever to reject the seven-point proposal."

Tho explains Viet Cong plan—In a clarification of the Viet Cong peace plan, Le Duc Tho said July 6 that the proposed simultaneous release of American prisoners and the withdrawal of U.S. forces was not dependent on reaching a political agreement on South Vietnam.

In an interview in Paris with New York Times correspondent Anthony Lewis, Tho said the withdrawal-prisoner issue could be negotiated separately at the Paris talks, with future political arrangements discussed later. When "the first batch of [American] soldiers" leaves Vietnam after an agreement is reached, "the first batch of prisoners will be released," Tho said. He called the 1971 target date for withdrawal of American troops "a reasonable one." But he warned that if President Nixon "prolongs the period of the troop withdrawal . . . then the American prisoners will be delayed in their release. . . ."

Other comments by Tho on the Viet Cong plan:

■ As part of its troop pullout, the U.S. must remove all its advisers attached to the South Vietnam army, halt the shelling of Vietnam by ships of the 7th Fleet and cease all bombing support action by planes based in Thailand. Refusal to halt these activities would only mean continued fighting.

■ The agreement on withdrawal of American troops and the freeing of captives applied only to Vietnam. "As to Laos and Cambodia, these are different questions."

■ Any future discussions on a political settlement in South Vietnam would be held between the Viet Cong's Provisional Revolutionary Government and the Saigon regime, "but a new one without" President Nguyen Van Thieu.

Tho said "the world knows that Thieu has been put in power by the U.S. Administration. And the U.S. will have the decisive voice in the forthcoming [presidential] elections [in South Vietnam in October]. It is the U.S. that will decide who wins."

Mrs. Nguyen Thi Binh said July 6 that the Viet Cong's seven-point plan was not an inflexible take-it-or-leave-it package. She urged Nixon to order his negotiators in Paris to take up the proposal with the Communist representatives. She warned that if Nixon rejected the formula, American troops would become involved in intensified fighting.

Kissinger visits Saigon—The Viet Cong proposal and related matters were discussed in Saigon July 4 by Henry A. Kissinger, President Nixon's national security adviser, and President Thieu. Kissinger had arrived in the capital July 1 on the first day of a 10-day fact-finding mission in the Far East. With other U.S. and South Vietnamese officials in attendance, Kissinger and Thieu were also reported to have discussed future American troop withdrawals and U.S. economic and military aid to South Vietnam.

Kissinger conferred July 5 with two possible presidential candidates—Vice President Nguyen Cao Ky and Gen. Duong Van Minh. Following his meeting with Kissinger, Ky named former National Assembly speaker Truong Vinh Le as his vice presidential running mate.

(In an interview made public July 5, Minh charged that Thieu was attempting "to manipulate" the presidential elections. "If President Thieu is re-elected through his dishonest maneuvers, South Vietnam would not have the smallest chance of survival," Minh said. He appealed to the U.S. to use its influence for a fair and honest election.)

U.S. criticizes Viet Cong plan. The Viet Cong peace plan was criticized moderately by the American delegation in its first official response July 8. Chief U.S. negotiator David K. E. Bruce then proposed further discussion of the proposal at a secret meeting the following week. The Communists rejected the suggestion as "a perfidious maneuver."

Bruce said study of the plan "indicates that despite some new elements, your proposals do not seem to change your long-asserted basic demands or indicate your intention to end the fighting." Bruce asked that the next scheduled meeting July 15 be "a restricted session at which we could further explore your proposals as well as discuss our own." A meeting of this kind, Bruce emphasized, would be "free from the glare of publicity" and "could provide a better atmosphere for productive discussions."

(In a restricted meeting, public statements would be made only in the form of a communique agreed to by both sides. The proceedings at regular sessions were made public by releasing texts of the delegates' prepared speeches and by delegation briefings of newsmen.)

Bruce described the Viet Cong demand for unconditional withdrawal of American troops from Vietnam as "so sweeping and categorical in nature that we cannot possibly accept" it "without any discussion or negotiation." He disapproved of the Viet Cong proposal for dealing only with the release of prisoners taken in North and South Vietnam and not with those captured in Laos and Cambodia. Bruce objected to the Communist call for a transitional regime in Saigon that would exclude President Nguyen Van Thieu as one that "fulfills your own criteria." "We will not impose any government on the people of South Vietnam, who must be allowed to determine for themselves their own future."

Mrs. Nguyen Thi Binh, chief delegate of the Viet Cong's Provisional Revolutionary Government, called on Bruce to respond to these questions:

"Do you agree to consider our seven points as a basis of negotiation?"

Of the seven points, "with which do you agree and with which do you disagree?"

Is the U.S. ready "to set immediately a final date for the withdrawal" of its troops from Vietnam?

Is the U.S. "disposed to stop supporting the warlike and corrupt group now in power in Saigon and led by Nguyen Van Thieu, or not?"

Bruce replied that those were the kind of questions that should be taken up in a restrictive session.

Describing her third question on troop withdrawal as fundamental, Mrs. Binh said "when we have the answer to that, we will take up the discussion of the form of the meeting."

A White House spokesman July 8 said Bruce's call for a clarification of the Viet Cong peace proposal was an attempt to start "meaningful negotiations." The chief delegate's response was said to be in compliance with instructions from President Nixon and Secretary of State William P. Rogers following their receipt of a number of high-level studies of the Communist plan ordered by the Nixon Administration.

According to the New York Times July 8, one of the studies, drawn up by the Central Intelligence Agency (CIA), warned that the Viet Cong formula was intended to make "things awkward for the United States government at home and overseas" and to encourage the political rivals of President Thieu. The CIA analysis, reportedly submitted to the President July 2, said the Viet Cong plan "softens the Communists' position on the prisoner-of-war release but retains a very tough line on United States disengagement from the war. In addition, it repackages Hanoi's demands for a political settlement in South Vietnam in a superficially more attractive form."

The CIA report was said to have noted "two nuances" in the Viet Cong plan: (1) instead of demanding a coalition regime in Saigon, it "simply demands that the United States 'cease backing the bellicose group' headed by Thieu"; (2) the Communists no longer insist on a "three-segment regime," including Communists, but ask for a broad "government of national concord" to be negotiated by the Viet Cong with a "post-Thieu administration."

Henry A. Kissinger, President Nixon's national security adviser, arrived in Paris July 12 and conferred with Bruce and other members of the American delegation.

U.S. presses Reds on peace plan. At the July 15 session of the Paris peace talks on Vietnam, the U.S. delegation continued to press the Communist delegation for clarification of the Viet Cong's seven-point peace plan, but did not reject the proposals outright. David K. E. Bruce, chief U.S. delegate, said: "We will need much more explanation from you as to what your points actually mean."

Bruce then called on the Communists to answer these five questions concerning the Viet Cong plan:

(1) Were the seven-points "the only basis for negotiation" or were "you willing to consider and discuss our proposals as well?"

(2) Must the allied delegation "agree to your series of arbitrary demands [in the first of the seven points] without any discussion or negotiation on them?"

(3) Did the proposal calling for agreement on the modalities of troop withdrawal and prisoner release mean that "we must take unilateral action first, i.e., fix a date for our withdrawal . . ., without any negotiation beforehand. . . .?

(4) Did the proposal to release prisoners "include those captured by your forces in Laos and Cambodia?"

(5) Were the "military and political questions" to be "dealt with separately" as the Communist side had recently indicated? "This is not apparent from your seven points, in which, for example, you still link the problem of cease-fire to the prior satisfaction of your political demands."

Xuan Thuy, North Vietnam's chief delegate, called Bruce's questions an attempt "to stall the negotiations by refusing to answer the seven points."

Mrs. Nguyen Thi Binh, head of the Viet Cong delegation, declared: "As I understand what the American delegate has said, they [the seven points] are all negative. Is that correct or not?" Bruce declined to answer.

(Nixon Administration officials had announced July 13 that Bruce would be replaced as chief delegate on or about Aug. 15 by William J. Porter, now U.S. ambassador to South Korea. Ill health was given as the reason for Bruce's impending resignation. Bruce had asked to be relieved effective July 1, but had agreed to stay at his post for another six weeks, the officials said.)

Peking for Asian parley on Indochina. Communist China had expressed interest in participating in a new international conference on Indochina, the Australian embassy in Washington informed the U.S. State Department July 14.

Australian opposition Labor party leader Gough Whitlam, who concluded a 12-day visit to China July 14, had discussed the matter with Premier Chou En-lai in Peking and communicated the substance of the conversations to Australian Prime Minister William McMahon. Whitlam indicated that the Chinese had advised him that the "administrative arrangements" of such a conference "would have to be more in an Asian framework than the framework set up in 1954." This was in reference to the 1954 Geneva conference which had ended the fighting between France and its allied Indochinese states and the Communist Viet Minh. That parley had been attended by China, the Soviet Union, Laos, Cambodia, South Vietnam, the U.S., Britain and France.

Vietnamese Communists oppose idea. China's readiness to take part in an international conference on Indochina evoked counterstatements by the Viet Cong and North Vietnam, who insisted the problem be handled by the Vietnamese themselves.

Duong Dinh Thao, a spokesman for the Viet Cong delegation at the Paris peace talks, said July 17 that the Paris meetings remained the best way of settling the Indochina war. Thao noted China's support for the Viet Cong's seven-point peace plan and that Peking "sustains our patriotic fight against American aggression."

North Vietnam inferentially affirmed its independence from Communist China's policy in articles appearing in the Communist party newspaper Nhan Dan July 19 and 20. An editorial in the July 20 issue marking the anniversary of the signing of the Geneva accords, said "the most important cause of our victories is our correct and creative independent and sovereign line." Predicting eventual American military defeat in Indochina, the newspaper stated that "the decisive voice only belongs to those who are defeating them."

The Vietnamese Communist stand appeared to be reflected in a Soviet statement made public July 20, reaffirming Moscow's opposition to an international conference on Indochina. The U.S.S.R.'s position was outlined in a letter (dated

July 13) of Foreign Minister Andrei A. Gromyko to U.N. Secretary General U Thant. Gromyko said "a constructive basis for solving the Indochina problem was found in the well-known proposals" of North Vietnam, the Viet Cong and the Pathet Lao of Laos. These proposals, he said, were aimed at permitting the people of that area "to settle themselves their internal problems without outside intervention."

Bruce ends peace talk role. David K.E. Bruce ended his role as chief American delegate to the Paris peace talks by attending his last session July 29.

In one of his final statements at the meeting, Bruce charged that the Communists had increased their activities in and around the demilitarized zone in "blatant violation of . . . previous understandings." He said "we have clear evidence that you are now engaged in building a road through the western part of the demilitarized zone connecting the road network of North Vietnam with roads in northwestern Quangtri Province of South Vietnam."

North Vietnamese press spokesman Thanh Le said after the meeting that Bruce's statement was a "caluminous allegation" aimed at covering up American military moves in Indochina.

In an interview July 30, Mrs. Nguyen Thi Binh, head of the Viet Cong delegation, July 30 offered to identify all American prisoners of war as soon as the U.S. set a deadline for the total withdrawal of its troops from Indochina. Mrs. Binh criticized William J. Porter, Bruce's successor, for what she called the "unheard-of savagery" of the pacification program in South Vietnam under his direction when he was deputy U.S. ambassador to Saigon. She also said it would be pointless for President Nixon to try to engage the Chinese in a discussion of a Vietnam settlement when he visited Peking.

U.S. officials disclosed July 31 that their latest figures, now a month old, indicated that 591 Americans were missing in South Vietnam. Many of them were assumed to be captives of the Viet Cong in jungle prison camps along the Vietnamese-Cambodian border.

Nixon reassuring on talks. At his press conference Aug. 4, President Nixon noted some criticism of Administration policy on the Paris talks, specifically with regard to the lack of a formal reply to the latest Viet Cong peace proposals. The Administration, however, was "very actively pursuing negotiations on Vietnam in established channels" and the record would eventually reveal this, Nixon declared. He said the U.S. was not missing any opportunity to negotiate. "It would not be useful to negotiate in the newspapers if we want to have those negotiations succeed."

POW release plan denied. A Swedish newspaper report Aug. 4 that the U.S. had asked the Scandinavian Airlines System (SAS) to fly 187 released American prisoners of war from Vientiane, Laos to Rome was denied the following day by the U.S., North Vietnam and Sweden.

The newspaper, Dagens Nyheter, said the plan had been secretly arranged by the U.S. command in South Vietnam at the end of July when it cabled SAS, asking for a chartered plane. The Swedish government probably had been involved in the negotiations, according to the newspaper. Dagens Nyheter said "the transport was originally planned to take place Aug. 6, but the departure was delayed till Aug. 12."

An unidentified West German businessman, with "contacts in both the East and the West," said Aug. 5 he had contacted SAS about the charter flight but that it had to be postponed "indefinitely" because of the "unwanted publicity." The man said the prisoner release plan had involved "no American, neither private nor military, organization."

The U.S. State Department Aug. 5 acknowledged that the SAS office in Bonn, West Germany had been contacted by a party unknown to the U.S. government and tried to arrange for the chartered flight. But the department insisted that the U.S. "has not been involved in, or a party to, any negotiations or contacts that would lead us to expect the release of any Americans at this time."

U.S. proposes secret talks. The U.S. delegation at the Paris peace talks Sept. 9 renewed its proposal to hold secret discussions in an effort to speed progress at the deadlocked conference. The North

Vietnamese and Viet Cong delegations rejected the suggestion.

The proposal was submitted by chief U.S. delegate William J. Porter in his first appearance at the talks. Porter urged the Communists to "depart from the practice of using this forum to produce a weekly press polemic" and requested that the following week's session be a restricted one in which only a communiqué agreed to by both sides would be issued after its conclusion.

The Viet Cong rejected Porter's proposal, asserting that the American chief delegate had brought with him an old plan previously turned down by the Communists. Dinh Ba Thi, sitting in for Mrs. Nguyen Thi Binh, accused Porter of trying to avoid answering the Viet Cong's seven-point peace plan that Mrs. Binh had put forward July 1. Thi said if the American delegation needed further clarification of the proposal "our delegation is ready to have private meetings" with the Americans alone.

U.S. press spokesman Stephen Ledogar said after the meeting that the American delegation would not confer with Viet Cong representatives without the South Vietnamese in attendance. Ledogar described the Viet Cong proposal as "a maneuver designed to prevent negotiation."

(Before assuming his post, Porter had conferred with President Nixon Aug. 24. Reporting on their discussions, White House Press Secretary Ronald L. Ziegler said Nixon had told Porter that he continued to place "a high priority" on a negotiated settlement and that he was sending him to Paris with "the widest flexibility" to reach an agreement.)

The U.S. had been represented at the previous sessions since Aug. 5 by Philip C. Habib, acting delegation chief.

Nixon vows prisoner release. President Nixon Sept. 28 assured the wives of American prisoners in North Vietnam that the U.S. would "eventually succeed" in securing the release of the captives.

In a surprise appearance before the annual convention in Washington of the National League of Families of American Prisoners and Missing in Southeast Asia, Nixon said the U.S. was employing "every negotiating channel" to obtain the freedom of the men. His ad-

ministration's efforts, he said, included "many private channels that have not been disclosed." But "we are dealing with a savage enemy, one with no concern for humanitarian ideals," Nixon said.

Sen. Edward M. Kennedy (D, Mass.) had told the convention earlier in the day that the captives were "rotting" in their camps because the Nixon Administration had failed to respond to the Viet Cong's July 1 peace proposal dealing with the exchange of prisoners.

Defense Secretary Melvin R. Laird, in an address to the group Sept. 28, rebutted claims that the Communist negotiators were prepared to be flexible and separate the POW issue from other issues. Official overtures on the matter had received "no response or a response veiled in ambiguity," he said.

2 prisoners released. The Viet Cong released an American prisoner of war Oct. 8 and the U.S. reciprocated Oct. 11 by freeing a North Vietnamese captive.

The U.S. soldier was S. Sgt. John C. Sexton, 23, who had been captured Aug. 12, 1969. He made his way to an allied base camp at Locninh, 70 miles north of Saigon. Sexton was the 24th American released by the Viet Cong and the first in 22 months, according to the U.S. command.

The North Vietnamese captive, a lieutenant, was set free in Cambodia.

At the Oct. 7 session of the Paris peace talks, William J. Porter, chief U.S. negotiator, had called on the Communist delegations for information about American prisoners known to be dead in Vietnam. The Viet Cong and North Vietnamese representatives did not respond. U.S. spokesman Stephen Ledogar later told newsmen that of the 1,618 American servicemen missing, only a third were believed to be still alive.

North Vietnamese press spokesman Nguyen Thanh Le insisted that the list of prisoners released December 1970 showing 20 American dead, was "complete."

Saigon frees Viet Cong POWs. In honor of President Thieu's inauguration, the South Vietnamese government Oct. 31 began releasing the first of 2,938 Viet Cong prisoners of war. The remainder were to be freed in the next few days. It was the largest such amnesty of the war.

Of the total number freed, 618 prisoners were being returned to their villages in South Vietnam. The others were being assigned to the government's Chieu Hoi (Open Arms) program, which called for a two–three month indoctrination period. On completion of their "political rehabilitation," the men were to be released but subject to future military service.

The South Vietnamese government had announced the amnesty program Oct. 28, describing it as "a major humanitarian gesture." At the 134th session of the Paris peace talks that day, the North Vietnamese and Viet Cong delegations refused to accept the release of the Communist captives. They assailed the Saigon action as a "farce" and a "perfidious maneuver."

William J. Porter, chief U.S. delegate to the Paris talks, welcomed the release of the Viet Cong prisoners "as a step toward peaceful solution of the prisoner-of-war question and we hope that it will lead to future releases on both sides."

Hanoi pressed on U.S. POWs. U.S. entertainer Bob Hope met with North Vietnamese officials in Vientiane, Laos Dec. 23 in an attempt to negotiate the release of American prisoners of war.

Hope, who was in Indochina for his annual Christmas show for GIs, said he had proposed freeing the American captives in exchange for a $10 million contribution to a North Vietnamese children's charity. Hope said he would raise the money through a charity show he would put on in the U.S. Hope said that in his discussions with Nguyen Van Tranh, first secretary of the North Vietnamese embassy in Vientiane, he requested a visa to Hanoi to discuss his proposal.

In other prisoner developments, the names of 18 American servicemen held captive by the Viet Cong in South Vietnam were released Dec. 22 by the Committee of Liaison With Families of Servicemen Detained in North Vietnam, a U.S. peace group.

Clash on peace talk date. Allied and Communist delegations at the Paris peace talks concluded their 138th session Dec. 9 and for the first time failed to reach agreement even on when to hold their next meeting.

The dispute arose when William J. Porter, chief American delegate, proposed that the next session be held Dec. 23 rather than the following week as would be the normal pattern. Porter told the Communist delegates, "We see no point in meeting next week for another sterile session when you obviously need more time to develop a constructive approach here."

The Communists rejected Porter's proposal as "sabotage." Xuan Thuy, chief North Vietnamese delegate, insisted that a meeting be held Dec. 16. According to the rules of procedure, all four parties to the talks must agree on a date.

The North Vietnamese and Viet Cong delegations inquired of the allied side Dec. 14 whether they were prepared to meet Dec. 16. A reply sent them by Porter Dec. 15 said he would not meet with them Dec. 16 and was also canceling his proposed new date. Porter suggested the meeting be held Dec. 30.

The North Vietnamese denounced the move as "utterably unreasonable."

A Dec. 30 meeting date was ultimately agreed on, but the onset of massive American air attacks on North Vietnam prompted the U.S. and Hanoi delegations Dec. 28 to cancel the Dec. 30 meeting. The North Vietnamese proposed that the next session be held Jan. 6, 1972 but the U.S. and South Vietnamese sides did not respond to the offer. The talks had been suspended since Dec. 9.

The note submitted by the American liaison officer at a meeting with his North Vietnamese counterpart said the cancellation "does not imply any intention on the part of our side to discontinue the Paris talks." The note cited the reasons U.S. Defense Secretary Melvin R. Laird had given for the bombings as the allied reason for not attending the meeting.

Fighting Continues

Cambodia operations. Fighting continued in Cambodia during early February before and after South Vietnam began its U.S.-aided drive in Laos.

A force of 2,500 South Vietnamese troops crossed the border into the Fishhook area of Cambodia to join 7,500 other Saigon troops there in the start of a new campaign to clear out what were described as Communist border sanctuaries, it was announced Feb. 3. The sweep, which had begun the previous week, was assisted by 7,500 Cambodian troops. American planes provided air support.

Although no major Communist activity had been detected in the area bordering part of South Vietnam's Military Region III, one official said the purpose of the drive was "to be sure that we haven't missed anything that would endanger the withdrawal of United States troops" from South Vietnam.

In an initial encounter with the enemy Feb. 4, Saigon reported that South Vietnamese and Cambodian troops had killed 69 Communist soldiers. South Vietnamese losses were placed at seven killed and 28 wounded.

The new operation centered in Kompong Cham Province where about 1,000 Cambodian troops Feb. 4 advanced about six miles north of the town of Suong. A Cambodian military spokesman said the first objective of the Pnompenh troops was to attack the command post of the 9th North Vietnamese Division at Chup.

In another development, a convoy of 34 trucks carrying gasoline arrived in Pnompenh from the port of Kompong Som Feb. 2. The convoy traveled over newly-opened Route 4 and was the first shipment of the fuel to reach the capital over the strategic road in more than two months.

Saigon headquarters reported Feb. 11 that South Vietnamese forces had killed 164 Communist soldiers in six engagements along Routes 1 and 7 in eastern Cambodia. South Vietnamese losses were listed at 21 killed and 67 wounded.

In fighting near Snoul Feb. 10, South Vietnamese troops threw back three Communist attacks, killing 73 North Vietnamese. Saigon's losses were put at 10 killed and 42 wounded.

Cambodian forces engaged in two clashes with the Viet Cong Feb. 13. One skirmish was fought at Samdech Yos airfield, 100 miles northeast of Pnompenh, and the other three miles southeast of Siem Reap, 140 miles northwest of the capital. No casualties were listed in either clash.

Communist forces Feb. 20 severed Highway 1, linking Pnompenh with Saigon, by damaging a bridge about 35 miles southeast of the capital, a government spokesman reported the following day.

Communist shells Feb. 22 blew up an ammunition barge on the Mekong River six miles from Pnompenh. Another barge was badly damaged and three Americans aboard a boat towing the barges were wounded. The attack occurred near Moat Krasas Krao, an area held for several months by the North Vietnamese and Viet Cong.

A force of 1,500 South Vietnamese troops entered Cambodia Feb. 25, raising the number of Saigon troops there to 24,500. The new operations were centered southeast of Kompong Trabek, northwest of Saigon.

The headquarters of three South Vietnamese task forces and a ranger battalion north of Route 7 came under heavy Communist shelling Feb. 28. The South Vietnamese, assisted by U.S. air strikes, struck back and killed 50 North Vietnamese, while their own losses were five dead and 30 wounded, a Saigon spokesman said.

2 allied generals killed. Two generals involved in the fighting in Cambodia— Cambodian Brig. Gen. Neak Sam and the commander of South Vietnamese forces in Cambodia, Lt. Gen. Do Cao Tri—were killed Feb. 12 and 23.

Neak Sam was killed with 14 other government soldiers in a clash with Communist troops 65 miles south of Pnompenh.

Gen. Tri and nine other persons died when their helicopter crashed shortly after taking off from Tayninh, South Vietnam for Kompong Cham, Cambodia. Also killed was Francois Sully, 43, Newsweek magazine correspondent. Tri also had been commander of Military Region III, the zone around Saigon.

Cambodia operations stalled. American sources in Saigon were quoted as saying March 8 that South Vietnam's offensive in Cambodia had virtually halted following the death of its commander, Lt. Gen. Do Cao Tri. The continuation of the drive was reportedly being held up while Tri's successor, Gen, Nguyen Van Minh, developed his battle plans.

In the last reported action, the South Vietnamese, with the aid of heavy American air strikes, were said to have killed 460 North Vietnamese soldiers in a battle March 3–4 on Route 75 between Chhlong and Route 7. The fighting erupted after a force of 4,000 Communists had cut the road south of the Vietnamese troops who were trying to get back to Route 7 after four days of operations near Chhlong. Saigon did not announce its losses.

According to a Saigon communique March 8, South Vietnamese losses since the start of the latest operations in Cambodia Feb. 24 totaled 249 killed and 1,644 wounded.

In previous actions in Cambodia, an American helicopter was shot down and destroyed over Kompong Cham Province March 8. Four crewmen were killed.

Viet Cong and North Vietnamese forces shelled the oil refinery at the port of Kompong Som March 2 and 4. The March 2 mortar shelling of four storage tanks was said to have destroyed 80% of the installation. Five Cambodian soldiers and a number of civilians were killed. Four Viet Cong were killed in a clash nearby.

A Communist ambush March 2 killed 11 South Vietnamese soldiers near the town of Suong. Thirty of the attackers were reportedly killed after air strikes and artillery were called in.

In other developments in Cambodia, government troops clashed March 15 with an enemy force of 200–300 men along the Tonle Toch River, south of Kompong Cham Lang, killing 30. Cambodian losses were placed at five killed and 10 wounded.

Two American helicopters were shot down March 31 while flying cover for an ammunition and gasoline ship convoy on the Mekong River on the way to Pnompenh. The convoy ran into heavy enemy fire from the riverbanks but reached the capital safely the following day.

Cambodian troops were reported to have killed seven enemy soldiers in a five-hour clash April 2 across the Mekong River from Kompong Cham, 49 miles northeast of Pnompenh. Government losses were two killed and 26 wounded. A fiercer clash was fought in Kompong Cham Province April 6 in which 130 Viet Cong were claimed to have been slain. Cambodia said its losses were six killed and 34 wounded.

ARVN abuse of Cambodians. Violent treatment of Cambodian civilians by ARVN (Army of the Republic of [South] Vietnam) troops was charged in a joint Cambodian-South Vietnamese report signed March 6 and made public March 20.

Since the start of their operations in Cambodia in April 1970, the statement said, South Vietnamese soldiers had engaged in "violence against . . . civilians, thefts and plunder, attempted rapes, gunfire causing dead and wounded, rocket fire causing destruction of homes." The report said these crimes were continuing despite strict orders and that South Vietnamese unit officers were not cooperating with their superiors in preventing such acts.

The report specifically cited 18 cases of crimes committed against civilians in three provinces. The most serious incident had occurred Dec. 30, 1970 near the district capital of Krivong where two South Vietnamese soldiers were arrested for stealing property and livestock. The arrests precipitated an armed clash between Cambodian and South Vietnamese troops that was quickly halted by the intervention of two U.S. generals.

In a move to prevent further acts of violence against· Cambodian civilians, the report proposed creation of a Cambodian-South Vietnamese commission in Pnompenh consisting of two high officers from each side. It also suggested establishment of permanent subcommissions in each province in which Saigon troops might be operating. The subcommissions could investigate all reported incidents and advise punishment and compensation immediately.

Route 4 blocked in Cambodia. North Vietnamese and Viet Cong troops March 30 captured a 10-mile stretch of Route 4 linking Pnompenh with Cambodia's only. deep sea port at Kompong Som. A joint Cambodian-South Vietnamese force had cleared the road in January after it had been under Communist control since November 1970.

The new fighting for Route 4 had erupted March 29 when a Cambodian convoy of several battalions, moving down the road about 58 miles from the capital, was ambushed by a Communist force. About 50 government soldiers were said to have been killed. The Cambodian convoy again came under attack the following day and retreated three miles to a fortified camp. The Communists were reported April 8 to have widened control of Route 4 by seizing another two-mile section.

North Vietnamese-Cambodian fighting along Route 4 continued through April. The clashes took place around Pich Nil Pass, 58 miles south of the capital, where a government force holding defensive positions was under North Vietnamese attack. An 8,000-man Cambodian force, attempting to relieve the besieged garrison, reached within two miles of the surrounded government soldiers April 28. A spokesman reported that 57 North Vietnamese were killed in four hours of hand-to-hand fighting, while government losses were placed at 12 killed and 51 wounded. Associated Press reported that the Cambodians were supported in the battle by U.S. fighter-bombers.

United Press International correspondent Catherine Webb, 28, of Australia, was captured by the Viet Cong in Cambodia April 8 but was released unharmed May 1. Miss Webb and five other foreign correspondents had been seized while covering a battle on Route 4.

Lon Nol suffers stroke. Cambodian Premier Lon Nol was partially paralyzed by a stroke suffered in Pnompenh Feb. 8. He signed an order Feb. 10 transferring his duties and authority as defense minister to Deputy Premier Sisowath Sirik Matak.

The premier was flown to Hawaii Feb. 13 for treatment at a U.S. Army hospital near Honolulu.

A U.S. embassy official in Pnompenh said Feb. 13 that Lon Nol's choice of an American convalescence was entirely his own and that of his advisers. He said "Washington does not want anyone to assume that the United States is taking any political responsibility for the general and his government."

Lon Nol resigned as premier April 20. Efforts to replace him led to a government crisis that was finally resolved May 3 with an accord under which Lon Nol would serve as titular premier while Lt. Gen. Sisowath Sirik Matak, deputy premier in the outgoing government, would hold the principal executive power.

Despite his decision to step down, Lon Nol received a mandate April 21 from Chief of State Cheng Heng to form a new government. Cheng Heng said he was urging the premier to stay on "because of the grave circumstances of our country today and in consideration of opinions emanating from various sectors."

Following several days of consultations with his political aides, Lon Nol submitted his final resignation April 29. At the same time, he was named chief of the Cambodian armed forces and Sirik Matak was appointed second in command. Cheng Heng then called on Sirik Matak to form a new government but the deputy premier declined the offer April 30. Chuop Hell, counselor to Cheng Heng, was mandated premier, but he informed the chief of state May 1 that he could not "fulfill his delicate mission." Brig. Gen. In Tam, National Assembly president, was called on to form a new government, but failed following consultations May 2.

A new cabinet submitted by Sirik Matak was approved by the National Assembly May 6. Sirik Matak held the principal executive power as premier-delegate, while Gen. Lon Nol was titular head of government, retaining his title as premier.

U.S. warns of DMZ buildup. The reported buildup of Hanoi's forces inside the demilitarized zone that divided North and South Vietnam prompted the U.S. State Department March 25 to warn of possible retaliatory air strikes if Communist artillery and rockets in the buffer area fired on allied positions to the south. The department said the massing of Communist equipment in the zone was the most extensive since 1968.

Defense Department spokesman Jerry Friedheim refused to comment on whether the Administration regarded the Communist actions as a violation of the so-called understanding in 1968 under which North Vietnam pledged to respect the neutrality of the DMZ in exchange for the American bombing halt of the North. Hanoi had repeatedly denied such an understanding.

Friedheim recalled Defense Secretary Melvin R. Laird's previous warnings that it was his "responsibility to recommend whatever protective reaction steps to protect allied and U.S. forces." The department spokesman said North Vietnam had started the DMZ buildup before the South Vietnamese invasion of Laos Feb. 8.

The U.S. command reported March 26 that the Communist movement of men and guns into the DMZ had increased 50% since February, with half of these activities reportedly occurring in South Vietnam's part of the zone. Saigon headquarters reported that Communist batteries March 26 fired from inside the zone and struck Dongha, a base 11 miles south. Several soldiers were killed or wounded.

A Hanoi communiqué had charged March 25 that U.S. raids over North Vietnam March 1-22 had caused 100 civilian casualties. During that period, the statement said, American aircraft had made 1,440 reconnaissance sorties and 220 tactical sorties, bombing several populated areas of the provinces north of the 17th Parallel. The reconnaissance flights had been conducted "over nearly all of the provinces and cities of North Vietnam, including Haiphong and Hanoi," the communique said.

U.S. jets bomb DMZ. American aircraft bombed North Vietnamese artillery positions in the northern section of the demilitarized zone March 30. Other military developments in Indochina through April 6 were marked by fierce ground clashes in the northern section of South Vietnam and by a South Vietnamese foray into Laos.

The U.S. command reported that the air strike on the DMZ was carried out by four planes because Communist artillery units there "were threatening United States and South Vietnamese personnel" inside South Vietnam. The command, describing the raids as "a protective mission," said they followed an increase in enemy artillery attacks in the northern part of South Vietnam in the past week. The command did not say the artillery fire had come from inside the DMZ. American planes were reported to have searched the DMZ March 27 for North

Vietnamese artillery but found the guns had been moved. The aircraft returned without dropping their bombs.

North Vietnamese attacks—Two North Vietnamese regiments carried out a devastating attack March 28–31 against the northern district capital of Ducduc, 25 miles southwest of Danang. Saigon said 43 civilians had been killed and 63 wounded and 800 houses burned. An Associated Press dispatch from Ducduc said 100 civilians had been killed and 150 wounded, with 20 regional militiamen slain and 51 wounded defending the town. The Saigon command said 50 enemy soldiers had been killed and two wounded in the fighting for Ducduc, but gave no casualties of the defenders.

South and North Vietnamese troops fought a protracted battle March 31–April 5 at Fire Base 6 in the Central Highlands near Dakto, six miles from the Laotian border. Saigon claimed that 1,914 North Vietnamese had been killed in the fighting, while South Vietnamese losses were listed as 61 killed and 82 wounded. Other sources said the South Vietnamese had suffered more than 200 killed and wounded in the first two days of fighting for Fire Base 6. South Vietnamese claims of enemy losses also were questioned by some military quarters.

The South Vietnamese were driven from Fire Base 6 March 31 and reoccupied it the following day before the enemy launched another attack. The commander of the military region covering the Central Highlands, Maj. Gen. Ngo Dzu, said the North Vietnamese had sent "wave after wave" of "suicide squads" against the base April 4 and "their bodies were piled in front of our guns." The enemy ground attacks tapered off and the Communists subjected the base to heavy shelling April 5.

Gen. Dzu said April 6 that the base remained surrounded by two North Vietnamese regiments, numbering 3,000 to 4,000 men. The installation was defended by 1,000 men.

U.S. artillery base raided—A U.S. artillery base in northern South Vietnam's Quangtin Province, about 50 miles south of Danang, came under Communist mortar and ground assault March

28. Thirty-three Americans were killed and 76 wounded. The base was partly overrun during the one-hour battle. U.S. authorities reported later that it remained "in friendly control" after the attackers were repelled with the aid of artillery and air strikes. The withdrawing enemy troops left behind 12 dead, an American spokesman said.

U.S. death toll at 9-month high. The U.S. command reported April 9 that 88 American soldiers had been killed in combat March 28-April 3. This was the highest U.S. weekly death toll since the week ended June 27, 1970 when 104 Americans were listed as killed in action.

Fire Base 6 battle continues. The fighting in South Vietnam was largely centered around Fire Base 6, the South Vietnamese stronghold in the northern Central Highlands, which had been under continuous attack by the North Vietnamese since March 31. The base was defended by 5,000–6,000 men, but its artillery pieces, destroyed in the initial Communist ground assault, were yet to be replaced. Meanwhile, U.S. planes continued to pound North Vietnamese troop concentrations around the base in an attempt to break the siege.

Saigon claimed the killing of 320 North Vietnamese in several engagements one mile north of the base April 7. Most of the casualties were said to have been caused by American air and artillery strikes.

Waves of U.S. bombers dropped explosives and napalm on enemy troops April 9 within two to three miles of the base, setting off jungle fires. North Vietnamese commandos, defying the severe raids, attempted to infiltrate Fire Base 6 April 10 but were repulsed with a loss of 12 killed. After the North Vietnamese were thrown back, South Vietnamese planes joined U.S. B-52 bombers in pounding enemy forces around the base.

An American helicopter attempting to bring in supplies was shot down by enemy fire April 11. The Communist guns also forced 11 other supply aircraft to turn back.

In a determined attempt to break the siege, U.S. planes April 12 began dropping seven-and-a-half ton bombs on

North Vietnamese troop concentrations around Fire Base 6. The huge explosives—one to a plane—were pulled from four-engined C-130 cargo transports by parachutes. A second chute stabilized the bomb during its descent. The bombs, which exploded laterally, normally were used to blast out heavy jungle growth to clear landing spaces for helicopters.

Among other military developments in South Vietnam:

North Vietnamese troops April 7 attacked Fire Base Lonely, 80 miles south of Fire Base 6, and were repulsed with a loss of 68 killed, half by air strikes. South Vietnamese losses were placed at one killed and three wounded, according to Saigon.

Enemy troops April 7 penetrated two hamlets 25 miles north of Danang, destroying 18 homes and a school and abducting 23 civilians.

Ten American soldiers were killed April 11 while attempting to secure a helicopter that had been shot down by the Viet Cong in northern Quangngai Province. One American died and two were wounded in the helicopter crash.

A North Vietnamese trawler was sunk and destroyed April 11 as it tried to slip through a U.S. Navy blockade at the southern tip of South Vietnam.

Allies probe Ashau Valley. U.S. and South Vietnamese forces launched a probe April 14 of the Ashau Valley, a 30-mile area used by the North Vietnamese as an infiltration corridor and supply transshipment point from Laos into northern South Vietnam.

Failure to establish significant contact with suspected enemy forces through April 21 apparently precluded the launching of an expected major offensive in the valley. About 400 U.S. and 5,000 South Vietnamese soldiers were reported committed to the sweep. The operation, code-named Lam Son 720, was described as a follow-up to the February-March thrust by South Vietnamese forces into Laos, code-named Lam Son 719.

President Nguyen Van Thieu had formally announced the drive April 17 at a ceremony in Hué marking the Laos "victory." After reviewing a parade of 23,000 soldiers, Thieu reiterated his political position on the war. He said:

"I want to repeat my four no's: no coalition, no neutralization, no territorial concessions, and never let Communist forces operate openly in South Vietnam." Recent operations were aimed at preventing these, Thieu said.

Gen. Creighton W. Abrams, commander of American forces in South Vietnam, attended the Hué ceremonies. He later told newsmen that a new South Vietnamese push into Laos from the Ashau Valley "could not be ruled out." Abrams provided little information on the latest operation, saying only that "it's against his [the North Vietnamese] supply system in South Vietnam, but don't narrow it to the Ashau."

About 60 miles north of the Ashau Valley, North Vietnamese forces were reported April 20 to have crossed into the northwestern corner of South Vietnam from Laos and seized material left behind at Khesanh by the allies after the Laos operations. Most of the equipment was believed to have been destroyed after Khesanh was abandoned by U.S. and South Vietnamese forces.

In another action involving Laos, the U.S. command reported that two fighter-bombers sought to protect other American aircraft bombing the Ho Chi Minh Trail April 19 by firing at two Communist missile sites, one in North Vietnam, 40 miles north of the demilitarized zone, and the other in the upper Laotian panhandle, 70 miles above the DMZ. The firing was aimed at thwarting anticipated Communist missile fire at the American planes, the command said. A U.S. Navy plane had bombed a radar station near the Bankarai Pass in North Vietnam April 12 in support of air missions in Laos.

In South Vietnam, the airborne arrival April 16 of 400 South Vietnamese troops at Fire Base 6 in the Central Highlands prompted the Saigon commander in the area to declare the North Vietnamese siege of the stronghold, in force since March 31, had been broken. However, 6,000–10,000 North Vietnamese troops continued to surround the base, making it difficult for reinforcements to reach the base on foot.

Enemy pressure on Fire Base 6 had begun to ease April 13–14 with the arrival of four South Vietnamese infantry battalions. The men were airlifted by

American helicopters to a landing zone two miles south and then made their way to the base on foot without encountering resistance. Heavy fighting broke out one half mile from the base April 14, with the South Vietnamese claiming that 96 North Vietnamese had been slain in the 16-hour clash. Meanwhile, an American helicopter April 14 lifted out four of the five U.S. military advisers at Fire Base 6. No reason for the evacuation was given. About 40 South Vietnamese seeking to flee the base swarmed around the 'copter as it was about to take off. Eight jumped aboard. Others tried to cling to the aircraft's landing skids, but the crew shoved them off.

The allied probe in and around the Ashau Valley continued but failed to make any contact with the enemy through April 25. U.S. helicopters April 21 flew about 1,500 South Vietnamese marines to landing zones 20–25 miles north of the valley. Another 525 government troops were air-lifted by U.S. 'copters April 23 to a mountain artillery base overlooking the Dakrong River valley, 18 miles north of the Ashau area.

According to South Vietnamese newspaper reports, the Ashau operations were only a "training exercise" for the many fresh troops that were sent to the 1st South Vietnamese Infantry Division to replace those lost in the February-March fighting in Laos. The commander of the Ashau operations, Brig. Gen. Vu Van Giai, said it would continue until October.

Five U.S. soldiers were killed and 10 wounded in an ambush just east of the Ashau Valley April 30. These were the first ground losses suffered by an American unit since the start of the Ashau Valley drive. U.S. B-52 bombers carried out raids May 1 in an attempt to strike at the North Vietnamese troops that ambushed the American reconnaissance unit. B-52s had carried out 18 raids the previous week near the Ashau Valley and two other areas in the north—15 miles northwest of Khesanh, near the demilitarized zone, and near Fire Base 6.

U.S. jets raid North Vietnam. American jets carried out several protective reaction strikes against missile bases in North Vietnam April 18–23. This brought to 30 the number of such raids conducted since Jan. 1. The bombings were the heaviest for a six-day period since the halt in raids over North Vietnam in November 1968.

Three missile bases and antiaircraft positions were struck April 22 and another was bombed just across the border in Laos. One mission flew 185 miles into North Vietnam for one of the deepest penetrations since the summer of 1970. The American command reported that two sites around the Quanglang airfield, 125 miles south of Hanoi, were destroyed or damaged. A follow-up announcement by the command April 24 said the attack "may have destroyed one or two MiG-21 aircraft located on the ground near the site."

Four Navy jets April 23 carried out two separate strike missions against two missile sites—48 miles northwest of Donghoi and further north, 15 miles southwest of Hatinh. The first attack came after at least one Communist missile was fired at the U.S. aircraft. None of the planes was damaged.

In another action April 23, two U.S. Phantoms on a routine bombing mission over the Ho Chi Minh Trail cut short their mission after spotting a North Vietnamese MiG-21. The MiG was chased into North Vietnam. While flying over the Quanglang airfield, the two American jets were fired on by three ground missiles and abandoned the chase. One of the planes was slightly damaged but returned safely to its carrier in the South China Sea.

The U.S. Defense Department reported April 26 that about six North Vietnamese MiG-21s had made limited flights into southern Laos in the last few weeks "on several occasions to threaten U.S. aircraft." The MiGs came from the Quanglang base, the department said.

Communists hit allied bases. Ending a long battle lull in South Vietnam, North Vietnamese troops carried out sharp attacks on allied bases and installations throughout the country April 24–27, inflicting heavy casualties.

Official but incomplete reports listed 54 South Vietnamese soldiers and civilians killed in the assaults and 185 wounded. U.S. losses totaled seven killed and 60 wounded.

The South Vietnamese suffered their heaviest casualties when North Vietnamese commandos April 24 overran part of the Hoanganh combat base 15 miles northwest of the coastal city of Quangngai. Twenty-two of the estimated 400 defenders were killed and 52 wounded. A Saigon statement said 21 North Vietnamese had been killed.

In one of two enemy ambushes of U.S. troops 20 miles northwest of Saigon, four U.S. soldiers were killed and 13 wounded. Two plows being used to clear jungle land to curb guerrilla activity were destroyed. Two more Americans were killed and four were wounded when North Vietnamese soldiers opened fire on a U.S. armored column six miles away. Two American tanks and one personnel carrier were destroyed in the seven-hour clash that ensued.

The Ducmy training center for South Vietnamese rangers, 150 miles north of Saigon, was pounded by 100 rocket and mortar shells April 24. The shelling was followed by a ground assault by 30 North Vietnamese sappers, but the attack was repulsed. The Communists then shelled a nearby housing area for military dependents, killing two civilians and wounding 32.

The heaviest North Vietnamese attack April 26 was directed at an ammunition dump at Quinhon, 265 miles northeast of Saigon. A mortar barrage blew up the depot, killing 10 government soldiers and wounding 26. Eighteen civilians also were wounded. The bombardment also struck a nearby U.S. Army support command post and a South Vietnamese military hospital. Six American servicemen were reported wounded. Other enemy activity that day included the shelling of three allied airfields and other minor ground attacks.

Several U.S. installations were shelled by enemy gunners April 27. Among the targets struck were a fuel storage tank at the Danang air base, the Camranh air base and airfields at Pleiku, Soctrang and Binhthuy, causing minor damage and some casualties. A direct hit was scored on the Danang air base tank, igniting 35,000 gallons of jet fuel and causing the fire to spread to other aviation fuel tanks.

The district headquarters of Dailoc, 15 miles south of Danang, was the scene of a sharp clash May 2. A North Viet-namese battalion struck the stronghold but was repulsed with a loss of 92 killed and five captured, according to a Saigon communique. Fourteen of the defending militia men were killed and 53 wounded. Five civilians were killed and 30 were wounded. Dailoc was shelled May 3, but little damage was reported.

U.S. deaths total 45,019. The U.S. command reported April 29 that 45 Americans had been killed in combat in Indochina April 18–24, bringing the total number of U.S. deaths to 45,019 since 1961. This figure was exceeded only by the U.S. death tolls in World War II (292,131) and World War I (53,513).

The 45 American deaths compared with 56 killed the previous week and reflected "a decrease in the level and intensity" of enemy attacks, the command said. The number of wounded—518—was a sharp rise from the 195 reported wounded in the previous seven-day period.

Other casualties incurred April 18–24: South Vietnamese—305 killed and 838 wounded (10-year death toll was 125,-995); North Vietnamese and Viet Cong—1,788 killed, bringing the 10-year total to 736,422, according to allied estimates.

The U.S. command announced May 6 that 68 American battlefield deaths had been recorded April 25-May 1, the highest fatality toll in five weeks.

The total included 21 who had been listed as missing, but who were subsequently verified as dead. Of this number, 13 were reported shot down in air operations over Laos. The command also listed 529 wounded in the same weekly period, 74 more than the previous week. An additional 20 Americans died April 25-May 1 as a result of accidents, illness and other non-hostile causes, bringing the 10-year total in that classification to 9,506.

The South Vietnamese government May 5 filed a protest with the International Control Commission, accusing North Vietnam of "intensified and indiscriminate" shellings of civilian targets. A Foreign Ministry note said there had been 151 shelling attacks the previous week in which 20 civilians were killed and 75 wounded.

The U.S. command announced May 10 that 6,300 American troops had been withdrawn from South Vietnam the previous week, reducing the total force to 267,100 men.

1970 black battle deaths drop. Figures released by the Defense Department May 19 showed that the combat death rate for black servicemen in 1970 was 8.8% of the total number of fatalities. This represented a drop from the 16% recorded for the 1962–66 period. The Negro death rate for the subsequent three years had been 12.7%, 12.9% and 10.8%.

1970 was the first year the percentage of black dead was lower than the percentage of Negroes in uniform, 9.8%. According to the Pentagon report, "Negro Participation in the Armed Forces," 5,521 men, or 12.5% of all those killed during 1961–70, were black.

Vietnam death toll report denied. The Defense Department denied April 29 a congressman's report that the number of noncombat deaths among U.S. servicemen in Vietnam had risen drastically in the past five years.

The Pentagon dismissed as inaccurate the statistics disclosed by Rep. William D. Ford (D, Mich.) showing a rise in the number of noncombat deaths per thousand soldiers in Vietnam from 1.95 in 1965 to 5.5 in 1970. A Pentagon spokesman said Ford's "mathematics are wrong." The correct figures, according to the Pentagon, were 3.71 deaths per thousand in 1966, 3.72 in 1967, 3.64 in 1968, 4.07 in 1969 and 4.54 in 1970.

The department spokesman said he denied "without any reservation that there is any manipulation of casualty figures. Casualties are a very serious thing to everyone. You simply don't play games with something that serious."

At the time he made his figures public, Ford had accused the Pentagon of playing a numbers game "for political purpose."

The Defense Department gave these reasons for the slight rise in combat deaths: combat units were being withdrawn from Vietnam more rapidly than noncombat units, the number of noncombat fatalities fluctuated according to total troop strength, and as the South Vietnamese took over more of the combat duties, American GIs had more leisure time, leading to more accidental deaths.

The Pentagon said the largest cause of noncombat deaths was airplane crashes, which accounted for 28% of the total noncombat fatalities over the 1965-1970 period.

Cease-fires violated. U.S. and South Vietnamese forces observed a 24-hour battlefield truce May 8-9 to mark the birth of Buddha. Viet Cong and North Vietnamese troops unilaterally declared a similar cease-fire but extended it another 24 hours until 7 a.m. May 10.

The allied commands claimed May 10 that the Communists had violated both cease-fires, initiating 66 attacks with a heavy loss of South Vietnamese lives. Saigon headquarters said 56 South Vietnamese soldiers and civilians had been killed and 36 wounded. A total of 34 North Vietnamese and Viet Cong soldiers were reported slain. American casualties were placed at two killed and six wounded.

The South Vietnamese fatalities included 41 civilians, 36 of whom had died May 9 in a mine explosion of a ferry boat on a river in northernmost Quangtri Province, three miles northeast of Dongha.

Following expiration of the truces, U.S. B-52 bombers resumed raids against Communist targets in South Vietnam. The B-52 missions had continued over Laos and Cambodia during the cease-fire periods. The raids over Laos, as they had for weeks, concentrated on the Ho Chi Minh Trail. Three such missions were flown May 7, striking at areas nine to 17 miles northwest of Khesanh. During one of the operations, U.S. fighter-bombers accompanying the B-52s flew over North Vietnam and destroyed three antiaircraft guns after being fired on near the Bankarai Pass, 40 miles north of the demilitarized zone, according to the American command. In another strike over North Vietnam, an American jet May 8 attacked an enemy antiaircraft battery 24 miles north of the Mugia Pass after the gun site had begun to track the U.S. plane.

U.S. jets hit North Vietnam. American jets struck antiaircraft sites in North Vietnam May 10-18. The air strikes brought to 40 the number of American attacks on North Vietnam's air defenses reported since Jan. 1.

In the May 10 attack, the U.S. command reported destruction of 13 antiaircraft guns around the Mugia Pass, 75 miles north of the demilitarized zone. The command said the attacks took place after a North Vietnamese MiG-21 had made two firing passes at a U.S. observation plane over the Plaine des Jarres in northern Laos.

Ashau fighting increases. In the first major battle since South Vietnamese forces launched an offensive in the Ashau Valley April 14, North Vietnamese troops May 12 attacked two South Vietnamese positions but were repelled with heavy losses. In the first engagement, about 400 Communists struck at a night bivouac of a 500-man Saigon marine battalion and lost 23 men. Six South Vietnamese marines were killed and 48 wounded. In the second assault, $10\frac{1}{2}$ hours later, the same battalion fought off another North Vietnamese thrust, reportedly killing 177. South Vietnamese casualties were listed at 36 killed or wounded.

The South Vietnamese earlier May 12 had claimed destruction of a North Vietnamese base camp and arms factory in the Ashau Valley area. The report said Saigon troops had destroyed 100 small structures with underground bunkers.

Sporadic fighting flared in and around the Ashau Valley May 19–23. Thousands of South Vietnamese troops fought a six-hour battle with North Vietnamese May 19, killing 14 of the enemy. Communist ground fire downed an American helicopter and damaged two other 'copters and a reconnaissance plane during the engagement. Government troops were reported to have killed 38 North Vietnamese on the southeastern end of the valley May 20. Twenty-eight Communist bunkers were captured. Government sources claimed the killing May 21 of 45 North Vietnamese in the valley with the aid of air strikes and artillery. Fifty enemy storage huts were reported destroyed and large quantities of ammunition were captured. Saigon headquarters reported the killing of 18 North Vietnamese soldiers in several encounters around the valley near the Laotian border May 23.

In other military developments in South Vietnam, an American personnel carrier May 14 struck a land mine 20 miles from Danang. Five of the occupants were killed.

North Vietnamese gunners May 17 shot down an American helicopter four miles east of the abandoned U.S. Marine base at Khesanh. One crewman was killed and the other rescued.

U.S. bases attacked. North Vietnamese forces heavily shelled U.S. positions along the demilitarized zone May 19–22 and Viet Cong sappers infiltrated the huge American air base at Camranh Bay May 23, blowing up 1,500,000 gallons of aviation fuel.

The worst enemy attack in the DMZ area occurred May 21 when 30 Americans were killed and 50 wounded in three rocket and mortar assaults. Nearly all of the fatalities were suffered at a position called Charlie 2, four miles southeast of the buffer zone. The base was hit by 15 100-pound rockets. Many of the victims were caught in a crowded bunker where they were having their meal. The bunker took a direct hit. The other two targets struck were an infantry bivouac area 17 miles southeast of Hue and an infantry field position about 30 miles south of Danang.

The casualties were said to be the heaviest from enemy shelling of U.S. units in at least 17 months.

In response to enemy shelling in the DMZ area May 22, American artillery struck at North Vietnamese rocket positions inside the southern half of the demilitarized zone. This attack was followed by strikes May 23 by U.S. fighter-bombers and B-52s against suspected Communist rocket-launching sites inside the zone and along the southern edge of the DMZ.

In the Camranh Bay incident, Viet Cong demolition experts, numbering about six men, slipped into the base May 23, planted satchel charges on six fuel tanks and blew them up, setting huge fires. Two Americans were injured in the attack. All six infiltrators escaped. Six hours after the explosion, enemy gunners fired 30 mortars into another part of the base, but caused no casualties or damage.

A spokesman at Camranh Bay said the fuel destroyed was enough to keep 850 helicopters flying for 24 hours. The fuel loss, however, did not halt air operations from the base. A spokesman said there was plenty of fuel available at two nearby bases, Nhatrang and Phanrang.

Gen. Creighton W. Abrams, commander of U.S. forces, was reported May 25 to have expressed anger over the DMZ and Camranh Bay attacks, charging a lack of proper security precautions on the part of the American defenders.

Among other military developments in South Vietnam:

An American cavalry base about 25 miles northwest of Saigon was attacked by Communist troops May 25. Eight Americans were killed and nine were wounded. The unit was stationed near the Cambodian border to prevent the increasing infiltration of Communist troops into the Mekong Delta area from Cambodia.

A U.S. helicopter carrying two allied generals was shot down by enemy gunners May 25 over the U Minh Forest in the Mekong Delta, but both officers were rescued uninjured. They were Maj. Gen. John H. Cushman, commander of the U.S. Military Assistance Command in the delta, and Maj. Gen. Ngo Quang Truong, commander of South Vietnamese forces in the region. The helicopter's pilot and crew chief were injured in the crash. All other passengers, in addition to the two generals, escaped unhurt.

U.S. and South Vietnamese forces reported the killing of 80 Communist troops in four clashes in the northern part of the country May 26. Five South Vietnamese were killed and 33 wounded in the fighting.

Communist forces May 28–29 shelled or assaulted eight U.S. and South Vietnamese positions ranging 85 miles north of Saigon to 100 miles west of the capital. Casualties were reported light.

Reds press Vietnam attacks. Saigon headquarters reported that Communist forces carried out 48 attacks in South Vietnam during a 24-hour period ending at 6 a.m. May 30, killing at least 20 government soldiers and 12 civilians. In addition, 101 South Vietnamese soldiers and 18 civilians were reported wounded.

One American was killed and eight were wounded. North Vietnamese and Viet Cong losses during the attacks were placed at 85 killed.

The Communist strikes included 30 rocket and mortar assaults against South Vietnamese positions. Most of the action centered in the five northernmost provinces. Four allied bases guarding the demilitarized zone were shelled. The U.S. command reported no casualties or damage in these attacks. The U.S. air base at Danang and the city itself were among the targets struck by the Communists. The U.S. command said 10 rockets hit the base without causing damage or casualties, but all 12 South Vietnamese civilian fatalities occurred during the shelling of the city. The Saigon command said the 13 Communist rockets that hit the city also destroyed five homes and wounded 11 other civilians.

Fighting again flared in the northern region May 30–31 with the South Vietnamese claiming they had killed 215 enemy infiltrators in a sweep through villages south of Danang. Six South Vietnamese soldiers were reported killed and 25 wounded in the two-day operation. U.S. advisers said 19 civilians were slain and 39 wounded by crossfire.

A Communist bomb May 31 destroyed a government building in Saigon, killing five civilians and wounding 12.

Seven Americans were killed in the crash of an Army helicopter 24 miles northwest of Saigon June 2. Another 'copter was lost the same day.

DMZ area attacks increase. Communist guns inside North Vietnam shelled allied positions along the demilitarized zone June 7 for the 17th consecutive day. Meanwhile, sharp ground clashes had been fought in the DMZ vicinity and in other sections in the northern provinces of South Vietnam.

South Vietnamese forces May 31 launched a sweep 15–20 miles south of the buffer zone in an effort to smash a North Vietnamese buildup and to clear and block Communist infiltration routes in western Quangtri Province. The operation was supported by American helicopters. Saigon, disclosing the action June 3, said the 2,500 government troops involved had made little contact with the enemy. The only significant action had occurred June 2 when enemy gunners shelled a South Vietnamese battalion near Khesanh for 10 hours. Field reports said six government soldiers were killed. North Vietnamese fatalities were placed at 10.

Two Americans were killed and 10 wounded June 3 when North Vietnamese troops ambushed a U.S. convoy near the DMZ and an infantry unit farther south, between Hue and Danang.

A U.S. base four miles south of the DMZ, Charlie 2, was struck by 15 rocket rounds June 4. American positions five miles northeast of the base were hit by 25 enemy missiles.

North Vietnamese rockets June 5 slammed into the American air base at Danang and the nearby city for the second time in a week. Five South Vietnamese civilians were killed.

Heavy fighting raged June 5–6 around Fire Base Sarge, a government stronghold 12 miles northeast of Khesanh. U.S. helicopter gunships reported killing 58 North Vietnamese in the area June 5, and Saigon's forces claimed they killed another 100 enemy soldiers. Government forces reported slaying 83 North Vietnamese in the same area June 6.

Waves of U.S. B-52 bombers struck North Vietnamese positions in the DMZ area June 7–8. Three of the raids June 8 were reported directed at enemy bunker complexes four and a half miles south of the zone. A fourth raid was said to have pounded newly improved infiltration routes near the Laotian border.

A Reuters report June 8, quoting military sources in Saigon, said North Vietnamese rocket and mortar teams were infiltrating in greater numbers through the central part of the DMZ to strike at allied artillery outposts. The infiltration seemed to have been rerouted into the buffer zone because monsoon rains had made travel difficult on the Ho Chi Minh Trail in Laos, the sources said.

Seven Americans were wounded June 10 when their armored column ran into a North Vietnamese force one and a half miles south of the DMZ. The U.S. command said three North Vietnamese were killed by artillery called in to shell the enemy positions during the five-hour battle.

A 6,000-man Saigon force operating in the Ashau Valley moved 35 miles north toward the DMZ June 12 to join two government marine brigades blocking infiltration south of the buffer strip. Five marines were reported killed when the enemy fired 200 mortar shells into their positions nine miles east of Khesanh.

A force of about 400 North Vietnamese opened an attack June 17 on Fire Base Sarge but were repelled with a loss of 95 men. The 200 government defenders, aided by American jet and helicopter strikes, were said to have lost 13 men. About 1,800 government reinforcements were sent into Fire Base Sarge June 18 to help the 200-man garrison. The expanded Saigon force seized the initiative and enemy attacks tapered off later in the day.

More than 300 North Vietnamese rockets were fired at South Vietnamese outposts near the DMZ June 19–20. The Saigon command claimed 173 enemy troops were killed in the two days of fighting, while South Vietnamese losses were light. Other sources, however, placed government casualties at 33 dead and 78 wounded.

A major confrontation between North and South Vietnamese forces erupted June 22 with an enemy attack on Fire Base Fuller, a government outpost four miles south of the demilitarized zone. Communist forces overran the base June 24, but Saigon claimed June 28 that its troops had reoccupied the outpost. The North Vietnamese 1,500-man assault had been preceded by heavy rocket and mortar shelling of Fire Base Fuller June 19. U.S. B-52s dropped 60 tons of explosives around the base June 21 in an attempt to smash enemy concentrations. The garrison's 500 defenders were reinforced June 24 by 800–1,000 government troops. The South Vietnamese, however, were forced to abandon the base because enemy bombardments had destroyed up to 80% of the bunkers, leaving the defenders with little protective covering. The North Vietnamese dispersed and left the base unoccupied after driving out the defenders.

South Vietnamese forces June 25 conducted a sweep near Fire Base Fuller for the enemy mortar and rocket emplacements that had contributed to the fall of the position. Some of the government troops clashed with the North Vietnamese, while American planes bombed enemy positions in the area. In announcing that a Saigon force of 120 men had moved back into Fire Base Fuller, a military spokesman said June 28 that the government troops had "no intention of rebuilding the fortifications of the base. We can come back any time we want." The Saigon command said in action around Fire Base Fuller since June 19 496 North Vietnamese had been killed, about 310 of them by air strikes. South Vietnamese losses were listed as 29 killed and 135 wounded.

The infiltration of at least two North Vietnamese regiments across the DMZ into South Vietnam, reported June 27, was said to have increased the number of enemy troops in Quangtri Province to about 10,000. Virtually all North Vietnamese troops had been pulled out of Quangtri when U.S. and South Vietnamese soldiers moved into the area in preparation for the February-March incursion into Laos. The increase in enemy attacks along the DMZ coincided with the arrival of the two North Vietnamese regiments in Quangtri.

The intensity of the attacks was pointed up by a report from Saigon June 27 that at least two North Vietnamese regiments had infiltrated across the DMZ into South Vietnam in the first large Communist thrust through the zone in three years. Meanwhile, U.S. B-52s continued to raid North Vietnamese infiltration routes and troop concentrations in the area in an attempt to blunt the Communist drive.

Elsewhere in South Vietnam, Saigon troops were reported to have broken a three-week enemy seige June 15 of Fire Base 5, a government artillery outpost in the Central Highlands. A government force of paratroopers fought a 12-hour battle with North Vietnamese troops and captured a huge enemy complex only 100 yards from the artillery base. Sixty-eight North Vietnamese bodies were found inside the complex, while the paratroopers said they suffered no casualties.

U.S. deaths at record low—The U.S. command announced June 10 that 19 Americans had been killed May 30-June 5, the lowest American weekly death toll since October 1965. Twenty-five

Americans were slain during each of the following two weeks.

DMZ battles continue. Fourteen U.S. F-4 Phantom fighter-bombers attacked the North Vietnamese section of the demilitarized zone June 30 in an attempt to knock out the Communist rocket sites that had been shelling U.S. and South Vietnamese bases just south of the DMZ for the past two weeks. The raid was the first in the DMZ since March 30. Military sources were quoted as saying that it was carried out after artillerymen had refused to fire into the North Vietnamese sector of the DMZ at what a spotter pilot described as a concentration of Communist troops. According to an announcement July 2, the American pilots participating in the raid estimated killing at least 50 and possibly as many as 300 North Vietnamese.

U.S. B-52 bombers had struck North Vietnamese positions just south of the demilitarized zone July 1 in the heaviest raid since August 1970. Four of the strikes were said to have concentrated on an area two to three miles from Fire Base Fuller, the scene of sharp fighting June 22-24.

The American air assaults followed intense battling just below the DMZ June 30. The North Vietnamese were said to have shelled a string of allied bases with rocket and mortar bombardments and attacked with ground troops. Responsive South Vietnamese assaults, accompanied by U.S. air and artillery support, were reported to have killed 92 North Vietnamese. Saigon's losses were listed at 15 killed. Another 38 North Vietnamese were said to have been killed in a flare-up of fighting on the western flank of the buffer zone near Fire Base Fuller. Three South Vietnamese were reported killed. Fighting continued around the government base July 1 as the defenders beat off an assault by 300 enemy troops with the aid of U.S. and South Vietnamese planes and helicopter gunships. The artillery outpost had been reinforced that day by 150 troops, doubling the size of the garrison.

North Vietnamese gunners July 5 struck at the U.S. air base at Danang for the 15th time since Jan. 1, killing three Americans and wounding 36.

Ground fighting along the DMZ came to a halt July 6 when a typhoon with 115-mile-an-hour winds swept the area. Despite the storm, B-52s continued their scheduled strikes along the zone, the only military activity reported during the day.

At a press briefing on the North Vietnamese DMZ drive, two South Vietnamese generals June 29 discounted the seriousness of the enemy attacks. Maj. Gen. Pham Van Phu, commander of the 1st South Vietnamese Infantry Division, and his deputy, Brig. Gen. Vu Van Giai, said there were actually fewer Communist troops in the area than in previous years and that the Communists had made little advance. Quoting allied intelligence estimates, the generals placed North Vietnamese strength in the two northernmost provinces at 18,500 men, compared with 24,500 in 1969. Phu and Giai said the purpose of the North Vietnamese attacks was to strengthen the Communist political base in the coastal lowlands of the northern provinces and to disrupt the August National Assembly elections and the October presidential elections.

U.S. ends DMZ area role. South Vietnamese troops July 9 assumed complete responsibility for defense of the area just below the demilitarized zone when they replaced American forces at Fire Base Charlie 2, four miles south of the zone. About 500 U.S. troops of the First Brigade, Fifth Mechanized Division, pulled out of the stronghold and soldiers of the South Vietnamese First Division moved in. The American withdrawal from Charlie 2 completed a turnover of border responsibilities begun in 1969.

Another stronghold nearby, Fire Base Alpha 4, had been turned over to South Vietnamese forces by American troops July 8. About 50 American artillerymen and technicians remained at Charlie 2 to operate a battery of guns and to monitor radar equipment. A similar U.S. contingent remained at Alpha 4.

U.S. military sources in Saigon reported July 7 that battle activity in South Vietnam had dropped to one of its lowest levels of the war the past week. Virtually no fighting was reported in the DMZ area, scene of intense Communist activity in the past month. U.S. B-52s, however, resumed bombing in the sector

around the buffer strip July 7-8 after being grounded for a day by bad weather.

Saigon drives in Cambodia. South Vietnamese forces had begun two separate drives against Communist concentrations in Cambodia May 11 and 15. Little contact was made with the enemy in either operation.

In the first action, announced May 15, a force of about 5,000 South Vietnamese troops, assisted by American air support, swept a 25-mile stretch from the Cambodian town of Kandol Chrum on Route 7 southward to Kompong Trach, an area ranging 75–100 miles northwest of Saigon. Operating up to 12 miles inside Cambodia, two task forces were moving southward from Kandol Chrum to meet a task force heading northward from Kompong Trach. Casualties through May 15 were listed as 14 enemy soldiers and one South Vietnamese killed.

Field commanders said the purpose of the offensive was to disrupt a complex of "Communist command and control facilities, headquarters and training areas" in eastern Cambodia that were being used to attack the two adjacent South Vietnamese provinces of Haunghia and Longan, west of Saigon.

The second South Vietnamese drive, disclosed May 16, was concentrated in the Parrot's Beak of eastern Cambodia to the south of the first operation. More than 1,000 Saigon troops were participating. In support of both operations, the U.S. May 14 flew 320 helicopter gunship missions and 32 bombing missions. The South Vietnamese air force flew 124 helicopter sorties and 32 bombing missions in the same sectors.

The Cambodian government May 20 announced the opening of a new drive to establish an alternate supply route from Pnompenh to the Gulf of Siam. The offensive was necessitated by the Communist control of Route 4, which connected the capital with Kompong Som, Cambodia's only deepwater port. In the new operation, one government column was moving down Route 3 (roughly parallel to Route 4), while another was moving north.

Press briefings dropped—A U.S. military official in Saigon announced May 16 the cancellation by American officers of press briefings on South Vietnamese military activities in Cambodia. Maj. George E. Martin explained that the decision was made following complaints of inaccurate press accounts of the Cambodian operations. The complaints were made by Lt. Gen. Nguyen Van Minh, commander of South Vietnamese forces in Cambodia.

North Vietnamese capture Snoul. North Vietnamese troops launched heavy assaults against the eastern Cambodian rubber plantation town of Snoul May 26 and drove out its 2,000 South Vietnamese defenders May 31. The Associated Press reported that the South Vietnamese had lost 200 men killed or wounded and had pulled back into South Vietnam, 10 miles to the southeast. A South Vietnamese military spokesman June 1 denied that Saigon troops had been routed and said they were still inside Cambodia. U.S. planes supported the South Vietnamese troops in the battle.

About 1,000 North Vietnamese had struck at Snoul May 26 and fought their way into the town the following day. The attackers at first were thrown back by the South Vietnamese with the aid of American air strikes. The South Vietnamese also claimed to have beaten back four other North Vietnamese assaults in the vicinity of Snoul. The North Vietnamese launched a heavy attack about a quarter of a mile west of the town May 27 but were stopped again by government troops. Saigon headquarters said 99 enemy soldiers were killed in the three-hour battle.

The Saigon command reported May 29 that the fighting for Snoul was over and that its forces were in complete conplete control. The battle, however, flared up again the following day and the North Vietnamese captured the town May 31. AP dispatches quoting field reports, said that 80 South Vietnamese tanks, armored personnel carriers, jeeps and trucks had been abandoned by the retreating defenders. They also were said to have destroyed 12 artillery pieces before pulling out.

Lt. Col. Le Trung Hien, a Saigon military spokesman, June 1 provided a contradictory version of the fighting at Snoul. Denying that the government

troops were driven out by heavy Communist attacks, Hien said the pullout was a "preplanned" "realignment" to cope with the coming rainy season. South Vietnamese troops had taken similar action at Snoul in May 1970, Hien recalled. The colonel said that during the latest withdrawal Saigon tanks and American and South Vietnamese air strikes had killed more than 700 North Vietnamese troops along Routes 7 and 13, the roads used by the South Vietnamese to withdraw. Hien said South Vietnamese casualties during the pullback were six wounded. He did not give government losses for the overall battle. Hien contradicted an AP report that government forces had pulled back to Locninh, South Vietnam. He insisted they were still in Cambodia. The U.S. Defense Department said June 1 that the South Vietnamese withdrawal "appears from here to be orderly and according to their plan."

The North Vietnamese capture of Snoul gave them control of parts of Routes 7 and 13 leading into the northern provinces of South Vietnam's Military Region III, which included Sagion and 11 surrounding provinces.

Snoul toll disputed—South Vietnamese forces, in their return from Snoul, suffered heavier losses than originally admitted by the government, according to a report by Saigon military sources June 3. The sources claimed that the 2,000-man government force involved in the fighting for the strategic rubber plantation town for five days had lost 100–200 killed and 400–500 wounded. About 380 were evacuated and 200 were missing. The retreating government forces were said to have left behind 50 trucks, 10 tanks, 14 armored personnel carriers, and 22 mortars. Most of the equipment was in operating condition. Some of the artillery was said to have been turned against the South Vietnamese by the Communists.

Maj. Gen. Nguyen Van Hieu, who had commanded the South Vietnamese 5th Division at Snoul, insisted June 3 that the official government casualty figures released in Saigon the previous day were correct. He said his forces had lost 37 killed, 167 wounded and 74 missing. North Vietnamese casualties were 1,043 killed, he said. Hieu was reported June 9 to have been relieved of his command.

Fighting near Pnompenh. A four-day lull in the fighting around the eastern approaches to Pnompenh was shattered June 8 when a Cambodian force sweeping an area near Prey Thom, 12 miles northeast of the capital, was attacked by about 1,500 North Vietnamese troops. At least 80 government soldiers were killed or wounded in a battle that continued through the day.

The battle lull had been preceded by 10 days of heavy North Vietnamese attacks along a 10-mile front across the Mekong River from Pnompenh. Four hundred Communists and 200 government troops were reported killed in these clashes. The Hanoi forces were attempting to seize a marshy area near the village of Vihear Sour that was part of the city's outer defenses. Enemy seizure of the strongpoint would bring Pnompenh within range of heavy mortar fire, government military sources said.

Cambodian troops were reported to have killed about 200 North Vietnamese and Viet Cong soldiers five miles from Pnompenh June 1. The all-day battle occurred in the marshes on the eastern bank of the Mekong River.

In other action in Cambodia, nearly 2,000 South Vietnamese troops June 2 opened a new drive five miles inside the country to block infiltration routes into the western part of the Mekong Delta in South Vietnam. The offensive was announced by Saigon headquarters June 8. A communique said in the first significant contact with the enemy June 6 a government battalion was struck by 100 rounds of mortar fire 17 miles southwest of Kompong Trabek. The shelling was followed by a Communist ground assault.

Communist attacks were directed at the eastern approaches to Pnompenh June 8–12 in the continuing battle for control of the strategic Vihear Suor marshes. Cambodian authorities claimed government troops June 8 killed about 200 North Vietnamese and Viet Cong soldiers. UPI reported that the Cambodians had withdrawn two miles—to within 10 miles of the capital—to regroup following the fighting.

Four government strongpoints 12 miles from Phompenh were struck by Communist rocket and mortar fire June 9. The shelling hit the villages of Prey Bang, Kompong Chamland, Kompong Ampil and Vihear Suor, all in the Vihear Suor marshes. The attack followed a Communist ambush of a government column in the center of the marshes. The attack killed or wounded 100 Cambodian soldiers. Heavy fighting continued in the area June 10. Cambodian authorities ordered a news blackout on the battle June 11. Heavy clashes erupted in the Vihear Suor area June 23 as government troops overran a North Vietnamese regimental headquarters within 15 miles of Pnompenh. A government spokesman said 120 North Vietnamese were killed, many of them by air strikes.

Hundreds of Viet Cong troops June 9 captured the district town of Srang, 25 miles southwest of Pnompenh. Although no official casualty report was issued, many Cambodian defenders were said to have been killed and wounded in the 10-hour clash. The defending government battalion was said to have been under strength because many of its men had been moved north to join the fighting at Vihear Suor, where the Cambodian command June 12 reported the killing of 350 North Vietnamese and Viet Cong troops.

Four Cambodian naval men were killed when 20 Communist commandos raided three naval guard posts four miles north of the center of Pnompenh June 16. It was the first enemy attack inside the capital since Jan. 21.

Cambodia urges peace talks. The Pnompenh government May 31 proposed talks to end the fighting in Cambodia if the Viet Cong and North Vietnamese withdrew all their troops from the country. Representatives of the North Vietnamese and Viet Cong at the Paris peace talks rejected the suggestion.

The proposal was advanced by Cambodian Chief of State Cheng Heng in the National Assembly in Pnompenh. Government sources said the suggestion was not new, but it was the first time Cambodia had publicly voiced the proposal since the ouster of Prince Norodom Sihanouk in March 1970.

In rejecting the proposal, a spokesman for the Viet Cong delegation said:

"We support the struggle waged by Prince Norodom Sihanouk and the Khmer people and will never have anything to do with the present Pnompenh administration."

Sihanouk's representative in France also rejected Cambodia's peace overture.

Laotian peace bids. The Pathet Lao Patriotic Front, in a broadcast from Hanoi May 12, announced what it called "new points" as preconditions for peace talks to end the fighting in Laos. The statement said:

1. The United States must end its intervention and aggression in Laos. As an immediate step, it must completely stop all bombing raids on the whole territory of Laos without posing any condition whatsoever.

2. After the United States stops the bombing:

(a) The armed forces in Laos [will] immediately realize a cease-fire and immediately stop all acts encroaching on, or nibbling at, the zone under the control of the other side.

(b) The Lao parties concerned will immediately discuss the formation of a provisional coalition government and other problems of mutual concern, including the guarantee of strict respect for the neutrality of the Kingdom of Laos as provided for by the 1962 Geneva agreements on Laos.

The Pathet Lao statement also claimed that the "defeat" of the February-March allied drive into Laos had resulted in "tipping the power balance in favor of the Lao and Indochinese revolutionary forces."

Laotian Premier Souvanna Phouma again proposed peace talks with the Pathet Lao "without delay."

Souvanna's proposal was contained in a letter sent May 26 to Pathet Lao leader Prince Souphanouvong. It did not mention Souphanouvong's recent demand for a U.S. bombing halt to be followed by a truce. The message stated that it was "urgent to arrive at a total and complete cease-fire, which presupposes ceasing ground as well as air combat." Souvanna also suggested that the Pathet Lao representative in Vientiane, Prince Souk Vongsak, be given a "more active role than that of simple messenger" so he could negotiate an end to the conflict with a Laotian government representative.

Hanoi forces seize Laos strongpoints. North Vietnamese forces May 16 captured Paksong and Ban Houei Sai to take virtual control of the entire Boloven Pla-

teau in southern Laos. The high ground had been used by Laotian troops as a principal base area for the surveillance and harassment operations against the Ho Chi Minh Trail.

The Laotian high command acknowledged the Communist seizure of the two strongholds May 17. It said government troops had abandoned the adjacent towns after fierce combat with the North Vietnamese force, estimated at eight battalions. The defenders, totaling about three battalions, were said to have lost about 50 men and large quantities of material. Laotian troops were still in control of Houei Kong, the last remaining stronghold on the Boloven Plateau, 20 miles southeast of Paksong. The North Vietnamese troops, however, were reported May 17 to have attacked the town and were said to be advancing on it in force. Three battalions of special forces recruited by the U.S. were stationed in the area.

A Vientiane military spokesman May 5 had reported the North Vietnamese capture of Muong Phalane, a government stronghold on the western flank of the Ho Chi Minh Trail. Sixty government troops were reported killed and 50 missing after two days of heavy fighting. Communist forces had captured Muong Phalane Feb. 11 but the Laotians retook it at the end of March.

In action north of the Boloven Plateau, North Vietnamese troops May 18 overran Dong Hene, about 70 miles west of Tchepone. The town was the headquarters of forward elements of Laotian troops on Route 9, the strategic road that cut across the panhandle from the Thai border along the Mekong River to the South Vietnamese border on the east. The North Vietnamese assault was preceded by a heavy rocket barrage that reportedly destroyed 75% of Dong Hene. The defenders as well as most of the civilians had abandoned the town before the North Vietnamese moved in. Its capture was said to pose a direct threat to the two principal towns of the panhandle to the south—Pakse and Savannakhet.

Meanwhile, North Vietnamese aircraft were becoming increasingly active against Laotian ground and U.S. air forces in Laos. The U.S. command reported May 11 that a North Vietnamese MiG-21 attacked an unarmed U.S. reconnaissance plane twice over the Plaine des Jarres in northern Laos May 8. This was the first report of a MiG attack on American aircraft supporting Laotian forces over the plain. The command said the U.S. aircraft was not damaged in the attack.

In another incident involving U.S. aircraft, North Vietnamese jets May 11 scored serious hits against American planes near Ban Ban and south of the Plaine des Jarres.

The Laotian government reported May 12 that North Vietnamese MiG-21s flew bombing and strafing missions against Laotian troop positions in the Plaine des Jarres for the first time.

North Vietnamese forces May 19 captured Houei Kong, the last Laotian stronghold on the Boloven Plateau. The Defense Ministry in Vientiane announced May 24 that Paksong was being reinforced by the Communists. Hanoi's forces were said to have moved artillery, antiaircraft guns and armored personnel carriers into the town.

The Defense Ministry announced May 24 that North Vietnamese troops had carried out heavy assaults against government positions in northern Laos May 22–23. In one clash, north of the Plaine des Jarres, government troops killed 36 North Vietnamese and lost six of their own killed in a six-hour battle for the town of Bouam Long. The North Vietnamese were said to have killed 22 civilians and wounded 28 others, all dependents of the government soldiers.

In another action, government troops abandoned Phou Pha Sai, 84 miles northeast of Vientiane, after massive North Vietnamese shelling and eight hours of fighting.

North Vietnamese troops May 28 overran a government blocking position on the Boloven Plateau seven miles west of Paksong. The strongpoint's capture forced Laotian troops to set up a new blocking position four miles west in an attempt to stop a threatened North Vietnamese drive down Route 23 toward Pakse. The Laotian Defense Ministry reported May 30 that govermemt soldiers had killed 64 North Vietnamese in their push toward Pakse. Many civilians were reported leaving the town for nearby Thailand as Pakse came under increasing Communist threat.

North Vietnamese supply buildup. According to American military analysts, the North Vietnamese were increasing the movement of war supplies through southern Laos, the New York Times reported June 4 and 7.

The heavy Communist mortar and rocket attacks against allied positions in northern South Vietnam since the end of Saigon's thrust against the Ho Chi Minh Trail in southern Laos was an indication that the campaign had failed to stem the flow of North Vietnamese supplies, the June 4 article said. North Vietnam's capture May 26 of the eastern Cambodian town of Snoul was attributed by the U.S. experts to the huge numbers of troops and equipment being funneled down the supply trail. North Vietnamese victories against Laotian government troops in the Boloven Plateau of Laos had secured the Communists' routes much to the west of the South Vietnamese borders, making them less vulnerable to Saigon attacks, according to the analysts.

The Times June 7 report, quoting American military experts, said that during the current rainy season the North Vietnamese were pushing their supply effort by repairing and widening Route 23 in Laos, well to the west of the Ho Chi Minh Trail. The improvement work was going on between Tchepone and the Boloven Plateau, 40–60 miles from the Vietnamese frontier. In an effort to keep all dirt roads open during the monsoon season, which would end in October, the North Vietnamese were reported for the first time to have set up fixed positions for most of their transportation and engineering units in southern Laos. One American general was quoted as saying: "As we continue to withdraw our troops, Hanoi is upgrading his combat capability."

Senate reviews U.S. role in Laos. The Senate met in secret session June 7 to review the extent of U.S. involvement in the war in northern Laos.

The unusual session had been requested by Sen. Stuart Symington (D, Mo.), who said May 28 the public and Congress had "little or no knowledge" of the Laotian situation and the Senate should ascertain the facts of the U.S. role before more funds were appropriated "for this clandestine war."

Symington said June 6 the U.S. was spending "hundreds of millions" of dollars on the war in Laos, much more than the $52 million acknowledged by the Administration as its economic aid for the area. In the secret session, Symington had said such spending was amounting to at least $350 million annually.

The use of B-52s for raids over northern Laos in support of the Laotian government troops was acknowledged May 3 by Undersecretary of State John N. Irwin 2nd, who told the Senate Foreign Relations Committee the B-52s were used on a regular basis to attack enemy troop formations and supply lines. Previously, the Administration had admitted use of the B-52s for such purpose on only one occasion in February 1970—during a battle for the Plaine de Jarres.

Committee Chairman J. W. Fulbright (D, Ark.) said May 21 that 4,800 Thai troops financed by the U.S., through the Central Intelligence Agency, were fighting in Laos in support of the Royal Laotian government. Fulbright charged that the U.S. role was "inconsistent with the spirit" of the "antimercenary" amendment enacted in 1970.

Sen. Edward M. Kennedy (D, Mass.), joining Symington June 6 in attacking U.S. policies in Laos, protested Administration "whitewashes" concerning its efforts in Laos and said the policy grounds for involvement there would justify "new military adventures by the President anywhere in Southern Asia." In a letter to Kennedy, the State Department had justified the Laotian role on the President's constitutional authority to "take reasonable measures" in northern Laos as part of his program to protect American forces withdrawing from South Vietnam. Kennedy had asked for the grounds of the U.S. military involvement.

In a statement issued just prior to the Senate's secret session June 7, the State Department said U.S. financial and material support of Thai "volunteers" fighting in Laos for the Laotian government was "fully consistent with all pertinent legislation." One of its arguments was that the program of using "volun-teers" in Laos predated enactment of the "anti-mercenary" amendment.

North Vietnamese campaign in Laos. North Vietnamese forces June 11 pushed to within 17 miles of the southern Laotian stronghold of Pakse after over-running the outpost of Ban Nhik on Route 23. The route was a major highway linking Pakse with the Boloven Plateau to the east.

Government defenders of Ban Nhik fled in disorder in the face of the North Vietnamese onslaught spearheaded by tanks, the Laotian command reported. No casualty figures were given, but two colonels were reported killed. A U.S. observation plane spotting targets for Laotian light bombers was shot down, but the pilot was reported rescued. Monsoon rains sweeping southern Laos prevented U.S. fighter-bombers from providing support for government ground troops.

Continued heavy fighting around Pakse was reported June 17. Defense Minister Sissouk Na Champassak said 700 enemy soldiers had been killed and three tanks and four antiaircraft guns were destroyed in the clashes there in recent days.

Pakse's capture would put the North Vietnamese on the Mekong River and within 20 miles of cutting across southern Laos to the Thailand border to the west.

Pathet Lao peace bid. The Pathet Lao renewed a proposal to end the fighting in Laos, it was announced by the North Vietnamese delegation to the Paris peace talks June 25. Laos in effect rejected the plan June 30.

The proposal had been sent by Pathet Lao leader Prince Souphanouvong to Laotian Premier Souvanna Phouma June 22. It called for an "immediate cease-fire on the whole of the Laotian territory, which would include the end of American bombing and a cease-fire on the spot by the armed forces of Laos, with an end to all military activities on land and in the air, all acts of violation or encroachment against the area under the control of the other side." The cease-fire would be followed by negotiations to bring about "peace and national agreement," according to the plan.

A new element in the Pathet Lao formula was the inclusion of a halt to the American bombing as part of the truce proposal; previously they had demanded the bombing halt as a precondition for a truce.

Premier Souvanna Phouma June 30 called for holding peace talks in Vientiane without preconditions. He also indicated that withdrawal of foreign troops from Laos was his condition for acceptance of the Pathet Lao proposal.

The Pathet Lao June 30 rejected Souvanna's suggestion for talks in Vientiane, asserting that his selection of that site indicated that he wanted the proposed discussions put off indefinitely.

New Saigon drives in Cambodia. A force of 1,500 South Vietnamese troops was transported into the Parrot's Beak of southeastern Cambodia by 40 U.S. helicopters July 8 in a new drive against Communist troop concentrations in the area. No contact was made with enemy units.

The South Vietnamese operation six to nine miles inside Cambodia had a twofold purpose: to meet up with another 1,500-man South Vietnamese force moving toward Svayrieng, 20 miles away, and trap an estimated 400-man battalion of North Vietnamese demolition men in the area; and to slow Communist infiltration through the Parrot's Beak toward the Saigon area.

The new thrust was called off July 15 after a fruitless search for Communist troops. Two-thirds of the force withdrew to South Vietnam, while 500 soldiers remained in the Parrot's Beak sector to operate a newly opened artillery and patrol base, Saigon spokesmen said July 16.

South Vietnamese forces began four separate drives in Cambodia July 19, 21, 26 and 28.

The July 19 effort was announced by Saigon authorities July 24. They said 2,-000 government rangers were searching the flatlands in the southeastern part of Cambodia to stem North Vietnamese infiltration into South Vietnam's Mekong Delta. An estimated 2,200 Communist soldiers were reported in recent months to have moved into the delta's U Minh Forest, long a stronghold of the Viet Cong.

The July 21 drive, described as the largest in six months, reportedly used 10,000 men already in Cambodia. It was reinforced by an armored brigade and spearheaded by 200 armored vehicles. The assault was centered 100 miles northeast of the first announced attack. In their first signifiaant contact with the enemy, government forces July 22 killed 37 North Vietnamese in a clash between the border towns of Krek and Mimot. U.S. artillery and helicopter gunships supported the attackers.

The commander of the Cambodian operation, Lt. Gen. Nguyen Van Minh, said July 21 that the objective was "to cut off North Vietnamese infiltration into South Vietnam and to prevent the enemy from sabotaging" the August National Assembly elections and the Oct. 3 presidential balloting.

The July 26 drive was centered 10 miles inside Cambodia and 90 miles north of Saigon. About 1,000 troops were participating in the sweep, with another 1,000 in reserve.

The July 28 drive, by a 3,500-man task force with 80 armored vehicles, took place 25 miles inside Cambodia and was centered about eight miles north of Kompong Trabek near Route 1, the main road connecting Pnompenh with Saigon.

The Saigon troops reported their first contact with enemy forces July 28 and said they killed 72 North Vietnamese and Cambodian guerrillas in a four-hour battle 12 miles north of the provincial capital of Svayrieng. Reports from the scene, however, said the bodies of 17 enemy soldiers were counted after the fighting. Another clash broke out Aug. 2 south of Route 1 with South Vietnamese claiming the killing of 21 men of a 100-man North Vietnamese force. Saigon casualties were listed at eight wounded.

Allied planes Aug. 3 leveled two Cambodian villages occupied by Communist forces blocking the South Vietnamese advance in the Parrot's Beak. Many of the enemy were reported killed, while government casualties were listed at two dead. The Cambodian villagers were said to have fled the area before the fighting started. The air strikes were carried out largely by South Vietnamese planes and helicopters. Two U.S. helicopter gunships had joined the attack but withdrew after they mistakenly fired close to the South Vietnamese troops. In two separate clashes about 70 miles apart, South Vietnamese soldiers Aug. 6 reported killing 79 enemy troops while losing 14, the Saigon command reported the following day. Twenty-four Communists were slain in sporadic clashes Aug. 9, according to the command.

Cambodian troops were reported Aug. 7 to have captured the strategic town of Preykry following an 11-day operation to sever a major Communist infiltration and supply route north of Pnompenh, a government military spokesman reported.

Cambodians accuse South Vietnamese. The Cambodian Foreign Ministry July 15 accused South Vietnamese troops of having mistreated Cambodian civilians in Kandal, Svayrieng and Preyveng provinces since March.

A ministry document submitted to the South Vietnamese embassy in Pnompenh alleged that the Saigon troops had killed one civilian, directed artillery against several villages, pillaged many homes and tortured a number of persons. The ministry demanded that South Vietnam "take adequate measures to punish the guilty parties, grant indemnities to the victims and put an end to such conduct."

Subsequent Pnompenh protests about alleged South Vietnamese atrocities led the Cambodian high command Aug. 15 to demand the evacuation of most of South Vietnam's troops from Cambodia, it was reported the following day. The command also was said to have called for the closing of the South Vietnamese military base at Neak Luong. The area was said to have been the scene of alleged South Vietnamese atrocities committed against civilians.

Cambodian authorities were reported Aug. 3 to have arrested 53 Vietnamese civilians in the village of Kbal Karlong and jailed them as prisoners of war. The Vietnamese had chosen to remain behind in Cambodia in 1970 when most of the country's 250,000 ethnic Vietnamese fled or were removed to South Vietnam.

Sirik Matak meets Nixon. Lt. Gen. Sisowath Sirik Matak, acting premier of Cambodia, conferred with President Nixon in Washington Aug. 10.

Sirik Matak, in the U.S. on a 19-day visit, told the National Press Club after the meeting that American military and economic assistance had enabled his country to resist Communist military intervention. The supply of U.S. small arms and materiel was partly responsible, he said, for the loss of "the initiative" by invading North Vietnamese forces in Cambodia.

Sirik Matak told a Washington news conference Aug. 11 that Cambodian forces would launch a winter offensive with the aid of U.S. air power and South Vietnamese ground forces. The objective of the proposed push would be to oust the Communists from four Cambodian provinces which they had been occupying since 1970, he said.

(The Defense Department disclosed Aug. 11 that the military team supervising U.S. arms aid in Cambodia had been expanded from 23 to 50 men. The increase was accomplished by shifting personnel from Saigon to the U.S. mission in Pnompenh.)

Sirik Matak said in New York Aug. 16 that Pnompenh would call on South Vietnam to withdraw its 10,000–12,000 troops from Cambodia by June 1972. He said the withdrawal would start in September from the eastern provinces and would be completed by June. The Cambodian leader said he had discussed the matter that day with U.N. Secretary General U Thant.

U.S. jets hit North Vietnam. The U.S. command reported two U.S. fighter-bombers July 11 attacked and knocked out seven guns at a cluster of antiaircraft sites in the Mugia Pass region of North Vietnam. It was the 46th "protective reaction" strike on the North since Jan. 1.

The American aircraft bombed the sites 80 miles northwest of the demilitarized zone after the Communist guns had fired at but missed another U.S. fighter-bomber attacking targets on the Ho Chi Minh Trail on the Laotian side of the border.

North Vietnamese antiaircraft guns July 10 had fired three missiles at a U.S.

R-4 reconnaissance plane around Dong-hoi, 45 miles north of the DMZ. The recon aircraft, on a mission photographing Communist defenses in the area, was not hit.

U.S. deaths reach 6-year low. The U.S. command reported July 22 that 11 Americans had been killed in combat July 11–17, the lowest weekly American death toll since August 1965. The command said the low total reflected the continuing withdrawal of American soldiers and the low level of combat.

The number of wounded in the July 11–17 period was placed at 81. Sixteen others died of "nonhostile causes," such as accidents, drug overdoses and disease, the command reported.

The little fighting that was reported in mid-July was centered in the northern provinces of South Vietnam and in the Saigon area. North Vietnamese artillery July 21 broke a lull of more than three weeks by shelling four South Vietnamese bases just south of the demilitarized zone. No casualties were reported.

U.S. bombers had carried out sporadic raids July 16–22 along the DMZ in a continuing effort to block a North Vietnamese buildup. The last American combat unit just below the buffer strip pulled out July 22. A 920-man force of the 1st Brigade of the 5th Infantry, Mechanized moved further south to await departure from Vietnam later in 1971.

In other developments in the north, an American helicopter carrying South Vietnamese rangers crashed in Quangtin Province July 21, killing 21 rangers and injuring 26 others, including the 'copter's five-man American crew. The aircraft crashed just as it was about to land at a fire base, Mary Ann, 28 miles south of Tamky.

U.S. helicopters July 26 airlifted a battalion of 1,600 South Vietnamese into the Ashau Valley. No significant contact was made with the enemy through July 28. Saigon spokesmen said the mission marked the fourth phase of Operation Lam Son 720, a clearing operation within South Vietnam that followed the thrust into Laos in February-March.

In the Saigon area, a Communist demolition unit July 28 infiltrated the airbase at Laikhe, 30 miles north of the capital, and blew up four American helicopters and damaged a fifth.

A helicopter repair depot at Phuloi, 13 miles north of Saigon, had been struck by Viet Cong rockets July 19, killing one American.

The U.S. continued to reduce its combat role in South Vietnam as seven more Army units, totaling 2,990 men, were

---

Most of enemy from South. Rep. Robert L. Leggett (D, Calif.) reported in the Congressional Record Aug. 4 that according to Pentagon figures, enemy forces in South Vietnam in 1964, "the year we felt compelled to intervene to save South Vietnam from a North Vietnamese takeover, ... were 3% North Vietnamese and 97% South Vietnamese. We then engaged in several years of bombing to 'halve the flow of men and supplies from the North.' We halted the flow so brilliantly that the mix of enemy forces changed ... to 42% North Vietnamese. . . .'"

Citing "another measure of enemy strength mix," Leggett said the Defense Department had reported that about 75% of enemy troops captured by U.S. and South Vietnamese forces were South Vietnamese. The year-by-year figures on estimated enemy strength and prisoners captured (NVA—North Vietnamese, VC—Viet Cong):

ENEMY MILITARY STRENGTH IN SOUTH VIETNAM

Year	South Vietnamese	North Vietnamese	Total enemy strength	Percen South Vietnamese
1961	63,400	0	63,400	100
1962	79,300	0	79,300	100
1963	91,700	0	91,700	100
1964	122,100	3,300	125,400	97
1965	159,000	10,000	169,000	94
1966	190,000	49,000	239,000	79
1967	203,000	55,000	258,000	79
1968	210,000	80,000	290,000	75
1968	140,000	106,000	240,000	58
1970	140,000	100,000	240,000	58
1971	140,000	100,000	240,000	58

POW CAMP INPUT BY YEAR AND POLITICAL ORIGIN

Year	NVA	VC
1965	165	202
1966	698	2,605
1967	1,088	7,143
1968	2,977	9,732
1968	2,380	7,311
1970	1,522	3,685
1971 (May)	61	218
Total	8,891	30,898

withdrawn Aug. 1. This was the largest phaseout in a month. The last troops of the first Army unit to enter the fighting in 1965 pulled out of the field Aug. 6 prior to returning home. The unit was the 4th Battalion, 503rd Infantry of the 173rd Airborne Brigade.

Communists warned on DMZ raids. A sharp increase in North Vietnamese activity along the demilitarized zone prompted the U.S. command Aug. 15 to warn it would take retaliatory action if the Communist attacks continued.

The command said: "Any enemy activity along the DMZ which threatens the safety of allied forces is viewed with deep concern by commanders who have the responsibility to exercise their inherent right of self-defense for their troops."

The North Vietnamese had stepped up their assaults against South Vietnamese bases along the buffer strip Aug. 12. The attacks broke a lull of several weeks of battle action in South Vietnam. At least 15 government troops were reported killed Aug. 12 as Hanoi forces launched three ground assaults against South Vietnamese positions. The North Vietnamese kept up their pressure the following four days. The hardest hit government bases were Alpha 1 and 2, which were struck by 300 shells Aug. 13; government casualties were light. The Saigon command acknowledged Aug. 16 that the marine outpost of Baho, two miles south of the DMZ, had been overrun by North Vietnamese forces the previous day. The 180 government defenders were believed to have suffered heavily, most being killed, wounded or missing. Enemy losses were placed at 200 dead, according to the Saigon command.

A U.S. helicopter was shot down less than two miles from the DMZ Aug. 14 and seven Americans were killed.

To counter the increase in North Vietnamese shelling of South Vietnamese bases along the buffer strip and to prevent massing of Communist troops for an offensive, U.S. B-52s were reported to have launched widespread raids along the zone in August. The B-52s also had been making unannounced strikes in the southern half of the DMZ for the first

time since the 1968 bombing halt, U.S. sources in Saigon said Aug. 15. The strikes were said to be concentrated in the western part of the zone, where the Communists reportedly were building a network of roads across the buffer strip to support their attacks against the South Vietnamese positions.

Other U.S. planes carried out attacks on missile sites in North Vietnam between July 30 and Aug. 15. The raids brought to 49 the number of "protective reaction" strikes on the North since January.

U.S. forces bomb DMZ. The U.S. command Aug. 17 acknowledged for the first time that B-52s had been bombing North Vietnamese targets in the southern half of the demilitarized zone "over a period of the last several months."

The report was followed by another command disclosure Aug. 19 that ships of the U.S. 7th Fleet also had been pounding North Vietnamese rocket and mortar positions in the southern sector of the buffer strip for the past six days. The command said such strikes had been going on periodically since November 1968, when the U.S. halted the bombing of North Vietnam, except for retaliatory attacks. The latest air and naval assaults were said by the command to be in response to the recent acceleration of North Vietnamese attacks against South Vietnamese positions just south of the DMZ.

A command spokesman said Aug. 17 that the American planes had flown no further than the Ben Hai River, which divided the six-mile buffer zone. The spokesman pointed out that since the southern part of the zone was South Vietnamese territory the raids on it were not a violation of the 1968 bombing halt on North Vietnam.

The command report on the naval strike said guns of a guided missile destroyer had touched off fires and explosions, indicating hits on ammunition dumps. U.S. Army authorities said Aug. 22 that the naval bombardment had continued for 10 days and helped slow down the North Vietnamese drive along the buffer strip.

U.S. B-52s staged massive raids on North Vietnamese positions just south of the demilitarized zone Aug. 19–24 in a concerted effort to blunt the Communist drive that had begun in the area Aug. 12. The discovery by South Vietnamese soldiers of 76 bodies of North Vietnamese troops Aug. 23 followed a B-52 attack that day on an enemy troop concentration outside an artillery base 15 miles south of the DMZ.

Intense North Vietnamese antiaircraft fire shot down four American helicopters along the DMZ Aug. 20. The loss prompted the U.S. command to ground all U.S. observation 'copters in the vicinity of the zone. Sharp ground clashes were fought along the DMZ Aug. 17–23. The fighting was marked by continued heavy North Vietnamese shelling of South Vietnamese bases. Among the major actions:

American artillery Aug. 17 was moved west into a position at Mailoc, 10 miles below the zone, to support government troops. The shift of the U.S. guns followed a heavy enemy rocket and mortar attack on nearby Fire Base Sarge, the second major barrage against the South Vietnamese base in less than 24 hours.

The Saigon command reported Aug. 19 that 142 North Vietnamese troops had been slain in battle Aug. 17–18 near a government regimental headquarters two miles southwest of Camp Carroll. Government losses were listed at 22 killed. U.S. bombers and artillery supported the South Vietnamese defense.

U.S. helicopters Aug. 19 arilifted American artillery pieces and a U.S. radio team of about six men out of Fire Base Sarge. A U.S. command spokesman said the action was "part of planned unit moves." All South Vietnamese artillery pieces were removed from the base Aug. 20. As a result of the withdrawal of the guns, a South Vietnamese spokesman said Aug. 21 that the stronghold was "no more a fire base."

South Vietnam claimed the killing of 37 North Vietnamese in a clash Aug. 23 one mile from a fire base near the DMZ. Saigon listed its losses at four killed.

Laotian tribesmen seize plain. Laotian Meo tribesmen were reported July 13 to have seized complete control of the Plaine des Jarres in northern Laos in a drive begun July 7. No significant resistance was met in the recapture of the strategic heights formerly held by North Vietnamese, Viet Cong and Pathet Lao forces, the Laotian Defense Ministry reported.

Laotian officers said the Meo offensive was coordinated by the U.S. Central Intelligence Agency and that some of the tribal commandos were led by American advisers. The U.S. State Department July 9 denied that any U.S. advisers were accompanying Laotian forces.

A Laotian Defense Ministry spokesman, Gen. Thongphanh Knoksy, July 8 had confirmed the Plaine des Jarres drive, but said his government "is not responsible for this operation." He added: "You should ask the American embassy. This is their affair."

U.S. officials in Vientiane July 9 acknowledged the sweep was under way, but declined comment on American involvement. They said the purpose of the operation was to destroy Communist supplies, not to occupy the plain. Large caches of enemy munitions, food, medicines and other supplies were said to have been found by the advancing forces.

Six Meo battalions were said to be participating in the offensive with two Thai battalions. Radio Pathet Lao had reported July 7 that three Meo regiments were involved and that they were supported by "mercenary Thai artillerymen" and U.S. bombers.

Thais build bases in Laos. The construction of several permanent bases in Laos by Thai troops with the aid of the U.S. Central Intelligence Agency (CIA), was reported by the Washington Post in a dispatch from Vientiane, Laos July 20.

According to the newspaper:

The bases had been erected in a large area of Sayaboury Province which bordered northeastern Thailand. The Thai unit had entered Laos from Nan Province of Thailand during a sweep against Thai guerrillas. The strongholds were built parallel to a complex of CIA-maintained Laotian bases extending eastward from Xieng Lom in a 40-mile arc to Hong Sa. U.S. sources in Sayaboury Province said it appeared that the Thai troops were permanently occupying a strip of Laos nearly 100 miles deep and 20 miles wide.

Sayaboury Province had been annexed by Thailand in World War II and then returned to Laos and the French as part of the war settlement.

The U.S. State Department insisted Aug. 9 that the Thai troops in Laos were volunteers. This statement contradicted a Washington Post dispatch the same day that the Bangkok units serving in Laos with irregular forces were regular Thai army troops. The department said it was entitled to withhold complete compliance with the Geneva agreement on Laos' neutrality since North Vietnam already was violating that neutrality with the presence of 80,000 troops in the country.

The department statement was issued following Congressional criticism of the presence of Thai troops in Laos. Senate Foreign Relations Committee Chairman J. W. Fulbright (D, Ark.) May 21 had questioned whether his "anti-mercenary" amendment of 1970 was being violated by the CIA support of Thai troops in Laos.

CIA force in Laos acknowledged. The Nixon Administration officially confirmed for the first time Aug. 2 that the U.S. Central Intelligence Agency (CIA) was maintaining an "irregular" force of 30,000 fighting men then engaged in battle throughout most of Laos.

The acknowledgment was made in a staff report prepared for the Senate Foreign Relations subcommittee on foreign commitments.

The report was written by two former foreign service officers who made a trip to Laos in April. Their report, once classified top secret, was released Aug. 2 after clearance by the CIA as well as the Defense and State Departments.

According to the report, the CIA-backed force had become "the main cutting edge" of the Royal Laotian army. Thai "volunteers" recruited and paid by the CIA were among those in the 30,-000-man force. The report indicated that the use of the "irregulars" was more widespread than had been generally reported in news accounts.

The report was made public by Sen. Stuart Symington (D, Mo.), subcommittee chairman. Symington said of the Administration's acknowledgment: "It is an encouraging sign that the executive branch has finally agreed that much of

what the United States government has been doing in Laos may now be made public."

The report also gave the first detailed description of the cost of U.S. involvement in the Laos war theater. In fiscal 1970 a "partial total" of U.S. expenditures in Laos was $284.2 million, of which $162.2 million was for military aid, $52 million for economic aid and $70 million was spent by the CIA exclusive of the amount spent on the Thai forces.

In fiscal 1972, the report said, the cost of military assistance had already "risen rapidly." The cost of military and economic aid plus the CIA expenses was expected to reach $374 million.

The report also noted increased Chinese Communist activity in northern Laos. The Chinese, the report said, had increased their defenses along a road they were building from Muong Sai in northern Laos sweeping towards Dienbienphu in North Vietnam. The road area, according to the report, was then "one of the most heavily defended in the world." New radar-directed anti-aircraft guns had been placed along the road, the report noted. Some of the guns were said to have a range of 68,000 feet.

More Chinese Communists were also said to be in the road-building area. In the last two years, the report said, the size of the Chinese contingent had increased from 6,000 to between 14,000 and 20,000.

House upholds secrecy on Laos—A proposal that the House be informed by the State Department about covert military operations in Laos was rejected by the House July 7 by a 261–118 vote. The proposal was offered by Rep. Paul N. McCloskey Jr. (R, Calif.), who also offered three other resolutions requesting information on Laos and Vietnam. They were rejected by voice votes.

U.S. planes hit North Vietnam. U.S. planes Aug. 22 struck antiaircraft and missile bases in North Vietnam after being threatened during bombing missions against the Ho Chi Minh supply trail in nearby Laos. The targets were 38 and 115 miles north of the DMZ. U.S. jets returned to North Vietnam Aug. 23 to pound antiaircraft sites that had fired on an unarmed reconnaissance plane. The incident occurred two miles north of the DMZ.

A Communist antiaircraft site 15 miles north of the demilitarized zone was struck Sept. 3 by one of two F-105s after the B-52s they were escorting on a mission over the Ho Chi Minh Trail in Laos were tracked by North Vietnamese radar.

In an air attack Sept. 6, two North Vietnamese antiaircraft positions 51 miles north of the DMZ were reported destroyed by F-4 fighter-bombers. The action followed the ground gunners' attack on a reconnaissance plane the F-4s were escorting.

Two antiaircraft sites two miles north of the buffer zone were hit Sept. 9 by two U.S. Phantom jets after a reconnaissance plane was fired on. The Soviet news agency Tass quoted a dispatch from Hanoi saying that one American plane had been shot down over Hatinh Province. A U.S. spokesman said he knew of no action occurring in Hatinh Province and said that day's incident had taken place in Quangdinh Province, south of Hatinh.

Election disruption attacks. Communist forces launched widespread attacks on civilian and military targets throughout South Vietnam Aug. 25 in an apparent attempt to disrupt the Aug. 29 National Assembly elections. The assaults continued one day beyond the balloting date.

The Saigon military command reported Aug. 31 that the Viet Cong and North Vietnamese had carried out 96 attacks Aug. 28–30, mostly in the northern section of the country from the Central Highlands to the demilitarized zone. According to official reports, at least 41 South Vietnamese soldiers and eight civilians were killed. The U.S. and South Vietnamese commands said 347 Communist soldiers had been killed Aug. 28–29, many in air raids and artillery barrages.

At the start of the enemy attacks, a series of explosions swept a huge ammunition dump at the U.S. base at Camranh Bay. The blasts, which continued for 13 hours, wounded five American servicemen and destroyed about 50% of the ammunition dump.

Other American bases came under attack Aug. 25, but little damage was sustained. They were the Danang base, Camp Faulkner, just south of Danang, the Laikhe base camp, about 30 miles north of Saigon and a number of installations 40 miles east of the capital.

North Vietnamese gunners Aug. 25 struck a hamlet on the outskirts of Danang, killing five civilians and destroying 100 homes.

In an attempt to head off enemy assaults against district towns in the Danang area, South Vietnamese forces Aug. 25 launched a general sweep 35 miles south of the city. Saigon headquarters claimed that government forces killed 46 North Vietnamese and Viet Cong.

American forces suffered their heaviest casualties for one engagement in several weeks when North Vietnamese troops Aug. 26 assaulted a unit of the Americal Division bivouacked 16 miles southwest of Danang. Five Americans were killed.

Sharp sporadic clashes continued just below the demilitarized zone as it had since Aug. 12. North Vietnamese gunners struck at government bases. U.S. B-52s pounded North Vietnamese targets along the DMZ and in the southern part of the buffer zone through Aug. 31. U.S. and Australian destroyers offshore joined the assault Aug. 26 and bombarded North Vietnamese gun sites inside the DMZ.

U.S. planes Aug. 24 bombed air defenses in North Vietnam for the 52nd time since January. The raid was in retaliation for an unsuccessful North Vietnamese artillery attack on two American reconnaissance planes near the Laotian border.

The U.S. command announced Aug. 26 that 10 Americans had been killed in combat Aug. 15–21, the lowest weekly toll in six years. It was the sixth consecutive week in which fewer than 20 Americans were killed in action.

U.S. casualties climb—The U.S. command reported Sept. 2 that 19 Americans had been killed Aug. 22–28, the highest weekly death toll in seven weeks. Ninety-seven others were wounded and four died of non-hostile causes. Other totals in that weekly period: 269 South Vietnamese killed and 585 wounded and 1,234 Communists slain. The American deaths during the following week of Aug. 29-

Sept. 4 dropped to 16, the eighth consecutive week in which U.S. battle fatalities fell below 20.

Allied drive near Laotian border. A South Vietnamese force of 12,000 men, heavily supported by U.S. soldiers, launched a major sweep Sept. 6 against 15,000 North Vietnamese troops believed deployed below the western end of the demilitarized zone near the Laotian border.

The purpose of the mission, called Operation Lam Son 810, was to destroy North Vietnamese supply bases, halt troop and supply movements into the northwest section of South Vietnam over roads of the Ho Chi Minh Trail and stave off "a new enemy high point" of attacks aimed at disrupting the Oct. 3 presidential elections.

The launching of the offensive was first reported by news agencies Sept. 7. The Saigon command reluctantly announced the new operation Sept. 8, complaining that the news agencies had prematurely disclosed the drive before significant contact with the enemy had been made and thus compromised the effectiveness of the mission.

The U.S. Defense Department Sept. 8 officially confirmed the American role in the campaign, but stressed that it was confined to providing government forces with security and was consistent with Vietnamization. The department also confirmed reports from Saigon that U.S. troops had moved into artillery bases abandoned by South Vietnamese forces in the area of the offensive. The American military commitment totaled 1,500–2,000 men, involving troop-carrying helicopters, artillery and air strikes and transport of war supplies. No U.S. ground troops were participating. Fifteen U.S. helicopters Sept. 9 flew 1,000 government reinforcements to within two miles of the Laotian border, raising the Saigon force in the area to 13,500 men.

B-52 raids against the North Vietnamese in the southern part of the demilitarized zone and just below since mid-August mounted in intensity as the new South Vietnamese drive progressed, with the heaviest assault launched Sept. 9. About 25 aircraft dropped more than 750 bombs on North Vienamese positions extending from the southern half of the buffer strip 20 miles southward below Khesanh, where the Saigon ground operation was centered. South Vietnamese patrols Sept. 12 reported finding the bodies of 32 North Vietnamese, apparent victims of a B-52 attack.

Operation Lam Son 810 was concluded Sept. 18. The Saigon command acknowledged that the drive had produced no significant contact with the enemy. The commander of the northern Military Region I, Lt. Gen. Hoang Xuan Lam, had said Sept. 16 that half of the 30,000 North Vietnamese threatening the northern provinces had withdrawn across the DMZ and Laotian border. Lam attributed the pullback to an apparent shortage of supplies.

In one of the heaviest shellings since mid-August on the northern front, North Vietnamese gunners Sept. 1 had pounded a South Vietnamese armored column near the DMZ and also struck five nearby bases with rockets and mortars. Government casualties were reported negligible. U.S. forces retaliated by bombarding enemy positions by land, sea and air.

Laotians retake Paksong. Laotian forces recaptured the strategic Boloven Plateau town of Paksong following a fierce battle with North Vietnamese troops Sept. 15–16. The Communists had first captured the village May 16. It overlooked the Ho Chi Minh Trail in southern Laos.

A Laotian Defense Ministry spokesman reporting on the two-day battle said Sept. 20 that two of seven government battalions had been put out of action with casualties totaling 202 killed, 745 wounded and 195 missing. North Vietnamese losses were estimated at 279 killed and about 600 wounded.

The drive to retake Paksong had been started in late July.

The government force reportedly met strong resistance in the vicinity of Ban Gnik, about 10 miles west of Paksong. In fighting in the area July 29, the advancing forces were reported to have overrun three North Vietnamese companies entrenched along Route 23. Air and artillery strikes that preceded the ground assault accounted for the death of 30 Communist soldiers; 15 more were slain by the advancing Laotians.

Laotian troops July 28 had captured the provincial capital of Saravane, in the southern panhandle northeast of Paksong. The town had been captured by Communist forces in June 1970. But when government soldiers were airlifted into Saravane, they met no significant resistance. The town, guarding a main junction on the Communists' Ho Chi Minh supply trail, was reported devastated by American and Laotian air strikes.

Mekong Delta battle. South Vietnamese forces, aided by U.S. air and artillery fire, Sept. 14 launched a drive against a Communist stronghold in the U Minh Forest of the Mekong Delta. Heavy fighting continuing through Sept. 21 resulted in the death of nearly 400 North Vietnamese and Viet Cong troops, according to Saigon estimates. Government losses through Sept. 18 were placed at 47 killed and 97 wounded. The Saigon command said the North Vietnamese had suffered their heaviest losses in fighting in the forest Sept. 18–19 with 207 killed. Ten U.S. helicopters were shot down by North Vietnamese gunners in the forest Sept. 14–19.

The Saigon command reported killing 35 more Viet Cong and North Vietnamese in the U Minh Forest Sept. 21. South Vietnamese losses since the drive had started were given as 113 killed and 183 wounded. A U.S. helicopter was downed in the U Minh Forest Sept. 21; this brought to 11 the number of American 'copters lost in the delta offensive.

Other military action—South Vietnamese troops suffered heavy losses in two Communist attacks around Saigon. A Viet Cong ambush Sept. 16 killed 15 government soldiers and three American advisers in the Michelin rubber plantation 35 miles north of the capital. Viet Cong losses were eight killed.

In the second incident, 21 government troops were killed and 64 were wounded Sept. 20 when a force of 600 Communist commandos, in a thrust from Cambodia, attacked a South Vietnamese base near Tayninh, about 55 miles northwest of Saigon. Enemy deaths were placed at 52. The base, 10 miles from the Cambodian frontier, was used in operations in eastern Cambodia.

A Saigon nightclub was struck by a terrorist bomb Sept. 16, killing 14 South Vietnamese and one American.

North Vietnamese troops carried out heavy attacks on South Vietnamese positions along the Cambodian-South Vietnamese border Sept. 26–27. In the first day's assault, 10 South Vietnamese positions and one U.S. base were hit in an area ranging 75–90 miles northwest of Saigon. Most of the attacks were around the Cambodian town of Krek, a key South Vietnamese base along Route 7, which led into the southern half of South Vietnam. Saigon forces were reported to have lost 20 killed in the two days of fighting. Enemy losses in that period were listed at 92 killed.

U.S. jets raid North Vietnam. A force of 200 U.S. fighter-bombers, accompanied by 50 protective escort planes, Sept. 21 carried out widespread attacks on North Vietnam in an area extending 35 miles north of the demilitarized zone. The raids, heaviest since the March 21–22 strike on the North, lasted eight hours.

The U.S. command in Saigon said the raids were "in response to recent increased evidence of North Vietnamese antiaircraft and missile activity" against American planes flying reconnaissance missions over the North and fighter-bombers passing over the North to strike at the Ho Chi Minh Trail in Laos. The U.S. Defense Department said in Washington Sept. 21 that the strike was launched because "the number of AA guns within 35 miles of the DMZ has increased almost 40% since August."

In describing the raids, the U.S. command said the targets posed "a threat to the safety of United States forces."

The U.S. added Sept. 23: In addition to missile sites, the American planes also had bombed military oil storage tanks. The command said the raids were centered just north of the demilitarized zone and were designed to prevent a possible "spectacular" North Vietnamese assault just before South Vietnam's Oct. 3 presidential elections.

It was announced by the White House Sept. 23 that President Nixon had personally ordered the Sept. 21 raid and that it did not violate the three-year old bombing halt. Press Secretary Ronald

Ziegler said the attack was aimed at protecting American troops "as they withdraw from Vietnam" and was therefore consistent with the policies previously outlined by Nixon.

Hanoi claimed Sept. 24 that the Sept. 21 raid had killed or wounded many North Vietnamese civilians.

The American air strike was condemned Sept. 25 by the Chinese Communist Foreign Ministry, which called it a "towering crime" and a "criminal act." The statement said the attack showed the U.S. was not interested in peace but in intensifying the war.

The raid on North Vietnam had prompted the Hanoi delegation to the Paris peace talks to announce Sept. 22 a protest boycott of the 130th session scheduled for the following day.

(In further action aimed at keeping up pressure on North Vietnamese troops and supplies, U.S. planes and warships Sept. 22 bombed the southern half of the demilitarized zone, striking at rocket sites and storage depots.)

In a Nov. 2 incident, a U.S. Navy jet bomber flying over the Ho Chi Minh Trail in Laos was fired on by an antiaircraft battery in North Vietnam, 105 miles north of the demilitarized zone. The bomber, unhit, attacked the missile site.

The North Vietnamese air base at Donghoi was struck by four fighter-bombers Nov. 7 in the heaviest air assault on the North since Sept. 21.

Two targets were pounded in a Nov. 8 assault—an airfield at Quanglang, 180 miles north of the DMZ for the deepest penetration of the North in 1971, and an antiaircraft position 40 miles south, at Vinh. Both raids were carried out after enemy ground gunners had fired on reconnaissance planes on a mission photographing airfields. The North Vietnamese Foreign Ministry claimed 2 American planes were downed in the Nov. 8 raids, but the U.S. command said all aircraft returned safely.

The North Vietnamese Foreign Ministry charged Nov. 3 that U.S. planes Oct. 30 had bombed Laichau Province, 160 miles north of Hanoi, on the Laotian-Chinese borders.

In a previous attack on the North, a U.S. jet Oct. 15 hit a gun position 95 miles north of the DMZ after the battery had fired on a reconnaissance plane.

Four U.S. Navy planes, in one of the deepest penetrations into the North in 1971, struck Nov. 21 at an antiaircraft-gun emplacement near Vinh, almost 150 miles north of the demilitarized zone. The jets, based on a carrier in the Tonkin Gulf, attacked after an unarmed Navy reconnaissance aircraft was fired on by the guns near Vinh.

Report on U.S. air war. The Nixon Administration was increasing the air war in Laos and Cambodia and maintaining a high level of bombing in South Vietnam as it reduced the American ground combat role in Indochina, according to a six-month survey sponsored by Cornell University's Center for International Studies. The survey, made public Nov. 7, said the heavy use of American airpower was not impeding the Communist advance in Indochina and was imperiling prospects for peace because it was destroying the societies of the target countries. Principal points of the report:

■ Although American bombing in Indochina was continuing at about half the rate of its peak period in 1968–69, the current rate averaged about 70,000 tons a month, almost the same level as in 1967. By the end of 1971, the U.S. would have dropped six million tons of bombs and other aerial ammunition on Indochina. This was three times the total tonnage used during World War II.

■ Air strikes on the Ho Chi Minh Trail in southern Laos had been increasing steadily and were now averaging about 400,000 tons of explosives a year.

■ About 90,000 tons of bombs a year were being dropped on Cambodia, reflecting a steadily rising rate following the U.S. incursion into the country in 1970. Civilian casualties were heavy.

■ The high level of bombing of South Vietnam was being maintained with an average of 300,000 tons annually, but the explosives were being dropped largely by the expanded South Vietnamese air force.

The Cornell survey was conducted by a team of 19 professors and students headed by Prof. Raphael Littauer, a physicist. It was based on Defense Department data and reports, including the Pentagon papers, and interviews with defense and foreign-policy specialists.

Vietnam civilian losses cited. At Boston hearings Oct. 7 held by the Vietnam Veterans Against the War, Sen. Edward M. Kennedy (D, Mass.) said that the number of civilian war victims treated in South Vietnam hospitals in the first half of 1971 had been as high as in any previous year.

The hearings were called to investigate the Nixon Administration shift's from ground fighting to what the group called "a highly destructive but politically supportable combination of electronic and air warfare."

Kennedy also reported that 75%–80% of refugees recently treated had fled allied bombing in Laos.

Cambodia oil tanks attacked. Cambodia lost 40% of its civilian fuel supply when Communist forces Sept. 20 fired rockets into big storage tanks on the Tonle Sap River in Pnompenh.

North Vietnamese or Viet Cong gunners were said to have ignited millions of gallons of gasoline, diesel oil and fuel oil. Other tanks were set afire by blazing fuel from punctured tanks. Three persons were reported killed. Tanks owned by Shell and Esso were struck. Tanks belonging to the Cambodian government oil company escaped damage. Fires in the storage dumps were finally extinguished Sept. 21.

On the military front, Cambodian forces fought scattered clashes with North Vietnamese and Viet Cong troops in August–September. Among the major developments:

Government troops Aug. 20 recaptured a major Communist base at Peaglong, 20 miles west of Pnompenh, the Cambodian command reported. The enemy strongpoint was retaken following intensive bombing and strafing by allied planes.

Cambodian soldiers Sept. 2 killed at least 100 North Vietnamese in a clash 65 miles northeast of the capital.

The Cambodian army Sept. 6 launched a new drive 42 miles north of Pnompenh. The objective was two abandoned rubber plantations along Route 21 used by the Communists as bases for more than a

year. No contact with the enemy was made.

Cambodia fighting intensifies. The sharp fighting that had erupted along the Cambodian-South Vietnamese frontier Sept. 26 intensified through Oct. 4. The South Vietnamese, with heavy American support, put up strong resistance to retain their toehold in eastern Cambodia, 50–90 miles west and northwest of Saigon.

U.S. and South Vietnamese troops Sept. 29 launched a counteroffensive against the North Vietnamese along the Cambodian frontier. Its purpose was to reopen the 30-mile stretch of road leading north along Route 22 from Tayninh, in South Vietnam, to Krek, just over the border inside Cambodia. Route 22 had been cut by the North Vietnamese in an apparent threat to overrun about six allied bases in the area. About 4,000 government troops were rushed into the area to reinforce 20,000 South Vietnamese soldiers already there on both sides of the frontier. The U.S. command reported moving 1,500 Americans and armored vehicles to the front but they stayed inside South Vietnam. Saigon estimated that 259 enemy soldiers were killed in the allied counter strikes.

Meanwhile, U.S. B-52 bombers Sept. 29 struck at North Vietnamese positions 17–19 miles southwest of Katum, a border town in Tayninh Province. Other B-52s bombed in eastern Cambodia against rear Communist bases in the Krek region. The B-52 raids were the heaviest since the bombers started pounding the North Vietnamese at the beginning of their border attacks.

The Cambodian fighting also was marked by the lifting of enemy sieges of two South Vietnamese bases that had been surrounded since the start of the North Vietnamese drive. A South Vietnamese relief column of 1,200 men Oct. 1 rescued the government garrison at Firebase Tran Hung Dao, 70 miles northeast of Saigon.

Three miles away, Saigon forces Oct. 4 fought their way through North Vietnamese lines to lift the siege of artillery base Alpha, inside Cambodia. Other government troops engaged the North Vietnamese near Krek. Saigon claimed that 154 North Vietnamese had been killed in both engagements and that government losses came to 19 killed and 49 wounded. After five days of inconclusive fighting, a force of 1,200 ARVN rangers Oct. 9 broke North Vietnamese resistance to reach Alpha. Saigon's forces reported that 97 North Vietnamese had been killed in the fighting and that their losses totaled one killed and eight wounded.

In other fighting in South Vietnam, Communist gunners Oct. 3 fired at least three rockets into Saigon in an attempt to disrupt that day's presidential elections. The U.S. command reported the attack, the first of its kind since Dec. 19, 1970, killed two civilians. At least 60 other Communist attacks occurred throughout South Vietnam to coincide with the presidential balloting.

A flareup of fighting near the Mekong Delta town of Kienthien Oct. 2 claimed the lives of 18 South Vietnamese soldiers. North Vietnamese losses totaled 16 killed, Saigon reported.

U.S. B-52s Oct. 7 dropped about 1,000 tons of bombs on North Vietnamese bunkers and gun emplacements near Krek and around Tayninh city, inside South Vietnam. It was the heaviest raid on North Vietnamese positions in more than a year.

A South Vietnamese offensive in Cambodia Oct. 20 involved a force of 2,500 men and was directed north of Krek where enemy strength was estimated at 1,600–2,000 men. A Saigon command report on the operation Oct. 28 said the government troops and armored units had failed to catch up with the withdrawing enemy troops.

A U.S. fighter-bomber Oct. 18 accidentally attacked a South Vietnamese position near the Cambodian border, killing 18 government soldiers and seriously wounding seven others. "Additional soldiers received lesser wounds," the U.S. command said in reporting the incident Oct. 19. The command said the plane, flying in support of South Vietnamese troops, had dropped two bombs of 500 pounds each on an "assigned target" near the government troop base at Thienhghon in Tayninh Province.

U.S. deaths at record low. Reflecting the continued disengagement of American troops from South Vietnam, U.S.

combat deaths Oct. 10–16 dropped to five, the lowest weekly fatality toll in more than six years, the U.S. command announced Oct. 21. Eighty-four Americans were wounded in the same period, an increase of 12 over the previous week. The number of American deaths Oct. 3–9 had totaled eight.

The U.S. command said Nov. 4 that two Americans had been killed Oct. 24–30. This would have made the number of deaths the lowest since March 1965. However, a spokesman conceded that another four U.S. soldiers had been slain in combat Oct. 24, but their deaths had not yet been "processed."

South Vietnamese battle deaths in the Oct. 24–30 period, reflecting the heavier burden of Saigon's fighting forces, remained high with 269 killed, and 562 wounded and missing.

GIs balk at combat patrol. A U.S. Army spokesman in Saigon said Oct. 11 that several U.S. soldiers had balked at going out on a night patrol Oct. 9 from an allied fire base near the Cambodian border.

According to the Army, the soldiers, who were part of a 1st Cavalry Division (Airmobile) patrol, "expressed a desire not to go" when they were ordered to take up an ambush position. The Army said the men began to move out, however, when the order was repeated. The order was withdrawn after it was learned that a South Vietnamese unit already occupied the position to which the Americans had been assigned.

Sen. Edward M. Kennedy (D, Mass.) asked the Pentagon Oct. 15 to look into a petition from 65 soldiers who had said they were being used in an offensive combat role on the Cambodian border. The 65 soldiers belonged to the same outfit as the other GIs who balked at going out on the night patrol from Fire Base Pace.

Richard Boyle, a free-lance writer who had been at Fire Base Pace, delivered the petition to Kennedy. In it, the soldiers said that "we are faced daily with the decision to take a court-martial or participate in an offensive role."

U.S. bars increased involvement. The U.S. State Department Oct. 18 reaffirmed its intentions of maintaining a "low profile" in Cambodia by limiting its military involvement in that country.

Department spokesman Charles W. Bray 3rd denied reports that the Administration was considering a major increase in aid to the Pnompenh government. A New York Times report Oct. 12 had said that the Joint Chiefs of Staff had devised a plan to carry out a "pacification", campaign and other unconventional warfare in Cambodia to protect South Vietnam's western flank as U.S. troop withdrawals continued.

The Joint Chiefs also were said to have proposed additional funds to finance the expansion of the Cambodian army in submitting their program to Defense Secretary Melvin Laird in September, it was reported.

Emergency rule declared in Cambodia. Premier Lon Nol Oct. 22 declared a state of emergency in Cambodia and abolished constitutional rule. At the same time, the premier announced the formation of a new Cabinet, which he said would govern by "ordinance." He said his action was aimed at preventing anarchy in the country, which he contended was threatened by a "fifth column."

In announcing his decision in a nationwide broadcast, Lon Nol asserted that "certain groups had launched acts aimed at creating confusion." He said he would no longer "vainly play the game of democracy and freedom" because it posed an obstacle to his country's efforts to defeat Communist forces on Cambodian soil.

A government statement Oct. 21 said Lon Nol's actions "cannot in any circumstances be taken to mean that our democratic ideal will be forgotten nor that a new dictatorship would ever be installed in our country."

The Cabinet had abolished the National Assembly Oct. 16 by decreeing that its five-year mandate, due to expire Oct. 18, would not be renewed. The Cabinet instead ordered the legislative body replaced by a constituent assembly, charged with drawing up a new constitution.

Twenty-eight opposition members Oct. 17 challenged the legality of the government's decision to deprive the assembly of its legislative powers. In a note to Chief of State Cheng Heng, the deputies urged the matter be reviewed and proposed that the assembly write a new constitution. Fifty-nine other deputies supported the abolition of the assembly.

U.S. supports Cambodia—The U.S. declared Oct. 21 that it would continue to support Cambodia despite the constitutional curbs it had invoked. A State Department statement denied the moves had brought "military dictatorship" to Cambodia and said the emergency powers put into effect by the Pnompenh government had been originally authorized by the National Assembly in 1970 after Prince Norodom Sihanouk's overthrow.

Cambodia military developments. Cambodian forces engaged in heavy combat with North Vietnamese and Viet Cong forces northeast of Pnompenh beginning in late October and sustained heavy losses.

Major clashes occurred Oct. 27–29 around the provincial capital of Kompong Thom and Rumlong, 50 miles northeast of the capital. The fighting broke out after Communist frogmen blew up a bridge on Route 6, cutting off supplies and reinforcements for the 20,-000 government troops on the northeastern front.

In an effort to reinforce the beleaguered garrison at Kompong Thom, more than 300 Cambodian soldiers were killed in a week of fighting, Pnompenh reported Oct. 29. Heavy casualties were suffered by government forces at nearby Romlong where at least 100 government soldiers were killed or wounded.

The Communist siege of another government town in the area, Prakham, was lifted Nov. 2 when a Cambodian relief force broke into the village 56 miles north of Pnompenh. The North Vietnamese and Viet Cong, who had encircled Prakham for more than a week, pulled back, losing 291 men, the Cambodian government reported.

The Saigon command reported Nov. 6 that 1,000 South Vietnamese troops had started a search-and-destroy operation Nov. 3 southwest of Kompong Trabek near the approaches to infiltration routes toward Saigon.

Communist attacks erupted Nov. 7 in an area northwest of Pnompenh, one of the quietest regions in Cambodia to date. The assault, directed at Bamnal, 70 miles from Pnompenh, resulted in the death of 10 government soldiers through Nov. 8, the Cambodian high command reported.

Pnompenh's international airport was struck by a Communist rocket barrage Nov. 10. The shelling killed 25 persons and wounded 30. Nine aircraft were reported damaged. While the attack on the field was in progress, other North Vietnamese forces raided a radio transmission station nine miles to the northwest, killing 19 Cambodians. The attack cut off international communications with Pnompenh for several hours.

Cambodians abandon Rumlong. Despite heavy American air support, Cambodian troops Nov. 13 were forced to abandon Rumlong to the Communists. The town, 52 miles northeast of Pnompenh, had been under North Vietnamese siege for nearly three weeks. The Cambodian high command said 30 of the defenders escaped and the rest of the 400 men in the town were killed or captured. Two other battalions left 400 dead or wounded behind when they retreated after an unsuccessful attempt to lift the enemy siege.

U.S. B-52s flying from Thailand had struck at enemy positions around Rumlong Nov. 10–11. Other American planes also were reported to have flown in support of the Cambodians.

Cambodian forces received American air support Nov. 16 in fighting close to Pnompenh. Helicopter gunships attacked North Vietnamese positions at Tuol Leap, a village 10 miles southwest of the capital.

North Vietnamese buildup. Military sources in Saigon reported Nov. 13 that Communist forces were building up supplies near the Benkarai and Mugia passes in North Vietnam in preparation for a major drive down the Ho Chi Minh Trail into Laos and Cambodia. The two passes were on the Laotian border. The reported massing of equipment was said to be the principal reason for President Nixon's warning Nov. 12 that the U.S. might intensify air strikes

against North Vietnam's infiltration trails.

Although enemy movement on and around the trails was said to be light, military sources said reconnaissance photographs showed extensive road-repair work and the deployment of more antiaircraft weapons, suggesting that a Communist thrust was in the offing.

Defense Secretary Melvin R. Laird Nov. 14 confirmed the reported North Vietnamese buildup, but said it was nothing new. Laird explained: "Those reports are true at this time of year every year. The North Vietnamese must make their logistic push as the rainy season comes upon us. This happens each year and the buildup is being made on those pass areas."

The reports apparently prompted an increase in U.S. B-52 attacks on enemy targets throughout the Indochina war sector. In one series of strikes Nov. 14, B-52s struck suspected enemy troop concentrations in Laos, Cambodia and South Vietnam.

B-52s Nov. 9 had pounded enemy positions near Quangtri in the northeastern part of South Vietnam for the first time in more than a year. The targets were said to be antiaircraft installations that had fired recently on allied helicopters and supply bunkers.

U.S. helicopter gunships Nov. 11 killed eight South Vietnamese soldiers and wounded 21 in an accidental attack while supporting a Saigon operation on the central coast about 280 miles northeast of Saigon. The U.S. command said Nov. 12 that the helicopters had fired on the targets "as directed" by South Vietnamese ground commanders.

In one of the heaviest actions in the South in recent weeks, defenders of a government infantry battalion camp in the Central Highlands Nov. 13 repulsed an attack by about 600 Communists attempting to overrun the base. A Saigon command report on the battle Nov. 15 said 163 North Vietnamese and Viet Cong were killed, while government casualties were 29 killed and 32 wounded. The action occurred 28 miles southwest of Pleiku.

Saigon opens two new drives—South Vietnamese forces launched two new operations—one in the Central Highlands Nov. 27 and the other in the Mekong Delta Nov. 22. The Central Highlands offensive, involving 15,000 troops, was aimed at weakening enemy base areas in the region where the South Vietnamese, Laotian and Cambodian borders meet. The U.S. was providing air and artillery support and three of its helicopters were shot down in the area after the start of the attack. Six American crewmen were wounded.

The Mekong Delta target was an estimated force of 5,000 enemy troops in the area stretching from the U Minh Forest to the Camau Peninsula to the south. A force of 25,000 South Vietnamese troops was committed to the drive, which was first reported Nov. 28. Only light fighting was reported.

In other developments in South Vietnam, a U.S. helicopter carrying 33 Americans disappeared during a thunderstorm Nov. 28 along the northern coast. The aircraft was enroute from Danang to Phubai.

U.S. losses at new low. U.S. forces suffered only nine casualties, five deaths and four wounded, in combat Nov. 14–20 for the lowest combined weekly loss recorded since 1965, the U.S. command reported Nov. 25. The command said 13 Americans died in the same period in accidents and from illnesses.

Saigon launches Cambodia drive. In a move aimed at relieving North Vietnamese pressure around Pnompenh, South Vietnamese forces launched a major drive into eastern Cambodia Nov. 22.

An initial force of at least 5,000 men, strengthened by 2,500 Cambodian soldiers, was said to have encountered little enemy resistance in the first day of the operations whose principal targets were the towns of Krek and Chup, 60 miles northeast of the Cambodian capital. The Saigon field command reported that 36 North Vietnamese had been killed in scattered clashes north of Route 7, about 90 miles northeast of Saigon. An additional 10,000 South Vietnamese troops were said to be poised along the border.

The key objectives of the new thrust were the rear headquarters and supply depots of three North Vietnamese divisions near Chup, 20 miles west of Krek, from which the Communists had been launching attacks around Pnompenh for two weeks. The Saigon operation also was aimed at thwarting possible North Vietnamese plans for attacks on South Vietnam's Tayninh Province.

The South Vietnamese drive followed a Cambodian appeal for assistance. South Vietnamese officials reported Nov. 19 that a delegation of eight Cambodian officers had flown to Saigon the previous week to request engineers and artillery to help ease Communist pressure on a Cambodian task force cut off northeast of Pnompenh.

In continued fighting around the capital, Cambodian troops Nov. 17 had attacked North Vietnamese positions near the western outskirts, only 10 miles from the center of the city. U.S. helicopter gunships continued to provide support to the Cambodian defenders, attacking North Vietnamese concentrations around the capital Nov. 16–17.

Official American sources in Saigon confirmed Nov. 18 that U.S. planes had increased their support of beleaguered Cambodian soldiers in the fighting around Pnompenh. According to the sources, the Cambodians had been provided with substantially more U.S. air support in the past 10 days than previously.

South Vietnam extended its operations in eastern Cambodia Nov. 24, airlifting several thousand paratroops from Krek to Chup. A total of 25,000 South Vietnamese troops were committed to the offensive.

Little enemy resistance was reported, however, through Nov. 30. The Saigon command reported Dec. 1 that 213 enemy soldiers had been killed in the week-long operation, all but 45 by U.S. and South Vietnamese air and artillery strikes. South Vietnamese casualties were put at 11 killed and 39 wounded.

U.S. forces were increasingly involved in the operation. American B-52s and other planes continued to attack enemy forces in the Cambodian border area. The U.S. command reported Nov. 28 that B-52s, helicopter gunships and mortars placed along the border provided support fire for the South Vietnamese. About 280 'copter missions had been flown in the previous 24-hour period, the command said. Some of the South Vietnamese troops brought into Cambodia were said to have been carried in U.S. helicopters, although both American and South Vietnamese military spokesmen insisted that only Saigon's helicopters were being used. An Associated Press report Nov. 23 said U.S. military advisors were in Krek despite the prohibition on their use in Cambodia. Newsmen reported seeing three uniformed Americans who identified themselves as members of the U.S. military equipment team in Pnompenh.

Cambodian military authorities reported Nov. 23 that the South Vietnamese offensive had relieved North Vietnamese pressure on the front northeast of Pnompenh, forcing some of the enemy troops to pull back to meet the South Vietnamese thrust. Hanoi's forces, however, resumed their heavy attacks against the Cambodian positions Dec. 1, forcing government troops to retreat from two towns. The Cambodians abandoned Baray, about 60 miles northeast of the capital, and were pulling out of Kompong Thmar, six miles to the north.

The deteriorating situation prompted Cambodia to call on the U.S. and South Vietnam to provide greater air support. Cambodian Air Force Commander Col. So Satto described the enemy attacks Dec. 1 as "a general offensive" and called the situation "very serious, but not yet alarming."

Cambodians routed near Pnompenh. Cambodian defenses northeast of Pnompenh were reported to have collapsed Dec. 2 in the face of heavy assaults by North Vietnamese troops. Half of the 20,000-man government force in the area, attempting to reopen Route 6 to the northern provinces, were said to have fled in disarray. North Vietnamese troops reoccupied a 30-mile stretch of Route 6 after the Cambodian retreat. Hundreds of government troops were reported to have been killed. In the wake of the government pullback, 10,-000 Cambodian troops and thousands of refugees were reported cut off in the Kompong Thom area to the north. The nearest Cambodian force was 25 miles away.

The rout began following the Cambodians' abandonment of the towns of Baray and Kompong Thmar, six and 12 miles north of Pnompenh. The remaining Cambodian defenders dug in at new positions in Tang Krasang.

At least 100 Cambodian soldiers were reported killed or wounded Dec. 5 in continued fighting in the northeastern sector. About half the casualties were suffered in a clash near Bat Doeung, 16 miles north of the capital. The Cambodians abandoned the village Dec. 6.

Hanoi radio claimed Dec. 6 that Cambodian forces had suffered more than 12,000 casualties in the past week of fighting northeast of Pnompenh.

Pnompenh came under Communist shelling Dec. 7 for the first time in several months. The city was struck by three rockets, wounding four civilians. At the same time, Pnompenh's airport was struck by eight rockets, killing two soldiers and wounding two.

Fighting raged within nine miles of Pnompenh Dec. 8 as 1,000 government troops moved to block a North Vietnamese advance near the hamlet of Sre Ngei. The Communist troops this time were moving in from the south in an attempt to encircle the city.

Refugees from villages surrounding Pnompenh continued to flee toward the capital Dec. 9 as North Vietnamese forces pounded government positions in the area. Meanwhile, the Cambodians Dec. 9 recaptured Kleah Sanday, 10 miles to the south of Pnompenh, after the North Vietnamese had occupied it for a day, but the village was leveled in the process.

Cambodian troops Dec. 11 evacuated a hill commanding Pnompenh's northern defenses perimeter, only eight miles outside the capital. Abandonment of the garrison, called Pnombaset, was ordered after it was cut off from a larger government force that had come to its support Dec. 8.

Saigon forces capture Chup. South Vietnamese forces captured Chup Dec. 14 in the deepest penetration of eastern Cambodia since the start of their offensive in the region in late November. Meanwhile, Cambodian forces continued to suffer setbacks in the face of

North Vietnamese attacks north and south of Pnompenh.

Chup, 35 miles inside Cambodia, was captured without opposition. The town's rubber plantation had been a base for elements of the North Vietnamese Seventh and Ninth Divisions. About 6,000 of South Vietnam's 25,000-man force in easter Cambodia were committed to the Chup operation. The drive toward the rubber plantation, supported by massive U.S. air support and 4,000 regular Cambodian troops, had been launched Dec. 13. U.S. airmen flew 300 helicopter missions at the outset of the offensive.

In the only area where the South Vietnamese encountered strong Communist resistance, the Saigon command reported Dec. 10 that its forces had killed 167 of the enemy in fighting around the hamlet of Dam Be since Dec. 8. South Vietnamese losses were placed at 10 soldiers and four airmen killed. Dam Be was on a supply route near the Chup plantation.

The Viet Cong radio announced Dec. 14 that the South Vietnamese had been dealt a major blow in the fighting at Dam Be. The broadcast said 500 South Vietnamese had been killed in the fighting and that 70 vehicles, including more than 40 tanks and armored trucks, had been destroyed.

The South Vietnamese force withdrew from Chup and other former enemy sanctuaries in the area Dec. 17. A Saigon informant said the purpose of the pullback was part of a "mobile third phase" of the offensive into Cambodia. The nearby ruined town of Suong also was abandoned to enable the Saigon force to consolidate "at well-defended positions closer to the border for mobile strike tactics," according to a senior officer. The capture of Chup had failed to find a trace of an estimated 9,000 North Vietnamese troops reported to be hiding in the area.

Allies meet on Cambodia threat. U.S. and South Vietnamese officers were reported to have arrived in Pnompenh Dec. 17, apparently to discuss Cambodia's deteriorating military situation.

Meanwhile, the Cambodian setbacks at the hands of the North Vietnamese in the fighting north of Pnompenh pre-cipitated new anti-government demonstrations. This prompted the regime of Premier Lon Nol to order another new ban on all political meetings and anti-government demonstrations and authorized police searches of private homes.

On the military front, refugees reaching Pnompenh Dec. 17 said major Communist forces had pushed into Vihea Suor, across the Mekong River about 10 miles north of the capital.

A Cambodian communiqué Dec. 17 said Communist forces continued the heavy bombardment of government positions at Prakham, 40 miles north of Pnompenh, and Taing Kauk, 12 miles further north. Both government garrisons in the two towns were reported Dec. 16 to have been surrounded. The Taing Kauk base was manned by 4,000 men.

In the fighting around Pnompenh Dec. 16, a U.S. Phantom jet was hit by enemy ground fire and crashed. The plane's two crewmen bailed out and were rescued. The attack occurred near Pnombaset, 14 miles northwest of Pnompenh. The U.S. command said the crash brought to 8,053 the number of American aircraft lost from all causes in the Indochina war.

Saigon ends Cambodia drive. The South Vietnamese offensive that had opened in eastern Cambodia in November ended Dec. 30. The Saigon command gave these figures on the 39-day operation: 1,336 North Vietnamese killed, many by American planes; 195 enemy weapons captured; 86 South Vietnamese soldiers killed and 226 wounded; and 17 South Vietnamese armored vehicles destroyed or damaged.

In other fighting, a Cambodian task force was reported Dec. 21 to have broken through to Prakham, a government garrison 45 miles northeast of Pnompenh that had been under North Vietnamese siege for 10 days. The task force was part of a 7,000-man operation aimed at clearing the enemy blockades of Prakham and the nearby town of Taing Kauk, which also had been beleaguered for 10 days.

Communists gain in Laos fighting. The strategic Plaine des Jarres in northern Laos was captured by about 15,000 North Vietnamese troops, Laotian officials reported Dec. 20. The Communist advance was supported by tanks and heavy artillery.

Meanwhile, North Vietnamese forces in southern Laos achieved military gains in an offensive that had started in that region in late November. Laotian forces Dec. 6 abandoned the strategic town of Saravane on the northern fringe of the Bolovens Plateau following an attack by two North Vietnamese battalions. The air strip at Ban Khot, six miles northeast of Saravane, also was abandoned. Government forces were reported Dec. 13 to be holding fast at a 20-mile defense perimeter in the eastern part of the plateau.

In a report on the Plaine des Jarres battle, Laotian Defense Minister Sissouk Champassak Dec. 21 said that 1,500 of the attacking 15,000-man North Vietnamese force had been killed in the two days of fighting. The government's 6,000–7,000 men on the plain and the Thai irregulars assisting them were said to have suffered heavy casualties.

With the capture of the Plaine des Jarres, Communist forces launched a new drive Dec. 21, posing a threat to the pro-government base of Long Tieng, 30 miles to the southwest. The base, defended by a CIA-sponsored Meo tribesman army, was attacked by 20 Communist commandos Dec. 21. The raiders were driven off. Government forces Dec. 25 abandoned two strongpoints 14 miles northwest of Long Tieng to the advancing Communist attackers. About 30,000 dependents of the Meo soldiers were reported Dec. 27 to have been evacuated from Long Tieng.

North Vietnamese and pro-Communist Pathet-Lao forces were in virtual control of the entire Boloven Plateau in southern Laos after capturing the town of Paksong Dec. 28. Laotian forces, however, reoccupied the town Dec. 29 after enemy forces withdrew. A Laotian Defense Ministry spokesmen said the seizure of the plateau and the North Vietnamese capture of the Plaine des Jarres constituted "a real Communist invasion." The spokesman said government forces had abandoned Paksong following a 12-hour mortar and ground attack by North Vietnamese troops.

MiGs challenge U.S. jets. The U.S. State Department confirmed Dec. 1 that a North Vietnamese MiG-21 fighter had attacked a U.S. B-52 bomber over the Ho Chi Minh Trail in southern Laos in late November, but its air-to-air missile missed. There had been at least 10 reported incidents of MiG passes at American planes but the department's statement was the first official confirmation of such an attack.

The incident was first reported by American pilots in Saigon Dec. 2. They said the attack had occurred 10 days previously and that the MiG had been chased back into North Vietnam. Reports in recent weeks had told of increased North Vietnamese MiG activity and the improvement of three airfields from which the planes operated in southern North Vietnam near the Laotian border. The Defense Department had warned Dec. 1 that the continued use of the MiGs could lead to retaliatory strikes at the three airfields at Donghoi, Vinh and Quanglang.

U.S. Air Force Secretary Robert C. Seamans, Jr., on a visit to South Vietnam, expressed concern Dec. 5 about the upsurge of MiG missions. But he said "it was too early to know now how intensive it was likely to become."

The U.S. command reported that American planes flying missions in the vicinity of the Laotian-North Vietnamese border Dec. 7 were fired at three times by surface-to-air missiles and antiaircraft artillery but no hits were scored.

The North Vietnamese Foreign Ministry claimed the downing of four U.S. F-4 Phantom planes over North Vietnam Dec. 18. The U.S. command Dec. 20 confirmed the loss of four aircraft but said they were shot down over northern Laos, three Dec. 18 and one Dec. 19. The loss of the three planes Dec. 18 was the heaviest in a single day since December 1967.

According to North Vietnam's account, three of the four American planes destroyed Dec. 18 were shot down during attacks "in a populated area" in

Nghean Province, about 145 miles south of Hanoi, and the fourth by antiaircraft fire in Vinhphu Province northeast of Hanoi. Four airmen were said to have been captured. They were identified by the North Vietnamese Dec. 20 as Lt. Kenneth R. Wells, Maj. Leland L. Hildebrand, Lt. Samuel R. Vaughan and Maj. Kenneth R. Johnson.

The U.S. command's version of the incidents said three planes had been downed over northern Laos in a two-hour period Dec. 18. One was believed to have been shot down in an engagement with a MiG-21 that flew across the border to challenge the American aircraft. It was not known how the other two planes were lost. The fourth plane was shot down Dec. 19 by antiaircraft fire along the Laotian-North Vietnamese border west of the Plaine des Jarres, the command said. The command reported that two of the downed airmen were rescued but six others were declared missing.

The U.S. command Dec. 22 reversed its account and conceded that one and possibly two of the four American jets had crashed inside North Vietnam while evading North Vietnamese MiGs that had shot down the third one over Laos. The U.S.-North Vietnamese jet clash over Laos—the first reported—occurred after a Phantom that had been flying bombing missions for Laotian forces on the Plaines des Jarres "was engaged and presumably downed by an enemy MiG," the command reported.

Two other F-4 Phantoms had been shot down over Laos by North Vietnamese surface-to-air missiles Dec. 10 and 17. The two crewmen of the second plane were rescued Dec. 18.

5 days of air attacks. U.S. Air Force and Navy planes carried out massive sustained attacks on military installations in North Vietnam Dec. 26–30. The raids, the heaviest on the North since the November 1968 bombing halt, involved 1,000 strikes.

Hanoi claimed 19 American jets were downed and said that "a number" of pilots were killed and three were captured. The U.S. command acknowledged the loss of only three aircraft and re-

ported one Navy pilot was rescued and three were missing.

The raids were in retaliation for what allied commanders charged was a huge buildup of military supplies by North Vietnam in preparation for a possible offensive against Cambodia and South Vietnam and for a sudden upsurge of North Vietnamese air and missile attacks on American planes that bombed the Ho Chi Minh Trail in northern Laos.

The U.S. command withheld information on the bombing until its termination Dec. 30. It said then that the strikes "were directed against surface-to-air-missiles, antiaircraft artillery units, air-defense radar sites, the enemy's logistics and P.O.L. [Petroleum-Oil-Lubricant] buildup north of the DMZ and particularly opposite major passes into Laos."

"Also included in the targets," the statement said, "were certain airfields south of the 20th Parallel from which there has been increasing aircraft activity in recent weeks." These targets were believed to have included airfields at Baithuong and Quanglang, both just below the 20th Parallel, and on the central coast at Donghoi. The command said most of the raids had been concentrated between the DMZ and the 18th Parallel. It warned of further raids if the North Vietnamese did not curtail their "significant" buildup.

A U.S. military spokesman reported Dec. 31 that 11 air defense sites had been destroyed by the raids.

The American raids were denounced by Hanoi radio Dec. 30 as an "insolent mad act of war that exposes more clearly the stubborn and warlike nature of the Nixon Administration." It said the planes had bombed "villages, cities, hospitals, schools and rice fields."

Another Hanoi broadcast Dec. 30 said of the 19 American planes destroyed, six had been shot down in Quangbinh Province, just north of the DMZ, six in Nghean Province, near the coastal city of Vinh, and two in Thanhhoa further north.

Previous air activity—In other American attacks on the North prior to the massive raids, a U.S. fighter-bomber attacked an antiaircraft battery 70 miles north of the DMZ Nov. 16 and damaged at least one enemy gun. The plane attacked the position after being fired on by the battery during a bombing mission over the Ho Chi Minh Trail in Laos.

U.S. fighter-bombers attacked three air defense radar sites in North Vietnam Dec. 4 in another "protective reaction" strike. One of the targets was 95 miles north of the demilitarized zone.

Two U.S. jets fired missiles Dec. 21 at an antiaircraft radar site 82 miles southeast of Hanoi. A U.S. military spokesman said Dec. 22 that the strike followed enemy radar tracking of the two planes involved in operations in northern Laos. Three more North Vietnamese radar sites, near the Laotian border about 75 miles southwest of Hanoi, came under attack by U.S. fighter-bombers Dec. 23 following "hostile action" by the installations.

Laird explains raids. U.S. Defense Secretary Melvin R. Laird declared at a news conference Dec. 27 that the raids on North Vietnam had "the primary emphasis of protecting the remaining forces of Americans" in South Vietnam. He said they were "of limited duration" and did not represent a basic change in the American bombing policy. But Laird warned that the attacks would be repeated whenever necessary to protect the American forces still in South Vietnam.

Laird also linked the raids to North Vietnam's alleged violation of the so-called understanding that had led to the 1968 bombing halt, an understanding whose existence Hanoi had repeatedly denied. The secretary said North Vietnam had violated that understanding by shelling cities in the South "quite recently," including Saigon Dec. 19; by constructing a road through the demilitarized zone; by failure to engage in serious negotiations at the Paris peace talks; by carrying out "very heavy attacks" on unarmed American reconnaissance aircraft; and by using North Vietnam as a sanctuary for attacks by MiG fighters against American planes operating in Laos.

Continued American air attacks in the Indochina war had been pledged by Secretary of State William P. Rogers Dec. 23. Speaking at a year-end news conference, Rogers said the U.S. would press its air strikes against Communist positions in Laos and Cambodia during 1972 in an effort to stop North Vietnamese drives in those two countries.

"We are going to continue the President's policy of supporting the South Vietnamese in Cambodia and we will continue to give air support in Laos to interdict the Ho Chi Minh Trail, and to give air support in northern Laos," the secretary said.

U.S. domestic criticism—The bombings of North Vietnam precipitated a barrage of criticism in the U.S. Dec. 29. Sen. J. W. Fulbright, chairman of the Senate Foreign Relations Committee, charged that in ordering the massive air raids, the Nixon Administration was "as dedicated as its predecessors to a hopeless quest for a military victory." Sen. Frank Church (D, Ida.) asserted that the air strikes were "further evidence that the President is not ending American involvement in Vietnam but simply changing its form."

Former Defense Secretary Clark M. Clifford said Laird's contention that the raids were in response to Hanoi's violation of the 1968 bomb halt understanding "makes no sense whatsoever." Clifford, who had headed the Defense Department at the time, said "part and parcel of the understanding was that we would not bomb North Vietnam." The current and previous bombings of the North had "breached the understanding to the point where there is no agreement left," Clifford said.

Communists denounce raids—The Soviet Union and China assailed the U.S. raids on North Vietnam.

The Soviet news agency Tass Dec. 27 called the air strikes "provocative and adventuristic," giving "fresh proof of the fact that Washington does not give up its attempts to solve the problem of Indochina by armed force."

The Soviet Union asserted Dec. 28 that the raids were a violation of the 1968 U.S. commitment to halt all bombing of the North. Moscow's critical statement also was directed at China, which was accused of keeping "silent, evidently not wishing in any way to darken President Nixon's forthcoming visit to Peking."

The Chinese Foreign Ministry issued a statement Dec. 29 expressing "utmost indignation at the United States imperialist crimes of aggression" against North Vietnam. The bombings of the North, the ministry said, "has once again exposed the falsehood of its [the U.S.] words of peace."

The Soviet Communist party newspaper Pravda had accused China Dec. 22 of giving the U.S. "a green light for the expansion of aggression in South Vietnam, Laos and Cambodia" by aligning its policies with Washington on a number of other issues.

South Vietnam holiday truces. Ground fighting in South Vietnam was relatively stilled by a 24-hour allied Christmas truce Dec. 24–25. The Communists had unilaterally declared a 72-hour Christmas truce Dec. 23–25. Another 24-hour truce for New Year's went into effect Dec. 31. The U.S. continued its air war over Indochina during the holiday truces.

The Saigon command announced on the expiration of the Christmas truce at 6 p.m. Dec. 25 that Viet Cong forces had committed 49 violations; the Viet Cong charged 170 truce breaches by allied forces.

The U.S. command reported Dec. 30 that one American had been killed in combat Dec. 19–25. It was the lowest weekly American fatality figure since February 1965 when no deaths were reported. Two Americans had been slain Dec. 12–18.

U.S. Policy Debate

Nixon leads policy defense. Faced with increasing attacks on his Administration's policy in Vietnam, President Nixon took his case to the nation April 7 with a televised address in which he announced his decision to increase the rate of troop withdrawals from Vietnam in order to bring home 100,000 more men between May 1 and Dec. 1.

The President stressed that the "American involvement in this war is coming to an end" and he was keeping his campaign pledge to end the involvement. "I expect to be held accountable by the American people if I fail," he said.

Utilizing charts, the President pointed to his record of withdrawing troops: 265,000 by May 1, "almost half of the troops in Vietnam when I took office," and 365,000 by Dec. 1, over two-thirds of the number in Vietnam when he assumed office. His decision to withdraw the additional 100,000 by Dec. 1 was fully supported by the South Vietnamese government, Nixon said.

The authorized force level when troop withdrawals were initiated June 15, 1969, was 544,000. It was 302,000 April 1. By Dec. 1 the target was 184,000. To achieve that, withdrawals would average 14,300 men a month compared to a 12,500 average over the last year.

The President also discussed the Cambodia and Laos invasions, his opposition to setting a deadline for ending U.S. involvement in Vietnam, his goal to end the war "nobly," and "two and a half million fine young Americans who have served in Vietnam," which he wanted to put "into perspective" against "the atrocity charges in individual cases."

Among his remarks:

Cambodia and Laos invasions—He said he had kept his pledge to get U.S. troops out of Cambodia in 60 days. Other fears expressed at the time "were wrong," he said. U.S. casualties "did not rise, they were cut in half." The pullouts "were not halted or delayed" but accelerated.

As for the Laos invasion, his conclusions were (1) that the South Vietnamese had "demonstrated that without American advisers they could fight effectively" against the best enemy troops, (2) that while the South Vietnamese suffered heavy casualties the enemy's casualties "were far heavier," and (3) that "the disruption of enemy supply lines, the consumption of ammunition and arms in the battle, has been even more damaging to the capability of the North Vietnamese to sustain major offensives in South Vietnam than were the operations in Cambodia 10 months ago."

He said: "Consequently tonight I can report that Vietnamization has succeeded."

Deadline for ending U.S. involvement—
Setting a deadline "would serve the enemy's purpose and not our own," Nixon said. It would throw away "our principal bargaining counter to win the release of American prisoners of war," it would "remove the enemy's strongest incentive to end the war sooner by negotiation" and would give the enemy "the exact information they need to marshal their attacks against our remaining forces at their most vulnerable time."

(State Secretary William P. Rogers had told newsmen Feb. 9 that American troops "by and large" would be out of a combat role in Vietnam by mid-1971. White House Press Secretary Ronald L. Ziegler informed the press the same day that 40,000 to 50,000 combat troops would remain in Vietnam after scheduled withdrawals had been completed in April. The Rogers and Ziegler remarks seemed to be contradictory, but Senate Republican Leader Hugh Scott explained later that while some 45,000 ground combat troops would remain in Vietnam after May 1, the Administration expected that number to be reduced to "a very bare minimum" by February or March 1972. It would be "midsummer," Scott said, before American troops were largely withdrawn from a combat role.)

Ending the war 'nobly'—"Our goal is a total American withdrawal from Vietnam" and it could and would be reached through Vietnamization if necessary, he said. "But we would infinitely prefer to reach it even sooner—through negotiations." He called again "on Hanoi to engage in serious negotiations to speed the end of this war" and especially "to agree to the immediate and unconditional release of all prisoners of war." "It is time for Hanoi to end the barbaric use of our prisoners as negotiating pawns and to join us in a humane act that will free their men as well as ours."

Nixon said he wanted to leave Vietnam in a way "that gives the South Vietnamese a reasonable chance to survive as a free people," in a way "that offers a brave people a realistic hope of freedom." He did not want to leave in a way "that by our own actions consciously turns the country over to the Communists." "We have the choice of ending our involvement in this war on a note of despair or on a note of hope." "We have it in our power to prove to our friends in the world that America's sense of responsibility remains the world's greatest single hope of peace" and "to close a difficult chapter in American history, not meanly, but nobly." If he moved to end the war "without regard to what happens to South Vietnam," it "would abandon our friends" and, "even more important, . . . abandon ourselves."

"We've come a long way in the last two years" toward the goal of "a full generation of peace." "With your continued support, I believe we will achieve that goal" and future generations "will be proud that we demonstrated that we had the courage and the character of a great people."

Atrocity charges put in perspective—"I understand the deep concerns which have been raised in this country fanned by reports of brutalities in Vietnam," Nixon said. These charges "should not and cannot be allowed to reflect" on the courage and self-sacrifice of the two and a half million "fine young Americans" who had served in Vietnam, he declared. Never in history "have men fought for less selfish motives—not for conquest, not for glory, only for the right of a people far away to choose the kind of government they want." While "we hear and read much of isolated acts of cruelty, we do not hear enough of the tens of thousands of individual American soldiers . . . who through countless acts of generosity and kindness have tried to help the people of South Vietnam. We can and we should be very proud of these men. They deserve not our scorn but they deserve our admiration and our deepest appreciation."

GOP rebuts war critics. An attack against critics of Administration war policy was mounted in the Senate April 1. It was led by GOP Leader Hugh Scott (Pa.), who charged some Democratic critics with "irresponsible mud-slinging" and with "giving comfort to the enemy" by "crying the same line of Moscow, Peking and Hanoi."

The organized attack, which featured praise for the Laos invasion, included speeches by Republican Sens. Robert Taft Jr. (Ohio), Lowell P. Weicker Jr.

(Conn.), William E. Brock (Tenn.), J. Glenn Beall Jr. (Md.), Clifford P. Hansen (Wyo.) and William B. Saxbe (Ohio).

Among their remarks: Taft said "we are on our way out" of Vietnam; Beall said the Nixon Administration, unlike the preceding administration, had "a plan" to get out of Vietnam; and Saxbe said that while he was "sick and tired" of the war, he was also "sick and tired" of "those who continually play politics" with the war.

Agnew attacks 'home-front snipers'— Vice President Spiro T. Agnew took a similar tack April 1, describing the war critics as "home-front snipers." Speaking to the Veterans Administration Volunteer Service in Washington, Agnew said the war critics—a group including leading senators, "prestigious columnists and news commentators, academic figures, some church organizations, as well as assorted radicals, draft card burners and street demonstrators"—made veterans feel they were fighting in a worthless and immoral cause. Although the majority of Americans felt the GIs in Indochina had served their country well, he said, the message did not get across as well as the "negative one," the "guilt-ridden view" that the GIs were "being exploited."

House approves draft law. The House ended its most intense floor debate on the war in Indochina by voting 293 to 99 April 1 to extend the military draft law to July 1973 and substantially raise servicemen's pay and benefits.

The vote ended three days of emotional debate during which a number of congressmen who had supported the U.S. war effort through the 1960s expressed antiwar opinion for the first time.

In addition to extending the draft law and raising service pay, the bill also included provisions requiring civilian service of conscientious objectors to be increased from two years to three and empowering the President to eliminate draft deferments for undergraduate college students.

President Nixon had sought the two-year extension to mid-1973, at which time, he said, he hoped the U.S. would no longer need a draft. He had asked in his budget for a $987 million increase in military pay and allowances but the House tripled that amount and approved $2.68 billion.

The three-day debate on the floor centered on a timetable for withdrawal of all U.S. forces from Indochina. Several long-time opponents of the war tried and failed to have a vote recorded on an amendment to force a troop pull-out by the end of 1971. Despite their failure, the House doves were backed by the antiwar votes of two Southern Democrats who had formerly been strong supporters of the U.S. role in Indochina.

Rep. John J. Flynt (D, Ga.), an 18-year veteran of Congress who had never voted against a military bill, was one of the two members to switch and vote against the bill. Flynt emphasized that he was still for a strong national defense, but was voting against the bill as his only means of trying to end the war.

"I will not now or ever again vote to start or continue an undeclared war," he said. "It is wrong to compound a six-year mistake and send young men half-way around the world to fight in a war we have not the fortitude to win or end. My people used to say 'Win the war.' Then they said, 'Win it or get out.' Now with one voice they say 'Get out.' The only way I know to end the war is to stop the draft."

He was joined by Rep. Phil Landrum (D, Ga.), Georgia's senior House member, who said Congress should recapture from the President the power to commit forces to combat.

Shortly before the final vote, the House voted down a series of amendments sponsored by the antiwar forces. One, turned down by a vote of 260–122, would have prohibited the assignment of a draftee to Indochina without his consent.

Fulbright: war leads to dictatorship. Sen. J. W. Fulbright (D, Ark.) warned April 3 that "neither constitutional government nor democratic freedoms can survive indefinitely in a country chronically at war, as America has been for the last three decades." "Sooner or later," he said, "war will lead to dictatorship."

Speaking in New Haven, Conn., Fulbright spoke out against "an expansion of presidential power at the expense of Congress" and called for a reversal of foreign policy based on "great-power militarism." "The real question," he said, "is not whether we can adapt democracy to the kind of role we are now playing in the world—I am sure we cannot—but whether we can devise a new foreign policy which will be compatible with our traditional values, a foreign policy which will give us security in our foreign relations without subverting democracy at home."

Fulbright stressed the balancing power of Congress, which, he said, despite "all its irrationalities, remains the strongest institutional barrier to presidential dictatorship." "Our best defense against creeping authoritarianism," he said, "is an assertive, independent legislature."

In a second speech in New Haven April 4, Fulbright called for a "new internationalism" with reliance on the United Nations rather than on power politics. U.S. policy in Vietnam, he said, represented "a grotesquely miscarried effort to apply traditional American values of self-determination and collective security" to outmoded concepts of power politics. He hoped the U.S. would "have the wisdom in any future Vietnams to make it clear at the outset that we will readily act in cooperation with other nations to implement decisions of the United Nations, but that we will not again attempt to substitute ourselves for it."

'Communist-baiting humbuggery'—In his April 4 speech, Fulbright said the U.S. had a "continuing obsession with communism" which permitted "client states like Israel and South Vietnam to manipulate American policy toward purposes contrary to our interest and probably to theirs as well." Although he was not saying the Russians lacked "ambitions in the Middle East," he doubted the validity of Israel's argument that she was "holding the line against a surging tide of Communist imperialism." He called this "Communist-baiting humbuggery."

Pullout date pressed. Advocacy of a deadline for ending U.S. involvement in

Indochina increased following President Nixon's April 7 announcement of his plan to withdraw another 100,000 U.S. troops by Dec. 1. The deadline also was a point of dispute between the Administration and Senate Republican leaders.

Three Senate leaders—GOP Leader Hugh Scott (Pa.), GOP Whip Robert P. Griffin (Mich.) and Democratic Whip Robert C. Byrd (W. Va.)—had a private briefing April 7 with Nixon prior to his speech. Scott reported the next day Nixon informed them "I have a date in mind. I have a plan and timetable for ending this war." Griffin and Byrd corroborated his report. Scott indicated that the date alluded to would be before the end of 1972, pointing out that if the war continued beyond then "another man may be standing on the platform" for the presidential inauguration in January 1973.

Griffin said "in a practical sense" the date indicated by the President was Nov. 7, 1972—election day. Byrd said that while Nixon "did not state a definite date," he had "the very definite impression from what was said that the President has a date in mind. . . . I think there's justification for thinking we'll be out by Dec. 31, 1972."

Scott also reported the President's intention to keep enough forces in Vietnam to induce release of prisoners but not to keep "residual forces" there on a long-term basis once the POW issue was resolved. "This is not a Korean-type situation," Scott declared.

The White House took exception to the senators' interpretation of the deadline. Press Secretary Ronald L. Ziegler told reporters later April 8 that while "the President has a plan in mind, he has not said that on 'X date' all Americans will be out of Vietnam." "It would be incorrect," Ziegler stressed, "to say the President at this time has a specific date he feels the plan will be completed."

Also prior to the President's speech, nine Republican senators had met April 5 with Defense Secretary Melvin R. Laird to urge the Administration to give the nation some indication of "finality" to the U.S. participation in the war. Their advice was that "we just can't hold the line anymore on numbers," or announcements of troop withdrawals over a period of months. The meeting was held at the home of Sen. Jacob Javits (R, N.Y.). Others attending were Scott, Sens. George Aiken (Vt.), John Sherman Cooper (Ky.), Charles McC. Mathias (Md.), Charles Percy (Ill.), Ted Stevens (Alaska), Richard S. Schweiker (Pa.) and Lowell P. Weicker (Conn.).

Aiken, in a Metromedia Radio interview April 6, had predicted that the President in his speech would announce a schedule that would lead to the removal of all U.S. forces from Vietnam by sometime in 1972 at a monthly withdrawal rate of about 18,000 men.

After the President's speech, Aiken commented April 7 that he doubted it was "enough to put the lid back on" war dissent. Scott called the speech April 7 a "continuation and acceleration of his determined plan to totally end this country's involvement in Vietnam." He added, "I know he has a timetable" and said, while the President could not reveal it and "tip his hand to the enemy," the most important fact was "that we are getting out of the war."

Some other senators attending the Laird meeting were disappointed with Nixon's speech. Javits said "to continue to base withdrawal policy on the process of Vietnamization [was] reaffirming Saigon's veto over the pace of U.S. disengagement." Percy said he "had hoped for a faster rate" of troop withdrawals. Mathias said "the gradual pace of reduction exposes us to all the risks of Vietnamization over an extended period of time."

A favorable assessment of Nixon's speech came from House Speaker Carl Albert (D, Okla.), who said Nixon was "acting responsibly," although he hoped he could "act a little faster."

Other comments April 7 were unfavorable: Sen. Harold E. Hughes (D, Iowa) said "we had been led to expect much more." Sen. George McGovern (D, S.D.) said Nixon failed to realize "that Vietnamization with its embrace of the Saigon regime perpetuates the war, confines our men to prison and continues the slaughter of the innocent." Sen. Edmund S. Muskie (D, Me.) noted the President "gave us no indication as to when our involvement would end"

and asserted his preference for "a fixed date to end our involvement."

Sen. Mark O. Hatfield (R, Ore.) said "the utter failure of the Paris peace talks demands that we set a specific date for our withdrawal in order to force action for the return of our prisoners of war. The casualty comparisons used to defend Vietnamization further reveals the moral insensitivity of this war policy." Sen. Frank Church (D, Idaho) said Congress "should now firm up an end-the-war policy" based on the principles of complete withdrawal and a terminal date in exchange for release of prisoners.

Further comment from the Administration on the pullout came from Vice President Spiro T. Agnew and Defense Secretary Laird. Agnew, in an interview published April 11, was quoted as saying if all American troops were immediately withdrawn from Vietnam "it would be disastrous" because it "would be followed by a wave of far-right, irresponsible sentiment that probably would do more harm to our democratic system than any of the left-wing excesses that are taking place today."

In a speech in Los Angeles April 7, Agnew denounced "the movement to plead America guilty," and said the dim view of the Laos invasion taken by the news media was a sign of growing American "masochism" that, if unchecked, "will destroy us as a nation." He said "most knowledgeable people" believed it was too soon to judge the effectiveness of the invasion.

Hartke sees pact if deadline set—Sen. Vance Hartke (D, Ind.) contended in Paris April 6, after talks with the four delegations attending the peace talks, that a settlement ending the combat and U.S. involvement in the war and providing for release of the prisoners could be reached if the U.S. would set the withdrawal date effective by the end of the year.

Laird cites U.S. presence—Defense Secretary Laird told newsmen April 13 the U.S. would maintain, after U.S. ground troops had been withdrawn, a naval and air presence in Southeast Asia as part of the Nixon Doctrine policy of "realistic deterrence." Asked if these units would continue to fight in South

Vietnam after the withdrawal of U.S. ground troops, Laird said, "I wouldn't care to discuss that question." He said, however, "we should not make the mistake of committing massive manpower to that part of the world. Military assistance, yes; manpower, no."

Laird predicted that combat responsibility in South Vietnam would be turned over to Saigon "sometime this summer."

(A report in the New York Times March 18 said the U.S. command in Saigon had informed Washington that a lack of funds for the Vietnam war was more crucial in determining the rate of troop withdrawals than the status of Vietnamization or enemy action. The report said Washington was informed that a lack of funds and manpower reductions had an adverse effect on Vietnamization.)

Mansfield vs. residual force—Senate Democratic Leader Mike Mansfield (Mont.) declared himself April 14 against Defense Secretary Melvin R. Laird's intention to keep U.S. naval and air power in Southeast Asia after the Vietnam war ended.

Mansfield said "we ought to pull out entirely from Indochina and Thailand as well" and rely on "the island-chain concept of defense." He mentioned Japan, the Philippines and "maybe Okinawa" as the islands he had in mind.

GOP senators urge pullout date. The issue of a specific deadline for total withdrawal of U.S. forces from Vietnam was pressed in the Senate April 15 by three Republican senators.

Sen. Clifford P. Case (R, N.J.) announced his intention to cosponsor pullout legislation being offered by Sens. George S. McGovern (D, S.D.) and Mark O. Hatfield (R, Ore.). He conditioned his sponsorship upon the understanding that the legislation's deadline of Dec. 31, 1971 was "subject to adjustment." The measure's sponsors had advised him, he said, that the adjustment in the final withdrawal date would be toward a year after enactment.

Sens. Charles McC. Mathias Jr. (R, Md.) and Edward W. Brooke (R, Mass.) suggested the possibility of an agreement between President Nixon and the Con-

gress on a "date certain" for total U.S. withdrawal. Brooke had called upon the President April 14 to set and announce a final pullout date, preferably the end of 1971.

Mathias and Case also voiced concern over a long-range military commitment and urged the Administration to clarify its attitude toward a residual force.

Two other Republicans defended the Administration's Indochina policy in the Senate April 15. Sen. William B. Saxbe (Ohio), a Vietnam war critic in the past, just returned from a trip to Vietnam, told the Senate the U.S. pullout was proceeding much faster than generally realized and he opposed setting a deadline as possibly giving the enemy an advantage.

Sen. Norris Cotton's (N.H.) defense of Administration policy took the form of an unusual personal attack in the Senate on another senator. He referred to McGovern as one of a group of senators encouraging antiwar demonstrators, disrespect for Congress and the enemy's intransigence in negotiations. Such senators, he said, were "impeding the President in his efforts to end the war." McGovern replied with a press release referring to Cotton as "one of those obsolete, self-styled experts whose patriotism consists largely of cheering from the sidelines while young men die in a foolish war he helped foster."

Total pullout conditions cited. President Nixon April 16 conditioned a total U.S. withdrawal from Vietnam upon release of the U.S. prisoners of war and South Vietnam's capacity to defend itself. The President said while total withdrawal was the U.S. goal, it would be necessary for the U.S. to maintain a residual force and "an air presence" until those two conditions were met.

Nixon stressed the conditions during a question and answer session, broadcast by radio, with a panel of six newspaper editors at the annual banquet of the American Society of Newspaper Editors in Washington.

Speaking of the POW issue, Nixon castigated the North Vietnamese for having been "the most barbaric in their handling of prisoners of any nation in modern history." He said no American president "could simply remove our forces" from Vietnam "as long as there's one American being held prisoner." There was the responsibility, he said, "to have some incentive on our side to get that man released." Without going into the details, Nixon said "we have some cards to play and we intend to play them to the hilt on the prisoner of war question."

As for the second condition—South Vietnam's capacity to defend itself against a Communist takeover—Nixon further defined that capacity as "not the sure capacity, but at least the chance."

Nixon defended his policy by contending that it would save many more Asian lives than were lost by U.S. bombing and combat-support operations. If the U.S. "were to fail in Vietnam," he said, "if the Communists were to take over, the bloodbath that would follow would be a blot on this nation's history from which we would find it very difficult to return."

Democrats ask public pullout date. A Democratic party rebuttal to President Nixon's April 7 television address on Vietnam troop withdrawals was broadcast by the American Broadcasting Co. April 22. Five of the six Democratic spokesmen, all senators and potential presidential nominees, advocated the announcement of a deadline for total U.S. withdrawal from Indochina by the end of 1971.

The sixth, Sen. Henry M. Jackson (Wash.), was against a public deadline—although he thought the President "should have certain dates in mind" in executing troop withdrawals—on the ground it would "weaken the bargaining leverage" in peace negotiations. Jackson favored "a vigorous diplomatic effort to achieve a mutual cease-fire, a return of American prisoners of war and an end to all the killing in South Vietnam, not simply an end to American involvement in it."

The advocates for a specific terminal date for U.S. involvement in Vietnam were Sens. Hubert H. Humphrey (Minn.), George S. McGovern (S.D.), Birch Bayh (Ind.), Harold E. Hughes (Iowa) and Edmund S. Muskie (Me.).

Muskie, appearing last, offered a summary of his colleagues' "compelling reasons for setting a date and bringing all our men home by the end of this year"—

the "bloodshed and terrible human suffering; the devastation of the lands of Indochina; the waste of our resources desperately needed here at home; the doubts it has created about the wisdom and word of our government."

"We have done as much for the South Vietnamese government as anyone could reasonably have asked of us," he continued. "It is not unreasonable now to ask that government to test its own ability to survive. Whatever you or I or any of us now think about the war, I believe we all agree on one terrible price it is making us pay. It is the price of division, fear and hatred in America. We must not go on like this."

Humphrey said the responsibility for U.S. involvement in Vietnam was "a national" one and "not a partisan one" and disengagement "must also be the task of all of us." A withdrawal in 1971 did not mean the nation was entering an "era of isolationism;" the U.S. had "extensive international responsibilities" and would honor them. The end of "our Vietnam obsession" would free the nation "to assume a far more balanced and productive role in the world community," he said.

McGovern said President Nixon's Vietnamization policy would not gain release of American POWs, end the danger to the U.S. forces remaining in Vietnam, break the negotiating stalemate nor end the destruction of people and countryside. "It only expresses the hope that by reducing our forces on the ground we can thereby reduce American casualties," he said. If "a flat commitment" on withdrawal were given, he felt, the negotiating stalemate could be broken and talks started on prisoner release and on safety of the forces remaining during withdrawal.

Bayh asked why it was necessary to wait until 1972 to end U.S. involvement in Vietnam. There was nothing to be gained by such a delay, he said, "unless the President hopes to enhance his own re-election prospects." He did not believe the U.S. had any commitment to the Thieu government "or to any particular government in South Vietnam." The commitment had been fulfilled with 53,000 American lives, more than $125 billion spent and a one-million-man army trained and equipped, he said.

Hughes felt there was no honor in prolonging the war "another week" nor in "sacrificing more American lives, even at a reduced rate."

The national television and radio network made available for the program by ABC was in response to a request from Democratic National Chairman Lawrence F. O'Brien. He asked for time to rebut the President's attempt to blame the "tragic conflict solely on the Democratic party" and to present the "clear difference" between the party and the Administration "on the critical issue of troop withdrawal." ABC demurred on the rebuttal aspect, considering it had complied with the "fairness doctrine" by "balanced coverage" of the Vietnam problem, but it granted "additional coverage" in the public interest because of the national importance of the war issue.

Similar requests from the Democrats for rebuttal time were rejected by the National Broadcasting Co. and the Columbia Broadcasting System.

Other Democrats urge pullout date— Senate Democratic Leader Mike Mansfield (Mont.) suggested April 24 the Nixon Administration privately communicate to North Vietnam a date for total withdrawal of U.S. troops from Vietnam.

Gov. Frank Licht (D, R.I.) April 25 urged withdrawal by Dec. 31 so the nation could concentrate on domestic problems.

GOP senators defend Administration— Four senators defended President Nixon's Vietnam withdrawal policy April 22 and spoke in the Senate against "a precipitous withdrawal" that "would betray the valiant effort made to date." The phrases were those of Conservative-Republican James L. Buckley (N.Y.). Joining him in defending Administration policy were Sens. William B. Saxbe (R, Ohio), who said he considered it unrealistic to name a specific pullout date; Clifford P. Hansen (R, Wyo.), who warned that troops remaining in Vietnam during the pullout could be "pinned down by the enemy"; and Robert Taft Jr. (R, Ohio), who berated "the Johnny-come-lately doves" for "the pure politics of their current dissent."

U.S. force at record low. The U.S. command announced April 26 that the number of American forces in South Vietnam dropped to 281,400 the previous week. This was 2,600 below the ceiling set by President Nixon for May 1 and constituted the lowest level in nearly five years. The previous low was July 16, 1966, when there were 280,000 American troops in South Vietnam.

Defense fund cut backed. The Gallup poll said April 14 that 50% of the Americans surveyed in a March poll believed the U.S. should reduce its military spending.

In the survey, which involved a sample of 1,556 persons over 18, 31% of those interviewed thought the present level of spending for defense and military purposes was about right, and 11% said they believed not enough was being set aside for the military; 8% said they had no opinion.

In a similar Gallup poll in 1960, 18% of those interviewed had said defense spending was excessive, while 45% said the funds were about right and 21% believed that spending for military purposes should be increased.

'End-the-war' hearings. The Senate Foreign Relations Committee opened hearings April 20 on legislative proposals to end the war. The Senate Refugees Subcommittee, headed by Sen. Edward M. Kennedy (D, Mass.), opened hearings April 21 on the Indochina refugee situation. Both hearings were attended by antiwar veterans who had come to Washington for a week of protest.

Sens. McGovern, Hatfield and Hartke were among the lead-off witnesses at the "end-the-war hearing" April 20. McGovern said "the very soul of this nation" demanded immediate positive action to end the U.S. war role in Indochina. Hatfield charged that a refusal to set a deadline and continued support of the Saigon regime made a negotiated settlement "impossible." Hartke insisted that a cease-fire could be arranged within 48 hours of a U.S. announcement of a withdrawal date, and a release of prisoners could probably be negotiated within three weeks.

Sen. Jacob K. Javits (R, N.Y.) told the panel April 21 that Congress should establish a pullout deadline and suggested mid-1972. The hearing was interrupted twice by demonstrations led by antiwar activist Rennie Davis.

In opening his hearing, Kennedy said the U.S. military activity, especially the air war, was contributing to a "bloodbath" and "agony" among "a rapidly growing number of civilians in Vietnam, Laos and Cambodia." He said the war operations, and largely the U.S.-supported operations, had spawned 150,000 refugees since November 1970. His view contrasted with testimony by William E. Colby, who was in charge of the pacification program in South Vietnam, that the refugee problem had decreased "enormously" in the last two or three years.

Opening testimony before the Kennedy panel was given April 21 by Rep. Paul N. McCloskey (R, Calif.), who recently returned from an eight-day trip to Indochina, including Laos. He charged that the State Department had deliberately concealed the extent of American bombing of villages in northern Laos since 1968 and that bombing was "the most compelling reason" for the refugee movement in Laos.

On the CBS "Face the Nation" broadcast April 18, McCloskey said the number of villages in Laos destroyed by U.S. bombing may have been in the "thousands." He urged an immediate halt to bombing throughout Indochina and said he would challenge President Nixon in primary elections in 1972 if the bombing were not ended.

'Dump Nixon' rally—McCloskey was one of the speakers at a "Dump Nixon" rally in Providence, R.I. April 18 attended by more than 10,000 persons. Sharing the platform with two potential Democratic presidential candidates— Sens. Edmund S. Muskie (Me.) and Birch Bayh (Ind.)—McCloskey renewed his Laotian bombing charges and said if a renomination bid by President Nixon could be defeated, "perhaps we can end this war and this bombing one or two months sooner."

Muskie disputed the President's contention that an abrupt pullout would bring on a right-wing reaction of recrimination. "The real nightmare of recrimination will come," he said, "if the war is perpetuated, if American and Vietnamese lives are thrown away long after a compelling reason for their sacrifice has vanished."

Bayh said he was "unwilling to accept the [Vice President] Spiro Agnew definition of patriotism" equating it with support of Administration Vietnam policy. "A man who loves his country must say stop this war and stop it now," he declared.

The rally, sponsored locally by a bipartisan group called Citizens for Alternatives Now, was the first of a projected series of "Dump Nixon" rallies organized by former Rep. Allard K. Lowenstein (D, N.Y.), leader of a similar effort against Lyndon B. Johnson in 1967–68.

Senate hearings. John F. Kerry, leader of Vietnam Veterans Against the War, which was holding a week-long protest in Washington, charged at the Senate Foreign Relations Committee's "end-the-war" hearings April 22 that Americans had been sent to die in Vietnam "for the biggest nothing in history." He urged "the earliest possible" date for ending the effort. Vietnamization was not the answer, Kerry contended, because it was "continuing the war."

Mayday Tribe, a radical youth group, whose leaders testified April 28, attacked the committee for "lack of initiative" in ending the war. It called Congress "the puppet of the madmen who are in power." Committee members advised the group that its planned disruptive tactics in Washington would be "counter-productive" to its goal. The group's organizer, Charles C. Marshall, 26, disagreed. "People have no way to vote on the war in Vietnam," he said, and "that's why we are saying that present methods are inadequate."

The committee also heard testimony April 23 and 26 on proposals to curb the war-making powers of the president. Sen. Barry Goldwater (R, Ariz.) testified April 23 that he felt such legislative restrictions would be "unwise" and could "utterly demolish" the nation's "dependability as an ally." He admitted a preference to put more faith in the presidency than in Congress. Testimony endorsing legislative curbs to the president's war-making powers was presented

April 26 by McGeorge Bundy, national security adviser to Presidents Kennedy and Johnson, and George E. Reedy, press secretary and later a consultant to Johnson. Bundy favored a partnership arrangement between the president and Congress, Reedy an "adversary position" for Congress to challenge the president on foreign policy direction.

Sen. Edward M. Kennedy's (D, Mass.) Senate Refugee Subcommittee continued its hearings April 22 with a denunciation from Kennedy of the "mindless use of power" in the U.S. military air operations in Indochina. Kennedy accused State Department witnesses of having no plan to help war refugees in Cambodia. One of them, William H. Sullivan, deputy assistant secretary of state for East Asian and Pacific affairs, disputed previous testimony that U.S. bombing was the major cause of the refugee movement in Laos. He attributed the abandonment of homes to North Vietnamese offensives.

Testimony against restricting the president's war powers was presented before the Senate Foreign Relations Committee May 14 by State Secretary William Rogers, who held that the issue should be dealt with in a spirit of cooperation between the executive and legislative branches. "Our constitutional system," he said, "is founded on an assumption of cooperation rather than conflict, and this is vitally necessary in matters of war and peace."

Sen. Clifford P. Case (R, N.J.) disagreed, observing that the Constitution provided for a division of powers "precisely to make it more difficult to get into war."

Rogers' position also was opposed by Committee Chairman J. W. Fulbright (D, Ark.), who told him "the message of your testimony is that Congress has no role to play and we should be good boys and receive your briefings." Fulbright said at the outset of the hearing that "the pendulum has begun to swing away from the dangerous practice of presidentially initiated warfare."

(A House Foreign Affairs subcommittee opened hearings June 1 on proposals to require the president to consult with Congress before involving U.S. forces in armed conflict. One of the suggestions, presented by Rep. Jonathan B. Bingham [D, N.Y.], was for Congress to decide, in the absence of a declaration of war, whether the president could continue using U.S. troops in hostilities outside U.S. territory.)

In testimony relating to "end-the-war" legislation, the McGovern-Hatfield proposal for withdrawing all U.S. forces by Dec. 31 was supported by ex-Sen. Joseph S. Clark May 25 and Princeton professor Richard A. Falk May 26. Falk said "the effects of troop withdrawal and so-called Vietnamization are to defer the evidence of defeat past the 1972 election date." Former U.S. Ambassador W. Averell Harriman, testifying May 25, urged Congress to use its "power over the purse" to compel a pullout, "preferably by the end of this year." Former U.S.Ambassador to the U.N. Charles W. Yost favored a firm pullout date in testimony May 26 but said the date should be conditioned to a North Vietnamese agreement to release U.S. POWs "no later than the date fixed for completion of our withdrawal."

Rep. Andrew Jacobs Jr. (D, Ind.) May 27 offered his own proposal, introduced March 17, for a U.S. pullout 60 days after the enemy signed an agreement to return American POWs.

H. R. Rainwater, commander in chief of the Veterans of Foreign Wars, testified May 27 against any proposals for an immediate, unilateral or unconditional withdrawal by the U.S.

In other testimony, Stanford professor John Wilson Lewis May 26 cited the "first Chinese-Indochinese coalition in history" begun after the Cambodian invasion and said the new role for China in the Indochina conflict posed "potential advantages" for the U.S. It offered, he said, "the opportunity for a genuine face-saving resolution of the Indochina war, for in the context of a change in U.S. policy toward China, there lies the opportunity for a negotiated international settlement of the war."

Rep. Paul N. McCloskey Jr. (R, Calif.), appearing before the Fulbright panel May 27, protested "deceptive briefings" during his tour of Vietnam and Laos and said such "deliberate withholding of information from the Congress presents a grave constitutional question as to whether the legislative branch can properly perform its own legislative responsibilities."

Senators back draft bill. The Senate Armed Services Committee April 27 unanimously approved a bill extending the draft law for two years to June 30, 1973. The committee, however, simultaneously voted to restrict a President's authority to raise troops for an undeclared war. It did so by approving a ceiling on the number of men that could be called up in the fiscal years 1972 and 1973.

The ceiling would permit no more than 150,000 men to be drafted in fiscal 1972, which would begin July 1. The same limit would be mandatory for fiscal 1973. Under the terms of the legislation, President Nixon could only raise the ceiling if he issued an executive order declaring that an expanded draft was necessary to meet urgent national security needs. If the ceiling became law, it would insure that the draft calls for fiscal 1972 and 1973 would be lower than in fiscal 1971, when 152,000 men would have been called for military service.

In other actions on the overall legislation:

■ The committee rejected a proposal that would have raised servicemen's pay and benefits by $2.7 billion at once in an effort to make military life more attractive for enlistees. The measure had been approved by the House. In voting down the measure the Senate committee instead adopted President Nixon's plan for a $987 million pay increase spread out through 1971.

■ The committee also approved a part of the bill that called for a reduction in the size of the military by June 30, 1972, to about 2.4 million men, about 100,000 below the level sought by manpower planners and the Nixon Administration.

■ The committee let stand the alternate service required of a conscientious objector at two years instead of the three recommended by the House.

Nixon firm on pullout policy. President Nixon April 29 reaffirmed his stand against setting a deadline for total withdrawal of U.S. troops from Vietnam.

Speaking at a news conference, the President held fast to his dictum that ending the U.S. involvement in Vietnam must await North Vietnam's release of American prisoners and South Vietnam's ability to defend itself.

Referring to the North Vietnamese proposal to open negotiations at once on a U.S. pullout date, the President said the end of U.S. involvement "will have to be delayed until we get, not just the promise to discuss the release of our prisoners but a commitment to release" them. "A promise to discuss means nothing from the North Vietnamese," he said. It required "action on their part and a commitment on their part with regard to the prisoners." "We'll be there as long as they have any prisoners in North Vietnam," he declared.

Ten of 17 questions at the televised White House news conference dealt with the war or war-related issues.

In his remarks April 29 on the withdrawal date, the President saw no gain—"when we get nothing for it"—in setting a date even so far in advance it might be considered safe. Although the U.S. was withdrawing, he said, and the goal was total withdrawal and no "permanent residual force" was planned, he refused to set a date because it was "not in our interest."

As for the residual force, Nixon said if the "North Vietnamese are so barbaric that they continue to hold our POWs regardless of what we do with regard to withdrawal, then we're going to keep a residual force no matter how long it takes." As for the ability of the South Vietnamese to defend themselves, he said, "we have a very good idea when that will occur, and as soon as that eventuality occurs we will be able to move on that."

Nixon stressed that the way the U.S. ended the war was "going to determine to a great extent whether we are going to avoid this kind of involvement in the future. If we end it in a way that encourages those who engage in aggression to try it again, we'll have more wars like this. But if we end it in a way that I have laid out, . . . then we'll have a chance to have peace" in future generations.

In response to a question about the possibility of naming a court of inquiry to investigate "just exactly who got us into this war," Nixon said, "I'm not going to cast the blame for the war in Vietnam on either of my predecessors." Presidents Johnson and Kennedy, he was sure, "were making decisions that they thought were necessary" for the security of the U.S.

Asked about the possibility of any new "Laotian or Cambodian type of operations," Nixon said the possibility was "quite remote" because of the reduced U.S. force in Vietnam. He saw "no need for any further actions" and noted "one indication of some effectiveness of previous actions"—the reduction of casualties. "As a result of Laos, as a result of Cambodia," he said, "the war is winding down."

Senate rejects pullout deadlines. The Senate rejected two attempts June 16 to set a deadline for the withdrawal of American troops from Indochina.

By a vote of 55–42, the Senate defeated the McGovern-Hatfield end-the-war amendment to the Selective Service bill that called for the withdrawal of all U.S. forces by Dec. 31. The House next day rejected a similar rider to a different bill.

In an earlier vote June 16, the Senate had rejected a compromise amendment to the same draft bill that would have set a withdrawal deadline of June 1, 1972. That proposal, sponsored by Sen. Lawton Chiles (D, Fla.), was defeated 52–44. But a week later and again in September the Senate approved measures calling for total withdrawal deadlines.

The June 16 refusal to set a date for the end of the U.S. combat role in Indochina was viewed as a victory for the Nixon Administration which had opposed any Congressional withdrawal date.

But there were indications that despite the rejection of the McGovern-Hatfield proposal and Chiles' compromise measure, there were an increasing number of senators who were ready to vote for some form of a Congressional resolution requiring an end to the U.S. combat role in Indochina by a specific date.

One indication was the vote of Sen. Milton R. Young (R, N.D.), a conservative and a staunch supporter of the President's Vietnam policies. When the Senate voted in 1970 on the McGovern-

Hatfield proposal, Young was one of those who voted against it. In the vote June 16, Young voted for the proposal co-sponsored by Sens. George McGovern (D, S.D.) and Mark O. Hatfield (R, Ore.). Young also voted June 16 for Chiles' compromise amendment.

Young was one of eight Republicans who voted for the McGovern-Hatfield proposal. The others were: Edward Brooke (Mass.), Clifford Case (N.J.), Hatfield, Jacob K. Javits (N.Y.), Charles Mathias (Md.), Charles Percy (Ill.) and Richard Schweiker (Pa.).

Thirty-four Democrats voted for the McGovern-Hatfield proposal, while 19 Democrats—almost all Southerners—voted against it. Thirty-six Republicans voted against the proposal.

The House action, taken by 254–158 vote June 17, was a refusal to set a Dec. 31 deadline for U.S. withdrawal from Indochina.

The House action came on an amendment—offered by Reps. Lucian N. Nedzi (D, Mich.) and Charles W. Whalen Jr. (R, Ohio)—to a military procurement bill. The Nedzi-Whalen amendment would have provided that none of the fund authorized in the procurement bill could be used to support U.S. forces in Indochina after Dec. 31.

Voting for the House amendment were 135 Democrats and 23 Republicans. Voting against it were 105 Democrats and 149 Republicans.

Senate calls for Vietnam pullout. The Senate adopted an end-the-war amendment June 22 calling for withdrawal of all U.S. forces from Indochina within nine months in return for the phased release of American prisoners of war.

Although it was provisional, it was the first time the Senate had set a deadline for the disengagement of American forces from Indochina.

By a vote of 57–42, the Senate accepted the pullout deadline as an amendment to the Selective Service Bill. The amendment was offered by Senate Majority Leader Mike Mansfield (Mont).

President Nixon did not publicly comment on the Senate's action. But White House Press Secretary Ronald L. Ziegler said the Mansfield amendment, even if enacted, was "not binding" and that the

President would "continue the policy which he has set forth of withdrawal of forces from South Vietnam and our efforts to get the other side to enter into serious negotiations."

To become law, the Mansfield amendment still required House approval.

Mansfield's amendment would establish the policy that the U.S. should "terminate at the earliest practicable date all military operations" in Indochina and "to provide for the orderly withdrawal" of all U.S. forces within nine months after enactment of the amendment. The disengagement would be contingent upon the release of all American prisoners.

The amendment called on the President to establish a final date for troop withdrawal, to negotiate with North Vietnam an immediate cease-fire to be followed by "phased and rapid" withdrawal of U.S. forces in return for phased release of American prisoners.

The Mansfield amendment was viewed as a moderate end-the-war plan since it would not cut off the funds to require a withdrawal by a certain date as other amendments had been designed to do. It was, however, stronger than a sense-of-the-Senate resolution since it established a policy of staged withdrawal within nine months subject only to the return of U.S. prisoners.

Ten senators who normally backed Administration Vietnam policies supported the Mansfield amendment. They were Lloyd Bentsen (D, Tex.), Alan Bible (D, Nev.), Howard Cannon (D, Nev.), Robert C. Byrd (D, W. Va.), David Gambrell (D, Ga.), Herman E. Talmadge (D, Ga.), William B. Spong Jr. (D, Va.), Ernest F. Hollings (D, S.C.), Len B. Jordan (R, Idaho) and John L. McClellan (D, Ark.).

In all, 45 Democrats and 12 Republicans voted for the Mansfield amendment. Ten Democrats and 32 Republicans opposed it.

The Mansfield amendment was passed after the Senate rejected a stiffer end-the-war amendment sponsored by Sens. Marlow W. Cook (R, Ky.) and Ted Stevens (R, Alaska). The Cook-Stevens amendment would have required withdrawal of all troops within nine months, with the provision that the withdrawal deadline would be suspended if North Vietnam within 60 days did not give a "firm commitment" to return all American prisoners. After some parliamentary maneuvering, the Administration forces, led by Sen. John C. Stennis (D, Miss.) succeeded in rephrasing the Cook-Stevens amendment, changing "firm commitment" to "release." Instead of the Cook-Stevens plan, the Senate accepted the watered-down version by a 50-49 vote. The Cook-Stevens amendment never came to a vote.

During discussion of the amendment, Mansfield June 9 had given the Senate a summary of his views on pullout and POW issues. He said:

The question of the POW's has been receiving significant attention in Paris and, most especially, in Hanoi and in this country. The number of POW's has been estimated at approximately 1,500 to 1,600 but figures which had been given by North Vietnam indicate that they hold approximately somewhere around 350 to 400 U.S. POW's.

The question of the POW's figures significantly and, in some respects, overridingly in the matter of ending the war in Vietnam. The administration has said that we will maintain forces in Vietnam until all POW's are released. Hanoi has said that they will not even begin to discuss the fate of the prisoners until a termination date has been set and then, according to press reports from the North Vietnamese delegation in Paris, they have indicated this matter could be settled promptly.

If a termination date were set and negotiations in earnest begun, there would be no useful reason, in my opinion, for North Vietnam to keep the U.S. POW's there. If a termination date is not set, then we are confronted with the paradoxial situation which results in more and more American casualties, perhaps more and more POW's and more and more of a determination on the part of North Vietnam to hang on to the POW's.

A terminal date for ending the war could lead to the release of the POW's. A continuation of the war with increased casualties and an increase in the number of POW's would make a bad situation worse. As it is now, it appears to me that both sides of the coin are the same as far as the POW's are concerned. The present approach makes hostages of the POW's with the result that the possibility of their release fades into the distance even as the casualties and the cost increase week by week, month by month, year by year. If we agree to a termination date and the prisoners are not released, we still retain all our options, and thereby lose nothing in the attempt.

On April 16, the President gave another reason in addition to the POW issue for not fixing a terminal date on the involvement. That was to give South Vietnam at least a chance to defend itself against North Vietnam. With an army which is larger than North Vietnam's, equipped, trained, supplied, paid and advised by Americans over a period extending from 1955 to the present, I would say that if they are not in a position now to have at least a chance to defend themselves, than they never will be. It is their country. It is their future. It is their decision, not ours.

Over the years, 17 years in fact, I have not deviated from my position that we had no business becoming involved, militarily, in Vietnam. We have no foundation and never have had for the pursuit of our intervention there.

As of May 22, 1971, 354,165 casualties, broken down to 54,731 dead and 299,434 combat wounded, $120 billion wasted, demoralization and divisiveness at home and abroad, drug addiction, graft, corruption, fraggings, the laying waste of a country and the wasting of lives—that is what Vietnam has entailed, that is what Vietnam means—even now. Let us grasp this nettle and bring this tragedy to a terminal ending—and do it now. I realize that this proposal is not in accord with the one that the President espouses and has espoused consistently. He has faced up to his responsibility. He is withdrawing our troops at a faster rate than announced. His policy may be correct, but there are at least two sides to every question, and I would hope that the Senate will face up to its responsibility and approve the McGovern-Hatfield amendment. I would be content to let history decide which course is the right one but, in the meantime, I would waste no time and make every effort to bring about the release of the POW's at the earliest opportunity and, at the same time, bring this tragedy to a final end.

Senate closes off draft debate—The Senate voted June 23 to shut off further debate on the bill to extend the draft.

Cloture was invoked by a 65–27 vote, three votes more than the two-thirds majority of those voting needed to cut off debate.

Many of the senators who voted to shut off debate said after the vote that if the Mansfield amendment was stricken from the bill in a House-Senate conference, they would not again vote for cloture when the bill was returned for final action.

Voting for cloture were 29 Democrats and 36 Republicans. Four Republicans and 23 Democrats voted against shutting off debate.

The cloture cut off a threatened filibuster by Sens. Alan Cranston (D, Calif.) and Mike Gravel (D, Alaska). They had argued that one way to end the war was to end President Nixon's authority to conscript men into the armed forces to fight it.

In an earlier action on the bill, the Senate voted June 17 against permitting potential draftees to bring lawyers when they appeared before their local draft board. The vote was 44–32. The measure had been sponsored by Edward M. Kennedy (D, Mass.), who said that under his proposal the lawyers would only have been allowed to advise their clients.

Mayors urge Vietnam pullout by 1972. The U.S. Conference of Mayors voted 54–49 June 16 to approve a resolution urging President Nixon to pull all U.S. troops out of Vietnam by Dec. 31, 1971.

The vote came on the final day of the organization's 38th annual conference, held in Philadelphia. Antiwar mayors had been active in past conventions, but this was the first time the organization, representing 400 mayors of U.S. cities with populations of at least 30,000, had taken an official stand against the war.

The Vietnam resolution stated that the war "has become a proper concern to city governments." It urged the President to do "all within his power to bring about the complete withdrawal of all American forces from Vietnam by Dec. 31, 1971, or sooner."

The resolution passed after a pro-Administration amendment failed in a 54–49 vote. The amendment, supported by mayors of smaller cities, called on the President to withdraw forces from Vietnam "as soon as national security permits." The debate on the war followed brief addresses by John F. Kerry of Vietnam Veterans Against the War and by John O'Neill of Veterans for a Just Peace, a group opposing Kerry's organization.

Biggest U.S. pullout. A total of 6,100 American troops left South Vietnam July 1. It was the largest single withdrawal of U.S. soldiers since the phased pullout was begun in 1969. The latest troop reduction brought the total of American servicemen remaining in South Vietnam to just over 236,000.

The units pulled out July 1 were in Military Region II in the Central Highlands and marked the start of the end of U.S. combat role in that sector. A majority of the remaining American combat soldiers in South Vietnam were in Military Region I, in the northernmost provinces, where the heaviest clashes were taking place.

Agnew's foreign tour. Vice President Spiro Agnew made a 32-day diplomatic tour of 10 nations in Asia, Africa and Europe June 27–July 28. The original purpose of the tour was a visit to South Korea to attend the inauguration of President Chung Hee Park.

In an overnight stay in Guam June 28 before leaving for Seoul, South Korea, Agnew said he was interested in visiting Communist China despite what he called his personal reservations about the country's diplomatic posture which he characterized as "basically hostile to the U.S."

Agnew's South Korean visit, which included two brief and informal discussions with Park and another with South Korean Defense Minister Jung Nae Huik, was described as low-key. Agnew assured Park June 30 that the U.S. would continue to underwrite the cost of maintaining South Korean forces in South Vietnam, while cautioning against "premature" withdrawal. The statement came after Huik announced earlier in the day that South Korea's contingent in Vietnam, estimated at 48,000–52,000 men, would be reduced by 15,000 before June of 1972 "unless we are requested to reconsider this timetable by South Vietnam." (Huik had stated June 29 that all Korean forces would be withdrawn by the end of 1972 "since there would be no reason for us to stay after the U.S. has left.")

Agnew also sought to reassure South Korean leaders that President Nixon's efforts to relax trade and travel restrictions to China would not endanger South Korea's economic strength or security.

Before leaving Seoul July 3, Agnew said that while he had hoped to discuss high-level matters with South Korean officials during his visit, no substantive discussions of major importance took place since President Park considered his appearance "a ceremonial one."

Agnew arrived in Singapore July 4 for a two-day visit. He paid a courtesy call on Singapore's new president, Dr. Benjamin Sheares, and met with Prime Minister Lee Kuan Yew July 5. The same day Agnew charged the U.S. news media with unintentionally assisting the North Vietnamese by some of their reportage of the Indochina war. He said the North Vietnamese were likely to launch a "high-risk, high-casualty" attack when U.S. forces were sufficiently reduced that would be a "public-relations coup" since the U.S. media would report it "as a failure of the Vietnamization program of the U.S." Agnew added that he was reassuring the leaders of the countries he visited that the Nixon Administration had no intention of leaving a vacuum in Asia or the Middle East and that the U.S. intended to remain a world power despite some "isolationist" voices in Washington.

Nixon on work for peace. President Nixon, speaking at the National Archives in Washington, said July 3 that the nation's greatest goal on the eve of its bicentennial anniversary should be world peace.

Nixon described the U.S. effort to end the war in Indochina as instrumental in securing world peace.

"We are already taking the first long step toward that goal by ending the difficult war in which we are engaged, in a way that will contribute not only to peace in the Pacific but to peace in the world—not only to peace for our generation, but to peace for the next generation."

Nixon warned the nation, however, that it should not forsake its role of world leadership after the Indochina war. Peace would only be reached, Nixon said, "if America continues to meet its responsibilities of leadership in building a structure of lasting peace in the world."

Nixon to visit mainland China. President Nixon announced to an astonished American public July 15 that he would visit Peking before May 1972 to confer with Communist Chinese leaders "to seek the normalization of relations between the two countries and to exchange views on questions of concern to the two sides." A follow-up announcement by the Western White House in San Clemente, Calif. July 16 said the President's trip might be made as early as late 1971 and that he would confer with both Communist Party Chairman Mao Tse-tung and Premier Chou En-lai. No American President had ever been received by a Chinese government.

In his address, broadcast from Los Angeles, Nixon disclosed that arrangements for the projected meeting with Chinese leaders had been worked out in secret talks held in Peking July 9–11 by Henry A. Kissinger, his national security affairs adviser, and Chou En-lai. Kissinger, on a fact-finding tour of Asia, had made the secret flight to Peking from Pakistan.

Nixon said the plan for the proposed trip was being announced simultaneously in the U.S. and Peking. Alluding to the Nationalist Chinese government on Taiwan, the President emphasized that "our action in seeking a new relationship with the People's Republic of China will not be at the expense of our old friends." Nixon called his forthcoming visit "a major development in our efforts to build a lasting peace in the world." He said it was in accord with his oft-stated belief that "there can be no stable and enduring peace without the participation of the People's Republic of China and its 750 million peoples."

Nixon said that Chou had extended the invitation to him to come to Peking in response to his [Nixon's] expression of interest in a visit to China. The Chinese premier was reported to have confirmed to a visiting French group July 17 that it was the President who had suggested the trip.

Premier Chou En-lai emphasized July 19 that an American military withdrawal from Indochina must take priority over improvement of U.S.-Chinese relations. Speaking to a visiting group of American graduate students, a 15-member delegation of the Committee of Concerned Asian Scholars, Chou said the demand in the U.S. and elsewhere for the removal of all American troops was "even stronger than the demand to restore the relations between the Chinese and American people, because the people of the United States do not want to sacrifice the lives of the American people for this dirty war."

Chou reiterated his support for the Viet Cong's seven-point proposal and went beyond it by insisting that American forces leave "all of Indochina," including Cambodia and Laos, according to the student spokesmen. (The Viet Cong plan demanded only a U.S. withdrawal from Vietnam.) Chou was said to have added that the U.S. withdrawal would have to include "not only troops, but all military forces and all military installations."

Kissinger mission described—Further comment on the President's plans to visit China and details of Kissinger's mission to Peking were outlined in the July 16 announcement.

In a press briefing, White House officials made these points:

■ There were "risks" in a meeting of Nixon and the Chinese leaders because of the enormous differences between the two countries, particularly over the issue of U.S. support of Nationalist China and Peking's demand that this backing be withdrawn.

■ No specific date had been set for Nixon's visit because it required considerable "preparatory work, . . . but it will be well before May 1972. May was set as the date because the President directed that a step of such importance for world peace . . . should not get mixed up" in the 1972 Presidential election campaign.

■ The Peking journey was not directly connected with the war in Indochina. However, when "countries of the magnitude and world concerns of the United States and the People's Republic of

China alter their relationship, it must affect other parts of the world."

■ Nixon would not extend his trip to include the Soviet Union: ". . . the occasion of a visit to Peking is not the best to also visit Moscow. The issues to be discussed between the two countries are too various. But in principle we are prepared to meet with the Soviet leaders whenever our negotiations have reached a point where something fruitful can be accomplished."

On the Kissinger mission, the White House officials disclosed that:

■ Preparations for it and the mission itself were shrouded in such secrecy that only Nixon, Kissinger, Secretary of State William P. Rogers and "a very few White House staff members" knew what was going on. The arrangements were drawn up between April and June. Nixon did not work out plans for the project in his office "for fear that papers would be left behind and people might walk in and see [the President and Kissinger] working on the papers. So they usually met in the Lincoln sitting room [of the White House]. . . ."

■ The negotiations leading up to the Kissinger trip were accomplished in two stages. The first required the establishment of a framework for negotiations and success in convincing the Chinese leaders that Americans were flexible and were "not prisoners of history." "The second phase started in April when we moved from this general framework to a more specific exploration of where we might go from here. Then in April, May and June this meeting was set up through a series of exchanges."

Congressional leaders briefed. President Nixon briefed Congressional leaders July 19 on his plans for the visit to China.

White House Press Secretary Ronald L. Ziegler said Nixon had told the eight senators and nine representatives present that he would not speculate on "the effect of these discussions [in Peking] on any other matters" including the war in Indochina, and that "general speculation on this matter would not be helpful."

The President's plans were discussed later at a Cabinet meeting attended by Nixon, Rogers and Kissinger.

Rogers held separate meetings July 19 with the envoys of nine countries to acquaint them with Nixon's plans for talks with the Chinese leaders. Rogers told them that despite Washington's move toward a rapprochement with Peking, the U.S. was still seeking ways of keeping Nationalist China in the U.N. Rogers met with the ambassadors of Nationalist China, Japan, Australia, Britain, New Zealand, Thailand, France and West Germany and the charge d'affaires of Italy.

Domestic political reaction. The announcement of Nixon's intention to visit China drew generally favorable comment, mainly within Congress, from U.S. political figures July 15–20.

Senate Majority Leader Mike Mansfield (D, Mont.) described himself July 15 as "flabbergasted, delighted and happy" that Nixon had accepted the Chinese invitation and said he was "looking forward to a new day" as a result of the decision. Sen. Hugh Scott, the Republican leader from Pennsylvania, called the planned visit "an extremely important step in producing world peace." Sen. Hubert H. Humphrey (D, Minn.) said the President's move was "a dramatic turn in American foreign policy and, in my mind, one that can lead to constructive developments." Sen. George S. McGovern (D, S.D.) said he hoped the trip would "mark the end of a long period of nonsense in our relations with China and the beginning of a new era of common sense."

A similar view was taken July 16 by Sen. John Sherman Cooper (R, Ky.), who said the planned trip was "a step that may help bring stability and peace to Southeast Asia." Cooper added, however, that "the prospects for an international settlement will be enhanced by a firm declaration on the part of the U.S. that it will remove all its forces from Indochina in order to bring about a political settlement and an end to all hostilities there." Sen. Edmund S. Muskie (D, Me.) remarked: "We should not, in the glow of this symbolic step, forget the two crucial questions . . . First, how are we going to end the fighting and the killing in Indochina at the earliest possible moment? And, second, how are we going to stop the arms race before it gets completely out of control?" While commending the President's move, Rep. Paul N. McCloskey Jr. (R, Calif.) noted that the announcement "in itself does not mean that we are any closer to getting out of Vietnam."

Sen. Jacob K. Javits (R, N.Y.) said July 19 that Nixon would not have planned the visit to China unless the two powers "were already on the way to agreement" on major issues. Javits also declared that he hoped Nationalist China would be given a U.N. General Assembly seat [see below] if Communist China took the Chinese seat in the Security Council. Expressing approval of Nixon's move, Sen. Edward M. Kennedy (D, Mass.) remarked: "Rarely, I think, has the action of any President so captured the imagination and support of the American people as President Nixon's magnificent gesture last week of the improvement in our relations with China."

Strong opposition to the move was voiced July 16 by Sen. James L. Buckley (R, N.Y.), who said he was "deeply concerned" over its possible results. Buckley added: "At home it will inevitably strengthen the hand of those seeking accommodation with the Communist world at almost any price" and in Asia "the grand scale of this overture to Peking will be anything but reassuring to those who have to live with the aggressive reality of mainland China." Sen. John G. Tower (R, Tex.) said he was "disturbed by the scheduled visit, which he said might be a result of "our steadily diminishing capability to cope with Soviet expansionism and . . . military might." Rep. John Schmitz (R, Cal.), who represented the President's home Congressional district, charged that Nixon was "surrendering to international communism."

Vietnamese, other foreign reaction. The response of other nations to President Nixon's announcement ranged from positive acclaim to sharp criticism in a few instances.

Mrs. Nguyen Thi Binh, chief Viet Cong delegate to the Paris peace talks, July 16 voiced confidence that China would not reach an Indochina agreement with President Nixon behind the backs of the Viet Cong leadership. She said "this would be inconceivable" in view

of China's support of "our struggle for independence."

A Viet Cong broadcast July 20 warned Nixon against attempting to impose an Indochina solution on the Vietnamese people with the aid of other nations. The statement said "Nixon should remember that the source of all his problems and misfortunes was and is in Vietnam and Indochina" and that he should deal directly with the Vietnamese people.

South Vietnamese Vice President Nguyen Cao Ky predicted July 18 that Nixon's move would bring about an early settlement of the Indochina war. Ky said he believed China would pressure North Vietnam to agree to a peaceful solution and already may have done so. President Nguyen Van Thieu said "I just nourish the hope" that Nixon's decision would lead to peace.

Japanese Premier Eisaku Sato July 17 said he trusted that Nixon's meeting with Peking's leadership would help improve relations between Japan and China.

The Soviet government newspaper Izvestia published a terse report on the Peking invitation July 16 without comment. Western diplomats in Moscow said Soviet officials had reacted with stunned surprise to the news.

Elsewhere in Eastern Europe comment varied. The Bulgarian state radio July 16 condemned Washington's action, charging that Nixon "does not view relations with the Chinese People's Republic as an instrument of peace and understanding between nations but rather as a means to keep disunited the anti-imperialist forces and the national liberation movement."

The Polish press foresaw a radical change in international relations resulting from a U.S.-Chinese rapprochement. One newspaper, Express Wieczorny, said July 16 that "Peking's shocking turn-about is not surprising at all."

Belgrade radio said July 16 that Nixon's "arrival in Peking will cause more thinking among the Chinese than among the American public, since the latter is accustomed to various political and diplomatic turns."

The Hungarian newspaper Esti Hirlap July 16 characterized Nixon's decision to establish contacts with Communist China as "baseball diplomacy." The journal said "it is hardly an accident that the Nixon trip is scheduled to take place five to six months before the Presidential election."

All Western European governments, including those of France, Britain and West Germany, July 16 welcomed Nixon's decision to visit China.

Congress specifies pullout date. The Senate, by a 57–38 vote Sept. 30, approved a policy declaration calling for total withdrawal of U.S. military forces from Indochina within six months conditional only on an agreement for release of all U.S. prisoners of war. The declaration, in the form of an amendment, was attached to a $21 billion defense procurement authorization. The House approved the measure in modified form Nov. 10, and the Senate gave final approval by 65–19 vote Nov. 11.

President Nixon said Nov. 17 that he would disregard the declaration. The amendment had no "binding force or effect," he declared. It "does not represent the policies of this Administration," and he had no intention of changing his policies, he asserted.

The amendment was introduced into the debate Sept. 27 by Senate Democratic Leader Mike Mansfield (Mont.), who had previously been successful in attaching a similar amendment to the draft bill. This had caused a delay in final passage of that bill before both houses accepted a weakened form of the rider devised by a House-Senate conference.

A Presidential statement deploring attachment of the Mansfield rider to the defense bill came Oct. 1 from White House Press Secretary Ronald L. Ziegler, who said, "It is our feeling that the Congress should not impose a fixed date on the President." Such an imposition, he said, "would lessen the opportunity for a negotiated settlement" of the war.

Laos aid ceiling approved—The Senate also approved as an amendment to the procurement bill a $350 million ceiling on the amount of military and economic aid to Laos. The amendment was proposed Oct. 4 by Sen. Stuart Symington (D, Mo.), who had brought out in hearings that the U.S. was supporting through the Central Intelligence Agency the Laotian government military effort against the Communists.

House sidesteps Viet pullout vote. A direct House vote on the Senate end-the-war amendment was averted by Republicans Oct. 19, who won a procedural vote dealing with the issue by a 215–192 vote.

Rep. Charles W. Whalen Jr. (R, Ohio) had been prepared to offer a motion to instruct the House conferees to accept the amendment.

But House Republican Leader Gerald R. Ford (Mich.) sought and obtained recognition for an instruction motion from Rep. Leslie C. Arends (Ill.), senior Republican on the Armed Services Committee. Arends' motion was to have the House conferees refuse to accept eight Senate amendments as non-germane to the bill and thus in violation of House procedure. This would cover the Mansfield amendment plus another controversial amendment, considered to have influenced some votes, to permit purchase of chrome from Rhodesia despite the United Nations embargo. Arends' proposal also brought in the issue of House prerogatives concerning Senate revision of House legislation.

An attempt to open Arends' motion to amendment and thus permit Whalen to offer his motion, was rejected 215–192. The 23-vote margin of defeat for the peace forces was considered a high-water mark, the biggest vote yet on the war issue in the House.

The later House vote, again by a 215–192 count, to reject Arends' motion was more difficult to interpret, involving as it did, the other issues.

The first vote in support of the Administration position drew a White House comment that President Nixon was "gratified" by this "vote of confidence in his initiatives for peace through negotiations."

An end-the-war move was defeated in the House again Nov. 17 in the rejection by 238–164 vote of a proposal to bar the use of funds from the $71 billion defense procurement appropriation for combat operations in Indochina after June 1, 1972. The House Nov. 17, by 211–183 vote, also rejected a proposal to prohibit the President from sending troops into combat for more than 60 days without

Congressional approval. An attempt to enact an end-the-war amendment in the Senate the following week did not get far enough for a vote.

Laird visits Vietnam. U.S. Defense Secretary Melvin R. Laird visited South Vietnam Nov. 3–6 to review American involvement in that country.

Before departing Saigon Nov. 6, Laird described the Vietnamization program as a "military success" and said the Communists were no longer capable of staging major countrywide operations. He made clear that although the U.S. force in Vietnam would be reduced considerably, a residual force would have to stay to protect U.S. airmen, gunners and supply personnel who would remain in a supportive capacity.

Laird had met with President Nguyen Van Thieu and other top South Vietnamese officials, Ambassador Ellsworth Bunker and Gen. Creighton Abrams, head of American forces in Vietnam. Laird said discussions largely focused on the economic situation in view of the U.S. Senate's action in killing the foreign aid bill. "We have helped the people of Vietnam to thwart Communist aggression," Laird said. "We need to help them further gain economic strength."

Laird repeated his praise for the Vietnamization program on returning to Washington Nov. 8. He said the South Vietnamese may not win every battle "but they are in a position where they are strong militarily and they can handle the military situation to an extent that I did not think was possible when this program started." The process of withdrawing American troops from Vietnam and turning the conduct of the war over to Saigon's soldiers was "on schedule or ahead of schedule in all respects," the secretary said.

Senate revises foreign aid program. The Senate approved, by a 61–23 vote Nov. 10, a bill to authorize $1.14 billion in foreign economic and humanitarian assistance. A companion bill, to authorize $1.185 billion in foreign military aid for fiscal 1972, was pending.

The two-bill aid package had been devised by the Senate Foreign Relations Committee following the surprise defeat of a $2.9 billion foreign aid authorization bill in the Senate Oct. 29. The two bills authorized $1.2 billion less than the Administration request. White House Press Secretary Ronald L. Ziegler said Nov. 4 that the revised total was considered "insufficient" by President Nixon.

The committee bills also included policy provisions to limit Central Intelligence Agency operations in Cambodia and put a $341 million ceiling on aid to Cambodia; to bar use of funds for mercenaries fighting in North Vietnam, Thailand or Laos; and to end the war in six months, the amendment proposed by Senate Democratic Leader Mike Mansfield (Mont.).

The Nixon Administration, which had firmly opposed the restrictive policy amendments, softened its stand somewhat Nov. 3 when Secretary of State William P. Rogers indicated to the Foreign Relations Committee that the ceiling on Cambodia aid could be acceptable. But he and Dr. John A. Hannah, administrator of the Agency for International Development (AID), appearing at a closed session, maintained the Administration's insistence on getting a resolution to continue the aid program at the funding level requested by the President. A State Department spokesman Nov. 5 cautioned that the committee's aid bills would seriously impair South Vietnam's economy and Cambodia's defense posture.

In presenting the committee's bills to the Senate Nov. 9, Chairman J. W. Fulbright (D, Ark.) called defeat of the earlier version "a salutary development" because it "should lead to a more rational foreign aid policy and a more realistic view of America's role in the world." The foreign aid program, he said, had become "a grab bag for everybody but the American people, who pay the bills."

A compromise stop-gap foreign aid bill from which the Mansfield amendment had been eliminated was passed by both houses Dec. 17.

Further U.S. troop cut announced. President Nixon announced Nov. 12 that 45,000 more U.S. troops would be withdrawn from South Vietnam by Feb. 1— 25,000 in December and 20,000 in January. The reduction in the authorized troop-level ceiling to a force of 139,000 men was announced during an unscheduled Presidential appearance at a regular White House news briefing. It was the first withdrawal announcement not made in a televised national address.

As for future withdrawals, the next announcement would be made before Feb. 1, 1972, Nixon said, and would be based on (1) the level of enemy activity, particularly the infiltration rate, (2) progress of the Vietnamization program and (3) progress "that may have been made" on gaining release of U.S. prisoners of war (POWs) and obtaining a cease-fire "for all of Southeast Asia."

The President cautioned that a substantial increase in enemy infiltration activity "could be very dangerous to our sharply decreased forces in South Vietnam." As U.S. forces were reduced, he said, "it is particularly important for us to continue our air strikes on the infiltration routes" and a "substantial stepup" in infiltration would cause the U.S. to step up its air strike activity.

Nixon pointed out that U.S. casualties had been reduced to less than 10 a week over the past five weeks, that 80% of the U.S. troops in Vietnam when he entered office had come home and that the remaining U.S. troops were "now in a defensive position," their offensive situation having been "concluded."

Reminded of his 1968 campaign promise to end the war, the President suggested he "be judged at the time of the campaign, rather than now" and that "every promise that I have made I have kept to this date and that usually is a pretty good example of what you might do with regard to future promises."

If negotiated settlement were attained, he said, it would mean a total U.S. withdrawal from Southeast Asia, including the Asian theater supporting the Vietnam effort, and an end to the air strikes. "If we do not get a negotiated settlement," Nixon continued, "then it is necessary to maintain a residual force" in order to maintain a negotiating position and to work toward a South Vietnam capable of defending itself.

"We have not given up on the negotiating track," he said, "and we are going to continue to press on that track because that is the track on which we eventually

are going to have success in getting our prisoners back." But Nixon stressed that he "would not like to leave the impression that we see the possibility of some striking breakthrough in negotiations in the near future." He reported that "we have not ... had any progress in our talks with the North Vietnamese in getting them to separate that issue [release of U.S. POWs] from the rest [of the issues]." The President said he had "no reason for encouragement that I can talk about publicly" concerning release of the POWs. The U.S. was pursuing the subject in a number of channels, he said, and had not and would never give up with regard to the prisoners.

In regard to his forthcoming trips to Peking and Moscow in relation to ending the war, Nixon said the U.S. would "welcome any assistance" but was "not counting on it from either source." "We will find our own way to bring it to a halt," he said.

In response to a query, the President did not foresee granting amnesty to young men who fled the country to avoid fighting in Vietnam.

Saigon concurs—President Nixon said the latest withdrawal plan had the "complete approval" of South Vietnamese President Nguyen Van Thieu. An official announcement from Saigon Nov. 13 said the new pullouts were being carried out under the Vietnamization program and "in consideration of the improved general security situation now prevailing in Vietnam."

(The U.S. force in Vietnam had dropped during the week of Oct. 31–Nov. 6 to 191,000 men, the lowest level since the 184,300 of December 1965. The number of men withdrawn the previous week was 5,600. The U.S. draft callup, declining as a result of the pullout and a new Army strength ceiling of 892,000 men, declined in 1971 to a total of 98,000 draftees, the lowest figure in almost a decade.)

Cambodia a case of Nixon Doctrine—In response to another question—whether the U.S. was "not sliding into another Vietnam in Cambodia" —Nixon said: "We will aid Cambodia," and "Cambodia is the Nixon Doctrine in its purest form" because "what we are doing is

helping the Cambodians to help themselves . . . rather than to go in and do the
fighting ourselves."

"We have made a conscious decision,"
he said, "not to send American troops
in. There are no American combat troops
in Cambodia. There are no American
combat advisers in Cambodia. There will
be no American combat troops or advisers in Cambodia."

The Pentagon Papers

Secret study of U.S. role in Vietnam. The New York Times June 13 began publishing a series of articles and documents based on a secret Pentagon study made during the Johnson Administration of the policy decisions drawing the U.S. into military involvement in the Vietnam war. The series was suspended June 15, after the third daily installment, in compliance with a temporary court order obtained by the Justice Department to bar publication of the material, which bore a "top secret" classification. The material published concerned 1964–65 policy decisions in the Tonkin Gulf incident, initiation of the air war against North Vietnam and commitment of U.S. ground combat troops to the war.

The "Pentagon papers" traced increasing U.S. involvement in the Vietnam war during the period ending in 1968. The study made such disclosures as Johnson Administration plans for major American military action against North Vietnam almost five months before the 1964 Tonkin Gulf incident, a covert commitment of U.S. ground combat troops to the war and an anxiety lest the escalation become publicized.

The Times printed three installments of the series June 13–15 covering 18 pages of newsprint with documents and analysis drawn from the Pentagon study. The study itself consisted of 3,000 pages of analysis and 4,000 pages of official documents on the policy decisions which led to U.S. involvement in the war. The Pentagon papers did not include Presidential papers and included only those State Department documents that turned up in the Defense Department files.

Commissioned by then-Defense Secretary Robert S. McNamara, the study was held confidential—only 15 copies reportedly were produced initially when it was written in 1968—and eventually committed by McNamara to the federal archives. The Times came into possession of 39 of its 40 book-length volumes.

Nixon Administration reaction—The Nixon Administration took the position on the Times articles that they involved unauthorized release of classified defense material. White House Press Secretary Ronald L. Ziegler pointed out June 14 that President Nixon had developed a "new Vietnam policy" and had decided upon assuming office in 1968 "not to engage . . . in a continuation or justification" of earlier policies. Questions about disclosure of the material were referred to the Defense Department.

The Pentagon issued a statement June 14 citing its concern about "the disclosure of publication of highly classified information affecting national security" and saying it had called "this violation of security" to the attention of the Justice Department. The material, it said, "remains classified and sensitive" despite its coverage of a period ending in 1968 and the government had "the responsibility to determine what individual or individuals, if any, violated the laws relating to national security information by unauthorized disclosure of classified material."

Earlier June 14, Defense Secretary Melvin R. Laird, appearing at a Senate hearing on foreign aid, called the disclosure of the Pentagon material "unauthorized" and a violation of security regulations. He opposed Sen. Stuart Symington's (D, Mo.) intention to seek a "full examination of the origins of the war" with the objection that it "would not serve the interests of the country and would not help us disengage from Vietnam." Laird said the documents would remain classified and would not be made available to the Senate panel, although Symington found it "shocking" that Congress had been uninformed about the material.

(Symington had expressed surprise June 13 at the "startling" information in the documents published by the Times of the U.S. role in Laos "well before any acceleration in Vietnam.")

Following the hearing, Symington put in the record letters in which Laird had refused a November 1969 request from Sen. J. W. Fulbright (D, Ark.) for the McNamara report to be made available to his Foreign Relations Committee.

Later June 14, Assistant Attorney General Robert C. Mardian, head of the internal security division, telephoned the Times to request that publication of the series be halted. He said court action would follow lack of compliance. The call came about two hours before press time for the edition scheduled to carry the third installment of the Vietnam series. An hour before press time, the Times received a telegram from Attorney General John N. Mitchell asking it to refrain from publishing any "further information of this character" on the ground it would "cause irreparable injury to the defense interests" of the U.S. Mitchell requested return of the documents to the Defense Department. The information, he said, related to national defense and "bears a top secret classification" and "as such," publication was

"directly prohibited by the provisions of the Espionage Law."

The Times refused. "It is in the interest of the people of this country to be informed of the material contained in this series of articles," it replied. The newspaper said it would oppose a U.S. court action but would "abide by the final decision of the court."

News curb debated—The Justice Department filed a civil suit June 15 to seek permanent enjoinment against publication of the articles. At a hearing before U.S. District Judge Murray I. Gurfein in New York that day, U.S. Attorney Michael D. Hess contended that the newspaper had violated a statute making it a crime for persons having "unauthorized possession" of federal documents to disclose their contents in a way that "could be used to the injury of the United States or to the advantage of any foreign nation." He cited a reference by Secretary of State William P. Rogers to concern over the disclosures expressed by several friendly nations. If the government was facing "irreparable injury" in its international relations, he said, it was not unreasonable to order a "slight delay" in the Times' publication schedule until the case could be further resolved.

At a news conference that day, Rogers had said the material had elicited diplomatic inquiries from foreign governments and could cause "a great deal of difficulty." "If governments can't deal with us in any degree of confidentiality," he said, "it's going to be a very serious matter."

The Times' attorney, Alexander M. Bickel, a Yale University professor, told Gurfein June 15 the issue involved was a "classic case of censorship" that was forbidden by the First Amendment's guarantee of a free press. He said court action to bar publication of an article was unprecedented in the U.S. and that the government's case, in any event, was based on an anti-espionage law never intended by Congress to be used against the press. "A newspaper exists to publish, not to submit its publishing schedule to the United States government," Bickel argued.

Gurfein urged the Times to consent to halt publication of the articles, but the Times, holding that this would be a precedent for federal action to curb news publications, refused.

Court hearings set—Gurfein agreed with the U.S. position that the temporary harm done to the Times would be "far outweighed by the irreparable harm that could be done" to the interests of the U.S. He ordered the Times June 15 to halt publication of the articles for four days, and he set a hearing for June 18 on the issue of continuing the ban. He declined at that time to order the Times to return the Pentagon material.

But Gurfein June 16 set another hearing on the Justice Department's request for an order to have the Times relinquish its Pentagon papers for government inspection, a procedure it held "important" to presentation of its case.

Public Senate hearings announced. Senate Democratic Leader Mike Mansfield (Mont.) said June 15 a Senate committee would hold public hearings on how the U.S. became involved in the war. The purpose would not be to find "scapegoats" concerning publication by the Times of the classified material, Mansfield said, but to "lay out the whole story" in the hope it would lead to closer cooperation between Congress and the Executive branch on foreign policy and thus "prevent future Vietnams." Mansfield intended not to restrict the probe to past Administrations but to provide a forum for examination of current policies and for Congressional advice to the President on how to end the war.

The Times articles, he said, had "surprised, shocked and astounded" him primarily because of the indication that crucial decisions to escalate the Vietnam war apparently had been made by the Johnson Administration without informing Congress. Mansfield expressed himself as "delighted" that the Times had been publishing the series.

Senate Republican Leader Hugh Scott (Pa.), while terming release of the Pentagon material "a bad thing, . . . a federal crime," viewed the articles June 14 as being "very instructive and somewhat shocking." He said the public had "never been told as much as they could digest about the war until President Nixon assumed office."

There was little immediate Congressional comment on the Times' articles. Sen. George S. McGovern (D, S.D.) said June 14 the series revealed an "almost incredible deception" of Congress and the public by the highest officials in government, including the President. McGovern cautioned that it would be a mistake to assume such deception "began and ended with the Johnson Administration" and was of the opinion that it would no longer be tenable for any senator to permit the Executive branch to make foreign policy alone. McGovern June 16 denounced the Justice Department effort to "harry the New York Times" and shut off "a free flow of vital information to the public."

Rep. Paul N. McCloskey Jr. (R, Calif.) commented June 14 that "the issue of truthfulness in government is a problem as serious as that of ending the war itself."

Sen. Gaylord P. Nelson (D, Wis.) asserted June 15 the documents "clearly show that those who made the decisions to deepen our involvement in the war in Vietnam were not only deluding the American public but deluding themselves as well." He did not consider release of the material a danger to national security. While the documents contained information "embarrassing to the political and military leadership of the country," he said, that was "no reason to deny the public information it is clearly entitled to have."

Congressional reaction builds. Reaction to the Times' articles and the U.S. action to curb them began building among members of Congress by June 16. Letters were sent by 62 representatives, most of them liberal Democrats, to the Defense and Justice Departments requesting the secret papers be made available to Congress and protesting "harassment" of the Times. The move was initiated by Rep. Jonathan B. Bingham (D, N.Y.).

Hearings on the government's classification procedures were announced by a House Government Operations subcommittee headed by Rep. William S. Moorhead (D, Pa.), who said the classification of the Pentagon papers involved in the dispute "was done not so much to save the security of the United States but to save some red faces."

Fulbright and McCloskey June 16 requested from the Times copies of unpublished material in the projected series, which the Times refused. Fulbright, traveling in England at the time, said in London the articles confirmed a "deliberate and flagrant deception" by the Johnson Administration that had done "serious injury" to the roles of Congress and the public in dealing with the issues of war and peace.

Sen. John G. Tower (R, Tex.) described the Times' articles June 16 as "particularly interesting" but questioned the propriety of publishing the information.

Comments by principals. Although a spokesman in Texas for former President Johnson, and former Secretary of State Dean Rusk in Atlanta June 15 refused comment on the Pentagon study, other major principals had these reactions:

Asked whether he believed the Johnson Administration had lied to the American people about further involvement in the Vietnam War, Sen. Barry Goldwater (Ariz.), Republican presidential candidate in 1964, replied, "I would have to say yes. It was too bad that the President would not level with the American people. It would have been better for the American people to have known about it." Goldwater made his comments in a television interview June 14. Goldwater said he had concluded one month before the Gulf of Tonkin incident that President Johnson planned to widen the war. Recalling his campaign, he said: "I was being called trigger-happy, war-monger, bomb-happy, and all the time Johnson was saying he'd never send American boys, I knew damn well he would."

Robert S. McNamara, former secretary of defense who had commissioned the Pentagon study in 1967, said he would not comment publicly because of his current position as president of the International Bank for Reconstruction and Development (the World Bank).

President Johnson's vice president, now Sen. Hubert H. Humphrey (D, Minn.), said the "real tragedy" of the New York Times articles was the doubt cast on the government's credibility. Commenting in Grand Rapids, Mich.

June 15, he said he was "shocked and surprised" by the information in the study, which he said had never been brought to his attention.

W. Averell Harriman, President Johnson's delegate to the Paris peace talks and a war critic, said June 16 that the public had been "misled by the publication of a lot of miscellaneous documents."

Another major figure and war opponent in the study, former Undersecretary of State George W. Ball was reached for comment June 16 in Salamanca, Spain where he was vacationing.

Ball said he had not yet read those parts of the study concerning his views and actions, but did recall: "I had special views on the subject [the war]. The view I consistently expressed was that Vietnam was a very poor place to commit American power, both from the political point of view and from the physical point of view, because of the terrain. I thought we should cut our losses before the point came where we could only get out with great breakage." Describing himself as a dissenter to the war, Ball stressed that President Johnson "rather than resenting my arguments, was grateful. He wanted me to speak my mind and thanked me a number of times for my disagreeing with him."

Gen. Maxwell D. Taylor, U.S. ambassador to South Vietnam in 1964–1965, accused The Times of having initiated "a practice of betrayal of government secrets." Interviewed by CBS June 16, Taylor said he did not believe in "the people's right to know" as a "general principle." He said: "You have to talk about cases. What is a citizen going to do after reading these documents that he wouldn't have done otherwise? A citizen should know those things he needs to know to be a good citizen and discharge his functions, but not to get into secrets that damage his government and indirectly damage the citizen himself."

Gen. Nguyen Khanh, leader of the South Vietnam government and commander of its armed forces in 1964, interviewed in Paris June 16, spoke of his conflict with Taylor during his regime when Taylor was U.S. ambassador in South Vietnam. Khanh described Taylor as the instigator in the South Vietnamese leader's ouster and exile from South Vietnam in February 1965. Khanh attributed the conflict to his opposition to the "Americanization" of the war and his desire for a political settlement among the opposing Vietnamese forces. Khanh said the National Liberation Front (Viet Cong) had been prepared to talk of a settlement "and still is." Another factor was his support of the Young Turks' dissolution of the legislative High National Council: "The council had gone beyond its attributions. How can one talk of a military coup when it was the army that had named the council in the first place?" Unhappy about references in the Pentagon study to intrigues by him and other generals, Khanh conceded instability during his regime but cited as a contributing factor confusion over the center of U.S. decision-making—CIA, Washington or Saigon officials.

Johnson reaction reported. Newsweek magazine reported June 21 that former President Johnson believed that the Pentagon papers presented a dishonest, distorted and biased picture of his role. In its June 28 edition, Newsweek reported "those in Austin [Tex.] privy to his feelings" said Johnson linked Robert Kennedy to the Pentagon study. They said Johnson considered McNamara, who ordered the study, a Kennedy man and that Kennedy was depending upon the Vietnam issue in his 1968 presidential campaign.

Time magazine, dated June 28, said Johnson was eager to "defend himself" against the contents of the Pentagon papers. Time did not reveal its sources but said Johnson believed the study was distorted because the documents included were mainly contingency plans, some not even known to himself or to Dean Rusk, his secretary of state.

The point that some of the documents in the Pentagon papers were merely contingency plans was also made by Roger Hilsman, assistant secretary of state in the Kennedy Administration, who figured prominently in the Chicago Sun-Times June 23 account of the 1963 coup against President Ngo Dinh Diem of South Vietnam. At a June 23 news conference, Hilsman, currently a Columbia University professor, acknowledged that

the Kennedy Administration was aware of the plotting against Diem and that "publicly our actions and statements encouraged the coup." Hilsman added that he approved the publication of the Pentagon papers because the nation's security was not involved in the disclosure of data about events that "are over."

Publication & printing bans spread. By June 18 other newspapers began to publish articles based on the Pentagon papers. Like the New York Times, these newspapers also were constrained to halt publication under court orders obtained by the Justice Department. The restraints against publication of the material, despite several decisions upholding the newspapers' right to publish it, were extended by the various courts pending appeals, which were expected to reach the Supreme Court.

The first of these other newspapers was the Washington Post. The Post June 18 began publishing a series of articles based on the same classified Pentagon papers. The Justice Department sought and obtained a court order stopping the series after its second installment the next day, although the Post article was distributed by the Washington Post-Los Angeles Times News Service to its 345 clients and was described in accounts carried by the New York Times, which was barred from carrying its own series, the Associated Press and United Press International, which were available to almost all the daily newspapers in the country, and by radio and television newscasters.

Publication of material, then barred in the Times and Post, spread June 22 to the Boston Globe, which published four and a half pages of material drawn from the study. A Justice Department suit to bar further articles was immediately filed with U.S. District Judge Anthony Julian, who issued a temporary restraining order later June 22 against further publication of such articles because of the possibility of "immediate and irreparable injury" to U.S. security. The judge, in a step not taken by the courts in New York and Washington, also ordered the documents or material from which the article was drawn impounded. He revised this requirement June 23 to permit the documents to be placed by the Globe in a bank safe deposit vault with restricted access. (The Justice Department suit against the Globe was dismissed Sept. 8.)

Publication of the material continued to spread. The Chicago Sun-Times June 23 published material it said it had received from "sources involving the Pentagon study," and the Knight newspaper group published in eight of its 11 newspapers June 23 stories claimed to be drawn from the controversial Pentagon study. The Justice Department made inquiry to the Sun-Times about its material but took no immediate action to bar further publication on a preliminary finding that the base documents had been declassified in 1968.

The St. Louis Post-Dispatch published material June 25 it said was based on the Pentagon report, and U.S. District Judge James H. Meredith, after the newspaper refused to halt publication voluntarily, issued a restraining order June 26 at the request of the Justice Department.

The Christian Science Monitor published June 29 what it said were excerpts from the Pentagon papers. The U.S. Attorney for the District of Massachusetts, Herbert F. Travers Jr., telephoned the Monitor, asked that two more planned articles not be published and was refused. The Justice Department announced later June 29 it would not seek to enjoin the future articles since the material did not include any "designated by the United States as potentially injurious to the national defense."

Monitor editor Erwin D. Canham said he had informed Travers that the future material consisted of an "analytical piece" on Ho Chi Minh, dating from the 1940s, and U.S. relations in the Far East in the mid-40s.

The Justice Department announced June 24 that no legal action would be taken "at this time" against the Los Angeles Times or Knight newspapers which published articles that day on the Pentagon papers. The articles had been reviewed and the decision made that the contents did not constitute a security threat.

The court action against the New York Times and Washington Post, meanwhile, continued. These were among. the developments:

New York Times—The Justice Department sought the surrender of the Pentagon papers by the newspaper for examination, contending it could not support its case that the national interest would be harmed by publication unless it knew what the newspaper planned to publish. The Times contended the government had copies of the material and inspection of the Times' material, much of it copied, could compromise its confidential source by facilitating identification of that source.

Judge Murray Gurfein ruled against a federal "fishing expedition into the files of any newspaper" June 17 and suggested the Times give the court and the Justice Department a list of descriptive headings of the documents in its possession. The Times complied.

Three Washington officials traveled to New York June 18 to present testimony to the court in secret. During the day Gurfein suggested the Times "ought to be willing to sit down" with the Justice Department and "as a matter of simple patriotism" determine whether publication of any of the classified documents "is or is not dangerous to the national security." But the Times attorney resisted with the point this would lead to self-censorship by the press or government censorship.

Gurfein June 19 denied an injunction against the Times series but extended the restraining order against publication pending appeal. While publication might cause "some embarrassment to the government in security aspects," Gurfein held, security "also lies in the value of our free institutions," such as the. free press. He found "no cogent reasons" advanced, aside from the overall embarrassment aspect, that public knowledge of the material would be a vital security breach.

Gurfein also rejected a contention that the case constituted a violation of espionage laws barring transmission of secret data with intent to harm the country. The Times' effort, he said, had been "in good faith" and for "the right of the public to know."

The restraining order against the Times was continued later June 19 by Judge Irving R. Kaufman to permit consideration of the issue by a three-judge panel of his 2nd Circuit Court of Appeals.

Further extension of the restraining order was effected June 21 by the three-judge panel, because of the "extraordinary importance" of the issue, to carry the case before the entire eight-member court. In a brief presented by U.S. Attorney Whitney N. Seymour Jr., the government contended that "national defense documents, properly classified by the Executive, are an exception to an absolute freedom of the press and should be protected by the courts against unauthorized disclosure." Seymour also submitted a sealed list of items in the Pentagon papers the government claimed would be security impairments if disclosed.

The appeals court issued a 5–3 decision June 23 that the Times could resume publication of the series after June 25 but could not use any material that the government held vital to national security. The court instructed Gurfein to hold secret hearings to determine what parts of the Pentagon papers posed "such grave and immediate danger" to U.S. security as to warrant enjoinment of publication.

Washington Post—As in the case of the Times, the Justice Department sought court restraint after the Post refused June 18 to voluntarily halt such publication.

U.S. District Judge Gerhard A. Gesell in Washington refused June 18 to sanction prior restraint of the articles with the observation "the court has before it no precise information suggesting in what respects, if any, the publication of this information will injure" the country. The proper recourse of the government in case of a security violation would be a criminal suit, he said.

Gesell regretted that the Post had refused his request for a delay in publishing the material to further weigh the issues involved. The Post's position, presented by its attorney, Roger A. Clark, was that the court would be "treading on dangerous ground if it tries to determine what is news."

Gesell's ruling was reversed June 19 by the U.S. Court of Appeals for the District of Columbia, which held in a 2–1 decision that the articles should be barred, pending a full hearing, and that

"freedom of the press, as important as it is, is not boundless." The majority claimed precedent for the government's position that prior restraint on publication might be appropriate in a case involving national security.

The dissenter was Judge J. Skelly Wright, who said "to allow a government to suppress free speech simply through a system of bureaucratic classification would sell our heritage far, far too cheaply."

After further hearings, some parts of which were secret at the government's request, much the same scenario was repeated. Gesell June 21 upheld the Post against prior restraint, permitting resumption of the articles, but the appellate court later June 21 continued the press curb and ordered a hearing before the full nine-man court. In rejecting the government's argument that "an immediate grave threat to the national security" was involved, Gesell noted his opposition to adjustment of the free-press guarantee to views of protesting foreign governments.

Hearings before the full appeals court, including secret sessions, were held June 22–23. U.S. Solicitor General Erwin N. Griswold entered the case for the first time June 22 and announced he had been authorized by the secretaries of state and defense and the military chiefs of staff to offer the solution of a "joint task force" to examine the documents involved for possible declassification within 45 days. The Post opposed such procedure with the view it would constitute "government by handout." In his presentation, Griswold stressed the gravity of the issue, which involved, he said, "the integrity of the institution of the presidency" itself.

The Appeals Court June 23 rejected the government's case that continued publication of the material would jeopardize security and upheld the Post's constitutional right to publish the articles. However, it continued the curb against the series to permit appeal.

In its ruling, concurred in by seven of the nine judges, the court referred to the Supreme Court's establishment of the "vitality of the principle that any prior restraint on publication comes into court under a heavy presumption against its constitutional validity." The appellate court said its rejection of the government's case was "fortified" by consideration of "the massive character of the 'leak' which has occurred," a reference to the number of newspapers carrying the material. This raised "substantial doubt," it said, "that effective relief of the kind sought by the government can be provided by the judiciary."

Ellsberg identified as source. Daniel Ellsberg, 40, a senior research associate at the Massachusetts Institute of Technology, was widely identified as the New York Times' source for the Pentagon documents. He disappeared from his home June 16 but, in a TV interview June 23, made his first public statement on the matter. Ellsberg was interviewed by Walter Cronkite of Columbia Broadcasting System at a secret location.

Ellsberg did not mention his suggested role in the release of the documents. Cronkite indicated that Ellsberg's delicate legal position prevented him from speaking directly on the subject.

Ellsberg, who had drafted a section of the controversial study, said one reason for the documents to be made public at this time was the possibility that "we were in for a replay of the year 1964."

Ellsberg laid the full responsibility for the war in Vietnam on the U.S., which had supplied the necessary supplies and money. He said he was disturbed by indications in the report that U.S. leaders never considered the effect of their policies on the Vietnamese in terms of overall casualties, refugees or the effects of defoliation.

Ellsberg had been named as the Times' source by Sidney Zion, a former Times reporter, on a WMCA radio program in New York June 16, and the next day in an article from the Washington bureau of the St. Louis-Post Dispatch.

Ellsberg reportedly was the principal object of an FBI investigation begun June 14 seeking the source which gave the Times the secret study. Two FBI agents had sought out Ellsberg at his home in Cambridge, Mass. June 17 after he had dropped out of sight. Justice Department officials stressed there was no warrant for his arrest.

The search for Ellsberg also led FBI agents June 22 to the office of Rep. Paul N. McCloskey (R, Calif.), a prominent war critic, who had disclosed June 17 that Ellsberg had given him a month ago copies of documents dealing with the U.S. involvement in the war. McCloskey said he could not determine whether his copy was part of the Times' series. He said the agents had asked him about his conversations with Ellsberg, which he declined to reveal.

In Los Angeles June 23, a federal grand jury, also conducting an investigation into how the documents reached the Times, subpoenaed as a witness a close friend of Ellsberg who had been associated with him at the Rand Corp. in Santa Monica, Calif. The witness, Anthony J. Russo, an economist and engineer no longer employed at Rand, refused to testify. (After several unsuccessful appeals against contempt charges, Russo was jailed Aug. 16 and not freed until Oct. 1 after he had agreed to testify.)

Ellsberg indicted, admits giving papers. Ellsberg surrendered to the U.S. attorney in Boston June 28 after admitting that he had leaked the documents.

After his arrest and arraignment on charges of unauthorized possession of secret documents, Ellsberg was released on $50,000 bail.

Later in the day, a Los Angeles federal grand jury indicted Ellsberg on two counts, violation of the Espionage Act and theft of government property. (He pleaded not guilty Aug. 16.)

Before surrendering at 10 a.m. as his lawyers had promised June 26, Ellsberg told newsmen that he had given the information contained in the documents to Sen. J. W. Fulbright (D, Ark.), chairman of the Senate Foreign Relations Committee. Ellsberg, accompanied by his wife Patricia, said his only regret was that he had not acted sooner in releasing the information to the press. He added: "I did this clearly at my own jeopardy and I am prepared to answer to all the consequences of these decisions. That includes the personal consequences to me and my family, whatever these may be." Interviewed later in the day at his home in Cambridge, Mass., Ellsberg refused to divulge whether he was the Times' source for the documents because of litigation in process before the Supreme Court. He also said he would not have released the documents if he had thought a single page "would do grave damage to the national interests."

On the advice of his lawyers, Ellsberg had eluded an intensive search by the Federal Bureau of Investigation after a warrant for his arrest was issued in Los Angeles late June 25. The warrant charged Ellsberg specifically with possession and failure to return the secret papers, under Title 18, Section 793E, of the U.S. Code. He was not charged with transmitting the documents to anyone else. The indictment June 28 briefly noted that Ellsberg in September and October 1969 had "had access to and control over copies of certain documents and writings relating to the national defense." The period described coincided with Ellsberg's employment at Rand Corp. in Santa Monica, Calif., the research organization that had received two of the 15 original copies of the 47-volume Pentagon study.

(Lynda R. Sinay, a freelance advertising agent described as a close friend of Ellsberg, had testified before the grand jury June 24 that Ellsberg had paid her $150 to Xerox copies of certain documents, but she said she did not know their contents.)

The second count of the indictment cited Section 641 of the U.S. Code and charged that Ellsberg had "willfully, knowingly and unlawfully" retained the Pentagon study and had failed to deliver it to the proper recipient.

(Ellsberg indicated Aug. 16 that he would base his defense on the importance of the papers and on the public's right to know what they contain. He intimated that this would be the core of a political defense that would go beyond the specific crimes with which he was charged and would include a sweeping indictment of U.S. policy in Southeast Asia. Ellsberg told newsmen that "obviously, my motive for whatever I've done closely depends on a reading of the papers." According to his interpretation, Ellsberg said, the papers reveal "high crimes by officials of our government.")

Nixon to release documents to Congress. President Nixon informed Senate Majority Leader Mike Mansfield June 23 that he would release to Congress two top-secret studies it had requested. The two documents were 47 volumes of the Pentagon papers and a 1965 Defense Department study of the Gulf of Tonkin incident.

According to White House Press Secretary Ronald L. Ziegler, the President specified that he was releasing the documents, which retained their top-secret classification, with the understanding that they would not be made public until their classification had been reviewed by the executive branch.

A Presidential directive Jan. 15, which the White House declined to make public because it was an "internal paper," had instructed government agencies to review existing classification procedures. Acting on that directive, Defense Secretary Melvin R. Laird disclosed June 22 that he had ordered a review of the controversial documents to determine which could be made public.

The same day, federal lawyers made an offer before appellate courts in Washington and New York to begin an interagency review of the already published documents to determine how much could be declassified. The lawyers were contesting lower court decisions upholding the right of the New York Times and Washington Post to publish the Pentagon study.

Ziegler, reporting on the Nixon-Mansfield meeting, said Nixon was releasing the studies because "the unauthorized publication of portions of the documents created a situation in which Congress would necessarily be making judgments in the meantime on the basis of incomplete data, which could give a distorted impression of the report's contents." Nixon had stressed to Mansfield that his decision reflected special circumstances and did not represent a change of policy. He indicated he would maintain his policy of refusing direct comment on the documents' substance, since they related primarily to the Johnson and Kennedy Administrations and he could not vouch for their accuracy or completeness.

The press secretary told newsmen there was no connection between the President's decision and the 57–42 Senate vote June 22 on an amendment to the Selective

Service bill calling for withdrawal of all U.S. forces from Indochina within nine months if U.S. prisoners of war were released.

Despite Nixon's action, Reps. John E. Moss (D, Calif.) and Ogden R. Reid (R, N.Y.) said they would press a court suit filed June 23 in Washington's U.S. district court to force Laird to make all or part of the documents public under the Freedom of Information Act of 1966, for which they had been principal sponsors. Moss, a member of the Foreign Operations and Government Information subcommittee of the House Government Operations Committee, had objected that the papers released by the President were referred to the House Armed Services Committee where members could read but not copy them.

The documents released to Congress were to be held by the secretary of the Senate pending a decision on how the Senate would conduct hearings on the origins of the war.

Meanwhile, the Senate leadership moved toward creating a special joint panel composed of eight members from the Foreign Relations Committee and eight from the Armed Services Committee. The select committee was a compromise (to avoid jurisdictional disputes) worked out by Mansfield with ranking Democratic and Republican members of the Foreign Relations Committee, a leading war opponent, and Armed Services, which had generally supported Johnson and Nixon Administration policies. The committee was expected to begin hearings in the fall. The Foreign Relations Committee said it still planned its own inquiry.

Congress gets documents. Two copies of the 47-volume Pentagon study were delivered to Congress June 28 on President Nixon's order and placed in locked vaults under 24-hour guard. A letter of transmittal from Defense Secretary Melvin R. Laird warned that disclosure of the contents would pose "grave and immediate danger to the national security."

The documents were received by Rep. F. Edward Hébert (D, La.), chairman of the Armed Services Committee, for the House, and Sen. Allen J. Ellender (D, La.), president pro tem of the Senate.

Hébert said rules which he would issue to House members would bar note-taking or disclosure of the contents.

In related developments, seven members of a House Government Operations subcommittee, acting under a 1928 statute, demanded that the Pentagon give the committee copies of the study, in addition to a report on the Gulf of Tonkin incident. The subcommittee, headed by Rep. William S. Moorhead (D, Pa.), was investigating government information and secrecy policies. The 1928 law required any executive agency to submit requested information pertaining to matters within a committee's jurisdiction.

A panel of newsmen appeared before the subcommittee June 25 to defend the newspapers that had published parts of the Pentagon study and to criticize what they described as the government's excessive secrecy.

The House Armed Services Committee June 29 rejected 25–2 a resolution by Rep. Bella Abzug (D, N.Y.) that would make the study available to all House members and security-cleared staff members and permit them to take notes.

Gravel reads papers to press—Sen. Mike Gravel (D, Alaska) read aloud to newsmen for over three hours June 29 portions of the Pentagon study. The act was deplored by many Republican colleagues, but Majority Leader Mike Mansfield refused to take disciplinary action against the freshman senator.

Gravel had intended to read the documents to the Senate in an all-night speech, but the Republican leadership thwarted attempts to raise the necessary quorum. Undaunted, Gravel hastily called a meeting of the Senate Public Works subcommittee of which he was chairman. Gravel chose the hearing as a forum to gain Congressional immunity from possible prosecution.

Gravel said he had received about half of the Pentagon study June 24 from an unidentified private source.

With Rep. John G. Dow (D, N.Y.) in the witness chair, Gravel began the hearing with the explanation, "I will not accept the notion that the President of the United States can manipulate the United States Senate into silence. It is my constitutional obligation to protect the security of the people by fostering the free flow of information absolutely essential to their democratic decision-making."

Gravel said he was convinced his action was "in no way jeopardizing this nation's security." During the reading, Gravel omitted supporting papers he considered sensitive material.

The documents disclosed by Gravel contained substantial material that had already been published. Some of the contents: an analysis of de-escalation efforts covering January-December 1967 that ended in President Johnson's announcement March 31, 1968 of limited bombing and his decision not to run for another term; summaries of the period 1940-60, including a conclusion that U.S. involvement in Indochina had begun over the choice to support the colonial policies of France rather than the communism of Ho Chi Minh; illustrations of the concerted drive by the Joint Chiefs of Staff for escalation of the war and opposition to any limitation of the bombing; and evidence of former Defense Secretary Robert McNamara's growing dissent to further escalation in the period prior to the Tet offensive in February 1968.

Visibly exhausted, Gravel stopped reading at 1:12 a.m. June 30 after he had broken into tears several times during the session. He then read an impassioned speech against the war. His staff made copies of the remaining papers available to the press.

Republican senators opened the Senate June 30 with heated demands that Gravel be disciplined for violating Rule 36 prohibiting senators from disclosing confidential information emanating from the executive branch. After meeting with Senate Minority Leader Hugh Scott (R, Pa.) and Minority Whip Robert P. Griffin (R, Mich.), Majority Leader Mansfield noted Gravel's sincere convictions and said he would take no action other than to have a "friendly talk" with Gravel.

On the Senate floor July 6 Gravel defended his public reading of portions of the Pentagon papers. Gravel declared that he had publicly read them because he deemed it "in the best interests of this nation we all love." Majority Leader Mansfield, who met with Gravel June 30 to discuss the incident, said later that he would oppose any move to censure or punish him.

Restraint on press rebuffed. The Supreme Court upheld by a 6-3 decision June 30 the New York Times and the Washington Post against the government's attempt to halt their publication of material from the Pentagon papers. Federal court stays against publication of the material were vacated.

The Times and Post resumed publication of the articles with their July 1 editions. Similar material was being published by other newspapers, although only four—The Boston Globe and the St. Louis Post-Dispatch in addition to the Times and Post—had been under federal court restraint not to publish the material.

The decision—The court's decision was brief and unsigned. It quoted precedents that "any system of prior restraints of expression comes to this court bearing a heavy presumption against its constitutional validity" and that the government "thus carries a heavy burden" of showing justification for the enforcement of such a restraint." It said that the district courts in New York and Washington and the appellate court in Washington had "held that the government had not met that burden" and "we agree."

Three members of the majority held that the First Amendment's free press guarantee was unassailable and the courts lacked the power to suppress press publication, no matter what threat to national security might be posed. Two of the three—Hugo L. Black and William O. Douglas—considered judicial restraint of the press altogether prohibited under the First Amendment. The third, Thurgood Marshall, stressed the principle of separation of powers, noting that prior restraint had never been authorized by Congress and Congress specifically had rejected bills to authorize restraint in 1917 and 1957.

A second group within the majority Justices William J. Brennan Jr., Potter Stewart and Byron R. White—asserted that the press could not be curbed except to prevent immediate and irreparable damage to the nation. They held that the material in question in this case did not pose such a threat.

Brennan held that the temporary restraints should not have been imposed because the government had alleged only in general terms that security breaches might occur.

Both Stewart and White, who concurred in their opinions, believed that publication of the documents was not in the national interest although publication could not constitutionally be prevented. Stewart held that protection of state secrets was "the duty of the executive" and not the duty of the courts through the banning of news articles. If publication would cause "direct, immediate and irreparable damage to our nation or its people," he said, he would uphold prior restraint, but he did not find that situation to exist in this case.

The Times and Post and other newspapers publishing the material were lauded by Black, who said they "should be commended for serving the purpose that the Founding Fathers saw so clearly" in the First Amendment's declaration that "Congress shall make no law . . . abridging the freedom of the press." A primary responsibility of the press, he said, was "to prevent any part of the government from deceiving the people." "In revealing the workings of government that led to the Vietnam war," he said, "the newspapers nobly did precisely that which the founders hoped and trusted they would do."

Justice Douglas said that the First Amendment's aim was to prevent "governmental suppression of embarrassing information." He said the temporary restraints on publication in the case "constitute a flouting of the principles of the First Amendment."

The separation-of-powers principle also was stressed by Brennan, Stewart and White, who held that the courts could not restrain publications except under extraordinary and extreme circumstances. Four justices commented on the issue of criminal laws, including the espionage laws, and their possible application of these to the case. White said that "the newspapers are presumably now on full notice" that federal prosecutions could be brought for violation of such laws. He added that he "would have no difficulty in sustaining convictions" in such an event even if the security breach

were not sufficient to justify prior restraint.

The dissents—The three dissenting justices were Chief Justice Warren E. Burger and Justices Harry A. Blackmun and John M. Harlan.

The three held that the decision was too precipitous—Burger referred to the "frenetic haste" of the case—and that the issue should be returned to trial with restraints upon publication continued. They asserted that the courts should uphold the executive branch's contention, at the cabinet level, that material should be kept confidential on a matter affecting foreign relations.

Burger and Blackmun were critical of the Times for failing to give sufficient time for proper consideration to the case. Burger said it was a breach of "the duty of an honorable press" not to have inquired about possible security violations before publishing the material. Burger said he had found this failing "hardly believable" and he saw no harm resulting if the issue were returned for additional testimony.

Blackmun asserted that if the war were prolonged and the return of American war prisoners were delayed as a result of the publication of the material, "then the nation's people will know where the responsibility for these sad consequences rests."

The third dissenter, Harlan, said: "The judiciary must review the initial executive determination to the point of satisfying itself that the subject matter of the dispute does lie within the proper compass of the President's foreign policy relations power. . .The judiciary may properly insist that the determination that disclosure of the subject matter would irreparably impair the national security be made by the head of the executive department concerned. . . . But in my judgment, the judiciary may not properly go beyond these two inquiries and redetermine for itself the probable impact of disclosure on the national security."

High court's acceptance of case—The New York Times brought its case before the Supreme Court June 24 with the argument that the court-ordered restraint on publishing the material already constituted a violation of the First Amendment. It pointed out that the Post had been freed to resume publication of the material and its articles, if they did resume, plus such articles appearing in other newspapers, would inflict "irreparable harm" on the Times' interests. It cited in addition the doctrine of separation of powers and the lack of Congressional sanction for courts to impose prior restraint on newspaper publication.

In the Post case, the Court of Appeals in Washington June 24 denied the Justice Department's request for a rehearing on the case and the court reaffirmed its June 23 ruling that the government had not demonstrated any grounds for preventing publication of the material. Both appellate decisions, the denial and the reaffirmation of its ruling, were by 7–2 votes. "The matter is now ripe for presentation to the Supreme Court," it said.

The Supreme Court accepted the Times and Post cases June 25. Because of the restraint continued upon the Times but not the Post from appellate decisions, it put both newspapers under equal publication restraints pending an ultimate decision. It marked the first time the Supreme Court had restrained publication of a newspaper article, and four justices —Black, Douglas, Brennan and Marshall —dissented in favor of freeing both papers to print the articles without hearing arguments. Although the court's order permitted both newspapers to publish information from the Pentagon study, it proscribed items the government considered "dangerous" to national security.

With Burger, Blackmun and Harlan dissenting, the court June 26 rejected the government's request for a secret hearing for presentation of details that publication of the material would be harmful to the national interest.

In a two-hour hearing June 26, the government presented its case that publication of the "top secret" documents could be barred as violations of the espionage laws and of statutes and executive orders under which the president had sole authority to control classified material. The power of the courts to block publication of government secrets that posed a "grave and irrevocable" security threat was claimed. And the government held that publication of the Pentagon study

involved diplomatic jeopardy because of the loss of confidentiality.

The government urged adoption of a standard permitting federal court intervention to halt publication whenever it would "affect lives," the "termination of the war" or "the process of recovering our prisoners of war."

Rusk denies deceit by LBJ. Former Secretary of State Dean Rusk strongly denied July 2 that there had been any "deliberate attempt" to deceive the American people about U.S. involvement in Vietnam during the 1964 Presidential campaign of Lyndon Baines Johnson.

He also denied there had been any deception about Vietnam policy while John F. Kennedy was President.

Rusk defended himself and the two Presidents he served in a lengthy televised interview with two National Broadcasting Company correspondents. He told Edwin Newman and Barbara Walters that "as far as general policy is concerned, there was no deception. I can't myself find any justification for the charge of deceit."

Rusk, a law professor at the University of Georgia, said that President Johnson had "made it very plain that we did not want a bigger war, but that we would fulfill our commitments."

In the course of the interview, Rusk conceded that he had underestimated the determination of the North Vietnamese to wage war. He also acknowledged that he had overestimated the willingness of the U.S. to sustain a protracted war in Indochina.

After previously refusing to comment publicly on the Pentagon papers, Rusk said he had agreed to the NBC interview because he could not "remain silent forever."

A similar view was expressed by George Ball, an under secretary of state in the Kennedy and Johnson Administrations. Ball, identified in the Pentagon papers as a critic of the rising U.S. combat role in Indochina, said June 28 that Johnson did not deceive the public during the 1964 election.

"What the President was saying," Ball said, "was entirely honest. . . . He didn't want a wider war. . . ."

In an interview broadcast by the Columbia Broadcasting System, Ball also said Johnson had expressed gratitude for his arguments against expanding the U.S. role in Vietnam.

Rostow defends U.S. role. Walt W. Rostow, one of President Johnson's key advisers on Vietnam, said July 11 that if the U.S. "had walked away from Asia" the nation could have faced the possibility of a nuclear war.

Appearing on an American Broadcasting Company television program, Rostow said that even knowing today that the war would cost $100 billion and take 50,000 lives, he thought it was worth the effort to maintain the balance of power in Southeast Asia.

Even today, Rostow said, the U.S. could not safely disengage from Indochina without running the risk of a nuclear war.

"If we had walked away from Asia or if we walk away from Asia now, the consequences will not be peace, the consequences will be a large war, fairly soon, and quite possibly a nuclear war."

Earlier July 11, in a meeting with newsmen, Rostow said that "the first initial effect" of publication of the Pentagon papers was to undermine faith in the presidency and strengthen an emerging mood of isolationism. Rostow added that he believed the publication of the documents distorted the truth about how the U.S. went to war in Vietnam.

Rostow singled out for criticism the New York Times for its part in the documents controversy. He said he regarded the Times' "performance" in its series of articles on the documents "as the shoddiest piece of journalism since I had any experience in public life, in 1941."

Rostow said that the Times' "headline writers, lead writers, editorial writers and columnists went beyond the Pentagon papers in purveying a sense of deceit by a President of the United States."

U.S. releases study. The government put on public sale Sept. 27 an expurgated version of the Pentagon papers.

The 12-volume set went on sale in Government Printing Office bookstores in Washington. The 7,800-page government version cost $50.

The study was released after specialists from the State and Defense Departments and the Central Intelligence Agency de-

classified the documents. According to a Pentagon spokesman, the security personnel struck from the documents data they considered would jeopardize national security. Additional portions were deleted to avoid embarassing other nations.

The government's version contained some previously unpublished material from the war study. Among the new data were eight letters and cablegrams from Ho Chi Minh, then the Communist leader in Vietnam and later president of North Vietnam, that went unanswered. In the correspondence, Ho appealed for help in his fight against France in 1945–46.

The official U.S. version, however, also deleted some material already published by the New York Times, the Washington Post and other newspapers in June.

Among those deletions were references to U.S. diplomatic contacts with the Soviet Union, data about U.S. discussions regarding relations with nations contributing troops to the Vietnam conflict, and material about covert military operations ordered by the Johnson Administration against North Vietnam.

Four volumes of the broad study, which dealt with secret diplomatic negotiations during the Johnson Administration, were withheld entirely. None of those volumes had been obtained by the newspapers involved in the Pentagon papers controversy.

The government's declassified version was made available to Congress Sept. 21. In a letter accompanying the volumes, a Pentagon aide said the four volumes dealing with the secret diplomatic talks during the Johnson years would not be made public. The aide said those volumes "deal exclusively with sensitive negotiations seeking peace and the release of prisoners" and "their disclosure would adversely affect continuing effort to achieve those objectives."

Judge denies release of war study. A U.S. district court judge in Washington denied Dec. 7 an attempt by two congressmen to compel the government to release the entire 47-volume set of the Pentagon papers.

Judge Gerhard A. Gesell granted a summary judgment in favor of the Defense Department, which had challenged a suit filed by Reps. Ogden R. Reid (R,

N.Y.) and John E. Moss (D, Calif.). The two congressmen, co-authors of the Freedom of Information Act, had asked Gesell Dec. 3 to examine the still classified segments of the study behind closed doors and decide whether all or part should be made public.

Reid and Moss had specifically asked Gesell to review those parts of the study which the government had withheld when it published a declassified version of the papers in September. Among the information withheld by the government were four volumes which included details of the secret diplomacy with North Vietnam during the Johnson Administration.

In rejecting their suit, Gesell said that an independent court review such as the one sought by Reid and Moss was neither required by the Freedom of Information Act nor desirable.

Gesell added that "government, like individuals, must have some degree of privacy or it will be stifled in its legitimate pursuits." He said that the Defense Department had made "an adequate showing that disclosure would be harmful to the national defense or foreign policy."

Ellsberg again indicted. The Justice Department Dec. 30 added 12 criminal charges, including conspiracy and violation of espionage statutes, to the list of charges against Daniel Ellsberg for releasing the Pentagon papers to the press.

The new charges were handed down by the same Los Angeles federal grand jury that had indicted Ellsberg in July on two counts of converting government property to his own use and illegally possessing government documents.

Also indicted Dec. 30 was Anthony J. Russo Jr., a former colleague of Ellsberg at the Rand Corp. in Santa Monica, Calif. Russo was indicted on four counts, including conspiracy.

The 25-page indictment also named Miss Linda Sinay and Vu Van Thai as co-conspirators. Neither Miss Sinay, a Los Angeles advertising woman, nor Thai, a former South Vietnamese ambassador to the U.S., were indicted.

Sen. Smith on papers' flaws. Sen. Margaret Chase Smith (R, Me.) told the Senate Sept. 17 that the time had come to realize that the Pentagon papers were not a complete or accurate record of U.S. involvement in Indochina. She rejected "the false image given to them of being literally a bible of gospel and unerring truth."

Mrs. Smith noted that flaws in the papers had been admitted by Leslie H. Gelb, chairman of the OSD (Office of the Secretary of Defense) task force that had produced the study. She had Gelb's introduction memo to the report printed in the Congressional Record for Sept. 17, and she italicized portions bearing on what she intimated was the unreliability of the papers.

Text of Gelb's memo (with italicization as directed by Mrs. Smith):

On June 17, 1967, Secretary Robert S. McNamara directed that a Task Force be formed to study the history of United States involvement in Vietnam from World War II to the present. Mr. McNamara's guidance was simply to do studies that were *"encyclopedic and objective."* With six full-time professionals assigned to the Task Force, we were to complete our work in three months. A year and a half later, and with the involvement of six times six professionals, we are finally done to the tune of *thirty-seven studies* and *fifteen collections* of documents contained in *forty-three volumes.*

In the beginning, Mr. McNamara gave the Task Force full access to OSD files, and the Task Force received access to CIA materials, and some use of State Department cables and memoranda. *We had no access to White House files.* Our guidance *prohibited personal interviews* with *any of the principal participants.*

The result was not so much a documentary history, as a history based solely on documents—checked and rechecked with antlike diligence. *Pieces of paper,* formidable and suggestive by themselves, *could have meant much or nothing.* Perhaps this document was never sent anywhere, and perhaps that one, though commented upon, was irrelevant. *Without the memories of people to tell us, we were certain to make mistakes.* Yet, using those memories might have been misleading as well. *This approach to research was bound to lead to distortions, and distortions we are sure abound in these studies.*

To bring the documents to life, to fill in gaps, and just to see what the "outside world" was thinking, we turned to newspapers, periodicals, and books. We never used these sources to supplant the classified documents, but only to supplement them. And because *these documents,* sometimes *written by very clever* men *who* knew so much and *desired to say only a part* and sometimes written very openly but also contradictorily, are not immediately self-revealing or self-explanatory, we tried both to have a number of researchers look at them and to quote passages liberally. Moreover, when we felt we could be challenged with taking something out of context, we included the whole paper in the Documentary Record section of the Task Force studies. (Parts V and VI. A and B). Again seeking to fend off *inevitable mistakes in interpretation and context*, what seemed to us key documents were reviewed and included in several overlapping in substance, but separate, studies.

The people who worked on the Task Force were *superb*—uniformly bright and interested, although not always versed in the art of research. We had a sense of doing something important and of the need to do it right. *Of course, we all had our prejudices and axes to grind and these shine through clearly at times, but we tried, we think, to suppress or compensate for them.*

These outstanding people came from everywhere—the military services, State, OSD, and the *"think tanks."* Some came for a month, for three months, for six months, and *most were unable,* given the unhappiness of their superiors, *to finish the studies they began.* Almost all the studies had several authors, each heir dutifully trying to pick up the threads of his predecessor. In all, we had *thirty-six professionals* working on these studies, with an average of four months per man.

The quality, style and interest of the studies varies considerably. The papers in Parts I, II, III, and IV.A, concerning the years 1945 to 1961 tend to be generally nonstartling—although there are many interesting tidbits. Because many of the documents in this period were lost or not kept (except for the Geneva Conference era) *we had to rely more on outside resources.* From

1961 onwards (Parts IV.B and C and VI.C), the records were bountiful, especially on the first Kennedy year in office, the Diem coup, and on the subjects of the deployment of ground forces, the decisions surrounding the bombing campaign against North Vietnam, US–GVN relations, and attempts at negotiating a settlement of the conflict.

Almost all the studies contain both a Summary and Analysis and a Chronology. The chronologies highlight each important event or action in the monograph by means of date, description, and documentary source. *The Summary and Analysis sections, which I wrote,* attempt to capture the main themes and facts of the monographs—and *to make some judgments and speculations which may or may not appear in the text itself.* The monographs themselves stick, by and large, to the documents and do not tend to be analytical.

Writing history, especially where it blends into current events, especially where that current event is Vietnam, *is a treacherous exercise. We could not go into the mind of the decision-makers, we were not present at the decisions, and we often could not tell whether something happened because someone decided it, decided against it, or most likely because it unfolded from the situation.* History, to me, has been expressed by a passage from Herman Melville's *Moby Dick* where he writes: "This is a world of chance, free will, and necessity—all interweavingly working together as one; chance by turn rules either and has the last featuring blow at events." Our studies have tried to reflect this thought; inevitably in the organizing and writing process, they appear to assign more and less to men and free will than was the case.

SUBSTANCE OF THE PENTAGON PAPERS
(As reported in the various publications carrying articles on and excerpts from the study.)

Ho Chi Minh's early pleas ignored. Eight direct appeals for aid were made by Ho Chi Minh, Communist leader of North Vietnam, in the five months following the end of World War II, and all were ignored by the U.S. This was revealed by the Pentagon papers, according to a Christian Science Monitor article June 30. Ho's messages, sent between October 1945 and February 1946, appealed for American help to prevent the post-war restoration of French colonial rule in Indochina.

Guerrilla fighting had broken out in Vietnam with the return of French troops in the south. Ho's messages cited among other things an October 1945 speech by President Harry S. Truman in which he endorsed national self-determination. After receiving no encouragement, reported the Monitor, Ho agreed to a

five-year return of the French in March 1946.

According to the Monitor's account, U.S. suspicion of Ho as a Communist underlay its refusal to deal with him as a nationalist leader. The report quoted a Dec. 5, 1946 State Department memo, included in the Pentagon papers, which told the U.S. representative in Hanoi to: "Keep in mind Ho's clear record as an agent [of] international communism . . . least desirable eventuality would be establishment [of a] Communist-controlled Moscow-oriented state."

The Monitor quoted the Pentagon analyst as saying the U.S. knew little about what was occurring in Vietnam and "certainly cared less about Vietnam than about France." The analyst said the U.S. offered Ho "only narrow options" and by the time the Indochina war began in earnest in late 1946, France had already used U.S. military equipment against the Vietnamese and the U.S. had arranged credit for the purchase of more equipment.

Early policy vacillating. The Christian Science Monitor July 1 quoted the analyst's assessment of U.S. Indochina policy during 1946-50 as marked by "indecision" and "an undertone of indifference." The U.S. saw danger in French colonial policies but refused to intervene until Mao Tse-tung's 1949 victory in China focused America's fears of the spread of communism.

The Monitor also said the study showed that the British opened the way for the French to return to power in Indochina after World War II. During the Japanese occupation of Vietnam, Ho Chi Minh's Viet Minh emerged as the only viable resistance force in the country.

The Monitor said the British, whose forces along with the Nationalist Chinese occupied Vietnam after the war, went along with French removal of the pro-Ho Chi Minh Committee of the South, touching off the first Indochinese war.

The Pentagon analysis said the Truman Administration tried to stay out of Indochinese affairs between 1946 and 1950, viewing it as one region "in which the U.S. might enjoy the luxury of abstention." However, America recognized that French colonial policies were headed toward defeat, and the U.S. pressured the French to give in to Vietnamese desire for autonomy. The Pentagon analyst saw America's actions in 1950— recognition of the new government the French set up to oppose Ho Chi Minh and agreeing to supply economic and military aid—as a "cohesive progression" from its 1946-50 policies rather than a sudden involvement in Vietnam.

Truman makes first 'crucial' move. Approval by President Truman May 1, 1950 of $10 million for French forces in Indochina was described by the Pentagon analysts as the first "crucial decision regarding U.S. military involvement in Indochina," according to a Washington Post article published July 3.

The growing U.S. concern with events in that part of Asia was reflected in a National Security Council paper No. 64, issued in February 1950, several months after Chinese Communist troops had reached the Indochinese border. The document concluded that "the Departments of State and Defense should prepare, as a matter of priority a program of all practicable measures designed to protect U.S. security interests in Indochina." The U.S. the same day extended recognition of the Indochinese regime of Bao Dai, a move Secretary of State Dean Acheson had recommended in a memo to Truman Feb. 3, 1950.

The Post reported that just prior to issuance of NSC 64 Deputy Undersecretary of State Dean Rusk had provided Maj. Gen. James H. Burns at the Defense Department with this statement of State Department policy:

> The Department of State believes . . . the resources of the United States should be deployed to reserve Indochina and Southeast Asia from further Communist encroachment, . . . The Department is now engaged in . . . examining what additional economic resources can effectively be engaged in the same operation.
>
> It is now . . . a matter of the greatest urgency that the Department of Defense assess the strategic aspects of the situation and consider, from the military point of view, how the United States can best contribute to the prevention of further Communist encroachment in that area.

A 1949 National Security Council paper cited by the Post had expressed concern with the Soviet Union's efforts "to gain control of Southeast Asia." The NSC expressed the belief that the Soviets were "motivated in part by a desire to acquire Southeast Asia's resources and communication lines, and to deny them to us." In what the newspaper decribed as the evolvement of what later became known as the domino theory, it further quoted the NSC paper as saying "if Southeast Asia also is swept by communism we shall have suffered a major political rout the repercussions of which will be felt throughout the rest of the world, especially in the Middle East and in a critically exposed Australia."

The North Korean attack on South Korea June 27, 1950 led to still further American involvement in Indochina. The Post recalled that Truman, in informing the American public of the North Korean assault, also said he had "directed acceleration in the furnishing of military assistance to the forces of France and the Associated States in Indochina and the dispatch of a military mission to provide close working relations with those forces." The Pentagon summary stated that despite the pressing needs of the Korean War, American military aid to Indochina rapidly increased and that by the time of the Geneva Accords in July 1954 it had totaled $2.6 billion.

According to the Post account, although the Truman Administration was reluctant to support France in recovering its lost colony in Indochina, it was nevertheless adamant in its opposition to the ascendancy of North Vietnamese leader Ho Chi Minh. The American ambassador to Paris was instructed to pass on these views to French Premier Paul Ramadier in February 1947. The Post quoted the ambassador as saying: "We cannot shut our eyes to the fact that there are two sides to this problem. . . ." One "side" was that "there is no escape from the fact that the trend of the times is to effect that colonial empires in XIX Century sense are rapidly becoming thing of past." The other "side" was "we do not lose sight of fact that Ho Chi Minh has direct Communist connections and it should be obvious that we are not interested in seeing colonial empire administration supplanted by philosophy and poltical organizations emanating from and controlled by the Kremlin. . . ." The statement concluded that "frankly, we have no solution of problem to suggest."

Vietnamese hated French, respected Ho. The Chicago Sun-Times June 25, the third day of a series based in part on the Pentagon papers, cited Central Intelligence Agency (CIA) documents of August 1954 in which the CIA advised that "the most significant particular political sentiment of the bulk of the population" of Vietnam was "an antipathy for the French combined with a personal regard for Ho Chi Minh as the symbol of Vietnamese nationalism."

Opposition to Vietnam elections in 1954. The Washington Post reported June 18 that the Pentagon analysis and appended documents of 1954 showed that the Eisenhower Administration strongly opposed early elections throughout Vietnam because U.S. officials were convinced they would bring victory to Ho Chi Minh. However, according to quotes from a summary in the Pentagon study, it was South Vietnamese President Ngo Dinh Diem who was responsible in 1955 for blocking the elections called for by the 1954 Geneva Convention.

The Post also reported portions of the Pentagon papers covering discussion in the months before the Geneva agreement in July about possible U.S. military intervention in Indochina. According to the Post's account of the study, President Eisenhower insisted early in 1954 on Congressional approval and allied support for such intervention to help the French, but the British resisted intervention.

The Post quoted a July 1954 cable, included in the Pentagon study, from John Foster Dulles, Eisenhower's secretary of state, which clearly set forth Dulles's objections to elections throughout North and South Vietnam. The cable, sent to various American diplomats, said in part:

". . . Thus since undoubtedly true that elections might eventually mean unification Vietnam under Ho Chi Minh this makes it all more important they should be only held as long after cease-fire agreement as possible and in conditions free from intimidation to give democratic elements best chance. We believe important that no date should be set now and especially that no conditions should be accepted by French which would have direct or indirect effect of preventing effective international supervision of agreement ensuring political as well as military guarantees."

The Post quoted other documents from the study indicating Dulles's displeasure with the Geneva Conference, which ended later in July with a "final declaration" stating that "general elections shall be held in July 1956." Shortly before the declaration was issued, Dulles cabled Undersecretary of State Walter Bedell Smith in Geneva that "we don't want to take responsibility of imposing our views on the French." But Dulles said he was "particularly concerned" that the conference would call for elections without U.N. supervision. Dulles cited a June 29 joint declaration by Eisenhower and British Prime Minister Winston Churchill stating that the U.N. should supervise such elections. Dulles said the declaration was going "down the drain with our apparent acquiescence."

In a previous cable quoted by the Post, Dulles complained to French Premier Pierre Mendes-France of a "whittling-away process" taking place in Geneva that went against an Indochina program agreed upon by the U.S. and Britain.

However, after the Geneva accords were issued, the Post narrative continued, the U.S. accepted the elections as inevitable, and it was Diem who decided to ignore the Geneva declaration, which Saigon had never accepted. The Pentagon survey stated in a summary:

As the deadline for consultations approached (July, 1955) Diem was increasingly explicit that he did not consider free elections possible in North Vietnam, and had no intention of consulting with the DRV (North Vietnam) concerning them. The U.S. did not —as is often alleged—connive with Diem to ignore the elections. U.S. State Department records indicate that Diem's refusal to be bound by the Geneva Accords and his opposition to pre-election consultations were at his own intiative.

However, the U.S., which had expected elections to be held, and up until May, 1955, had fully supported them, shifted its position in the face of Diem's opposition, and of the evidence then accumulated about the oppressive nature of the regime in North Vietnam. "In essence," a State Department historical study found, "Our position would be that the whole subject of consultation and elections in Vietnam should be left up to the Vietnamese themselves and not dictated by external arrangements which one of the parties never accepted and still rejects."

The Pentagon study, according to the Post, said the Eisenhower Administration discussed the possibility of sending military aid and men to help the French forces before the Geneva Conference. The study related discussions at a January 1954 meeting of the President's Special Committee on Indochina concerning sending aircraft as well as 200 military mechanics.

The Pentagon study's report of the meeting said Deputy Defense Secretary Roger Kyes "questioned" whether sending the men "would not so commit the U.S. to support the French that we must be prepared eventually for complete intervention, including use of U.S. combat forces." Undersecretary of State Smith disagreed and said, according to the study, "we were sending maintenance forces, not ground forces. He felt, however, that the importance of winning in Indochina was so great that if worst came to worst he personally would favor intervention with U.S. air and naval forces—not ground forces."

Further discussion and planning produced a January 1954 National Security Council policy statement that was approved by President Eisenhower. The first part of the statement, on general considerations of U.S. objectives and courses in Southeast Asia, set forth

what has been called the domino theory of Communist domination:

1. Communist domination, by whatever means, of all Southeast Asia would seriously endanger in the short term, and critically endanger in the longer terms, United States security interests.

a. In the conflict in Indochina, the Communist and non-Communist worlds clearly confront one another on the field of battle. The loss of the struggle in Indochina, in addition to its impact in Southeast Asia and in South Asia, would therefore have the most serious repercussions on U.S. and free world interests in Europe and elsewhere.

b. Such is the interrelation of the countries of the area that effective counteraction would be immediately necessary to prevent the loss of any single country from leading to submission to or an alignment with communism by the remaining countries of Southeast Asia and Indonesia. Furthermore, in the event all of Southeast Asia falls under communism, an alignment with communism of India, and in the longer term, of the Middle East (with the probable exceptions of at least Pakistan and Turkey) could follow progressively. Such widespread alignment would seriously endanger the stability and security of Europe.

c. Communist control of all of Southeast Asia and Indonesia would threaten the U.S. position in the Pacific offshore island chain and would seriously jeopardize fundamental U.S. security interests in the Far East.

The statement went on to cite "serious economic consequences" for free world nations and "significant resources" that would be added to the Soviet bloc if Southeast Asia were to fall to the Communists. It said the loss of Malaya and Indonesia "could result in such economic and political pressures in Japan as to make it extremely difficult to prevent Japan's eventual accommodation to communism."

The statement set as an immediate aim to help the French in a program to "eliminate organized Viet Minh forces by mid-1955" and in "developing indigenous forces . . . which will eventually be capable of maintaining internal security without assistance from French units."

The paper suggested military actions to be taken by or directed by the U.S. in the event of Chinese intervention. The Pentagon study cited an "Army position" based on the National Security Council statement that said, "seven U.S. divisions . . . with appropriate naval and air support would be required to win a victory in Indochina if the French withdrew and the Chinese Communists did not intervene."

The Pentagon analysis, reported the Post, said Eisenhower approved the planning but would not sanction intervention without allied participation. A quote from an April 1954 telegram from Dulles to Douglas Dillon, U.S. ambassador to France, said the "U.S. is doing everything possible" to "prepare public, Congressional and Constitutional basis for united action in Indochina. However, such action is impossible except on coalition basis with active British Commonwealth's participation. Meanwhile U.S. prepared, as has been demonstrated, to do everything short of belligerency."

On his failure to get British agreement, Dulles said later in April, as quoted in the study, "UK attitude is one of increasing weakness. British seem to feel that we are disposed to accept present risks of a Chinese war and this, coupled with their fear that we would start using atomic weapons, has badly frightened them."

The Post said none of the papers available to it cited a decision by Eisenhower not to intervene. However, the Post quoted a May 1954 memo by a presidential adviser reflecting Eisenhower's feeling: "The United States will not agree to a 'white man's party' to determine the problems of the Southeast Asian nations."

Geneva accords undermined. The New York Times reported July 5 that the Pentagon study concluded that the U.S. had "a direct role in the ultimate breakdown of the Geneva settlement" of the Indochina conflict in 1954. The study indicated that in August, immediately after the Geneva convention, the Eisenhower Administration decided to replace French advisers and supply direct aid to the South Vietnamese government of Ngo Dinh Diem.

The Times report also said that Col. Edward G. Lansdale of the Central Intelligence Agency, who had been sent to Saigon in June, headed a team of agents that began covert sabotage operations against North Vietnam soon after the close of the Geneva conventions. Included in the Pentagon papers was a lengthy report in the form of a diary describing the operations of Lansdale's Saigon Military Mission (SMM) from June 1954 through August 1955.

The Pentagon study showed that the basic rationale for the U.S. commitment

in Indochina, which the study said was "never questioned" during the Eisenhower Administration, was first clearly stated by the National Security Council in February 1950. The 1950 statement, expressing what came to be known as the domino theory, said, "It is important to U.S. security interests . . . that all practicable measures be taken to prevent further Communist expansion in Southeast Asia. Indochina is a key area and is under immediate threat. The neighboring countries of Thailand and Burma could be expected to fall under Communist domination if Indochina is controlled by a Communist government."

The premise was restated in National Security Council documents throughout the 1950s. A policy statement approved by Eisenhower in January 1954 warned that a "loss of any single country" in Southeast Asia would lead to the loss of all the area, then Japan and India, and would finally "endanger the stability and security of Europe."

Leading up to the Eisenhower period, as reported in the Times, the Pentagon papers described the "indecision" of policy toward Indochina in the '40s. The study cited a May 8, 1950 announcement that the U.S. would supply economic and military aid to the French in Indochina. It said that "the U.S. thereafter was directly involved in the developing tragedy in Vietnam."

The Pentagon study said that twice in the spring of 1954, the U.S. very seriously considered direct intervention of U.S. troops to help the French. During the second intervention debate, in May and early June after the fall of the French fortress at Dienbienphu, the study indicated that a draft Congressional resolution was prepared to allow for commitment of U.S. troops. However, the French military situation deteriorated, and on June 15 France was informed that the time for American aid had run out.

According to the Pentagon study, "except for the United States, the major powers were satisfied" with the Geneva agreements as concluded July 21, 1954. The analysis said France, Britain, the Soviet Union and Communist China believed that the conflict had been taken into the political realm and that the

French would "remain in Vietnam" and insure that the 1956 elections specified in the accords would be carried out.

The Pentagon account said, however, that the National Security Council, in meetings Aug. 8 and 12, concluded that the settlement was a "disaster" that "completed a major forward stride of communism which may lead to the loss of Southeast Asia." On Aug. 20, President Eisenhower approved a National Security Council program of direct aid to Diem. The Pentagon study said the decision was taken despite intelligence warnings that Diem was too weak to prevent a further deterioration of anti-Communist forces. According to the analyst, "the U.S. decided to gamble with very limited resources because the potential gains seemed well worth a limited risk."

Besides the direct aid, the study described Lansdale's SMM team and its "paramilitary operations" and "political-psychological warfare" against North Vietnam. The French were scheduled under the Geneva agreement to evacuate Hanoi Oct. 9, 1954. The Lansdale report included the following description of the team's activities immediately before:

The northern team had spent the last days of Hanoi in contaminating the oil supply of the bus company for a gradual wreckage of engines in the buses, in taking the first actions for delayed sabotage of the railroad (which required teamwork with a CIA special technical team in Japan who performed their part brilliantly), and in writing detailed notes of potential targets for future paramilitary operations (U.S. adherence to the Geneva Agreement prevented SMM from carrying out the active sabotage it desired to do against the power plant, water facilities, harbor, and bridge). The team had a bad moment when contaminating the oil. They had to work quickly at night, in an enclosed storage room. Fumes from the contaminant came close to knocking them out. Dizzy and weak-kneed, they masked their faces with handkerchiefs and completed the job.

One of the team's operations in South Vietnam, described in the report, was to hire Vietnamese astrologers to predict doom for the Communists and publicize good omens for Diem. According to the Pentagon study, Lansdale also had a hand in rallying Diem's prospects in April 1955 when Secretary of State John Foster Dulles had decided to stop supporting his regime.

The Times described the Pentagon study's conclusion that although the U.S. did not "connive" with Diem to prevent elections called for in the Geneva accords, the Eisenhower Administration did wish to postpone the elections as long as possible and these views were communicated to Diem.

Communist insurgency in South Vietnam grew in 1957 and particularly in 1959, according to the Pentagon study. Although U.S. intelligence reports continued to indicate the weakness of the Diem regime, the Pentagon study said the U.S. resolves were stated by the National Security Council in "virtually identical" language in 1956, 1958 and 1960. These goals as stated in 1956 were as follows:

Assist Free Vietnam to develop a strong, stable and constitutional government to enable Free Vietnam to assert an increasingly attractive contrast to conditions in the present Communist zone....

Work toward the weakening of the Communists in North and South Vietnam in order to bring about the eventual peaceful reunification of a free and independent Vietnam under anti-Communist leadership....

Support the position of the Government of Free Vietnam that all-Vietnam elections may take place only after it is satisfied that genuinely free elections can be held throughout both zones of Vietnam.

(In another story published July 5, the Times reported the Pentagon analyst's conclusion that the U.S. official view that war was forced on South Vietnam because of North Vietnamese aggression was "not wholly compelling." The study cited intelligence estimates in the 1950s indicating that the war began as a rebellion in the South against Deim's oppressive regime. However, the Pentagon study also rejected the argument of critics of U.S. policy who held that Hanoi's involvement came directly in response to large-scale U.S. intervention in 1965. The study said: "It is equally clear that North Vietnamese Communists operated some form of subordinate apparatus in the South in the years 1954–1960.")

According to the Pentagon analyst, when President Kennedy took office in 1961, he was confronted by a "special commitment" in South Vietnam. The analyst said that without U.S. support, "Diem almost certainly could not have consolidated his hold on the South during 1955 and 1956.

"Without the threat of U.S. intervention, South Vietnam could not have refused to even discuss the elections called for in 1956 under the Geneva settlement without being immediately overrun by the Vietminh armies.

"Without U.S. aid in the years following, the Diem regime certainly, and an independent South Vietnam almost as certainly, could not have survived."

The Pentagon analyst concluded, "South Vietnam was essentially the creation of the United States."

1961 pressure on Diem. The Sun-Times, in its June 24 editions, said President John F. Kennedy sent Vice President Lyndon Johnson to Saigon in May 1961 to persuade South Vietnam to request U.S. ground troops. The article, which the paper said was based in part on the Pentagon papers and in part on other government documents, said South Vietnamese President Ngo Dinh Diem originally opposed U.S. troops except to answer direct aggression by North Vietnam. The paper said Diem finally agreed and in October 1961 made the request.

Push toward commitment. The Washington Post July 1 outlined the dire view of the South Vietnam crisis at the beginning of 1961 and the assessments by military leaders that pushed President Kennedy toward a U.S. commitment to South Vietnam. Kennedy was said to have been persuaded that a commitment in support of Diem "should make it obvious to the Vietnamese and the rest of the world that the United States is committed to preventing Communist domination of South Vietnam and Southeast Asia."

The Joint Chiefs viewed the Vietnam situation as part of "a planned phase in the Communist timetable for world domination," the control of Southeast Asia providing access "to the remainder of Asia and to Africa and Australia" just as control of Cuba provided access to South and Central America.

If the Viet Cong could not be "brought under control" with Diem's forces, the Chiefs saw "no alternative to the introduction of U.S. military combat forces along with those of the free Asian nations that can be persuaded to participate."

The Chiefs also viewed the U.S. forces as excelling in "a peninsula and island-type" of warfare that would be waged in Southeast Asia and the Communist forces "limited" because of "natural logistic and transportation problems."

However, McNamara informed Kennedy, he was "not prepared to endorse the views of the Chiefs until we have had more experience with our present programs" in South Vietnam. Kennedy was concentrating more on a counter-insurgency movement. A National Security Action Memorandum at the time ordered a study of the feasibility of "increased use of third-country personnel in paramilitary operations" in Laos, indicating the prior utilization there of such forces.

The indeterminate nature of the long-range prospect of the U.S. effort also was stressed in the documents. Assistant Secretary of State Roger Hilsman wrote Rusk Dec. 3, 1962 that "elimination, even significant reduction, of the Communist insurgency will almost certainly require several years" and require a "considerably greater effort" by South Vietnam "as well as continuing U.S. assistance."

An April 1963 report from intelligence sources noted indications "that the Viet Cong can be constrained militarily" but added "we do not believe that it is possible at this time to project the future course of the war with any confidence. . . . No quick and easy end to the war is in sight. Despite South Vietnamese progress, the situation remains fragile."

The complexities of the imminent coup became added to the web of crisis and by October 1963, Lodge was cabling the State Department in agreement "that a miscalculation could jeopardize position in Southeast Asia. We also run tremendous risk by doing nothing."

JFK and 1961 commitment—The Globe reported June 22 on some policy recommendations in 1961 leading to an eventual commitment by President John F. Kennedy of some 16,000 American advisers in Indochina. On the basis of cablegrams (whose texts were published) from Gen. Maxwell D. Taylor, Kennedy's special adviser on Vietnam, the Globe reported that, at a time when the U.S. had about 1,000 soldiers in South Vietnam serving as advisers to the South Vietnamese army, Kennedy had approved by May 11, 1961 programs for covert actions against North Vietnam.

These actions reportedly included dispatch of agents into North Vietnam, aerial supply of the agents through civilian mercenary crews, infiltration of South Vietnamese units into Southeast Laos to attack Communist bases and lines of communication, formulation of sabotage teams and bases for light harassment inside North Vietnam, and overflights of North Vietnam for dropping leaflets. The Globe reported from the Pentagon study that Kennedy called for initiation of "guerrilla ground action, including the use of U.S. advisers if necessary" against Communist aerial resupply missions in the vicinity of Tchepone, Laos.

The Globe article reported Kennedy's refusal to commit an 8,000-man U.S. military task force to South Vietnam as recommended in October 1961 by Taylor to bolster the Saigon regime and South Vietnamese "national morale" in its opposition to the Communist military position. Taylor had pictured use of the U.S. force as engaging in flood relief work, which would at least present, he said, "a specific humanitarian task as the prime reason for the coming of our troops."

In an October, 1961 cable, Taylor recommended introducing the U.S. military force into South Vietnam but warned of the possible disadvantages: the strategic reserve of U.S. forces was then weak, U.S. prestige was "already engaged" in South Vietnam and would "become more so by the sending of troops," it would "be difficult to resist the pressure to reinforce" if it became necessary, and the introduction of the U.S. military forces "may increase tensions and risk escalation into a major war in Asia."

But Taylor was reported to have advised Kennedy that it was doubtful "our program to save Vietnam" could succeed without the U.S. military commitment. According to the same cable listing the disadvantages, Taylor claimed that "the risks of backing into a major Asian war by way of SVN [South Vietnam] are present but are not impressive," that North Vietnam was "extremely vulnerable to conventional bombing, a weakness which should be exploited diplomat-

ically in convincing Hanoi to lay off SVN," and both the North Vietnamese and Chinese Communists "would face severe logistical difficulties in trying to maintain strong forces in the field" in Southeast Asia, "difficulties which we share but by no means to the same degree."

Tide toward 'partnership.' The Washington Post July 2 focused on the initial move by the Kennedy Administration in 1961 to a "limited partnership" with Saigon amidst a seemingly irreversible tide of advice toward a military commitment. The article portrayed the increasing tug of Vietnam events on a President already immersed in global vexations with the Soviet Union over Berlin and distracted by the peaking, peripheral crises of Communist inroads in Laos and Thailand.

By May, 1961, there was a task force report suggesting implementation of a SEATO contingency plan "providing for military intervention in South Vietnam should this become necessary to prevent the loss of the country to communism." By May 10, there was a Joint Chiefs of Staff recommendation, pinned on the assumption "that the political decision is to hold Southeast Asia outside the Communist sphere," for "immediate deployment of appropriate U.S. forces to South Vietnam."

In the fall there was an opinion from Assistant Defense Secretary William Bundy "that it is now or never if we are to arrest the gains being made by the Viet Cong." Bundy estimated the probability of success would be 70% for "an early and hard-hitting operation" and 30% for winding up "like the French in 1954," adding that "white men can't win this kind of fight." On the 70–30 basis, he suggested the "odds" would "slide" down within a month if the U.S. did not "move" to "60–40, 50–50 and so on," all of which, taking cognizance of the Laotian problem, "underscores the element of time."

By October, Gen. Maxwell Taylor, after his investigatory mission to Vietnam, was proposing a U.S. force, "largely military in composition," of about 8,000 men as "an essential action if we are to reverse the present downward trend of events" in Vietnam.

In transmitting his report to the President, Taylor stressed the U.S. "must decide how it will cope with [Soviet leader Nikita] Khrushchev's 'wars of liberation' which are really para-wars of guerrilla aggression." This was "a new and dangerous Communist technique which bypasses our traditional political and military responses," Taylor warned, and it was clear "that the time may come in our relations to Southeast Asia when we must declare our intentions to attack the source of guerrilla aggression in North Vietnam and impose on the Hanoi government a price for participation in the current war which is commensurate with the damage being inflicted on its neighbors to the South."

On Nov. 8 President Kennedy received endorsement of the Taylor recommendation from McNamara and the Joint Chiefs with McNamara's estimate that "we can assume that the maximum U.S. forces required on the ground in Southeast Asia will not exceed six divisions, or about 205,000 men," even if Hanoi and Peking were to "intervene overtly."

This was followed by a Nov. 11 joint memorandum from McNamara and Secretary of State Dean Rusk recommending that "we now take the decision to commit ourselves to the objective of preventing the fall of South Vietnam to communism and that, in doing so, we recognize that the introduction of United States and other SEATO forces may be necessary to achieve this objective." "We should be prepared," it declared, "to introduce United States combat forces if that should become necessary for success."

All this preceded a National Security Action Memorandum Nov. 22 providing Kennedy's approval for sending to Vietnam helicopters, light aircraft and transport planes manned by uniformed U.S. personnel in a new "partnership" between the U.S. and South Vietnam. The advance crews arrived in Saigon Dec. 11, 1961 and an accelerated aid program for South Vietnam was announced Dec. 15.

The Kennedy years. The New York Times resumed its interrupted series on the Pentagon papers July 1 with articles on policy planning by the Kennedy Administration in 1961–63. One article dealt with events leading up to the coup d'état against South Vietnamese President Ngo Dinh Diem, the second with Diem's overthrow.

Among the conclusions of the pre-coup article, the Pentagon study found a transformation during the Kennedy years from a "limited-risk gamble" of the Eisenhower Administration into a "broad commitment" to bar Communist domination of South Vietnam.

The study also reported that "the dilemma of the U.S. involvement dating from the Kennedy era" was to use "only limited means to achieve excessive ends." According to the study, Kennedy resisted pressures for putting U.S. ground combat troops in Vietnam but combat support and advisory missions were built up, in a decision made "almost by default" because of the intense debate in 1961 over the question of ground combat forces.

Starting from a decision in the spring of 1961, not given publicity, to send 400 Special Forces troops and 100 other American military advisers to South Vietnam, the American involvement grew to 16,732 men by October 1963. The Pentagon study found the original expansion as signaling "a willingness to go beyond the 685-man limit on the size of the U.S. [military] mission in Saigon, which, if it were done openly, would be the first formal breach of the Geneva agreement," which cited the 685-man limit. It also found that the decision to increase the combat aid and advisory missions had been reached "without extended study or debate" or precise expectation of its possible results.

Kennedy left President Johnson as least as critical a Vietnam situation as he had inherited, according to the study. As for what policy Kennedy might have pursued had he lived, it said "no reliable information can be drawn."

A strange aspect of this period was a drive by Defense Secretary Robert S. McNamara, when events seemed to subside in 1962 from the chronic crisis of 1961, to begin planning for American withdrawal. On July 23, 1962, the day a Laotian peace agreement was signed in Geneva, McNamara ordered the planning begun because of "tremendous progress" with the U.S. operations in Indochina and a concern about indefinite retention of public support. The study commented that the withdrawal planning, seen in the midst of the political struggle against Diem that began in May, 1963, had an "absurd quality" predicated on "the most Micawberesque predictions" of progress. The continuing political deterioration attending the Diem struggle caused the eventual demise of all phaseout planning in early 1964.

Another aspect of the period was Diem's reaction to the possibility, broached by Vice President Johnson during his 1961 Asian tour, of U.S. combat units being sent to Vietnam and a defensive security alliance drawn between the U.S. and South Vietnam. As told in an embassy report, Diem was uninterested and said he wanted American combat troops only in the event of an open invasion. In his private report to Kennedy May 23, Johnson said "we must decide whether to help these countries to the best of our ability or throw in the towel in the area and pull back our defenses to San Francisco."

In a June 9 letter to Kennedy, however, Diem asked for a "considerable" buildup of U.S. forces and a 100,000-man expansion of the South Vietnamese army, and by Sept. 29, according to a cablegram from the U.S. ambassador in Saigon, Diem was asking for a bilateral defense treaty.

On the U.S. side, the study revealed the ascendancy of the "domino" theory —that if South Vietnam fell, all of Southeast Asia would follow—and inaccurate estimates of the ultimate, maximum U.S. strength requirement. A Joint Chiefs of Staff estimate in October 1961 was "that 40,000 U.S. forces will be needed to clean up the Viet Cong threat." Also in 1961, the chiefs and McNamara were reporting estimates that the maximum U.S. ground force requirement "will not exceed six divisions."

McNamara and Secretary of State Rusk joined in a report to Kennedy Nov. 11, 1961, warning that the loss of South Vietnam "would make pointless any further discussion about the importance of Southeast Asia to the Free World." Kennedy asked the importance of South Vietnam and Laos at a Nov. 15 National Security Council meeting, and, according to notes reported in the Pentagon study, Gen. Lyman L. Lemnitzer, chairman of the Joint Chiefs, replied, "We would lose Asia all the way to Singapore."

The Diem coup. The Times July 1 dealt with the plans, decisions and events of the military coup that overthrew President Diem in 1963 and resulted in his murder. The study detailed the U.S. "complicity" in the coup, its support for the plotters and its discovery that the war against the Viet Cong was going much worse than previously thought. The resultant trend, according to the Pentagon analysis, was to do more rather than less for Saigon. By supporting the coup, it said, "the U.S. inadvertently deepened its involvement. The inadvertence is the key factor."

President Kennedy was kept abreast of the coup planning and gave no direct countermand, at least from the Pentagon account, to the strong pro-coup support of the U.S. ambassador in Saigon, Henry Cabot Lodge.

According to an Aug. 30, 1963 cable obtained by the Times along with the Pentagon study, Kennedy privately informed Lodge of his support for "everything possible to help you conclude this operation successfully" but requested continuing reports in order to permit the contingency of a "reverse" signal. "We must go to win," Kennedy warned, "but it will be better to change our minds than fail."

Later, in October 1963, the question of an aid cutoff to the Diem regime was suggested, a course the Pentagon study determined left "ambiguous" the matter of whether such a course would be construed as a "green light" for the coup. The aid cutoff was begun in a context of working with the Diem regime but not supporting it, as recommended by McNamara and Gen. Maxwell D. Taylor, chairman of the Joint Chiefs. At about the same time, a White House message to Lodge (Oct. 5) called for "surveillance and readiness" without "active promotion" of coup to leave room for "plausibility of denial" of U.S. involvement. Another White House message to Lodge (Oct. 25) stressed the necessity for the "option of judging and warning on any plan with poor prospects of success." In reply Oct. 25, Lodge opposed any effort to "pour cold water" on the plot. Still another White House message (Oct. 30) urged Lodge to "discourage" the plot if "quick success" were unlikely, but Lodge replied the same day that the U.S. was unable to "delay or discourage a coup" by now.

As the coup proceeded, according to a Lodge cable to the State Department Nov. 1, Diem telephoned Lodge to inquire of the "attitude of the U.S." and Lodge replied he was not "well enough informed to tell you," and, since it was 4:30 a.m. in Washington, "the U.S. government cannot possibly have a view." Lodge did express concern "about your physical safety" and said, "If I can do anything for your physical safety, please call me." Diem's reply was, "I am trying to re-establish order." Lodge also told Diem he had "a report that those in charge of the current activity offer you and your brother safe conduct out of the country if you resign."

Diem and his brother, Ngo Dinh Nhu, were shot to death by armored units after accepting a safe-conduct offer from the generals staging the coup.

The Washington Post July 1 quoted the analyst as saying: For two months before the coup the U.S. "variously authorized, sanctioned and encouraged the coup efforts of the Vietnamese generals and offered full support for a successor government."

The study held that the decision on the coup was one of the "fundamental choices" made by the U.S. in the Vietnam involvement. It could have continued to "plod along" with Diem, or encouraged a coup or seized the opportunity of political instability to disengage from South Vietnam. Decisions on the first two choices were based, the report held, on the consideration that "we could not win" with Diem and his brother Nhu. The third alternative, it said, was "never seriously considered" because of the underlying assumption that an independent, non-Communist South Vietnam was "too important a strategic interest to abandon."

The authors of the Pentagon analysis found the event of the coup a significant

deepening of the U.S. commitment to South Vietnam, an assumption of responsibility for the incoming regime and for the fight against the Communist menace.

The article attributed much of the impulse toward the coup to Diem and Nhu and their violent action against the Buddhist opposition, including the midnight assaults on pagodas throughout Vietnam Aug. 21, 1963 despite a public pledge of conciliation by Diem.

The Administration's insistence on Nhu's removal from a position of power was transmitted to Lodge, who was told by cable to give Diem a chance to drop Nhu from the regime. That Diem's tenure was conditioned on it was made explicit: "If in spite of all your efforts," the cable continued, "Diem remains obdurate and refuses, then we must face the possibility that Diem himself cannot be preserved."

The U.S. attitude toward Nhu and the "obvious implication" that Diem's future was tied to the issue were to be relayed to key Vietnamese military leaders, who were also to be informed that the U.S. "will give them direct support in any interim period of breakdown central government mechanism." The cable further directed Lodge to "urgently examine all possible alternative leadership and make detailed plans as to how we might bring about Diem's replacement if this should become necessary."

Lodge's return cable expressed certainty of Diem's refusal to remove Nhu and advised taking the matter directly to the generals.

In succeeding cables, the U.S. made clear its intention to remain completely clear of direct involvement in coup events and its concern that any coup attempted after encouragement from the U.S. should not fail. The U.S. "will support a coup which has a good chance of succeeding," the embassy in Saigon was informed. Later, when prospects of a coup receded temporarily, the advice was "that no initiative should now be taken to give any active covert encouragement to a coup. There should, however, be urgent covert effort with closest security under broad guidance of ambassador to identify and build contacts with possible leadership as when it appears." The activity was to be secretive and "fully deniable." "Surveillance and readiness" were the passwords.

Later, word was to be passed to the plotting generals that "while we do not wish to stimulate coup, we also do not wish to leave impression that U.S. would thwart a change of government or deny economic and military assistance to a new regime if it appeared capable of increasing effectiveness of military effort, ensuring popular support to win war and improving working relations with U.S."

Shortly before the coup, the cabled policy to Lodge was to "take action to persuade coup leaders to stop or delay any operation which, in your best judgment, does not clearly give high prospect of success." The U.S. was not to be directly involved with either side in any coup action, but if a coup were initiated under responsible leadership, it said, "It is in the interest of the U.S. government that it should succeed."

The Chicago Sun-Times June 23 published a partial text of a secret State Department memo revealing that the Kennedy Administration took part in the planning of the coup.

The paper also printed part of a second State Department communication recommending that the U.S. put pressure on Diem to remove from power Ngo Dinh Nhu, his brother and chief of South Vietnam's secret police.

Both memorandums were from Roger Hilsman, then assistant secretary of state, to Secretary of State Dean Rusk. The first, on Aug. 30, 1963, recommended that the U.S. encourage and assist a coup against Diem and Nhu.

Hilsman wrote the Aug. 30 memorandum at a time when U.S. officials believed a military coup—or action by Diem against his dissident generals—was imminent. The coup took place Nov. 1, 1963.

In his Aug. 30 communication, Hilsman charted what he saw as the likely courses of action which Diem and Nhu could take to crush a coup and maintain themselves in power. For each course of action, Hilsman proposed counter-moves by the U.S.

In the event that Diem sought to have North Vietnam intervene on his side in a coup, Hilsman recommended swift U.S. action.

"If the DRV [North Vietnam] threatens to respond to an anti-Diem coup by sending troops openly to South Vietnam, we should let it know unequivocally that we shall hit the DRV with all we have to force it to desist."

Hilsman also proposed a U.S. response should Diem appeal to French President Charles DeGaulle for the neutralization of Vietnam:

We should point out publicly that Vietnam cannot be effectively neutralized unless the Communists are removed from control of North Vietnam. If a coalition between Diem and the Communists is suggested, we should reply that this would be the avenue to a Communist takeover in view of the relative strength of the two principals in the coalition. Once an anti-Diem coup is started in South Vietnam, we can point to the obvious refusal of South Vietnam to accept a Diem-Communist coalition.

According to Hilsman, the U.S. objective was clear:

". . . .to bring the whole Ngo family under the control of the coup group."

The goals of the coup's participants were also clear, Hilsman wrote:

"We should warn the coup group to press any military advantage it gains to its logical conclusion without stopping to negotiate."

Hilsman advised Rusk to urge the coup's generals to seek total victory even if Diem and his forces chose to make a final stand at the Presidential palace.

"We should encourage the coup group to fight the battle to the end and to destroy the palace if necessary to gain victory."

In the closing paragraphs of the Aug. 30 memorandum Hilsman recommended that if Diem and his family chose to flee, the U.S. should provide them with a plane but only if Diem agreed to go to France or another European country. The Sun-Times quoted the memo as having said that "under no circumstances should the Ngos be permitted to remain in Southeast Asia in close proximity to Vietnam because of the plots they will try to mount to regain power. If the generals decide to exile Diem, he should also be sent outside Southeast Asia."

The second Hilsman memorandum, on Sept. 16, 1963, reflected a shift in U.S. policy. According to the excerpts published by the Sun-Times, the U.S. no longer was seeking to oust Diem but rather had decided to support him but force Nhu out. The Sun-Times said the documents made it clear that there was unanimous agreement among President Kennedy and his top advisers that pressure should be applied to Diem to purge Nhu.

Hilsman put his views to Rusk in two cables—one on the "Reconciliation Track" and one on the "Pressures and Persuasion Track."

Hilsman wrote that he thought Nhu had already decided on an "adventure," in which case the "reconciliation track" would not work. Nhu, Hilsman said, "feels that the progress already made in the war and the U.S. material on hand gives him freedom to launch on a course that has a minimum and a maximum goal." According to Hilsman, Nhu's minimum goal would be to reduce the American influence in the South Vietnamese government, and his maximum to deal with North Vietnam for a truce.

The "pressure track" called for the careful testing and probing of U.S. policy as developments unfolded.

A Los Angeles Times report June 24 also dealt with Kennedy Administration discussions in the last months before the coup. The Los Angles paper focused on an August 1963 National Security Council memo recording the recommendation of a State Department expert that the U.S. should quit Vietnam rather than continue supporting the Diem regime.

The memorandum, written by Marine Maj. Gen. Victor C. Krulak, pertained to a Security Council meeting to discuss options following an unsuccessful coup attempt against Diem. Krulak reported that the State Department expert, Paul H. Kattenburg, said "if we undertake to live with this repressive regime, . . . we are going to be thrown out of the country in six months." The memo said Kattenburg "stated that at this junction it would be better for us to make the decision to get out honorably."

According to the Los Angeles Times, the Pentagon analysis showed that Kattenburg's assessment was rejected by Secretary of State Dean Rusk as "speculative." Rusk, reportedly supported by Vice President Johnson and Defense Secretary Robert McNamara, was recorded as saying: "It would be far better for us to start on the firm basis of two things—that we will not pull out of Vietnam until the war is won, and that we will not run a coup" against Diem.

The Los Angeles Times said the documents indicated that while the U.S. was unwilling to "run" a coup, the Administration decided not to intervene on Diem's behalf and, according to an Oct. 2, 1963 document, to undertake "urgent covert effort with closest security. . . to identify and build contacts with possible alternative leadership."

Saigon regimes trouble LBJ. Reports published in the Washington Post July 1 and 2 dealt with the Pentagon analysis of Washington's difficulties with a succession of regimes in Saigon beginning with the ouster and assassination of Diem in November 1963.

According to the Post, fear that pro-French politicians and generals in Saigon might embrace French President Charles de Gaulle's August 1963 call for "neutralization" of Vietnam colored the U.S. attitude toward the Diem ouster and the January 1964 coup against its pro-U.S. successor, Gen. Duong Van Minh.

The Post said the Diem overthrow destroyed the "entire mandarin-style political structure of South Vietnam." The Pentagon papers revealed that the weakness in Saigon that followed was a major problem of the war from 1964 through 1967, when U.S. forces in Vietnam grew from 15,000 advisers to nearly 500,000 troops.

In its July 1 report, the Post said the study indicated that in 1963 and 1964 the U.S. was struggling more to stay in the war than to get out of Vietnam. A March 16, 1964 memo from Defense Secretary Robert McNamara to President Johnson was cited as illustrating Washington's attitude that negotiation on the basis of de Gaulle's neutralization proposal "would simply mean a Communist takeover in South Vietnam," And Johnson, in late March 1964, sent word to Ambassador Henry Cabot Lodge in Saigon that "your mission is precisely for the purpose of knocking down the idea of neutralization wherever it rears its ugly head."

McNamara and Gen. Maxwell D. Taylor, chairman of the Joint Chiefs of

Staff, in an Oct. 2, 1963 report to President Kennedy following a survey trip to Vietnam, voiced Washington's distrust of the Diem regime. The memo said that a "disturbing feature of [Ngo Dinh] Nhu," Diem's brother, "is his flirtation with the idea of negotiation with North Vietnam."

However, the Diem coup and takeover by Gen. Duong Van Minh did not end Washington's fears that the U.S. would be frozen out by a forced neutralization of Vietnam. The Pentagon papers indicated that the justification used by Gen. Nguyen Khanh for the Jan. 30, 1964 bloodless coup that toppled Minh was that he had moved against Minh to frustrate the ambitions of "pro-French" generals in Saigon who wished to seize power and negotiate for neutralization. An explanatory cable from Ambassador Lodge to the White House expressed skepticism about Khanh's motives but also cited an opinion from diplomatic circles that "the Minh government was actively in support of Gen. de Gaulle's ideas and would turn overtly neutralist at the proper time."

Lodge expressed the hope that Khanh might turn out to be the "tough and ruthless commander" needed in Saigon. However, the Pentagon analyst said the U.S. "recognized that it was a severe blow to the stability of the government that we had believed was so necessary for South Vietnam, and we doubted the charges that Khanh used as a justification for his actions."

The political difficulties in South Vietnam following the Diem ouster were such that there were six major changes of government in 18 months, the last being the mid-1965 military coup that brought Nguyen Cao Ky and Nguyen Van Thieu to power. According to the July 2 Post report, in contrast to the Diem coup, the U.S. was not informed in advance about four major coups or coup attempts between early 1964 and mid-1965.

During this period, the Pentagon papers showed U.S. preoccupation with strengthening the Saigon government in order to successfully pursue the war in the South. However, the Saigon regimes pressed for military action outside South Vietnam—for action in Laos and a

"March North" campaign. According to the Post, the U.S. was drawn into increased military involvement, partially in order to encourage and improve the morale of the weak leaders in Saigon.

Declaring that U.S. military actions depended upon stability in Saigon, Taylor, who had replaced Lodge as ambassador, upbraided dissident Saigon generals in December 1964. The Pentagon analyst said that during a crisis in the spring of 1966, when the generals used force against a popular general and his Buddhist supporters, the State Department "authorized the threat of total U.S. withdrawal" in an attempt to force a reconciliation. But according to the Post account, efforts to obtain national unity in South Vietnam failed in 1966 and again following the Viet Cong's Tet offensive in 1968.

1962 pullout plan abandoned. The Christian Science Monitor's first story in its Pentagon papers series, published June 29, told of a five-year plan to pull U.S. troops out of Vietnam. The plan, according to the Monitor, was formulated and abandoned during "a crucial 21 months spanning the Kennedy and Johnson Administrations."

Quoting from the Pentagon analysis, the article said planning for a "phased withdrawal" began "amid the euphoria and optimism of July 1962 and was ended in the pessimism of March 1964." The plan was abandoned in what the Pentagon analyst called "the sinking aftereffects" of the November 1963 coup in Saigon and assassination of South Vietnamese President Diem.

Although the pullout was "overtaken by events," said the Pentagon study, the plan was flawed from the start by "some basic unrealities." According to the Pentagon analyst, the Kennedy Administration based the phase-out plan on a belief that "the fight against the guerrillas would have clearly turned the corner by Fiscal Year 1965." The study also said the planners were overly optimistic about the effectiveness of the South Vietnamese.

The study said, "the political situation in South Vietnam itself should have prompted more realistic contingency plans against failure of the Vietnamese, in order to give the U.S. some options other than what appeared as precipitous withdrawal."

In a conclusion, the Pentagon analysis sized up the plan as follows:

Phased withdrawal was a good policy that was being reasonably well executed. In the way of our Vietnam involvement, it was overtaken by events. Not born of deep conviction in the necessity for a U.S. withdrawal or in the necessity of forcing the GVN [Saigon government] to truly carry the load, it was bound to be submerged in the rush of events. A policy more determined might have used the pretext and the fact of the Diem coup and its aftermath as reason to push for the continuation of withdrawal. Instead, the instability and fear of collapse resulting from the Diem coup brought the U.S. to a decision for greater commitment.

LBJ alternatives. The Washington Post said July 3 that the Pentagon papers revealed that Johnson, during his first year as President, was confronted with conflicting advice from his advisers adding up to a dilemma that whatever course he chose in Vietnam would lead to a risk of nuclear war. While some advisers cautioned that inaction in Southeast Asia, leading to the loss of Vietnam, could cause the U.S. to slip into a nuclear confrontation, others warned that massive intervention could trigger a nuclear war with Communist China.

The risk of nuclear war through inaction was stated in a November 1964 analysis entitled "Courses of Action in Southeast Asia." (The Post explained that this particular document, written by Assistant Secretary of State William P. Bundy and Assistant Defense Secretary John T. McNaughton, was a draft that may have reached Johnson only in the form of Cabinet-level recommendations for action.) The document presented a modification of the "domino" theory, that Communist victory in South Vietnam would almost automatically topple non-Communist adjoining nations.

After projecting various consequences of defeat in South Vietnam, the document stated: "There are enough 'ifs' in the above analysis so that it cannot be concluded that the loss of South Vietnam would soon have the totally crippling effect in Southeast Asia and Asia generally that the loss of Berlin would have in Europe; but it could be that bad, driving us to the progressive loss of other areas or to taking a stand at some point [so that] there would almost certainly

be major conflict and perhaps the great risk of nuclear war."

The Post said the Pentagon study showed, however, that the possibility that U.S. military action on a large scale could trigger intervention by Communist China was constantly under consideration. The Pentagon analysis referred to contingency plans that were made to meet such intervention. Options for specific military actions were weighed with Chinese reaction in mind.

The Post cited a Jan. 22, 1964 memo from the Joint Chiefs of Staff to Defense Secretary Robert S. McNamara that urged the "adoption of a more aggressive program" of military action. The memo was reassuring on the problem of Chinese intervention: "It appears probable that the economic and agricultural disappointments suffered by Communist China, plus the current rift with the Soviets, could cause the Communists to think twice about undertaking a large-scale military adventure in Southeast Asia."

In the memo Gen. Maxwell D. Taylor, chairman of the Joint Chiefs of Staff, advised McNamara that the Joints Chiefs believed the U.S. "must be prepared to put aside many of the self-imposed restrictions which now limit our efforts and to undertake bolder action" in order to win the war in South Vietnam. In his memo, entitled "Vietnam and Southeast Asia," Taylor proposed the following military moves:

a. Assign to the U.S. military commander responsibilities for the total U.S. program in Vietnam.

b. Induce the Government of Vietnam to turn over to the United States military commander, temporarily, the actual tactical direction of the war.

c. Charge the United States military commander with complete responsibility for conduct of the program against North Vietnam.

d. Overfly Laos and Cambodia to whatever extent is necessary for acquisition of operational intelligence.

e. Induce the Government of Vietnam to conduct overt ground operations in Laos of sufficient scope to impede the flow of personnel and material southward.

f. Arm, equip, advise, and support the Government of Vietnam in its conduct of aerial bombing of critical targets in North Vietnam and in mining the sea approaches to that country.

g. Advise and support the Government of Vietnam in its conduct of large-scale commando raids against critical targets in North Vietnam.

h. Conduct aerial bombing of key North Vietnam targets, using U.S. resources under Vietnamese cover, and with the Vietnamese openly assuming responsibility for the actions.

i. Commit additional U.S. forces, as necessary, in support of the combat action within South Vietnam.

j. Commit U.S. forces as necessary in direct actions against North Vietnam.

11. It is our conviction that any or all of the foregoing actions may be required to enhance our position in Southeast Asia. The past few months have disclosed that considerably higher levels of effort are demanded of us if U.S. objectives are to be attained.

The Post said no adviser seemed able to guarantee just what Communist China's reactions would be. After calculating the risks of various military options considered by the Johnson Administration, a study by a working group of the National Security Council said in November 1964: "Nevertheless, there is always a chance that Peiping might so intervene either for reasons that seem irrational to us or because it miscalculated the objectives of U.S. moves in the area."

Tonkin period. The period from the beginning of 1964 to the Tonkin Gulf clashes in August 1964 was considered in the Pentagon study as a pivotal phase, according to the Times report June 13. The Pentagon papers described the escalation of a three-phase covert war against North Vietnam. Simultaneously, according to the Pentagon analysis, the Johnson Administration authorized extensive planning for an overt military campaign culminating in air attacks against North Vietnam.

Because of the extensive plans for overt action, said the Pentagon analyst, the Johnson Administration was able to order retaliatory air strikes on less than six hours notice during the Tonkin incident. A list of targets for the air strikes already existed as well as a draft resolution to provide Congressional support.

The Pentagon study, according to the Times, cited the following three elements of a growing clandestine war against North Vietnam: (1) a series of destructive and harassment actions—ground, air and sea raids—conducted under the code name Operation Plan 34A and beginning Feb. 1, 1964; (2) air operations in Laos; and (3) destroyer patrols in the Gulf of Tonkin, under the code name De Soto patrols.

Military planning for the 34A raids was the joint responsibility of the U.S. command in Saigon and the South Vietnamese. The raids were performed, said the Pentagon analyst, by the South Vietnamese or "hired personnel," but they were directed by the U.S. military command in Saigon.

A Jan. 2, 1964 report, quoted in the Pentagon study, from the head of a Joint Chief of Staff unit to President Johnson, described an overall plan for the 34A "destructive undertakings." The report said the raids were designed "to result in substantial destruction, economic loss and harassment" and the strikes were to escalate through 1964 to include "targets identified with North Vietnam's economic and industrial well-being."

The Laos bombing phase of the covert war included strikes by T-28 fighter-bombers carrying the markings of the Laotian Air Force. The report said, however, that some of the planes were manned by pilots of Air America, described as a private operation run by the Central Intelligence Agency, and by Thai pilots. In addition, reconnaissance flights over Laos were conducted by regular U.S. Air Force and Navy jets. After two Navy jets were shot down by enemy ground fire June 6 and 7, 1964, Washington added armed escort jets.

The first destroyer patrol in the Tonkin Gulf was conducted without incident in February and March of 1964 and was completely separate, according to the Pentagon report, from 34A raids occurring at the same time. The analyst admitted that the presence in the gulf of the U.S. destroyer Maddox, on the second De Soto patrol, resulted in the Tonkin incident—attacks by North Vietnamese torpedo boats on Aug. 2 and 4, 1964. However, the study contended that no deliberate provocation was intended.

Of the three phases of covert war, the Pentagon analyst emphasized the importance of the 34A raids in crossing a "firebreak." The study said the "unequivocal" U.S. responsibility for the raids "carried with it an implicit symbolic and psychological intensification of the U.S. commitment."

In addition to the clandestine military operations, the Johnson Administration prepared detailed plans for the "increasingly bolder actions" against North Vietnam advocated by Gen. Maxwell D. Taylor, chairman of the Joint Chiefs, in a memo to McNamara Jan.

22, 1964. After a trip to Vietnam, McNamara March 16, 1964 also advised planning for two programs of "new and significant pressures upon North Vietnam."

In a memorandum submitted to President Johnson March 16, 1964, Secretary McNamara asserted that the military and political situation in South Vietnam "has unquestionably been growing worse." The report, "South Vietnam," cited civilian apathy, large numbers of military desertions and draft-dodging and North Vietnam's increasing support of the Viet Cong.

In order to provide the Saigon regime with greater political and military assistance, McNamara recommended that President Johnson "instruct the appropriate agencies of the U.S. government:

1. To make it clear that we are prepared to furnish assistance and support to South Vietnam for as long as it takes to bring the insurgency under control.

2. To make it clear that we fully support the Khanh government and are opposed to further coups.

3. To support a Program for National Mobilization (including a national service law) to put South Vietnam on a war footing.

4. To assist the Vietnamese to increase the armed forces (regular plus paramilitary) by at least 50,000 men.

5. To assist the Vietnamese to creat a greatly enlarged Civil Administrative Corps for work at province, district and hamlet levels.

6. To assist the Vietnamese to improve and reorganize the paramilitary forces and increase their compensation.

7. To assist the Vietnamese to create an offensive guerrilla force.

8. To provide the Vietnamese Air Force 25 A-1H aircraft in exchange for the present T-28s.

9. To provide the Vietnamese Army additional M-113 armored personnel carriers (withdrawing the M-114s there), additional river boats, and approximately $5–10 million of other additional material.

10. To announce publicly the Fertilizer Program and to expand it with a view within two years to trebling the amount of fertilizer made available.

11. To authorize continued high-level U.S. overflights of South Vietnam's borders and to authorize "hot pursuit" and South Vietnamese ground operations over the Laotian line for the purpose of border control. More ambitious operations into Laos involving units beyond battalion size should be authorized only with the approval of Souvanna Phouma. Operations across the Cambodian border should depend on the state of relations with Cambodia.

12. To prepare immediately to be in a position on 72 hours' notice to initiate the full range of Laotian and Cambodian "Border Control" actions (beyond those authorized in Paragraph 11 above) and the "Retaliatory Actions" against North Vietnam, and to be in a position on 30 days' notice to initiate the program of "Graduated Overt Military Pressure" against North Vietnam.

At a National Security Council meeting the next day, President Johnson ordered that the planning "proceed energetically."

A National Security Action Memorandum 288, "U.S. Objectives in South Vietnam," dated March 17, 1964, said U.S. policy was to "prepare immediately to be in a position on 72 hours' notice to initiate the full range of Laotian and Cambodian 'Border Control Actions' . . . and the 'Retaliatory Actions' against North Vietnam." The memo, however, cautioned against "U.S. intervention on a large scale and/or GVN [South Vietnam] actions against the North" and against a full American take-over of the military command in the South. It said these actions "would disturb key allies and other nations" and would have an "adverse psychological impact."

In response, Administration officials produced a scenario dated May 23 outlining a 30-day program leading to full-scale, open bombing of North Vietnam. The program included a plan for air strikes and included lists of targets. The May 23 scenario, quoted by the Pentagon analyst, was never put into operation as planned, but elements of it were adopted before and after the Tonkin incident.

One element of the plan was carried out June 18, 1964, when a Canadian diplomat visited Hanoi. According to the Pentagon analyst, the diplomat's message was that U.S. intentions in Southeast Asia were "essentially peaceful" but that "in the event of [Vietcong] escalation the greatest devastation would of course result for the D.R.V. [North Vietnam] itself."

A U.S. note delivered to the Canadian embassy in Washington Aug. 8, 1964 urged that J. Blair Seaborn, Canadian member of the International Control Commission, transmit to Hanoi Washington's version of the North Vietnamese attacks on American destroyers in the Gulf of Tonkin Aug. 2 and 4.

Another element of the scenario, securing passage of a joint Congressional resolution to back the Administration, was delayed although a draft resolution was prepared May 25. Obtaining the resolution "prior to wider U.S. action in Southeast Asia," said the analyst, was a major topic at top level strategy sessions in Honolulu June 1 and 2, 1964.

Also in June, the study related, President Johnson submitted a formal question to the CIA: "Would the rest of Southeast Asia necessarily fall if Laos and South Vietnam came under North Vietnamese control?" The CIA memo in reply challenged the widely held "domino" theory: "With the possible exception of Cambodia . . . it is likely that no nation in the area would quickly succumb to Communism" if the two countries fell. "Furthermore," continued the CIA memo, "a continuation of the spread of Communism in the area would not be inexorable, and any spread which did occur would take time."

The analyst described how the preparation of the May 23 scenario, including the drafting of a Congressional resolution, allowed the Administration to act quickly following the Tonkin incident. The Pentagon report said, "the Tonkin Gulf reprisal constituted an important firebreak and the Tonkin Gulf resolution set U.S. public support for virtually any action."

Air strikes following the incident, said the analyst, "marked the crossing of an important threshold in the war, and it was accomplished with virtually no domestic criticism, indeed, with an evident increase in public support for the Administration."

The study concluded that the "precedent for strikes against the North was thus established and at very little apparent cost." The analyst, however, cites a "real cost . . . in that the Administration was psychologically preparing itself for further escalation. . . . Greater visible commitment was purchased at the price of reduced flexibility."

In a cablegram March 20, 1964 to Henry Cabot Lodge, U.S. ambassador to Saigon, President Johnson stated that escalating the war against North Vietnam "at the present would be premature." Such action against the North "is on a contingency basis at present and immediate problem in this area is to develop the strongest possible military and political base" in South Vietnam "for possible later action," Johnson said.

Gen. Maxwell D. Taylor cautioned the State Department in a cablegram July 25, 1964 against support of South Vietnam's "public campaign for 'Marching North.'" He recommended that:

"We would try to avoid head-on collision with the GVN which unqualified U.S. opposition to the 'March North' campaign would entail. We could do this by expressing a willingness to engage in joint

contingency planning for various forms of extended action against [North Vietnam]. Such planning would not only provide an outlet for the martial head of steam now dangerously compressed but would force the generals to look at the hard facts of life which lie behind the neon lights of the 'March North' slogans. This planning would also gain time badly needed to stabilize this government and could provide a useful basis for military action if adjudged in our interest at some future time. Finally, it would also afford U.S. an opportunity, for the first time, to have a frank discussion with GVN leaders concerning the political objectives which they would envisage as the purposes inherent in military action against the DRV [North Vietnam]. . . ."

William P. Bundy, assistant secretary of state for Far Eastern affairs, Aug. 11, 1964 drafted a memorandum, "Next Courses of Action in Southeast Asia," following the Tonkin Gulf incidents. In an introduction to the document, a summary of which was cabled Aug. 14 to the Pacific command and the U.S. embassies in Saigon and Vientiane, Laos, Bundy said:

"This memorandum examines the courses of action the U.S. might pursue, commencing in about two weeks, assuming that the Communist side does not react further the [sic] the events of last week.

We have agreed that the intervening period will be in effect a short holding phase, in which we would avoid actions that would in any way take the onus off the Communist side for escalation . . ."

Adm. U.S. Grant Sharp, commander of Pacific forces, reviewed past American military actions and possible future moves in a cablegram sent Aug. 17, 1964 to Joint Chiefs of Staff. The document, "Next Courses of Action in Southeast Asia," said "an essential element of our military action . . . is to proceed in the development of our physical readiness posture: deploying troops, ships, aircraft, and logistic resources. . . . We must maintain this posture; to reduce it would have a dangerous impact on the morale and will of all people in Southeast Asia."

In a cablegram to the U.S. embassy in Vientiane, Laos, Secretary of State Dean Rusk Aug. 26, 1964 authorized the use of of U.S. Air America pilots in search and rescue missions directed at U.S., Thai or Laotian pilots downed in bombing operations against Communist forces in Laos. Rusk said the bombing missions by T-38 planes were "vital both for their military and psychological effects in Laos and as negotiating card in support" of Laotian Premier Souvanna Phouma.

In a cablegram to the U.S. embassy in Vientiane, Laos Aug. 7, 1964, Rusk had raised the possibility of proposing a peace conference to end the hostilities in Laos. "We would insist that the conference be limited to Laos and believe that it could . . ., if necessary by our withdrawing from the conference room if any other subject brought up . . .," Rusk said. Copies of the cable also were sent, with a request for comment, to the American missions in London, Paris, Saigon, Bangkok, Ottawa, New Delhi, Pnompenh and Hong Kong, and to the Pacific command and the mission at the U.N.

Maxwell D. Taylor replied to Rusk in a cablegram Aug. 9, 1964 that "we see very little hope that results of such conference would be advantageous to the U.S." Taylor argued that the talks would lead to "increased political instability" in South Vietnam and would undermine the Saigon forces' "morale and will to fight" in South Vietnam.

Sustained bombing undertaken. Although concentrated U.S. bombing of North Vietnam did not begin until the launching of Operation Rolling Thunder in February 1965, the Pentagon analysis related that the Johnson Administration reached a "general consensus" at a Sept. 7, 1964 strategy meeting that air attacks would probably have to be initiated. The Pentagon study, as reported by the Times June 14, cited President Johnson's election campaign as the first of a "set of tactical considerations" that "prevented action for the time being."

In the words of the Pentagon analyst, "the President was in the midst of an election campaign in which he was presenting himself as the candidate of reason and restraint as opposed to the quixotic Barry Goldwater," who was advocating full-scale bombing of North Vietnam. The study said "from the September meeting forward, there was little basic disagreement" among the principal Johnson Administration policy makers on the need for air attacks against North Vietnam and that it was expected that "these operations would begin early in the new year."

Before the Sept. 7 White House meeting, Maxwell D. Taylor—who had succeeded Lodge as ambassador in Saigon—in an Aug. 18 cablegram to Johnson designated as a joint U.S. mission message, said counterguerrilla measures in the

South were not enough and counseled "a carefully orchestrated bombing attack" on North Vietnam. The Joint Chiefs of Staff, in a memo to Secretary McNamara Aug. 26, agreed with Taylor's assessment of the need for bombing.

In its Aug. 18 cablegram to the State Department, the U.S. mission in Saigon said that the "present in-country pacification plan [in South Vietnam] is not enough in itself to maintain national morale or to offer reasonable hope of eventual success." The statement cited four objectives "which U.S. policy in South Vietnam should take during the coming months":

The first and most important objective is to gain time for the Khanh government to develop a certain stability and to give some firm evidence of viability. Since any of the courses of action considered in this cable carry a considerable measure of risk to the U.S., we should be slow to get too deeply involved in them until we have a better feel of the quality of our ally. In particular, if we can avoid it, we should not get involved militarily with North Vietnam and possibly with Red China. . . .

A second objective in this period is the maintenance of morale in South Vietnam particularly within the Khanh government. . . . Thirdly while gaining time for Khanh, we must be able to hold North Vietnam in check and restrain a further buildup of Viet Cong strength by way of infiltration from the North. Finally, throughout this period, we should be developing a posture of maximum readiness for a deliberate escalation of pressure against North Vietnam, using January 1, 1965 as a target D-Day. We must always recognize, however, that events may force U.S. to advance D-Day to a considerably earlier date. . . .

With these understandings reached, we would be ready to set in motion the following:

(1) Resume at once 34A [raids on North Vietnam] (with emphasis on Marine operations) and Desoto patrols [destroyer patrols in Tonkin Gulf]. . . .

(2) Resume U-2 overflights over all NVN.

(3) Initiate air and ground strikes in Laos against infiltration targets as soon as joint plans now being worked out with the Khanh government are ready . . . .

To avert the possible collapse of the Khanh government in Saigon, the mission offered an alternative plan, called "Course of Action—B." It said "we need an accelerated course of action, seeking to obtain results faster than under the course" outlined above. This program would include the following measures:

Again we must inform Khanh of our intentions, this time expressing a willingness to begin military pressures against Hanoi at once, providing that he will undertake to perform as in course of action A. However, U.S. action would not await evidence of performance.

Again we may wish to communicate directly on this subject with Hanoi or awaiting effect of our military actions. The scenario of the ensuing events would be essentially the same as under Course A but the execution would await only the readiness of plans to expedite relying almost exclusively on U.S. military means.

Further proposed military measures against Communist forces in Indochina were suggested in the Joint Chiefs of Staff memo, "Recommended Courses of Action—Southeast Asia," sent to McNamara Aug. 26. A four-point plan said the U.S. policy should be able to seek:

(1) improvements in South Vietnam, including emphasis on the Pacification Program and the Hop Tac plan to clear Saigon and its surroundings; (2) interdiction of the relatively unmolested VC lines of communication (LOC) through Laos by operations in the Panhandle and of the LOC through Cambodia by strict control of the water-ways leading therefrom; (3) denial of Viet Cong (VC) sanctuaries in the Cambodia-South Vietnam border area through the conduct of "hot pursuit" operations into Cambodia as required; (4) increased pressure on North Vietnam through military actions. As part of the program for increased pressures, the OPLAN 34A operations and the Desoto patrols in the Gulf of Tonkin should be resumed, the former on an intensified but still covert basis.

A list of strategic targets in North Vietnam to be struck by U.S. planes and naval forces and by South Vietnamese infiltration teams Sept. 1–30, 1964 was contained in a memorandum, "OPLAN 34A-September." The memo was transmitted Aug. 27 to Assistant Secretary of State Bundy and Assistant Defense Secretary John T. McNaughton by Maj. Gen. Rollen H. Anthis, an Air Force aide to the Joint Chiefs of Staff.

Political proposals were also under consideration. Asserting that "the situation in South Vietnam is deteriorating," a memo dated Sept. 3 and apparently drawn up by Assistant Defense Secretary John T. McNaughton recommended a series of political measures to stabilize the Saigon government, which was shaken by internal unrest, as well as certain military moves "outside the borders of South Vietnam" to reverse the "the downward trend."

The proposals to improve the situation inside South Vietnam:

(a) to press the presently visible leaders to get a real government in operation;

(b) to prevent extensive personnel changes down the line;

(c) to see that lines of authority for carrying out the pacification program are clear.

(d) to establish a U.S. Naval base, perhaps at Danang;

(e) to embark on a major effort to pacify one province adjacent to Saigon.

A separate analysis is being made of a proposal:

(f) to enlarge significantly the U.S. military role in the pacification program inside South Vietnam—e.g., large numbers of U.S. special forces, divisions of regular combat troops, U.S. air, etc., to "interlard" with or to take over functions of geographical areas from the South Vietnamese armed forces. . . .

As for military measures, the memorandum proposed that activities:

. . . . in addition to present continuing, extra-territorial, actions (U.S. U-2 reconnaissance of North Vietnam, U.S. jet reconnaissance of Laos, T-28 activity in Laos), would be by way of an orchestration of three classes of actions, all designed to meet these five desiderata—(1) from the U.S., GVN and hopefully allied points of view, they should be legitimate things to do under the circumstances, (2) they should cause apprehension, ideally increasing apprehension, in the DRV, (3) they should be likely at some point to provoke a military DRV response, (4) the provoked response should be likely to provide good grounds for us to escalate if we wished, and (5) the timing and crescendo should be under our control, with the scenario capable of being turned off at any time. . . .

While not rejecting this advice, the analyst said, the Johnson Administration decided against immediate bombing or any "provocation strategy" also under discussion at the Sept. 7 meeting. Besides the pressures of the election, said the analyst, the weakness of the Saigon government also led to the decision for delay. The President's orders resulting from the meeting, related in a Sept. 10 memo from McGeorge Bundy, were for a resumption of De Soto patrols in the Tonkin Gulf, reactivation of the 34A coastal raids and arrangements for Laotian ground operations, air strikes and possible U.S. reconnaissance flights.

The memo also urged discussions with Laos "for limited South Vietnamese air and ground operations into the corridor areas of Laos, together with Lao air strikes and possible use of U.S. armed aerial reconnaissance."

Bundy Sept. 8 had sent President Johnson a memo, "Courses of Action for South Vietnam," that recorded "the consensus reached in discussions between Ambassador Taylor and Secretary Rusk, Secretary McNamara and General Earle Wheeler, for review and decision by the President."

The proposals:

1. U.S. Naval patrols in the Gulf of Tonkin should be resumed immediately (about September 12). They should operate initially beyond the 12-mile limit and be clearly dissociated from 34-A maritime operations. . . .

3. Limited South Vietnamese air and ground operations into the corridor areas of Laos should be undertaken in the near future, together with Lao air strikes as soon as we can get [Premier] Souvanna's permission.

These operations will have only limited effect, however.

4. We should be prepared to respond on a tit-for-tat basis against the DRV in the event of any attack on U.S. units or any special DRV/VC action against South Vietnam. The response for an attack on U.S. units should be along the lines of the Gulf of Tonkin attacks, against specific and related targets. The response to special action against SVN should likewise be aimed at specific and comparable targets. . . .

The aim of the above actions, external to South Vietnam, would be to assist morale in South Vietnam and show the Communists we still mean business, while at the same time seeking to keep the risks low and under our control at each stage. . . .

Pressure for immediate bombing of North Vietnam intensified, according to the narrative, following a Nov. 1 Viet Cong attack on U.S. planes and facilities at Bienhoa airfield near Saigon. Although President Johnson refused to order air attacks, he set up an inter-agency working group under William Bundy, assistant secretary of state, to recommend options for Vietnam policy.

Although the Bundy group was mandated to reconsider the entire U.S. policy in Vietnam, the Pentagon papers said "there appears to have been, in fact, remarkably little latitude for reopening the basic question about U.S. involvement in the Vietnam struggle." The analyst said the objective of "an independent, non-Communist South Vietnam . . . did not seem open to question."

The Bundy group came up with three options; all involved bombing: (A) reprisal air strikes and covert military pressures; (B) bomb the North, according to the analyst, "at a fairly rapid pace and without interruption" while resisting "pressures for negotiations"; and (C) a gradual escalation of air strikes "against infiltration targets, first in Laos and then in the DRV [North Vietnam], and then against other targets in North Vietnam" with a further possibility of "significant ground deployment to the northern part of South Vietnam." The Bundy group's paper, in its final form, was presented to the National Security Council Nov. 21, 1964.

The Pentagon narrative cited a William Bundy memo on a Nov. 24 Security Council meeting to discuss the options. The record said Undersecretary of State George W. Ball "indicated doubt" that bombing of the North would improve things in the South and "argued against"

the position that a Viet Cong victory in South Vietnam would have the falling-domino effect of producing Communist victories in Asia.

The consensus of the Security Council, reached after two more meetings Nov. 27 and 28, rejected Ball's view and advised a two-part operation: a 30-day program of Option A type attacks followed by the first phase of Option C, bombing of infiltration targets in North Vietnam. William Bundy was assigned to write a draft policy paper based on the Security Council recommendations, to be presented to President Johnson Dec. 1.

In an assessment of the bombing plan, dated Nov. 29, the Pentagon analyst said, "There is some reason to believe that the principals thought that carefully calculated doses of force could bring about predictable and desirable responses from Hanoi. Underlying this optimistic view was a significant underestimate of the level of the DRV [North Vietnam] commitment to victory in the South and an overestimate of the effectiveness of U.S. pressures in weakening that resolve."

After the Dec. 1 presentation of the bombing plan, the Pentagon account said, President Johnson approved the plan and immediately authorized implementation of the first 30-day phase. But he tied any further action to a strengthening of the Saigon government, which was overthrown later in December by dissident military officers.

According to the Pentagon papers, Administration thinking in the final months before the launching of Operation Rolling Thunder was influenced by the fear of a "final collapse" of the Saigon government, making a Viet Cong takeover a "distinct possibility." The narrative cited a Jan 27, 1965 memo from Assistant Defense Secretary John T. McNaughton to McNamara advocating, according to the chronicler, "initiating air strikes." The Pentagon analyst said NcNaughton contended "and Mr. McNamara agreed" that the U.S. objective in South Vietnam was "not to 'help friend' but to contain China."

The initial U.S. bombing strike came Feb. 7 following a Viet Cong attack on a U.S. compound at Pleiku. The Pleiku attack, said the Pentagon study, "triggered a swift, though long-contemplated

Presidential decision to give an 'appropriate and fitting response.' " Although executed as a "one-shot, tit-for-tat reprisal," said the analyst, "the drastic U.S. action . . . precipitated a rapidly moving sequence of events that transformed the character of the Vietnam war and the U.S. role in it."

There was a second U.S. reprisal raid Feb. 11 following a guerrilla attack on U.S. barracks at Quinhon. Johnson gave the order Feb. 13 that launched a sustained air war against North Vietnam, Operation Rolling Thunder.

A Nov. 5, 1964 paper by Assistant Secretary Bundy, "Conditions for Key Actions Surrounding Any Decision," called for "international soundings" on any "decision for stronger action" in Southeast Asia.

The paper proposed that:

a. We should probably consult with the U.K., Australia, New Zealand, and possibly Thailand before we reach a decision. We would hope for firm moral support from the U.K. and for participation in at least token form from the others.

b. SEATO as a body should be consulted concurrently with stronger action. . . .

c. The NATO Council should be notified on the Cuban model, i.e., concurrently, by a distinguished representative.

d. For negative reasons, France probably deserves VIP treatment also.

e. In the UN, we must be ready with an immediate affirmative presentation of our rationale to proceed concurrently either with a single reprisal action or with the initiation of a broader course of action.

f. World-wide, we should select reasonably friendly chiefs of state for special treatment seeking their sympathy and support. . . .

g. USIA must be brought into the planning process not later than early next week, so that it is getting the right kind of materials ready for all our information media, on a contingency basis. . . .

The second draft of a paper, "Action for South Vietnam," by Assistant Defense Secretary McNaughton, Nov. 16, 1964, listed American aims in Southeast Asia and three options "open to us" to cope with a "deteriorating" situation.

The aims:

(a) To protect U.S. reputation as a counter-subversion guarantor.

(b) To avoid domino effect especially in Southeast Asia.

(c) To keep South Vietnamese territory from Red hands.

(d) to emerge from crisis without unacceptable taint from methods.

The options:

OPTION A. Continue present policies. Maximum assistance within South Vietnam and limited external actions in Laos and by the South Vietnamese covertly against North Vietnam. The aim of any reprisal actions would be to deter and punish large VC actions in the South, but not to a degree that would create strong international negotiating pressures. Basic to this option is the continued rejection of negotiating in the hope that the situation will improve.

OPTION B. Fast full squeeze. Present policies plus a systematic program of military pressures against the north, meshing at some point with negotiation, but with pressure actions to be continued at a fairly rapid pace and without interruption until we achieve our central present objectives.

OPTION C. Progressive squeeze-and-talk. Present policies plus an orchestration of communications with Hanoi and a crescendo of additional military moves against infiltration targets, first in Laos and then in North Vietnam, and then against other targets in North Vietnam. The scenario would be designed to give the U.S. the option at any point to proceed or not, to escalate or not, and to quicken the pace or not. . . . .

At a meeting in Washington Nov. 27, 1964, Ambassador Taylor delivered to senior officials a prepared briefing, "The Current Situation in South Vietnam—November, 1964."

Taylor said "After a year of changing and ineffective government, the counter-insurgency program countrywide is bogged down and will require heroic treatment to assure revival."

Taylor suggested that:

"To change the situation, it is quite clear that we need to do three things: first, establish an adequate government in SVN; second, improve the conduct of the counterinsurgency campaign; and finally, persuade or force the DRV to stop its aid to the Viet-Cong and to use its directive powers to make the Viet-Cong desist from their efforts to overthrow the government of South Vietnam. . . ."

An airgram sent by Ambassador Taylor to the State Department Dec. 24, 1964 described his meeting the previous day with a group of Saigon generals following the South Vietnamese military's Dec. 19 ouster of the civilian High National Council. Criticizing their actions, Taylor said: "I made it clear that all the military plans which I know you would like to carry out are dependent on government stability. Now you have made a real mess. We cannot carry you forever if you do things like this."

Walt W. Rostow, chairman of the State Department's Policy Planning Council, stated his views on committing U.S. troops to the war in South Vietnam and escalating action against North Vietnam, at the risk of retaliatory moves by Communist China. The views were outlined in a letter sent Nov. 16, 1964 to

Secretary McNamara. Highlights of the letter, titled "Military Dispositions and Political Signals":

The signal consists of three parts:

(a) damage to the North is now to be inflicted because they are violating the 1954 and 1962 accords;

(b) we are ready and able to go much further than our initial act of damage;

(c) we are ready and able to meet any level of escalation they might mount in response, if they are so minded.

Four points follow.

1. I am convinced that we should not go forward into the next stage without a U.S. ground force commitment of some kind:

a. The withdrawal of those ground forces could be a critically important part of our diplomatic bargaining position. . . .

b. We must make clear that counter escalation by the Communists will run directly into U.S. strength on the ground. . . .

2. The first critical military action against North Vietnam should be designed merely to install the principle that they will, from the present forward, be vulnerable to retaliatory attack in the north for continued violations for the 1954 and 1962 Accords. . . .

3. But our force dispositions to accompany an initial retaliatory move against the north should send three further signals lucidly:

a. that we are putting in place a capacity subsequently to step up direct and naval pressure on the north, if that should be required;

b. that we are prepared to face down any form of escalation North Vietnam might mount on the ground; and

c. that we are putting forces into place to exact retaliation directly against Communist China, if Peiping should join in an escalatory response from Hanoi. . . .

4. The launching of this track, almost certainly, will require the President to explain to our own people and to the world our intentions and objectives. This will also be perhaps the most persuasive form of communication with Ho and Mao. . . .

In a Nov. 23 memo to Secretary Rusk, titled "Some Observations as We Come to the Crunch in Southeast Asia," Rostow said: The "most basic problem" was how to persuade the Communists "that a continuation of their present policy will risk major destruction in North Vietnam; that a preemptive move on the ground as a prelude to negotiations will be met by U.S. strength on the ground; and that Communist China will not be a sanctuary if it assists North Vietnam in counter-escalation."

Rostow advocated bringing some American ground forces into South Vietnam, and possibly into Laos and introducing into the Pacific Theater "massive forces to deal with any escalatory response, aimed at Communist China as well as North Vietnam."

The U.S. embassy in Vientiane, Laos had been authorized by the Defense and State Departments in October "to urge the Laotian government to begin air attacks against Viet Cong infiltration routes and facilities in the Laos Panhandle by Royal Laotian Air Force T-28 aircraft as soon as possible." The cablegram authorizing this action, received Oct. 6, further authorized the embassy to inform the Laotian government that American planes would conduct "suppressive fire strikes against certain difficult targets in the Panhandle."

American objective in South Vietnam remained "unchanged," according to a "Draft Position Paper on Southeast Asia" circulated to top-level officials Nov. 29, 1964.

The objectives were to:

1. Get Hanoi and North Vietnam (DRV) support and direction removed from South Vietnam, and, to the extent possible, obtain DRV cooperation in ending Viet Cong (VC) operations in SVN.

2. Re-establish an independent and secure South Vietnam with appropriate international safeguards, including the freedom to accept U.S. and other external assistance as required.

3. Maintain the security of other non-Communist nations in Southeast Asia including specifically the maintenance and observance of Geneva Accords of 1962 in Laos.

B. We will continue to press the South Vietnamese Government (GNV) in every possible way to make the government itself more effective and to push forward with the pacification program.

C. We will join at once with the South Vietnamese and Lao Governments in a determined action program aimed at DRV activities in both countries and designed to help GVN morale and to increase the costs and strain on Hanoi, foreshadowing still greater pressures to come. Under this program the first phase actions within the next thirty days will be intensified forms of action already under way, plus (1) U.S. armed reconnaissance strikes in Laos, and (2) GVN and possible U.S. air strikes against the DRV, as reprisals against any major or spectacular Viet Cong Action in the south, whether against U.S. personnel and installations or not.

D. Beyond the thirty-day period, first phase actions may be continued without change, or additional military measures may be taken including the withdrawal of dependents and the possible initiation of strikes a short distance across the border against the infiltration routes from the DRV. . . .

E. Thereafter, if the GVN improves its effectiveness to an acceptable degree and Hanoi does not yield on acceptable terms, *or if the GVN can only be kept going by stronger action* the U.S. is prepared—at a time to be determined—to enter into a second phase program, in support of the GVN and RLG, of graduated military pressures directed systematically against the DRV. . . .

Key decision in 1965. The Los Angeles Times June 26 quoted part of the Pentagon study concerning a "watershed" decision made by the Johnson Administration to deploy 3,500 Marines in March 1965 to defend the air base at Danang. This decision, said the analyst, "breached" a "mighty commandment of U.S. foreign policy—thou shalt not engage in an Asian land war." The Pentagon study said, however, that except for Gen. William C. Westmoreland, "who did see it as a first step and welcomed it," and Ambassador Maxwell D. Taylor, "who saw it as an unwelcome first step, official Washington regarded the deployment as a one-shot affair to meet a specific situation."

Increasing ground combat involvement.

The Pentagon study, as reported by the Times June 15, related that in the months after the Feb. 13, 1965 order authorizing the Rolling Thunder bombing campaign, the Johnson Administration swiftly lost hopes for its success. President Johnson decided April 1 to use U.S. ground troops for offensive action, a "pivotal" change, according to the study. However, the analyst said, "President Johnson was greatly concerned that the step be given as little prominence as possible."

With a series of Viet Cong successes in May and June, the Johnson Administration decided on a troop buildup for offensive action in mid-July, once more concealing the decision, according to the analyst. The decision, involving commitment of 44 battalions (193,887 troops), provided the means for a change in the role of U.S. combat forces—from the base and enclave security activity of the spring to search-and-destroy operations. "The acceptance of the search-and-destroy strategy," said the Pentagon study, "left the U.S. commitment to Vietnam open-ended. The implications in terms of manpower and money are inescapable."

A major influence behind President Johnson's Feb. 13 order for Operation Rolling Thunder, according to the Pentagon account, was a Feb. 7 memo by McGeorge Bundy, special assistant for national security affairs. Calling for a "policy of sustained reprisal against North Vietnam," Bundy argued that "episodic responses" lacked the "persuasive force of sustained pressure" in terms of the "political values of reprisal."

In an introduction to a four-point statement, Bundy said:

We believe that the best available way of increasing our chance of success in Vietnam is the development and execution of a policy of *sustained reprisal* against North Vietnam—a policy in which air and naval action against the North is justified by and related to the whole Viet Cong campaign of violence and terror in the South.

While we believe that the risks of such a policy are acceptable, we emphasize that its costs are real. It implies significant U.S. air losses even if no full air war is joined, and it seems likely that it would eventually require an extensive and costly effort against the whole air defense system of North Vietnam. U.S. casualties would be higher—and more visible to American feelings—than those sustained in the struggle in South Vietnam.

Yet measured against the costs of defeat in Vietnam, this program seems cheap. And even if it fails to turn the tide—as it may—the value of the effort seems to us to exceed its cost.

A cablegram from the State Department to Ambassador Taylor Feb. 13, 1965 told of President Johnson's approval that day of a decision to "intensify by all available means the program of pacification within South Vietnam" and the carrying out of "measured and limited air action jointly with South Vietnam against selected military targets in North Vietnam, remaining south of the 19th Parallel until further notice." At the same time, the U. S. would "go to the U.N. Security Council to make clear case that the aggressor is Hanoi."

Taylor in Saigon welcomed the order, the Pentagon analyst said, but he spoke of problems caused by "the condition of virtual nongovernment" in Saigon. In fact, the first Rolling Thunder assault was delayed until March 2 partly because of instability and coups in Saigon.

A draft paper by William P. Bundy, "Where Are We Heading?" Feb. 18, 1965, examined possible developments and problems arising from pursuit of following U. S. policies in South Vietnam: "a. Intensified pacification within South Vietnam," accompanied by possible large increase of American forces; "b. A program of measured, limited, and spaced attacks, jointly with the South Vietnamese, against the infiltration complex in North Vietnam. . . . c. That the U.S. would take no initiative for talks, but would agree to cooperate in consultations . . . undertaken by the U.K. and U.S.S.R. as co-chairmen of the Geneva Conference. . . ."

The paper foresaw possible Chinese Communist air defense equipment supplied to North Vietnam, but discounted actual Chinese involvement in air operations.

A decision adopted Feb. 18, 1965 for continuing joint U.S.-South Vietnamese air and naval action against North Vietnam was cabled by the State Department to heads of nine U.S. diplomatic missions in the Far East. The heightened war effort also called for "intensification by all available means of the pacification program within South Vietnam" and a "detailed presentation to nations of the world and to the public of documents case against North Vietnam as the aggressor."

The Pentagon papers spoke of a shift in the rationale for the bombing from assaults "dominated by political and psychological considerations," such as emphasized in Bundy's Feb. 7 memo, to a "militarily more significant, sustained bombing program" designed to destroy Hanoi's capability to support a war in the South. In the beginning, said the analyst, Washington hoped the air assaults "would rapidly convince Hanoi that it should agree to negotiate a settlement to the war in the South." However, the study said, "once set in motion . . . the bombing effort seemed to stiffen rather than soften Hanoi's backbone."

In a March 24 memo, Assistant Defense Secretary John T. McNaughton answered "probably no" to this question posed by Defense Secretary McNamara: Could the deteriorating situation in South Vietnam be remedied without (a) "extreme measures" against Hanoi or (b) "without deployment of large numbers of U.S. [and other] combat troops inside SVN [South Vietnam]?"

A detailed plan for widespread air strikes on North Vietnam and a "program of large U. S. ground effort in South Vietnam and Southeast Asia" was outlined in a first draft of "Annex—Plan for Action for South Vietnam," appended to McNaughton's March 24 memo. The memo also advanced arguments for and against holding negotiations on halting North Vietnamese military activities and withdrawing U.S. forces.

A request for 17 battalions of U.S. combat troops was made in a detailed report March 26 by Gen. William C. Westmoreland, American commander in Saigon. The Joint Chiefs backed his request, and McNamara gave his "qualified approval," according to the Pentagon analyst.

President Johnson made his decision for deployment of more troops and for "a change in mission" for Marine battalions "to permit their more active use" April 1. The decision was recorded in National Security Action Memorandum 328 dated April 6. The Pentagon analyst, referring to a U.S. maxim dating back to the Korean conflict that land war in Asia should be avoided, said of the April 1 decision: "The fact that this departure from a long-held policy had momentous implications was well recognized by the Administration."

From two opposite poles, the decision met with dissent within the Administration. John A. McCone, director of the Central Intelligence Agency, argued in an April 2 memo that the planned actions were not strong enough. McCone said it was unwise to commit ground troops unless the U.S. was willing to bomb the North "with minimum restraint." Otherwise, he argued, "we will find ourselves mired down in combat in the jungle in a military effort that we cannot win and from which we will have extreme difficulty extracting ourselves." The raids have not caused a change in the North Vietnamese policy of directing Viet Cong insurgency, infiltrating cadres and supply material," McCone said. He recommended intensifying the air war, hitting "them harder, more frequently, and inflict[ing] greater damage. We must strike their airfields, their petroleum resources, power stations and their military compounds."

Prime Minister Harold Wilson of Great Britain cabled President Johnson June 3, 1965 to warn him about the political disadvantages of bombing raids against oil targets near Hanoi and Haiphong.

Wilson said that although "I wholly understand the deep concern you must feel at the need to do anything possible to reduce the losses of young Americans in and over Vietnam . . . . I am bound to say that, as seen from here, the possible military benefits that may result from this bombing do not appear to outweigh the political disadvantages that would seem the inevitable consequence."

The bombing, Wilson added, "may only increase the difficulty of reaching an eventual settlement. . . ."

Wilson said that if the petroleum raids went off, "we shall have to dissociate ourselves from it."

Undersecretary of State George W. Ball, who had dissented before to Vietnam policies, argued in a memo circulated June 28 that neither bombing the North nor fighting guerrillas in the South would effectively advance U.S. interests. According to the analyst, Ball was "convinced that the U.S. was pouring its resources down the drain in the wrong place," and he proposed, in the words of the study, that the U.S. "cut its losses" and withdraw from South Vietnam. The study said Ball's compromise solution, presented to the President July 1, reflected these beliefs. Ball recommended that the U.S. seek a political solution with the North Vietnamese. Ball based his suggestions on the fact that "the South Vietnamese are losing the war to the Viet Cong" and that there was no guarantee "that we can beat the Viet Cong or even force them to the conference table on our terms."

In his memo, "A Compromise Solution in South Vietnam," Ball urged adoption of the following program:

(a) Military Program
(1) Complete all deployments already announced—15 battalions—but decide not to go beyond a total of 72,000 men represented by this figure.
(2) Restrict the combat role of the American forces to the June 9 announcement, making it clear to General Westmoreland that this announcement is to be strictly construed.
(3) Continue bombing in the North but avoid the Hanoi-Haiphong area and any targets nearer to the Chinese border than those already struck.
(b) Political Program
(1) In any political approaches so far, we have been the prisoners of whatever South Vietnamese government that was momentarily in power. . . .
(2) So far we have not given the other side a reason to believe there is *any* flexibility in our negotiating approach. And the other side has been unwilling to accept what *in their terms* is complete capitulation.
(3) Now is the time to start some serious diplomatic feelers. . . .
(4) I would recommend approaching Hanoi rather than any of the other probable parties, the NFL [Viet Cong]—Peiping. Hanoi is the only one that has given any signs of interest in discussion. . . .
(5) There are several channels to the North Vietnamese but I think the best one is through their representative in Paris, Mai Van Bo. Initial feelers of Bo should be directed toward a discussion both of the four points we have put forward and the four points put forward by Hanoi as a basis for negotiation. . . .
(6) If the initial feelers lead to further secret, exploratory talks, we can inject the concept of self-determination that would permit the Viet Cong some hope of achieving some of their political objectives through local elections or some other device.
(7) The contact on our side should be handled through a non-governmental cutout (possibly a reliable newspaper man who can be repudiated).
(8) If progress can be made at this level a basis can be laid for a multinational conference. . . .
(7) Before moving to any formal conference we should be prepared to agree once the conference is started:
(a) The U. S. will stand down its bombing of the North
(b) The South Vietnamese will initiate no offensive operations in the South, and
(c) the DRV will stop terrorism and other aggressive action against the south.
(8) The negotiations at the conference should aim at incorporating our understanding with Hanoi in the form of a multinational agreement guaranteed by the U.S., the Soviet Union and possibly other parties, and providing for an international mechanism to supervise its execution.

The April 1 decision received no publicity, reported the Pentagon analyst, "until it crept out almost by accident in a State Department release on 8 June." A White House statement the next day insisted "there has been no change in the mission of U.S. ground combat units in Vietnam." But the statement did say Westmoreland had authority to employ U.S. troops "in support of Vietnamese forces faced with aggressive attack" when other reserves were unavailable.

In a National Security memorandum 328, McGeorge Bundy April 6, 1965 notified Secretary of State Rusk, Secretary of Defense McNamara and John A. McCone, director of the Central Intelligence Agency (CIA) that President Johnson had approved an increase in the U.S. ground force and a change in the scope of missions for all Marine battalions in South Vietnam.

Bundy said the ground force buildup approved by Johnson called for an "18–20,000 man increase in U. S. military support forces to fill out existing units and supply needed logistic personnel."

For the Marines, Bundy said, Johnson had approved a change of mission to permit their "more active use" under conditions approved by McNamara and Rusk.

The memorandum also disclosed that Johnson had approved "the urgent exploration, with the Korean, Australian, and New Zealand Governments, of the possibility of rapid deployment of significant combat elements from their armed forces in parallel with the additional Marine deployment. . . .

In another part of the document, Bundy said Johnson desired that with respect to the orders for the force buildup—including the additional deployment of the Marine battalions—and shift in Marine missions "premature publicity be avoided by all possible precautions. The actions themselves should be taken as rapidly as practicable, but in ways that should minimize any appearance of sudden changes in policy. . . ."

Walt W. Rostow, chairman of the State Department's Policy Planning Council, prepared for Secretary Rusk May 20, 1965 a memorandum on guerrilla warfare. The report, "Victory and Defeat in Guerrilla Wars: The Case of South Vietnam," sought to explain that the U.S. could stop the Communists and attain a clear victory in South Vietnam.

Rostow said there were four routes to victory in a guerrilla war:

a. Escalation to all-out conventional war and winning (as in mainland China);

b. Political collapse and takeover (North Vietnam);

c. Political collapse and coalition government in which the Communists controlled the security (police) and armed forces branches of the government;

d. Converting the bargaining pressure applied by guerrilla successes into a partial victory by splitting the country as in Laos in 1954.

McNamara July 20 recommended to President Johnson an immediate decision to increase the number of U.S. and third-country forces in South Vietnam from the 16 maneuver battalions (15 U.S., one Australian) there.

Ambassador Taylor, in a cablegram dated April 17, 1965 from Saigon, sought to define for Secretary Rusk and McGeorge Bundy how he interpreted instructions issued to him about the introduction of third-country combat forces in South Vietnam.

Taylor cabled that he understood that the decision to commit more U.S. Marines had been approved but that a decision "for bringing in more U.S. combat forces and their possible modes of employment was withheld. . . ."

As to a third-country force, Taylor said he understood "State [Department] was to explore with the Korean, Australian and New Zealand govts the possibility of rapid deployment of significant combat elements in parallel with the [U.S.] Marine reinforcement."

Taylor notified Rusk that on April 8 he had received concurrence from the government of South Vietnam for the introduction of the U. S. Marine reinforcements and to an expanded mission for all Marines in the Danang-Phu Bai area.

Taylor also asked Rusk to provide him with Washington's "purposes and objectives" with regard to the introduction of third-country (as well as U.S.) forces.

"The air campaign in the North," he said, "must be supplemented by signal successes against the VC in the South before we can hope to create that frame of mind in Hanoi which will lead to the decisions we seek."

McNamara also proposed a change in the mission of the 16 battalions from one of providing support and reinforcement for the South Vietnamese Army to one of aggressive pursuit of the enemy's main force units in South Vietnam.

McNamara concluded his July 20 memo with an optimistic forecast:

"The overall evaluation is that the course of action recommended in this memorandum—if the military and political moves are properly integrated and executed with continuing vigor and visible determination—stands a good chance of achieving an acceptable outcome within a reasonable time in Vietnam."

Responding to successful Viet Cong "summer offensive" attacks, Westmoreland sent a request June 7 for more troops, a message that was known within the Administration as the "44-battalion request." It was in response to Westmoreland's recommendation, said the Pentagon account, that Undersecretary Ball presented his compromise solution July 1. On the same day, Assistant Defense Secretary William Bundy advised in a memo, summarized by the analyst, that the "U.S. needed to avoid the ultimatum aspects of the 44 battalions and also the Ball withdrawal proposal."

Assistant Defense Secretary McNaughton reported in a July 2, 1965 memorandum to Lt. Gen. Andrew J. Goodpaster, assistant to the Chairman of the Joint Chiefs of Staff, his views on the forces needed for winning the war. McNaughton said in the memo, entitled "Forces Required to Win in South Vietnam," that he believed the U.S. should think in terms of a 44-battalion buildup by the end of 1965, with added forces in 1966.

McNaughton also brought up the question of the introduction of third-country forces in South Vietnam. He said Gen. Westmoreland had equated nine Korean battalions with nine U.S. battalions, and that if the nine Korean battalions were not introduced, he wanted the nine other U.S. battalions.

President Johnson approved deployment of 34 battalions July 17 with others to be requested later if needed. On July 30 the Joint Chiefs approved 44 battalions for deployment and by the end of the year, 184,314 U.S. troops were in South Vietnam.

In a conclusion, the Pentagon study said, "the major participants in the decision knew the choices and understood the consequences." The deployment "was preceived as a threshold—entrance into an Asian land war. The conflict was seen to be long, with further U.S. deployments to follow." The analyst also preceived a "subtle change of emphasis. . . . Instead of simply denying the enemy victory and convincing him that he could not win, the thrust became defeating the enemy in the South. This was sanctioned implicitly as the only way to achieve the U.S. objective of a non-Communist South Vietnam." The Pentagon study said that Johnson and McNamara "were prepared for a long war."

1965–66 escalation analyzed. The Pentagon study, according to the New York Times July 2, said the massive buildup of U.S. troops in 1965 and 1966 occurred because "no one really foresaw what the troop needs in Vietnam would be" and the enemy's ability to expand forces was "consistently underrated." The Pentagon analysis also said the U.S. air war expansion was based on a "colossal misjudgment" of the effect of bombing on Hanoi's capabilities and will.

The Times also said the Pentagon papers indicated that in 1965-66 U.S. military leaders were confident of victory, and that although civilian leaders expressed doubts about the effectiveness of both the air and ground efforts, they continued to recommend escalation. The Times reported on an August 1966

evaluation by a non-government scientific panel declaring the bombing effort a failure and urging that an electronic barrier be established to stop infiltration and supplies from North Vietnam.

The Times said Gen. William C. Westmoreland's troop requests increased from a total of 175,000 in June 1965, to 275,000 in July 1965, 443,000 in December 1965 and 542,000 in June 1966.

Neither the requests nor President Johnson's approval of all but the last request were made public. The Times pointed out that on Feb. 26, 1966, when there were 235,000 U.S. troops in Vietnam and after Westmoreland's request for more than 400,000, Johnson said at a news conference, "We do not have on my desk at the moment any unfilled requests from General Westmoreland."

According to the Pentagon analyst, when Johnson in July 1965 decided to approve Westmoreland's request for 44 combat battalions and to endorse his search-and-destroy strategy, he "left the U.S. commitment to Vietnam open-ended" because "force levels for the search-and-destroy strategy had no empirical limits"—they "depended entirely" on the enemy's response."

The Pentagon study suggested that Westmoreland's battle plan in July 1965 "was derived from what would be available rather than the requirement for manpower being derived from any clearly thought out military plan." Westmoreland's strategy, as quoted in the study, had three phases:

Phase I—The commitment of U.S./F.W.M.A. [United States/Free World Military Assistance] forces necessary to halt the losing trend by the end of 1965.
Phase II—The resumption of the offensive by U.S./F.W.M.A. forces during the first half of 1966 in high-priority areas necessary to destroy enemy forces, and reinstitution of rural-construction activities.
Phase III—If the enemy persisted, a period of a year to a year and a half following Phase II would be required for the defeat and destruction of the remaining enemy forces and base areas.
Withdrawal of U.S./F.W.M.A. forces would commence following Phase III as the GVN [Government of Vietnam] became able to establish and maintain internal order and to defend its borders.

Thus, said the study, Westmoreland expected "to have defeated the enemy by the end of 1967."

Gen. Earle G. Wheeler, chairman of the Joint Chiefs of Staff, also expected victory. Asked by Defense Secretary

Robert McNamara in July 1965 what "assurance" the U.S. could have of winning, Wheeler's answer, based on a Pentagon study group, was: "Within the bounds of reasonable assumptions—there appears to be no reason we cannot win if such is our will." In connection with this, the Pentagon group received the following working definition of "win" from Assistant Defense Secretary John T. McNaughton: to win "means that we succeed in demonstrating to the VC [Viet Cong] that they cannot win."

According to the Pentagon analyst, Westmoreland would revise upward his estimate of the number of troops needed at each phase of his plan because the original strategy "did not take escalatory reactions into account." By November 1965, Phase I seemed near its goal, but the enemy had built up its forces with unexpected rapidity. Westmoreland said he would need 154,000 more men than previously estimated for Phase II.

To evaluate the troop request, McNamara visited Saigon, returning to Washington Nov. 30, 1965. On his return he wrote a memo to Johnson recommending that the U.S. send a total of nearly 400,000 men to Vietnam by the end of 1966, but he expressed doubts over the military's confidence in ultimate victory. McNamara said:

5. Evaluation. We should be aware that deployments of the kind I have recommended will not guarantee success. U.S. killed-in-action can be expected to reach 1,000 a month, and the odds are even that we will be faced in early 1967 with a "no-decision" at an even higher level. My overall evaluation, nevertheless, is the the best chance of achieving our stated objectives lies in a [bombing] pause followed, if it fails, by the deployments mentioned above.

The Pentagon study said that in the summer of 1965, the U.S. bombing campaign against North Vietnam, begun in February 1965 under code name Rolling Thunder [see p. 441C1], changed from an attempt to break Hanoi's will to fight to a more modest effort to stop infiltration and the flow of supplies to the South. This change, said the analyst, occurred because it was recognized that "as a venture in strategic persuasion the bombing had not worked."

The Times cited a November 1965 Defense Intelligence Agency evaluation,

quoted in the Pentagon study, of the effect of bombing on North Vietnam. It said the enemy's industrial performance had been reduced but that "the primarily rural nature of the area permits continued functioning of the subsistence economy" and that Hanoi's "determination to continue supporting the war in South Vietnam" appeared unaltered. The Pentagon analyst commented, "The idea that destroying, or threatening to destroy, North Vietnam's industry would pressure Hanoi into calling its quits, seems, in retrospect, a colossal misjudgment."

The Times also discussed a 1965 debate between McNamara and the military leaders over the merits of using bombing pauses to put pressure on Hanoi.

At the beginning of 1966, both McNaughton and McNamara clearly expressed doubts about U.S. strategy both in the air and ground wars. McNaughton, in a Jan. 19, 1966 memo, suggested that the U.S. did not need to achieve full victory because "the U.S. end is solely to preserve our reputation as a guarantor." McNamara, in a Jan. 24, 1966 memo to Johnson, said troop deployments would not guarantee success. He said the Communists "continue to believe that the war will be a long one, that time is their ally and that their own staying power is superior to ours." He added:

It follows, therefore, that the odds are about even that, even with the recommended deployments, we will be faced in early 1967 with a military standoff at a much higher level, with pacification still stalled, and with any prospect of military success marred by the changes of an active Chinese intervention and with the requirement for the deployment of still more U.S. forces.

A "major policy dispute" in the spring of 1966, said the Pentagon study, was whether the U.S. should bomb North Vietnam's oil storage facilities, a plan encouraged by the Joint Chiefs of Staff and endorsed in a May 5, 1966 memo to Johnson by Presidential Assistant Walt W. Rostow. Adm. U.S. Grant Sharp, U.S. commander in the Pacific, said the program would "bring the enemy to the conference table or cause the insurgency to wither from lack of support." Against this advice, the Central Intelligence Agency advised repeatedly that it was unlikely that bombing oil tanks would "cripple" the enemy.

The attacks, however, were ordered June 22 and began June 29. By the end of July, the Defense Intelligence Agency reported that 70% of North Vietnam's original oil storage capacity had been destroyed. However, said the Pentagon study, it "became clearer and clearer" that Hanoi "retained enough dispersed capacity . . . to meet her ongoing requirements." The strikes were a failure, said the analyst, and McNamara realized it. "The attack on North Vietnam's P.O.L. [petroleum, oil, lubricants] system," said the analyst, "was the last major escalation of the air war recommended by Secretary McNamara."

Westmoreland's final troop request of the 1965–66 period, for a total of 542,588 men in 1967, was met by a challenge from McNamara. He said in an Aug. 5, 1966 memo to the Joint Chiefs that "it is our policy to provide the troops, weapons, and supplies requested by General Westmoreland at the time he desires them." But he continued:

Nevertheless, I desire and expect a detailed, line-by-line analysis of these requirements to determine that each is truly essential to the carrying out of our war plan. We must send to Vietnam what is needed, but only what is needed.

The Pentagon narrative said that this marked the end of automatic approval of troop increases.

The Times also reported on a secret seminar of scientists that met during the summer of 1966 to evaluate technical aspects of the war. The Pentagon analyst said the panel's recommendations had "a powerful and perhaps decisive influence in McNamara's mind." The panel proclaimed the bombing campaign a failure and said that to stop infiltration and supplies, the U.S. should build an electronic barrier device across the demilitarized zone. The Pentagon study suggested that McNamara seized the idea as a possible alternative to past strategies, which he viewed with "disenchantment."

McNamara despair in '66 reported. The St. Louis Post-Dispatch, in its June 25 editions, published the text of an Oct. 14, 1966 memo to President Johnson in which Defense Secretary McNamara called the pacification program "a bad disappointment."

In his memo, written about 18 months after the initiation of the pacification program, McNamara said "pacification has if anything gone backward." He said guerrilla forces were larger, terrorism had increased, crops were smaller and added, "we control little, if any, more of the population."

The Post-Dispatch said the memo was written at a time when both McNamara and President Johnson were speaking publicly of the progress that had been made in Vietnam since U.S. military escalation in the spring of 1965.

The McNamara memo also said the bombing of North Vietnam had neither "significantly affected infiltration or cracked the morale of Hanoi." He said: "This important war must be fought and won by the Vietnamese themselves. We have known this from the beginning. But the discouraging truth is that, as was the case in 1961 and 1963 and 1965, we have not found the formula, the catalyst, for training and inspiring them into effective action."

McNamara turnabout 1966–67. The New York Times reported July 3 that McNamara, in his Oct. 14, 1966 memo, recommended a reduction in the bombing of North Vietnam and a cutback in U.S. troop reinforcements. In a May 19, 1967 draft proposal, McNamara went further and urged that Saigon be persuaded to negotiate for a political settlement—a coalition government—and a cease-fire.

The Pentagon narrative described how McNamara's proposals, born of a deepening disillusionment with the course of the war, opened a rift in the Johnson Administration. Military advisers met McNamara's recommendations with requests for troop increases and demands for a wider war. A third party, consisting of some senior White House and State Department officials but primarily the President himself, chose the middle ground of piecemeal escalation.

McNamara's Oct. 14, 1966 memo was written on his return from a trip to Saigon.

In his recommendations, McNamara asked Johnson to "limit the increase in U.S. forces" in 1967 to a total of 470,000 men. This was 100,000 fewer than requested by the military. He asked that a portion of the troops be used for "construction and maintenance of an infiltration barrier" [see above]. He also recommended a program to "stabilize" the bombing attacks on North Vietnam and said "we should consider" a decision to "stop bombing all of North Vietnam" or to shift targets away from Hanoi, Haipong and areas to the north and concentrate instead "on the infiltration routes."

The Pentagon narrative said the Joint Chiefs of Staff—which had on Oct. 7 urged what the analyst called a "full-blown" mobilization of Army, Navy, Air Force and Marine reserves—reacted with a "predictably rapid—and violent" response to McNamara's proposal.

A memo to McNamara dated the same day as McNamara's report to Johnson said:

"The Joint Chiefs of Staff do not concur in your recommendation that there should be no increase in level of bombing effort and no modification in areas and targets subject to air attack. They believe our air campaign against NVN [North Vietnam] to be an integral and indispensable part of overall war effort. . . . The bombing campaign is one of the two trump cards in the hands of the President (the other being the presence of U.S. troops in SVN [South Vietnam]). It should not be given up without an end to NVN aggression in SVN."

McNamara's proposal to limit the air war was rejected by President Johnson. However, the President did order a territorial limit on the bombing of North Vietnam on March 31, 1968—17 months after McNamara made his proposal.

A wider debate within the Administration took place over troop requests. Gen. Westmoreland, on March 18, 1967, notified the Joint Chiefs that he needed at least 100,000 men "as soon as possible but not later than 1 July 1968." The request said that for an "optimum force" he would need 200,000 troops, which would increase the total strength to more than 670,000 men.

The Joint Chiefs formally transmitted the request to McNamara in an April 20 memo. Paraphrasing the Joint Chiefs' request, the Pentagon analyst said, "What they proposed . . . was the mobilization of the reserves, a major new troop commitment in the South, an extension of the war into the VC/NVA [Viet Cong/Army of North Vietnam] sanctuaries (Laos, Cambodia and possibly North Vietnam), the mining of North Vietnamese ports and a solid commitment in manpower and resources to a military victory. The recommendation not unsurprisingly touched off a searching reappraisal of the course of U.S. strategy in the war."

Setting forth his argument for a narrowing of the war, McNamara, with the help of Assistant Defense Secretary McNaughton, prepared his draft memo for the President dated May 19, 1967. In it, said the Pentagon analyst, McNamara "pointedly rejected" the traditional "high blown formulations of U.S. objectives" and "came forcefully to grips with the old dilemma of the U.S. involvement dating from the Kennedy era: only limited means to achieve excessive ends."

McNamara and McNaughton said in the memo:

The time has come for us to eliminate the ambiguities from our minimum objectives—our commitments—in Vietnam. Specifically, two principles must be articulated, and policies and actions brought in line with them: (1) Our commitment is only to see that the people of South Vietnam are permitted to determine their own future. (2) This commitment ceases if the country ceases to help itself.

It follows that no matter how much we might *hope* for some things, our *commitment is not*:

—to expel from South Vietnam regroupees, who are South Vietnamese (though we do not like them),

—to ensure that a particular person or group remains in power, nor that the power runs to every corner of the land (though we prefer certain types and we hope their writ will run throughout South Vietnam),

—to guarantee that the self-chosen government is non-Communist (though we believe and strongly hope it will be), and

—to insist that the independent South Vietnam remain separate from North Vietnam (though in the short-run, we would prefer it that way).

(Nor do we have an obligation to pour in effort out of proportion to the effort contributed by the people of South Vietnam or in the face of coups, corruption, apathy or other indications of Saigon failure to cooperate effectively with us.)

The memo recommended that Saigon be moved:

To seek a political settlement with the non-Communist members of the NLF [National Liberation Front]—to explore a cease-fire and to reach an accommodation with the non-Communist South Vietnamese who are under the VC banner; to accept them as members of an opposition political party, and, if necessary, to accept their individual participation in the national government—in sum, a settlement to transform the members of the VC from military opponents to political opponents.

The Joint Chiefs responded immediately with three memorandums renewing the recommendation for 200,000 new troops and air attacks. In their sharpest rebuttal, a May 31 memo, the Joint Chiefs said the "drastic changes" in American policy advocated by McNamara "would undermine and no longer provide a complete rationale for our presence in South Vietnam or much of our efforts over the past two years."

President Johnson disregarded McNamara's advice and launched a spring air offensive against North Vietnam in 1967. However, the President's decisions on troop reinforcements were much closer to McNamara's recommendations than to the demands of the Joint Chiefs of Staff and the military commanders. According to the Pentagon analysis, the real ceiling on U.S. troop commitment was Johnson's refusal to ask Congress to mobilize reserve forces. This represented "a political sound barrier," said the Pentagon study, that Johnson would not break.

Motives for Johnson bombing lulls. According to the Washington Post's June 19 account of the Pentagon study, the Johnson Administration initiated pauses in the bombing of North Vietnam between 1965 and 1968 with little expectation that peace talks would result. The Post said the Pentagon analysis revealed that the Johnson Administration considered the bomb pauses not as peace initiatives but rather as moves that would placate domestic and world opinion, and that some strategists hoped to use the unproductiveness of the lulls to justify escalating the war.

In a discussion of President Johnson's decision for a partial bombing halt, announced in an historic speech March 31, 1968, the Post said the study confirmed Johnson's later assertion that Secretary of State Dean Rusk advocated the move. However, the Post said, the Pentagon papers indicated that as the bombing halt was being planned, the expectation at the State Department was that there would be another "pause," which would risk little militarily and would probably be unproductive.

The Post cited a March 1968 State Department cable to U.S. embassies, which preceded and, according to the article, did not anticipate Johnson's end-of-the-month announcement that he would not run for re-election in 1968. The cable told the ambassadors that in explaining the partial bombing halt:

. . . You should make clear that Hanoi is most likely to denounce the . . . project and thus free our hand after a short period . . .

In view of weather limitations, bombing north of the 20th Parallel will in any event be limited at least for the next four weeks or so—which we tentatively envisage as a maximum testing period in any event. Hence, we are not giving up anything really serious in this time frame.

The message also said "air power now being used north of the 20th can probably be used in Laos . . . and in SVN [South Vietnam]." And it continued:

Insofar as our announcement foreshadows any possibility of a complete bombing stoppage, in the event Hanoi really exercises reciprocal restraints, we regard this as unlikely . . .

A Central Intelligence Agency memo February 1968, said the Post, reflected the U.S.'s feeling that no negotiated settlement would result from peace talks because the Hanoi position was irreconcilable with U.S. interests. The CIA said if the U.S. stopped bombing North Vietnam, Hanoi would engage in "exploration of issues, but would not moderate its terms for a final settlement or stop fighting in the South."

According to the Pentagon analyst, as reported by the Post, almost all of Johnson's advisers viewed political initiatives as secondary to military moves. Commenting on a July 1965 memo by Defense Secretary Robert McNamara, the analyst said he thought of diplomatic overtures as "channels for the enemy's discreet and relatively face-saving surrender when he decided the game had grown too costly. . . . This was, in fact, what official Washington (again with the exception of [Undersecretary of State [George W.] Ball) meant in mid-1965 when it spoke of a 'political settlement.'"

The first bombing lull, in May 1965, lasted five days—an impossibly short time, according to the Pentagon analyst, for "a meaningful response" from Hanoi. A longer pause—37 days—began Dec. 24, 1965. The Post quoted a Nov. 30, 1965 McNamara memo to Johnson regarding the planning for this longer pause:

It is my belief that there should be a three- or four-week pause ... in the program of bombing the north before we either greatly increase our troop deployments to Vietnam or intensify our strikes against the north.

The reasons for this belief are, first, that we must lay a foundation in the mind of the American public and in world opinion for such an enlarged phase of the war and, second, we should give North Vietnam a face-saving chance to stop the aggression.

The Pentagon analyst, as reported by the Post, said Assistant Defense Secretary John McNaughton, in July 1965, caught "Washington establishment's view of a bombing pause" when he used the "image of a ratchet, such as the device which raises the net on a tennis court, backing off tension between each phase of increasing it." The Pentagon analyst said the only danger, in the view of Johnson's strategists, was voiced by McNamara in his Nov. 30, 1965 memo —the danger of "being trapped in a status quo cease-fire or in negotiations which, though unaccompanied by real concessions by the VC [Viet Cong], made it politically costly for us to terminate the pause."

The Pentagon study, said the Post, recorded disillusionment in the Johnson Administration in 1966 and 1967 regarding the likelihood of its policies bringing victory in Vietnam. The study cited a McNaughton memo early in 1966 which spoke of "lowering of sights from victory to compromise." McNaughton stated that the U.S. objective "is to avoid humiliation," advocating, in the analyst's words, that the U.S. and Hanoi "should consider coming to terms" because "we are in an escalating military stalemate."

Coalition suggested in '67. Knight Newspapers Inc. published an article in eight of its 11 papers stating that Defense Secretary McNamara proposed a coalition government in Saigon in May 1967. The story, which appeared in the Philadelphia Inquirer June 24, said McNamara had become discouraged with the progress of the ground war, and he urged a coalition government for Saigon that would include non-Communist members of the National Liberation Front, the political arm of the Viet Cong.

The story, purportedly based on the secret Pentagon study, said that after becoming discouraged with the bombing of North Vietnam, McNamara ordered an electronic barrier erected in October 1966 to halt infiltration into South Vietnam.

Policy change follows Tet offensive. The Pentagon papers account of the Johnson Administration decisions surrounding the Communist Tet offensive in February 1968, as reported by the New York Times July 4, showed that the Joint Chiefs of Staff and Gen. William C. Westmoreland pressed for a national mobilization to achieve victory in Vietnam. The study said that "a fork in the road had been reached" with the military's demand for a "full-scale call-up of reserves" and "putting the country economically on a semiwar footing."

A bitter policy debate followed, resulting in the opposite of the desires of the Joint Chiefs and Westmoreland, commanding general in the field. Westmoreland was relieved of his command, and on March 31, 1968, President Johnson announced a cutback in the bombing of North Vietnam to the 20th Parallel. Johnson also announced that he would not seek re-election.

Before Tet, the Pentagon study indicated, Johnson had tended to discount "negative analyses" of U.S. strategy in the war offered by top civilian advisers in 1967. The study said he embraced "optimistic reports" such as a year-end assessment offered by Westmoreland Jan. 27, 1968, just four days before the Tet attacks began. Westmoreland said: "The year ended with the enemy increasingly resorting to desperation tactics in attempting to achieve military/psychological victory; and he has experienced only failure in these attempts."

Another year-end report, offered by Adm. U.S. Grant Sharp, commander in the Pacific, in a cablegram to the Joint Chiefs Jan. 1, said that although the air war had failed to halt the supplies sent from North to South Vietnam, the bombing had reduced the flow of external supplies into North Vietnam. Sharp also said the distribution of materials in both the North and the South had been disrupted.

A Jan. 31 attack on the U.S. embassy at Saigon began the enemy offensive during Tet, the Lunar New Year. Although Johnson said at a Feb. 2 news conference that the attack had been "anticipated, prepared for and met," the Pentagon analysis said the offensive took the White House and Joint Chiefs "by surprise, and its strength, length and intensity prolonged this shock."

Defense Secretary McNamara asked for plans to supply emergency reinforcements to Westmoreland, and on Feb. 12, the Joint Chiefs presented three alternatives, all of which they said would leave the strategic reserve in the U.S. dangerously thin. The Joint Chiefs recommended that "a decision to deploy reinforcements to Vietnam be deferred at this time." The Pentagon analyst commented: "The tactic the Chiefs were using was clear: by refusing to scrape the bottom of the barrel any further for Vietnam, they hoped to force the President to 'bite the bullet' on the call-up of the reserves—a step they had long thought essential, and that they were determined would not now be avoided."

McNamara, despite the advice, approved Feb. 13 an emergency deployment of 10,500 troops, a brigade of the 82nd Airborne Division. Johnson went to North Carolina to see the men off Feb. 14. The Pentagon study described the President, "shaking hands with the solemn but determined paratroopers" who were "seasoned veterans returning to an ugly conflict." The analyst said the "experience proved for him to be one of the most profoundly moving and troubling of the entire Vietnam war. . . . It may well be that the dramatic decisions of the succeeding month and a half that reversed the direction of American policy in the war had their genesis in those troubled handshakes."

To determine exactly how many men Westmoreland would need, the President sent Gen. Earle G. Wheeler, chairman of the Joint Chiefs, to Saigon in late February. Wheeler returned and filed an immediate report Feb. 27 that Westmoreland "has stated requirements for forces over the 525,000 ceiling" set in 1967. "The add-on requested totals 206,756 spaces for a new proposed ceiling of 731,756."

Wheeler's report was not optimistic. He said the Tet drive had gained the initiative for the enemy. The South Vietnamese forces had been forced into "a defensive posture around towns and cities" while the Viet Cong was "operating with relative freedom in the countryside." To hold the northern provinces, Wheeler said, Westmoreland had been forced to send half the U.S. maneuver battalions, "stripping the rest of the country of adequate reserves" and robbing himself of "an offensive capability."

Westmoreland wanted about half the reinforcements by May 1 and all 206,756 additional troops by the end of 1968. The Pentagon study said:

Now the alternatives stood out in stark reality. To accept and meet General Wheeler's request for troops would mean a total U.S. military commitment to SVN [South Vietnam]—an Americanization of the war, a call-up of reserve forces, vastly increased expenditures. To deny the request for troops, or to attempt to again cut it to a size which could be sustained by the thinly stretched active forces, would just as surely signify that an upper limit to the U.S. military commitment in SVN had been reached.

Clark Clifford, designated to be sworn in as defense secretary March 1 to replace McNamara, was asked by Johnson Feb. 28 to gather senior advisers for a complete review of U.S. policy. The men, who came to be known as the Clifford Group, included top officials from various departments as well as personal advisers to the President.

Development of draft memos for the President, to be approved by the group, was the work of the International Security Affairs (ISA) office of the Defense Deparment, headed by Assistant Secretary Paul C. Warnke. Warnke had succeeded John T. McNaughton, one of McNamara's chief lieutanants and supporters. McNaughton had died in late 1967 in a plane crash.

An ISA draft memo produced Feb. 29 said that even with the 200,000 additional troops requested, "we will not be in a position to drive the enemy from SVN or to destroy his forces." The memo said if further escalation occurred, "it will be difficult to convince critics that we are not simply destroying South Vietnam in order to 'save' it and that we genuinely want peace talks. . . . This growing disaffection accompanied, as it certainly will be, by increased defiance of the draft and growing unrest in the cities because of the belief that we are neglecting domestic problems, runs great risks of provoking a domestic crisis of unprecedented proportions."

The ISA recommended that the U.S. mission be to "buy the time" needed by the South Vietnamese army to "develop effective capability" rather than wage offensive war. This approach was strongly opposed by the military advisers.

The initial draft was discussed by the Clifford Group March 3 and rejected. A revised memo indicated that the group came to no conclusions about bombing policy. It did not even mention what was to be Johnson's decision at the end of March, a territorial limitation on bombing. This had been suggested before by McNamara and was brought up again by Rusk.

On the question of troops, the new memo, completed March 4, recommended deployment of 22,000 more troops; reservation of a decision to deploy the other 185,000 men requested by Westmoreland; and approval of a reserve call-up of about 262,000 men.

The Pentagon papers said President Johnson decided March 13 to approve deployment of 30,000 men, in addition to the 10,500-man emergency reinforcement already made. This decision involved total reserve call-ups of 98,451 men, but the 30,000 was reduced to 13,-500 by the time Johnson made his announcement March 31.

A number of outside events were cited as examples of public pressure on the President in March. The press, beginning with the New York Times, published leaks of Westmoreland's 200,000-man request. A floor debate in the Senate March 7 was interrupted with the demand from several prominent senators that Congress be consulted on troop increases. Returns from the Democratic Presidential primary in New Hampshire began coming in with evidence of Eugene McCarthy's strength as an antiwar candidate. On March 16, Sen. Robert F. Kennedy announced his candidacy.

In an epilogue to the narrative of the events of February and March, the Pentagon study gave a summation of what the analysts believed led Johnson to his March 31 announcement. Mentioning "large and growing elements" of the American public who were dissatisfied, the summation said:

The political reality which faced President Johnson was that 'more of the same' in South Vietnam, with an increased commitment of American lives and money and its consequent impact on the country, accompanied by no guarantee of military victory in the near future, had become unacceptable to these elements of the American public. The optimistic military reports or progress in the war no longer rang true after the shock of the Tet offensive.

Thus, the President's decision to seek a new strategy and a new road to peace was based upon two major considerations:

(1) The conviction of his principal civilian advisers, particularly Secretary of Defense Clifford, that the troops requested by General Westmoreland would not make a military victory any more likely; and

(2) A deeply felt conviction of the need to restore unity to the American nation.

Johnson 'Vietnamization' plan reported

—The Globe, in its June 22 edition, reported that the Pentagon study and accompanying documents showed that President Johnson, when he announced March 31, 1968 that he would not run for re-election, was also deciding on a policy of Vietnamization, similar to that adopted by President Nixon.

According to the Globe's account, the enemy's Tet offensive at the end of January 1968 led to a sweeping re-evaluation of U.S. Vietnam policy and to a decision to limit U.S. commitment and to build up the effectiveness of the South Vietnamese government and army.

The Globe cited a State Department cable issued the day before Johnson's announcement. The article contended that the following paragraph in the cable pointed the way toward a Vietnamization policy: "Major stress on importance of GVN [Saigon government] and ARVN [South Vietnam army] increased effectiveness, with our equipment and other support as first priority in our own actions."

The Globe also noted that Johnson said in his announcement: "We shall accelerate the re-equipment of South Vietnam's armed forces in order to meet the enemy's increased firepower. This will enable them progressively to undertake a larger share of the combat operations against the Communist invaders."

The Globe said the Pentagon narrative explained that Johnson's decision followed two months of what the analyst described as a "reassessment from A to Z" of America's policy. Discussing the effect of the enemy's Tet offensive, the Pentagon study said:

The possibility of military victory had seemingly become remote and the cost had become too high both in political and economic terms. Only then were our ultimate objectives brought out and re-examined. Only then was it realized that a clear-cut military victory was probably not possible or necessary, and that the road to peace would be at least as dependent upon South Vietnamese political developments as it would be on American arms.

The re-evaluation was initiated by a request by Gen. William Westmoreland, U.S. commander in Saigon, for 206,000 additional troops over the 525,000 ceiling that had been placed on American forces in Vietnam. The Globe printed excerpts from a Feb. 27, 1968 report by Gen. Earle G. Wheeler, chairman of the Joint Chiefs of Staff, on the situation following the Tet offensive. Speaking of the enemy's situation, Wheeler said:

Although many of his units were badly hurt, the judgment is that he has the will and the capability to continue. . . . His determination appears to be unshaken.

Wheeler's assessment of the situation in South Vietnam was in part:

(1) Psychological—The people in South Vietnam were handed a psychological blow, particularly in the urban areas where the feeling of security had been strong. There is a fear of further attacks.

(2) The structure of the government was not shattered and continues to function but at greatly reduced effectiveness.

The Pentagon narrative said the Joint Chiefs of Staff recommended against Westmoreland's request. The analyst commented that it was unprecedented in the history of America's involvement in Vietnam that the Joint Chiefs spoke against additional forces requested by a field commander.

The study said that Clark Clifford, sworn in March 1, 1968 as defense secretary, was under presidential mandate to conduct "a complete and searching reassessment of the entire U.S. strategy and commitment in South Vietnam."

In a memo dated March 4, Clifford called for a small deployment in response to Westmoreland's request and further recommended: "Either through Ambassador [Ellsworth] Bunker or through an early visit by Secretary Clifford, a highly forceful approach to the GVN [Thieu and Ky] to get certain key commitments for improvement, tied to our own increased effort and to increased U.S. support for the ARVN."

The reassessment also took note of domestic opinion. The Pentagon analysis cited a study by Phil Goulding, assistant defense secretary for public affairs, recommending that Westmoreland's request be denied. He said this would "show change" if not progress and would "prevent the middle-of-the-roaders from joining the doves."

The Pentagon papers said a March 18 White House meeting between Johnson and "a group of his friends and confidants" outside the government moved him closer to his March 31 decision. The group produced a recommendation March 19, in the words of the analyst, to "forget about seeking a battlefield solution . . . and instead intensify efforts to seek a political solution at the negotiating table."

U.S. Dissent

Antiwar veterans demonstrate. About 1,000 antiwar veterans began five days of demonstrations in Washington April 19. While the demonstrators held rallies, lobbied in Congress and staged guerrilla theater protests, their lawyers fought government attempts to prevent the veterans from using the Mall area near the Capitol as a campground.

Organized by the Vietnam Veterans Against the War, the demonstrators arriving April 18 called their protest Operation Dewey Canyon III and described it as a "limited incursion into the District of Columbia." (Dewey Canyon II was a code name used for the Laos invasion.)

The chief spokesman for the veterans in their Washington demonstration was John F. Kerry, 26, a former Navy lieutenant in Vietnam. Former Sp. 4 Jan Crumb, 28, the organization's president, was one of the founders. The group gained momentum and decided to bring its case to Congress following a three-day war crimes inquiry it sponsored in Detroit in February 1971.

After a march to the Capitol April 19, the veterans held a rally in which they demanded Congressional action on a 16-point program to end the war. Among their demands, the protesters urged "immediate, unconditional and unilateral" withdrawal of U.S. military and intelligence forces from Vietnam; a formal war crimes inquiry; amnesty for all Americans who had refused to serve in Vietnam; and improved benefits for returned veterans.

Reps. Bella Abzug (D, N.Y.) and Paul N. McCloskey Jr. (R, Calif.) spoke at the rally, which broke up as the veterans separated into state delegations for lobbying efforts. Earlier the protesters had been barred from entering the Arlington National Cemetery for a memorial service, but the gates were opened for the ceremony April 20. The service was a solemn, single-file march to lay wreaths to the Indochinese and allied dead in Vietnam.

Sens. Edward M. Kennedy (D, Mass.) and George S. McGovern (D, S.D.) visited the campsite April 21. Kennedy congratulated the veterans for their service to their country and said, "Now I think you are serving it better by being here in Washington."

Delegations of veterans attended a Senate Foreign Relations Committee hearing April 20 and a Senate Judiciary Subcommittee hearing on Vietnam refugees and civilian casualties April 21. They staged mock "search and destroy" missions and smashed toy M-16 rifles April 20. A delegation of protesters went to the Pentagon April 21 and tried to surrender themselves as war criminals.

One hundred and ten veterans were arrested on the steps of the Supreme Court April 22 as they demanded a ruling against the war as unconstitutional. Washington police refused the demands of two legless veterans to be arrested along with their "brothers." The city prosecutor dropped disorderly conduct charges against those arrested after Superior Court Judge William Stewart found April 23 that there was "no evidence of any violent act."

The veterans continued lobbying activities and guerrilla theater protests April 22, and a group joined their spokesman, John F. Kerry, in an appearance before the Senate Foreign Relations Committee. Joined by supporters, the veterans held a candlelight march to the White House that evening.

The high point of the protest came April 23 when 700 veterans discarded their military medals and ribbons at a demonstration at the Capitol.

The veterans broke camp on the Mall April 23, ending what Sen. George McGovern (D, S.D.) said was "the most effective protest to date" against the war in Indochina.

Many civilian demonstrators echoed McGovern's sentiment about the effectiveness of the veterans' protest. Asked to explain its impact, Mike Milligan, 22, a former Marine who was wounded in Vietnam, told a Washington Post reporter April 23: "People have never seen protesters like us. . . . We didn't dodge the draft. Our guerrilla theater is effective because we were the guerrillas. Nobody is going to doubt the sincerity of a guy who got both his legs blown off in the Nam. We're finally bringing the war home."

The injunction against camping on the Mall had been dissolved April 22 by the federal judge who had issued the order. Judge George L. Hart Jr. rebuked the Justice Department for seeking the injunction and then, after it was upheld by the Supreme Court, failing to enforce it. The department had asked Hart to dissolve the order.

Hart said the judiciary had been "improperly used" by the executive branch, and he said to Justice Department lawyers: "You have put the Vietnam veterans in a situation of openly defying the courts of this country." Afterwards, the department said it had "taken note of the fact that the order related to men who have served their country honor-

ably" and that "for practical as well as humanitarian reasons," it had been considered unnecessary to continue the injunction.

(Some 600 active duty servicemen, many in uniform, joined thousands of persons April 23 for a memorial service "for all Indochina war dead" at Washington Naval Cathedral. The judge advocates general of the Army and the Air Force had warned earlier in the day that soldiers attending the service in uniform could face prosecution for violating regulations against engaging in a political demonstration while in uniform.)

Veterans tell their story to Congress. Several Congressional panels, in addition to the Senate Foreign Relations Committee, provided a forum for the protesting antiwar veterans.

A special one-day hearing was held April 23 by Sens. George S. McGovern (D, S.D.), Walter F. Mondale (D, Minn.) and Philip Hart (D, Mich.), and Rep. Charles A. Vanik (D, Ohio). They heard a former Marine lieutenant, Everett B. Carson, disclose that he had been a platoon commander in Gulf Company in the 7th Battalion of the 9th Marine Regiment when it crossed into Laos in February 1969 as part of a two-week "interdiction and ambush" mission. He reported that the military command had listed the operation as having taken place entirely in South Vietnam and he had been told not to discuss the Laos portion with newsmen.

A House hearing April 23 called by Reps. Jonathan B. Bingham (D, N.Y.) and Paul Findley (R, Ill.) heard two former Marines from a graves registration unit in Vietnam charge that the official toll of U.S. battle deaths was far lower than their own count and they were under orders not to discuss the count outside the chain of command.

An unofficial, ad hoc committee, headed by Rep. Ronald V. Dellums (D, Calif.), heard allegations of atrocities in unsworn testimony April 26–29. Three former Army officers told April 26 of an artillery bombardment, condoned by the commanding general, of an enemy hospital. Other witnesses told of prisoners tortured and murdered, civilians hit with fire bombs and of a "body-count mania."

A witness said a general had ordered his battalions to meet monthly "body-count" quotas.

Danny S. Notley, a former Army sergeant, told the group April 28 that his unit, a platoon of the Americal Division, 4th Battalion, 21st Infantry, had participated in the killing of about 30 Vietnamese men, women and children in a village called Truong Khanh, near Mylai, in April 1969. He had not publicly talked about it before.

Vietnam veterans testified before the ad hoc group April 29 about U.S. bombing and shelling of villages.

(Six Vietnam war veterans appeared with David Susskind on a WNEW-TV program April 25. They were all dubious of the reasons given by the government for being in the war. Former Marine Corps Lt. Robert O. Muller, paralyzed from the chest down from a war wound, said he was not bitter "because I got shot through the chest" but because he found out "that I was betrayed by my government." The veterans agreed that the South Vietnamese troops were not capable of handling the combat alone and that the war had racial overtones of "Americans versus Orientals.")

Antiwar vets march in Boston. About 400 Vietnam veterans marched from Bunker Hill (Charlestown, Mass.) to the Boston Common May 31, Memorial Day, on the last leg of a 20-mile trek to protest the war in Indochina. The marchers, organized by the Vietnam Veterans Against the War, had started from Concord May 29, tracing in reverse the route of Paul Revere's ride, to "spread the alarm" against the current war.

Arthur Johnson, the group's New England coordinator, explained May 28 their choice of the route Paul Revere took in 1775 to warn that British soldiers were coming at the start of the American Revolution. Johnson said the veterans hoped "to publicize the parallels between the actions of the revolutionary citizen-soldiers and our actions." The group named their march "Operation POW," Johnson said, to point out "that all Americans are prisoners of this war."

About 100 of the veterans and more than 300 sympathizers were arrested May 30 for violating curfew in Lexington.

The arrests took place following a heated town meeting May 29 when the Lexington selectmen refused to suspend the curfew for the veterans camping on Lexington Green. Townspeople who opposed the decision left the meeting to join the veterans. State and local police moved in at 3 a.m. to clear the green.

Marching onto the Boston Common May 31, the veterans chanted "Bring our brothers home" and smashed toy rifles they had carried from Concord. Former Sen. Eugene J. McCarthy, in an address to the rally that followed, said "This is a bearing-witness to life and what we want to be manifest as the true spirit of America."

Antiwar vets condemned by rival group. A group calling itself Vietnam Veterans for a Just Peace claimed June 1 that it represented the "great majority" who supported President Nixon's Vietnamization and withdrawal program. Spokesmen for the group, at a Washington news conference, condemned the "relative handful" of veterans who participated in "irresponsible" protests in Washington organized by the Vietnam Veterans Against the War.

Former Marine Sgt. Bruce N. Kessler, speaking for the new group, said the organization was formed in a "sort of spontaneous reaction" to the antiwar veterans. He said it had 5,000 members. Kessler challenged John F. Kerry, spokesman for the Vietnam Veterans Against the War, to a televised debate.

Also speaking at the press conference, which was arranged with the help of an officer of the Veterans of Foreign Wars (VFW), was former Navy Lt. John O'Neill, who said he had served in the same unit as Kerry in Vietnam. Commenting on Kerry's testimony before the Senate Foreign Relations Committee —that he saw crimes committed on a day-to-day basis by American forces in Vietnam—O'Neill said "I never saw one war crime committed by allied forces."

O'Neill said he had written the Senate committee to ask to testify but had been refused. A spokesman for the committee commented that the panel had heard testimony from a Navy lieutenant who supported the Administration's Vietnam policy and from Herbert Rainwater, national VFW commander.

Rainwater, testifying May 27, had called the antiwar veterans "a very confused minority" and Kerry "an opportunist." Rainwater had said he was particularly bitter about the "120 minutes" of national television coverage devoted to the antiwar vets during their five-day demonstration.

POW relatives clash. At a Vietnam Veterans Against the War news conference in Washington July 22, called to demand a set date for withdrawal of U.S. forces from Vietnam in exchange for release of American prisoners of war, four women relatives of POWs interrupted to shout that antiwar veterans' leader John F. Kerry was using the POW issue to promote his own political ambitions. "Mr. Kerry is using your families," the critics cried to six other relatives of POWs introduced by Kerry.

Kerry charged that the Nixon Administration's position on the POW issue was "a part of a macabre policy of rationalization" and that the American prisoners were "being used to continue the war." After the four women critics walked out, Kerry introduced Delia Alvarez, whose brother, a prisoner since 1964, had been held in Indochina longer than any other American. She said the U.S. government "is stalling" and asked, "Why is my brother still a prisoner in North Vietnam if our government has not betrayed its men?"

Richard Sigler of Lakewood, Colo., whose son was a prisoner, said the Administration had put "tremendous pressure" on POW families to prevent dissent from official policy. Sigler claimed that at a July 3 briefing in Colorado, he was told not to make any public statements because they might upset secret negotiations.

In another development, about 500 Vietnam veterans and their supporters marched three miles through Kansas City, Mo. July 4 on an antiwar candlelight parade. Johnny Upton, 24, of the Vietnam Veterans Against the War, said the march was "to counteract the rockets' red glare" of traditional Independence Day fireworks. The antiwar veterans group had announced the Kansas City protest June 6 as "a limited incursion of Vietnam veterans into middle America." Upton had said then, "we feel the East and West Coasts have been barraged with antiwar sentiment, and middle America is being neglected."

Mass marches on both coasts. Hundreds of thousands of marchers massed in Washington and San Francisco April 24 and held peaceful rallies urging Congress to bring an immediate end to the war in Indochina. Although radicals seized control of the speakers' platform for a portion of the West Coast rally [see below], there was none of the violence and large-scale arrests that marred some of the previous mass protests against the war.

As in the past, most of the protesters were young, with high school and college students making up the largest contingent. However, more adults participated than in former antiwar rallies. Many in Washington told reporters it was their first march against the war, and on the West Coast, a group marched under a Parents for Peace banner.

Many labor union locals were represented in the D.C. rally, and longshoremen served as parade marshals in San Francisco. There was only a sprinkling of blacks in the Washington protest, but minorities, particularly Mexican Americans, played a major role in the West Coast demonstration.

Washington protest The turnout for the April 24 Washington march was at least double the expectation of the Justice Department and Washington police officials. D.C. Police Chief Jerry V. Wilson said 200,000 attended the rally, but the National Peace Action Coalition (NPAC), chief sponsor of the march, estimated the crowd at 500,000.

At 11 a.m. the day of the march, when thousands had already started along Pennsylvania Avenue toward the rally site at the Capitol, police reported a three-mile traffic backup near Baltimore of cars and buses headed for Washington. As the march route filled up, thousands of protesters were diverted to other streets. Throughout most of the afternoon, the crowds that had reached the rally site cheered announcements that more were still coming along Pennsylvania Avenue.

The Washington demonstrators, with relaxed tolerance, accepted fellow marchers walking under banners promoting women's liberation, gay liberation and a variety of radical causes. Students for a Democratic Society (SDS) organizers used bullhorns to urge protesters to abandon the "so-called liberal politicians" and attend a counter rally. Later SDS led an uneventful march to Dupont Circle, the scene of a police-protester clash during the November '69 demonstration.

Of the numerous rally speakers—including congressmen, civil rights and labor leaders, spokesmen for women's rights and Puerto Rican independence—former Navy Lt. (j. g.) John F. Kerry drew one of the most enthsiastic responses. Kerry, the major spokesman for the antiwar veterans who had been protesting in Washington for the preceding week, told of the veterans' "determination to undertake one last mission, to reach out and destroy the last vestige of this barbaric war . . . and so when in 30 years from now our brothers go down the street without a leg, without an arm, or a face, and small boys ask why, we will be able to say 'Vietnam' and not mean a desert, not a filthy obscene memory, but mean instead the place where America finally turned and where soldiers like us helped in the turning."

Coretta Scott King urged the nation to pay tribute to her slain husband, the Rev. Martin Luther King, by ending the war by Aug. 28, the eighth anniversary of King's historic civil rights march on Washington. George Wiley, director of the National Welfare Rights Organization, urged the protesters to remember "the other war" against racism, poverty and injustice, a theme also voiced by Mrs. King.

In another major speech, Sen. Vance Hartke (D, Ind.) said, "The only way to bring our prisoners of war home is to get out now; the only way we can renew our commitment to mankind is to get out now. . . . Let our voices sound the two great words of peace in no uncertain terms—out now."

Other Congressional speakers, including New York Reps. Bella Abzug and Herman Badillo, emphasized the significance of the site of the rally, on the Capitol lawn. Mrs. Abzug said, "Your presence here today means that you're going to force the Congress to undeclare this war."

Other speakers included the Rev. Ralph Abernathy, president of the Southern Christian Leadership Conference; pacifist David Dellinger, a leader of the Peoples Coalition for Peace and Justice; Reps. Abner Mikva (D, Ill.) and John Conyers (D, Mich.); and labor leaders such as Harold J. Gibbons, a vice president of the International Brotherhood of Teamsters.

Singers Peter, Paul and Mary, Country Joe McDonald and Pete Seeger were joined by the demonstrators in favorite hymns of the antiwar movement. They also entertained at a dusk-to-dawn rock and folk concert that evening on the Washington Monument grounds, sponsored by the Peoples Coalition.

While thousands stayed on in Washington for the protests scheduled the next week, the majority left after the rally or after the all-night concert. Traffic was halted for four hours on the New Jersey Turnpike April 25 by about 1,000 returning antiwar protestors who stopped their cars on the road and built a bonfire that halted traffic coming the other way.

Among related developments:

■ Vice President Agnew, at a New Orleans press conference April 25, praised the march organizers for a "very well-controlled rally" but added, "The American people must not be misled simply because some 200,000 demonstrators marched in the streets of Washington. After all, they are less than 2% of the population." President Nixon was out of Washington for the entire weekend, most of the time at the Presidential retreat at Camp David, Md.

■ Washington police April 25 reported only 25 arrests in connection with the march, all for minor offenses. The largest group arrest since the beginning of the current Washington protests came April 25 when police detained 151 Quakers, who were among 300 who staged a silent peace vigil in front of the White House.

■ The National Peace Action Coalition (NPAC) and the Justice Department, in separate press conferences April 16, had announced agreement on details of the April 24 activities in Washington. In contrast, the Peoples Coalition for Peace and Justice continued to disagree with government officials over its plans for protests in Washington April 26–May 5.

The Peoples Coalition and the NPAC represented the radical and more moderate factions of the New Mobilization Committee to End the War in Vietnam (New Mobe), the sponsor of major peace demonstrations before it split over tactics in the summer of 1970. Reflecting a continued belief in the efficacy of mass marches, the NPAC formulated plans for the April 24 Washington rally and a similar demonstration the same day in San Francisco. The Peoples Coalition, focusing not only on the war but on poverty and charges of political repression, planned to combine rallies with acts of civil disobedience in Washington.

At the Justice Department press briefing April 16, officials praised the NPAC leaders for their "cooperativeness" in planning the protest. Vice President Spiro T. Agnew, in his capacity as president of the Senate, had agreed April 15 to let the marchers congregate for a rally on the west lawn of the Capitol, space denied to former large antiwar protests.

The NPAC, at a press conference April 21, claimed the endorsement of eight U.S. senators and 33 representatives for the D.C. and San Francisco protests. Sen. Vance Hartke (D, Ind.) spoke at the conference and urged President Nixon to take note of the rallies and to have "the courage to speak the voice of the American people."

The April 24 march had also been endorsed by numerous individuals and organizations, among them Mrs. Coretta King, Americans for Democratic Action and many labor union locals. In an advertisement in the New York Times April 11, 49 members of the Army's 1st Air Cavalry Unit stationed in Vietnam were listed as signers of a plea that read, "We urge you to march for peace April 24. We would do it ourselves, but we're in Vietnam."

The Interior Department announced April 9 that it would not allow the Peoples Coalition to use Washington's Rock Creek Park for an encampment and base of activities during its protests beginning April 25. A department spokes-

man cited federal regulations against camping in U.S. park land in the District of Columbia. (But the Justice Department April 22 gave it permission to use West Potomac Park as a staging area for its week of demonstrations.)

In a press release April 21, the Mayday Movement, one of the groups in the Peoples Coalition, called on Congress to legislate total withdrawal from Vietnam by May 1 or face massive civil disobedience designed to close down Washington. The group said protesters would bodily block commuter traffic into Washington May 3 and 4 in an effort to create massive traffic jams.

■ D.C. police arrested 92 protesters near the White House April 5 for disorderly conduct and blocking the sidewalk. The protesters, many of them young seminarians, called their demonstration a "Holy Week witness against the war" and planned to fast during the week leading up to Easter and Passover.

■ Some 500 women marched on the Pentagon April 10 calling for an end to the war and oppression against women.

Radicals take over Coast rally—The scheduled program at the San Francisco peace rally was disrupted when militant Chicanos and radicals seized the platform and held the stage for more than an hour. Led by Abe Tapia, president of the Mexican American Political Association and a scheduled speaker, dissidents including Chinese, Japanese and Indian protesters charged that the ralliers ignored "third-world" issues. David Franchez, prime minister of a militant Mexican-American group called the Brown Berets, called the peace movement "a conspiracy to quench the revolution."

Scheduled speakers including draft resister David Harris, husband of folk singer Joan Baez, and Rep. Paul N. McCloskey Jr. (R, Calif.) left the rally without delivering addresses. McCloskey said later he had left before the disruption because of his heavy speaking schedule.

The march and rally was the largest peace demonstration ever held on the West Coast. Police estimated the rally crowd at 156,000. The NPAC claimed 300,000 participants.

The marchers, led by servicemen on active duty, had the backing of San

Francisco mayor Joseph A. Alioto, who called the demonstrators loyal Americans. Earlier in the week, the city's Board of Supervisors had passed a resolution establishing April 24 as "a day of public determination to end the war in Vietnam."

(Leaders of the opposition New Democratic party in Canada staged a demonstration of 400 people in Ottawa April 24 to show "solidarity" with the U.S. antiwar protesters. In London, 1,500 persons gathered outside the U.S. embassy for the city's first antiwar protest in more than a year.)

Nixon's comment. At his press conference April 29, President Nixon said: The Washington demonstrators were "listened to." "They indicated they wanted the war to end now, that they wanted peace. That, of course, is what I want. It's what ... everybody in this nation wants." While he respected those "who disagree with my policies," his responsibility was "to bring peace but not just peace in our time but peace ... for our children...."

Nixon cautioned that neither Congress nor the President was "intimidated" by the demonstrations and that the government was "going to go forward." It did not mean "we're not going to listen to those who come peacefully," he said, but "those who come and break the law will be prosecuted to the full extent of the law."

Nixon added at his May 1 press conference: It was an "American principle that while everybody has a right to protest peacefully, ... policy in this country is not made by protests." If illegal conduct occurred in the Washington demonstrations, "we're prepared to deal with it. We will arrest those who break the law. ... The right to demonstrate for peace abroad does not carry with it the right to break the peace at home."

The Philadelphia Yearly Meeting of the Religious Society of Friends, the largest Quaker organization in the U.S., approved April 3 and sent to President Nixon a letter protesting that his public claims to a Quaker heritage and commitment to pacifism, coupled with defense of his Indochina war policy, was a misuse of the basic Quaker peace testimony against outward strife. It requested him "most respectfully" to cease "further distortion" of the tenet.

Mass arrests in Washington. At least 12,000 demonstrators were arrested in Washington May 3-5. The more than 7,-000 detained in sweeping arrests May 3 constituted a record for the city. The demonstrators, conducting large-scale civil disobedience protests designed to close down the capital, were organized by the Peoples Coalition for Peace and Justice, particularly the coalition's radical Mayday Tribe constituent.

A week-long Peoples Lobby protest marked by limited civil disobedience April 26-30 led into the Mayday phase, when demonstrators attempted massive traffic disruptions combined with marches on the Pentagon May 3, the Justice Department May 4 and the Capitol May 5.

Washington police prepared for the threatened disruptions by ordering 30,-000 protesters out of West Potomac Park in a pre-dawn raid May 2. The demonstrators' permit to use the park was canceled, according to D.C. Police Chief Jerry V. Wilson, because of "numerous and flagrant" violations of the permit and "rampant" use of drugs. Later, government and city officials and demonstration leaders credited the failure of the protesters' aim to close down the city to the clearing of the park and dispersal of the demonstrators.

With a mandate from President Nixon to keep the city "open for business," the 5,100-man Washington police, backed up by federal troops, used tear gas and made mass arrests May 3 to keep Washington traffic moving and to prevent the demonstrators from reaching their announced target, the Pentagon. Four thousand federal troops were deployed in the city, some of them transported by helicopter to the Washington Monument. Other forces included 1,-400 National Guardsmen and Park and Capitol police.

The police arrested 2,000 of the protesters by 8 a.m., successfully stifling an attempt to tie up traffic at targeted bridges leading into Washington and at downtown traffic circles. Antiwar leader Dr. Benjamin Spock was one of the earliest arrested as he, with 300 others, tried to march to the Pentagon. Lacking jail facilities, police detained thousands outdoors in the Washington Redskins football practice field near Robert F. Kennedy Memorial Stadium.

Throughout May 3, protesters, splintered into small groups, roamed through the city and blocked intersections, using their bodies, trash cans, and disabled or parked cars. Chased by police, they regrouped on other corners. There were no reports of looting or window-breaking, but some property damage resulted from the protesters' tactic of slashing the tires of cars, including one belonging to Sen. Paul Fannin (R, Ariz.).

In a few incidents, rocks were thrown at police, but such violence was rare as compared with other disruptive protests in Washington and elsewhere. There were 155 reported injuries of police and protesters. Police used their nightsticks, aiming mostly at protesters' legs, but some of those imprisoned at the Redskin practice field were treated for head injuries.

Following the morning rush hour, Attorney General John N. Mitchell declared the demonstrations a failure: "The city is open . . . The traffic is flowing. The government is functioning." Several top government officials, however, were in their offices well before 6 a.m. in order to avoid the protesters.

Mayday leader Rennie Davis, speaking at a mid-afternoon press conference shortly before he was arrested on conspiracy charges, agreed that the protest had failed. He said, "We want to make clear that we failed this morning to stop the U.S. government," but he added that they had succeeded in building "a people's organization" and described the days action as "almost the most major nonviolent demonstration" in the country's history.

Federal Bureau of Investigation agents arrested Davis for conspiring to keep federal employes from their jobs and to violate the civil rights of others. Similar charges were lodged against John Froines, who was arrested the next day. Abbie Hoffman, who along with Davis and Froines was a "Chicago Seven" defendant on conspiracy charges arising from riots at the 1968 Democratic National Convention, was arrested in New York May 5 on charges connected with the D.C. protests.

The protesters changed their tactics May 4 and did not attempt to block the heavily-guarded bridges leading into Washington. Two thousand more were arrested during the day—most during a rally at the Justice Department, which was watched from the windows by Mitchell and other department officials.

Others were arrested in incidents throughout the day as police scattered groups of protesters, but without the sweeping arrests and tear gas used the day before. Protesters marching to the Justice Department cooperated with authorities by stopping for traffic lights and keeping to the sidewalks.

The arrests at the Justice Department were peaceful. Protesters sat in the street, then rose to be arrested while a demonstration leader called through a bullhorn, "Keep it cool, man . . . The whole world is watching."

More than 1,000 demonstrators were arrested May 5 after they had forced officials to close the Capitol to visitors. A rally on the steps of the House was addressed by four representatives, who called the demonstrators their "guests." Reps. Bella Abzug (D, N.Y.), Ronald V. Dellums (D, Calif.), Parren Mitchell (D, Md.) and Charles B. Rangel (D, N.Y.) delivered speeches, and protest leaders demanded that Congress ratify a "people's peace treaty" negotiated by student antiwar leaders during a December 1970 trip to Hanoi.

Meanwhile, 500–1,000 government workers gathered in Lafayette Square, across from the White House, in a protest organized by Federal Employes for Peace. Rep. Paul N. McCloskey (R, Calif.) spoke at the rally.

Nationwide demonstrations May 5 paralleled the Washington protests as antiwar groups proclaimed a "moratorium" on business as usual. Demonstrators in several cities met to commemorate the killing of students at Kent State University and Jackson State College a year ago as well as to demand an end to the war in Indochina.

A court battle developed during the three days of protests as attorneys challenged the mass arrest procedures used by the Washington police. Public defenders, representing the thousands detained in the Redskin practice field, charged in a habeas corpus petition filed May 3 that many of those detained were "non-demonstrators who without notice were swept off the sidewalk by police without just cause" in "dragnet" fashion.

Superior Court Judge Harold H. Greene ruled May 4 that the police must release those arrested May 3 who were not charged with a specific offense. A federal appeals court panel, ruling May 5, upheld Greene's finding that the police had illegally detained protesters May 3. However, the appeals court reversed Greene's order that fingerprints and photographs of persons arrested but not charged should be destroyed and not sent to the FBI.

D.C. Police Chief Wilson, in a press conference May 5, denied published reports that the Justice Department and White House decided on the mass arrest procedures. Wilson said, "The decision to temporarily suspend the use of field arrest forms [citing specific offenses] and to immediately arrest all violaters of the law was mine and mine alone."

However, antiwar congressmen blamed the Nixon Administration for allegedly violating the constitutional rights of protesters and by-standers. At a speech in New Rochelle, N.Y. May 5, Sen. Edward Kennedy (D, Mass.) said the Administration "undermined the Constitution" by forcing the D.C. police to use illegal mass arrest procedures May 3. "It all added up to a game of pride," Kennedy said. "The object was to enable John Mitchell to say at 10 a.m. on Monday morning that he had made the city safe for automobiles. Of course the city may have been safe for cars at the time," Kennedy said, "but it was a very unsafe place for citizens."

Mayday tactics described—The Mayday Tribe explained its goals and philosophy in a "tactical manual" read by protesters gathered in West Potomac Park to prepare for the protests. According to the manual, "Mayday is an action, a time period, a state of mind and a bunch of people."

"The aim of the Mayday actions is to raise the social cost of the war to a level unacceptable to America's rulers. To do this we seek to create the specter of social chaos while maintaining the support or at least toleration of the broad masses of American people." The tactic chosen was nonviolent civil disobedience, the manual said, in order to keep a broad base of support and in order to lessen "the likelihood of coming into violent conflict with the GIs who will be ordered to disperse us and who we wish to win on our side."

Peoples Lobby: April 26–30—The mass arrests of May 3–5 followed a week of antiwar protest activity called the Peoples Lobby, when demonstrators lobbied in Congress April 26 and on subsequent days brought specific demands to various government agencies. Focusing on the issues of the draft, war taxes, poverty and repression, the lobbyists visited Selective Service headquarters April 27, the Internal Revenue Service April 28, the Health, Education and Welfare Department April 29 and the Justice Department April 30.

Joining in the lobbying effort were the Southern Christian Leadership Conference (SCLC), the National Welfare Rights Organization (NWRO) and the National Action Group (NAG). The NAG was a constituent of the Peoples Coalition representing such pacifist organizations as the War Resisters League, the Fellowship of Reconciliation and the American Friends Service Committee. The lobbyists engaged in limited acts of civil disobedience, such as sitting in at the offices of congressmen who refused to talk to the protesters and blocking the doors of federal agencies.

A new tactic was demonstrated in the Congressional lobbying April 26 when protesters, splattered with red paint representing blood, wandered through the halls outside Congressional offices wailing and sobbing and begging for peace. Mock war maneuvers were staged, and there was a brief disruption in the spectators' gallery above the Senate floor. Demonstrators organized by NWRO visited congressmen and held a rally on the House steps to push for a $6,500 guaranteed annual income for a family of four.

Arrests were kept to a minimum April 26 and the next day, when protesters, by previous arrangement with Draft Director Curtis W. Tarr, visited Selective Service headquarters. However, arrests on a larger scale began April 28 when police detained more than 200 protesters who had conducted an all-night vigil outside draft headquarters.

A similar number were arrested April 29 during an attempted march from HEW to the White House. The marchers followed an SCLC mule train that had arrived in Washington that day after leaving New York City April 2. Earlier, Ralph D. Abernathy and Hosea Williams of SCLC and George Wiley of NWRO spoke at a "teach-in" at HEW. Williams was among those arrested after the demonstrators tore down a temporary wall in the HEW lobby that had been erected to block the protesters from department offices.

Williams was rearrested April 30 along with some 370 demonstrators who were blocking the entrances to the Justice Department. Outside the building Abernathy read a "poor people's bill of particulars" against the Justice Department, accusing the agency of undermining voting rights, failing to act against police repression and "intimidating the people with illegal searches."

War protests staged nationwide. Protesters estimated at 20,000–40,000 gathered in Boston and 10,000 rallied in New York City May 5 in the largest of numerous antiwar protests held outside of Washington in a "moratorium" on business as usual declared by the Peoples Coalition and other antiwar groups. While most of the protests were peaceful, police used tear gas to disperse thousands of University of Wisconsin protesters in Madison and thousands of University of Maryland students who blocked traffic near their College Park, Md. campus.

Sen. Vance Hartke (D, Ind.) spoke in Boston and New York. In Boston he called President Nixon's Vietnamization policy "a plan to continue the war indefinitely, using South Vietnamese conscripts to carry out the Nixon program for American domination in Southeast Asia."

In San Francisco, protesters clogged the streets, and 76 demonstrators were arrested after a confrontation between police, armed with nightsticks, and protesters, armed with rocks. In Seattle, a protest march by 3,000 youths was dis-

persed by police. Other disruptions and arrests occurred during protests in Waukegan, Ill., Lakewood, Colo., Rochester, N.Y. and in Minneapolis, where 10 students and the chaplain from Macalester College (St. Paul) were arrested for blocking the entrance to the federal building.

Three fire bombs broke the windows of a building at Arizona State University (Tempe) May 5, and a small explosive device went off in the Chico, Calif. branch of the Bank of America. (A bomb had shattered windows at the Bank of America's Santa Cruz, Calif. branch May 1, in an incident reported to be the 35th assault on properties of the bank within the last 15 months.)

At Kent State University in Ohio, demonstrators ended an overnight sit-in in front of the Reserve Officers Training Corps headquarters May 5. The Kent ROTC building had been burned in 1970 in violence which preceded the killing of four students by National Guardsmen. A four-day memorial service was held at the campus May 1–4 marking the first anniversary of the shootings.

The protests continued at the University of Maryland May 6–10. National guardsmen, who had left campus after helping quell disruptions May 5, returned May 7 and used tear gas against 2,000 protesters. Gov. Marvin Mandel declared a general state of emergency May 7 and imposed a curfew. The guardsmen remained on campus through May 10.

An estimated 2,000 to 4,000 protesters staged a sit-in that completely surrounded the John F. Kennedy Federal Building in Boston May 6 in the second day of antiwar protests in the city organized by the Peoples Coalition for Peace and Justice. Officials reported 130 arrests. At one point, police charged the crowd of protesters. Numerous injuries were reported, none serious.

D.C. protests concluded. The three weeks of antiwar protest in Washington appeared at an end May 6 when a scheduled march on the South Vietnamese embassy drew only about 60 demonstrators. However, Mayday leader Rennie Davis said at a news conference that day, "This is literally a beginning. We are coming back again. They are going to have to jail every young person in America before we can be stopped."

D.C. Superior Court Judge James A. Belson ruled May 7 that 600 demonstrators were being held in jail under conditions constituting "cruel and unusual punishment." He said the prisoners were subjected to "irreparable injury" in conditions "which grossly violate the minimum standards properly applicable even to temporary detention facilities."

Belson, referring to protesters detained in the cellblock of the U.S. Courthouse, cited as minimum standards "a place to sleep—a place to lie down—one place per person, and blankets and things of that nature." A Justice Department spokesman, commenting on the ruling May 7, said "jails around the country are overcrowded" and "we don't feel that any cruel or irreparable harm came to the people detained there." In his ruling, Benson ordered immediate court proceedings for the remaining prisoners, and by the end of the day, fewer than 200 demonstrators were left in jail.

In another court action, Superior Court Judge Charles W. Halleck dropped charges May 7 against 200 persons arrested outside the Health, Education and Welfare Department April 29, ruling that the charge of parading without a permit was unconstitutional. Halleck accused prosecutors May 10 of "pressuring" those arrested into entering no-contest or guilty pleas in order to dispose of the 6,000 cases arising from the demonstrations. He criticized "the intractable insistence of somebody in the prosecutor's office to bring everybody to trial," putting pressure on defendants "so authorities can say, 'You see, they were guilty after all.'"

(Many of those arrested May 3-5 obtained their release without appearing at court by posting a $10 "collateral," in a procedure similar to that used for traffic violations.)

Victory marchers rally in capital. Thousands of demonstrators, calling for a military victory in Vietnam, marched behind the Rev. Carl McIntire and attended a rally at the Washington Monument May 8. It was McIntire's third victory march in Washington, but the turnout,

estimated at 15,000 by U.S. Park Police, fell below the 20,000 drawn by the last march in October of 1970.

The demonstrators, armed with Bibles and American flags, marched in evenly spaced ranks behind a "victory" band of members of the Veterans of Foreign Wars.

In addition to protesting what McIntire called the policy of retreat in Vietnam, the marchers carried placards calling for prayers in schools, an end to abortions and freedom for Army Lt. William Calley, convicted of murdering South Vietnamese civilians at Mylai.

At the Washington Monument rally, McIntire urged President Nixon to repent his Indochina policy and "use the sword as God intended" to "stop the Communists." He said the President's duty was "to lead us not in flight and in fear, but in triumph to victory."

McIntire broadcast to the demonstrators telephone calls of support from Gov. George C. Wallace of Alabama and Lt. Gov. Lester Maddox of Georgia. A planned telephone call from South Vietnamese Vice President Nguyen Cao Ky, however, could not be put through from Saigon. Reps. John Rarick (D, La.) and John G. Schmitz (R, Calif.) participated in the march. So did Gene Shaffer, a member of Ironworkers Local 361 in New York City. McIntire described Shaffer as one of the originators of the "hardhat movement."

Mitchell lauds D.C. police. Attorney General John N. Mitchell compared the Mayday antiwar protesters to Hitler's Brown Shirts May 10 and defended the mass arrest tactics of the Washington police. In a San Francisco speech before the California Peace Officers' Association, Mitchell said, "I hope that Washington's decisive opposition to mob force will set an example for other communities."

Mitchell denied Sen. Edward M. Kennedy's assertion that the Nixon Administration forced the D.C. police to make mass arrests. Mitchell said that "courageous decision" was made at the scene of the disturbances by Police Chief Jerry V. Wilson. Mitchell added, "Nothing else could have been done unless the police were to let the mob rule the city."

Stating that his sentiments were "fully shared by the President," Mitchell said the Mayday protesters were "rights robbers" whose "wretched tactic" of civil disobedience constituted a "growing threat to civil rights in this country." Noting that Sen. Lee Metcalf (D, Mont.) had compared police tactics with those of the Nazis, Mitchell said the protesters reminded him of "another group of civilians who roamed the streets of Germany in the 1920s, bullying people, shouting down those who disagreed with them, and denying other people their civil rights. They were called Hitler's Brown Shirts."

In response to Mitchell's statement, Kennedy asked May 10 why the attorney general was "so anxious to disclaim the Administration's responsibility" if he was "so pleased" with the Washington police performance. Kennedy said Mitchell "apparently believes that it is a model of law enforcement fairness to arrest masses of innocent pedestrians, to detain people against whom there is no evidence of criminal conduct, to hold them incommunicado . . . and to manufacture fraudulent arrest papers."

Vice President Spiro Agnew also praised the Washington police in a speech May 11 to the Illinois General Assembly in Springfield. He called the Mayday protesters "the same scruffy individuals that caused the disruptions in Chicago in 1968" at the Democratic National Convention, and he lauded the D.C. police for "deftly" using the same crowd control measures employed in '68 by Chicago's police force.

The controversy over police and protester tactics was the subject of a debate in the House May 6, where Rep. Joe D. Waggoner Jr. (D, La.) said the congressmen who had supported the protesters did a "disservice to this body and disservice to the country." Rep. Dan Kuykendall (R, Tenn.) accused four congressmen of inviting the protesters to a May 5 rally on the steps of the House in defiance of police orders. Rep. Bella Abzug (D, N.Y.), one of the four representatives who addressed the rally, replied that the House steps were a traditional meeting place and that the protesters were nonviolent and their arrests illegal.

The Senate passed by voice vote May 10 a resolution commending the D.C.

police. Sen. Metcalf, who was presiding at the time, declared, "the chair votes 'no.' "

The mass arrests of May 3 were challenged as illegal May 13 in a suit filed by 15 Washington residents who were arrested. The suit, filed in U.S. district court, named Mitchell, Wilson, Deputy Attorney General Richard G. Kleindienst and the D.C. government. The suit claimed the plaintiffs' arrests were "false and unreasonable," the charges "malicious and wholly unsupported" and that they were confined under "inhumane conditions." The federal and D.C. officials were accused of a "predetermined conspiracy . . . to disregard and deny the legal and constitutional rights of citizens."

U.S. prosecutes protest leaders—Yippie leader Abbie Hoffman was indicted May 13 by a grand jury in Washington on charges of interstate travel "with intent to organize, promote, encourage, participate in and carry on a riot" in connection with the Mayday protests. He was also accused of interfering with a policeman during a civil disorder.

Another D.C. grand jury, acting the same day, indicted a coordinator of the Peoples Coalition for Peace and Justice on various counts of assault. In connection with the May 3 protest, the jury accused Bradford Lyttle Jr. of assaulting a policeman with a dangerous weapon and interfering with a policeman. The indictment identified the dangerous weapon as "an audible portable speaker."

On charges brought by the Justice Department, U.S. Magistrate Arthur L. Burnett ruled May 19 that Mayday leaders Rennie Davis and John R. Froines be held for grand jury action. Burnett ruled that the government had demonstrated "sufficient linkage" between speeches by Davis and Froines and the May 3 demonstrations. The Justice Department had charged the two with conspiring to deprive persons of their civil rights and conspiring to interfere with government workers.

Court reports first 1,999 cases—Figures made public May 18 by Arnold M. Malech, executive officer of the D.C. Superior Court, showed that the court had dismissed charges in 712 of the first 1,-

999 Mayday antiwar demonstrator cases to be processed. In another 420 cases, the D.C. corporation counsel's office decided not to file charges and the corporation counsel decided not to prosecute another 131 of those arrested.

The court records showed that 588 persons were found guilty but that only one of these defendants was convicted after a trial. Almost all those found guilty—584 persons—pleaded no contest to disorderly conduct charges. Three others pleaded guilty.

In 93 of the initial cases, those arrested chose to forfeit collateral posted upon their release rather than stand trial or enter a plea. Of those who pleaded guilty or no contest, 347 were released on the basis of time already spent in jail, 218 were given suspended sentences and 22 were fined. The court said 5,200 Mayday demonstrator cases were still pending. Other persons who had been arrested were not scheduled for court because they initially forfeited their collateral.

Mitchell charges Communist leaders. Attorney General John N. Mitchell said May 13 that some of the leaders of the recent antiwar demonstrations in Washington had backgrounds of "Communist association." Mitchell told newsmen that Communists and Communist sympathizers "have been part of the leadership and makeup of every mass demonstration."

Asked how important to the protests was Communist leadership, Mitchell answered, "Important enough to be one of the major stimulants in bringing these people to Washington." He said "Communist sources" had provided "some of the resources that have been used for some of these demonstrations."

Court halts some Mayday trials. The U.S. Court of Appeals for the District of Columbia, in a ruling May 26, ordered the Washington corporation counsel to suspend prosecution of persons arrested during the Mayday demonstrations unless there was "adequate evidence to support probable cause for arrest and charge." The city prosecutor said the next day that about 2,500 of the remaining cases would be dropped.

The appeals court was ruling on an emergency appeal brought May 24 by the American Civil Liberties Union (ACLU), which argued that most of the 12,000 persons arrested May 3–5 had been illegally detained. D.C. Superior Court officials said May 26 they had no exact figures on convictions, but according to unofficial estimates, there had been no more than 10 convictions out of some 3,000 cases already processed by the court.

The ACLU had argued that many Mayday defendants had been forced needlessly to undergo "economic and physical hardship in returning to Washington" to find their cases dismissed at the last minute. The appeals court ordered the corporation counsel to "take all reasonable steps . . . to notify those who are not required to appear." The court said its order did not prevent "further bona fide prosecution" in cases where there was sufficient evidence. The order was to remain in effect until a hearing could be held on the ACLU charge that the city was conducting Mayday prosecutions "for purposes of harassment and . . . with no hope of securing convictions."

Most of the defendants affected by the ruling were persons arrested May 3 when police suspended standard "field arrest procedures" and therefore could not tell where and when the alleged "disorderly conduct" offense occurred. In the majority of these cases, the arrested demonstrators were released after posting a $10 collateral at the police station.

D.C. Corporation Counsel C. Francis Murphy said about 3,000 collateral cases remained in which the defendants elected to stand trial rather than forfeit the fee and have automatic convictions entered on their records. He said about 2,500 of these would be dismissed. In about 2,000 additional cases, Murphy said, authorities had field arrest forms and the cases would be prosecuted.

Murphy's office argued May 27 that it would be "burdensome and expensive" to notify the estimated 2,500 defendants whose cases were being dropped, and the ACLU offered to undertake the job. However, the ACLU said June 1 that many names on the photocopied lists provided by the corporation counsel were illegible and said the prosecutors did not supply addresses for more than half of the names.

Nixon lauds police. At his televised press conference June 1, President Nixon said: The Washington police handled the "very difficult" situation "properly with the right combination of firmness and restraint." There were demonstrators, whose right to demonstrate was recognized and protected, and there were "vandals and hoodlums and lawbreakers" who "should be treated as lawbreakers." "I approve the action of the police in what they did" and "in the event that others come in, not to demonstrate for peace but to break the peace, the police will be supported by the President and the attorney general in stopping that kind of activity."

The President, pressed on the subject, was asked about the mass arrests and whether the suspension of constitutional rights was justified. He responded that individuals attempted to block traffic and "stop the government" and they were halted without significant injuries and a minimum amount of force.

He was asked why the courts released many of those arrested if they were lawfully arrested. "Arrest does not mean that an individual is guilty," he said. After arrest a person had an opportunity for trial and if evidence was lacking could be released. A questioner pointed out, however, that the releases were made on the grounds the arrest was not proper. Nixon reaffirmed his endorsement of the firmness and restraint shown by the police during Mayday and expressed hope such situations could be handled the same way in future protests in Washington or elsewhere.

Leaders of the Peoples Coalition for Peace and Justice criticized Nixon June 2 for endorsing the mass arrests. Coalition organizers, at a Washington news conference, charged that the atmosphere in America was becoming similar to that of Germany in the 1930s.

Referring to Nixon's description of the Mayday protesters, Bradford Lyttle, a coalition coordinator, called the President "the chief vandal, the chief hoodlum and the chief lawbreaker in the United States today." David Dellinger said "Nixon, like an American Hitler, is willing to kill another half-million people" in Indochina to stay in power.

Nixon's comments were also criticized by the American Civil Liberties Union (ACLU) in a statement issued June 2 that said: "It is shocking that the President, sworn to uphold the Constitution, believes he can turn it on and off like a traffic light on the corner to keep the cars moving." The ACLU said the Mayday tactic of stopping traffic was "disruptive" and "must be dealt with firmly . . . but hardly anybody is still being deceived into believing that the national existence was at stake."

Yippie leader Abbie Hoffman, after pleading innocent June 2 to government charges in connection with the Mayday protests, also criticized Nixon's statement and Nixon Administration tactics. Hoffman, who was indicted by a Washington grand jury for promoting and participating in a riot, said his indictment was part of a plan by Attorney General John N. Mitchell "to tie up" radical leaders with grand juries.

At a news conference May 25, Mayday leaders had charged that the Nixon Administration was using grand juries as a "star-chamber" to intimidate protesters. They said they would discuss Mayday plans in public but would refuse to testify before a grand jury.

Among other protests:

■ Five antiwar protesters scuffled with Curtis W. Tarr, Selective Service director, June 4 as they tried to handcuff Tarr and perform a citizens' arrest. Rosemary Reilly, a member of a New York City draft resistance organization, read Tarr a "summons to public accountability" for war crimes and demanded a moratorium on all draft activities. The others involved in the protest in Tarr's office were two Jesuit priests and two former Roman Catholic seminarians.

■ A group calling itself the Potomac Revolutionary Gang served an "eviction notice" on the South Vietnamese embassy in Washington July 6 demanding that the officials move out to make way for the Provisional Revolutionary Government of South Vietnam. A delegation of four protesters presented embassy officials with copies of the antiwar movement's people's peace treaty while about 40 demonstrators remained outside.

■ More than 150 war protesters were arrested during a demonstration in Bedford, Mass. Aug. 6 organized by the Peoples Coalition for Peace and Justice. The demonstration took place outside Hanscom Field, site of government research laboratories that employed about 3,000 Air Force and about 8,000 civilian personnel.

800 Mayday cases dropped. The federal government entered a motion Aug. 26 to drop criminal charges against 800 protesters who had been arrested May 5 on the steps of the Capitol during the Mayday antiwar protests in Washington. A spokesman for the U.S. attorney's office said the decision not to proceed with the cases had been "significantly influenced" by the acquittal by jury of eight of those arrested at the Capitol protest.

The disposal of the 800 cases left only a few hundred unresolved cases resulting from the 12,000 arrests May 3–5. Formal charges had been filed in 7,802 cases, and convictions had been obtained in fewer than 200.

■ A study by the District of Columbia Human Relations Commission, reported by the New York Times July 5, said that more than half of the persons arrested during the Mayday demonstrations did not violate any law and that only about a quarter of them had been apprehended while breaking the law. The 59-page report said the principal criterion for arrest seemed to have been "evidence of youthfulness," such as long hair, beards or casual clothing, rather than "evidence of an unlawful act."

The report said that despite "isolated instances of police brutality" May 3, most police officers behaved "in a manner becoming officers of the law in carrying out an extremely unenlightened policy" of indiscriminate mass arrests. It said "a substantial number" of police had failed to wear badges or nametags and that due process rights of the demonstrators were violated by the suspension of field arrest procedures by the metropolitan police department, "on the advice and counsel of the Justice Department and without approval of the city administration."

Mayday prosecutions restrained. The U.S. Court of Appeals for the District of Columbia ruled Oct. 1 that police must refund collateral to almost all of the protesters who forfeited it in the more than 12,000 arrests during the Mayday antiwar demonstrations. The ruling, which included other restraints on Washington prosecutors, was hailed as an "almost total victory" by American Civil Liberties Union attorneys who had brought suit as a class action on behalf of the protesters.

The three-judge panel also warned that unless prosecutors could show "legitimate governmental interests" against such a procedure, the court might order all Mayday arrest records completely expunged except for those of persons convicted after trial.

The court totally banned dissemination of Mayday arrest records, even to the Federal Bureau of Investigation, except in the fewer than 200 cases where protesters were convicted of illegal acts. The court also ordered the D.C. corporation counsel to trace any copies of arrest records already given to other agencies and retrieve them for metropolitan police files.

The ruling temporarily enjoined further prosecution of the estimated 325 Mayday cases still pending until the cases had been thoroughly screened by the corporation counsel.

During a hearing on the case Sept. 22, Washington officials were unable to provide what the court considered necessary information on the arrests. The metropolitan court records were unclear because forfeitures and no contest pleas had been counted as convictions. The court ordered the corporation to supply the information within 20 days.

Clifford offers peace plan. Clark M. Clifford, secretary of defense under former President Johnson, proposed a plan June 8 for ending American involvement in Indochina by the end of 1971.

Speaking to a coalition of peace groups in Washington, Clifford suggested withdrawal of all American troops and an end to U.S. military activity in Indochina by Dec. 31. All American prisoners held by North Vietnam were to be released within 30 days of a joint Washington-Hanoi announcement of the accord. The Viet

Cong and North Vietnamese in turn would agree to refrain from attacking American soldiers during the pullout period. U.S. obligation to remove its troops would be suspended if the Communists failed to release the captives within the specified 30 days.

Clifford said his formula was based on a "number of conversations and meetings I have had in recent weeks with different people, some of them Americans and some of them not." Clifford declined to say whether he had been in direct contact with North Vietnamese, Viet Cong or even Soviet officials.

White House Press Secretary Ronald L. Ziegler took issue with Clifford's proposal June 8. He said: "We have no indication from them [the North Vietnamese] that they are prepared to do anything more than discuss the release of our prisoners if a withdrawal deadline is set. In their official statements they remain hard in their posture."

Ziegler also said that the Dec. 31 deadline proposed by Clifford was "so precipitate that it would not give the South Vietnamese the opportunity to defend themselves and determine their own future."

Lawyers lobby against war. Hundreds of lawyers gathered in Washington June 7 for several days of lobbying sponsored by the National Convocation of Lawyers to End the War. The group backed legislation to withdraw U.S. troops from Vietnam by the end of the year.

Amid a day of lobbying appointments with congressmen from their home districts, the lawyers rallied on the steps of the Capitol June 8 and heard speeches by Sens. Birch Bayh (D, Ind.) and Mike Gravel (D, Alaska) and Reps. Robert Drinan (D, Mass.), Paul N. McCloskey Jr. (R, Calif.) and Lucien N. Nedzi (D, Mich.) and former Rep. Allard Lowenstein (D, N.Y.).

At a Wall Street antiwar demonstration in New York City April 30, 2,000 lawyers gathered a day in advance of Law Day to protest that the conduct of the war in Indochina had led to a loss of faith in the law among the American people. Taking part in the protest were Reps. McCloskey, Herman Badillo (D, N.Y.) and Bella Abzug (D, N.Y.) and former Justice

Bernard Botein, president of the New York City Bar Association, and Francis T. P. Plimpton, Botein's predecessor.

ABA rejects antiwar resolution. The assembly of the American Bar Association rejected a resolution July 7 calling for a withdrawal of U.S. troops from Vietnam "as soon as physically and logistically possible." The resolution, submitted by a group of young New York lawyers, was defeated by a 173 to 105 vote at the closing business session of the ABA's 94th annual convention.

The antiwar group also asked for an ABA study of the "respective powers under the Constitution" of the President and Congress in going to war and an inquiry into the question of American war crimes in Indochina. The assembly, in a compromise, approved a resolution for a study of government war powers.

In defeating the end-the-war resolution, the assembly approved a statement that the ABA should not become "a forum for partisan political debate and action."

The objection had been raised July 6 in the ABA resolutions committee as Rep. Paul McCloskey (R, Calif.) and others argued in favor of the antiwar measures. The resolutions committee recommended disapproval of the pullout measure but said it "agrees with the sense and spirit of the resolution in that the association hopes, as all Americans hope, for a speedy conclusion to the war."

Sidney Peck, another coalition leader, said publication of the Pentagon Papers had "vindicated" the contention of the peace movement that "a conspiracy to deceive the people" existed. Dellinger said the disclosure of the papers generated a "new spirit on confidence" among the 800 delegates at the meeting.

Fall protest crowds meager. A "fall offensive" of antiwar demonstrations scheduled for October and November drew relatively meager crowds despite planning that had been started at the end of the spring protest campaign.

A three-day planning meeting had been held in Milwaukee by the Peoples Coalition for Peace and Justice. Coalition leaders June 27 then announced plans for a fall mobilization against the war and against Nixon Administration domestic policies.

David Dellinger said the activities would include "Mayday type" nonviolent civil disobedience in Washington designed to "close down the military aspects of the government."

After further planning, the Peoples Coalition Oct. 1 announced a Washington campaign for October and November that would include mass civil disobedience Oct. 26. Spokesman Rennie Davis said demonstrators would surround the White House and other buildings, serve an "eviction notice" on President Nixon and declare a "national mourning service" for war dead.

Leading up to the Oct. 26 protest, Davis said, a "grass roots" grand jury of welfare mothers, members of the religious community, ex-prisoners and others would convene Oct. 22 to investigate Administration policies. Rallies and protests on following days would be centered around the jury's findings.

The Washington protests would come after a national work strike and "moratorium on business as usual" called for Oct. 13 by the Peoples Coalition and National Peace Action Coalition (NPAC). National peace rallies were scheduled for Nov. 6 in 16 cities including Washington. Jerry Gordon, an NPAC coordinator, had announced endorsement of the Oct. 13 and Nov. 6 demonstrations by 150 labor union leaders, according to a Sept. 12 report. Gordon released a statement signed by the union leaders, who argued that "to check inflation, we must end the war in Vietnam—not freeze wages."

As part of the fall program, relatively poorly attended Vietnam Moratorium Day protest rallies were held in several cities and various college campuses Oct. 14.

About 300 antiwar demonstrators were arrested Oct. 26 in Washington after sitting down in the middle of Pennsylvania Avenue during the evening rush hour. The demonstrators had been on their way from a Washington Monument rally to the White House to deliver an "eviction notice" to President Nixon. Policemen filled out field arrest forms and photographed each of those arrested, who were charged with disorderly conduct and blocking the street. Bail was

set at $50. The procedures were designed to meet criticism of the mass arrests during the spring protest. Over 1,000 police had been deployed, and city officials had prepared a "demonstration contingency plan" for the first time. The plan provided for federal-city enforcement coordination and first aid, food, amenities, psychiatric help and a 100-lawyer Legal Defense group for arrested demonstrators.

At the Washington Monument rally, protest leaders Rev. James Groppi and David Dellinger spoke by long distance telephone to North Vietnamese and National Liberation Front (NLF) representatives to the Paris peace talks, who urged support for the NLF seven-point peace plan.

Thousands of antiwar protesters demonstrated in cities across the U.S. Nov. 6, in rallies coordinated by the NPAC, as the culmination of the movement's "fall offensive."

War challenge review refused. The Supreme Court declined Oct. 12 to review a 2nd Circuit U.S. Court of Appeals decision upholding the constitutionality of the Vietnam war. Only two justices, William O. Douglas and William J. Brennan Jr., voted to hear the case, viewed as the most important constitutional challenge to the war to reach the court.

In the war challenge case, the New York and American Civil Liberties Unions had argued on behalf of two Vietnam-bound soldiers that the conflict was unconstitutional because Congress had never formally declared war. In April, the U.S. appeals court had held that Congress, through the Tonkin Gulf resolution and appropriations, implicitly condoned the war. The Supreme Court refused to hear an appeal of that ruling brought on behalf of the two soldiers, Salvatore Orlando and Douglas Kaplan.

ACLU attorney Leon Friedman said Oct. 12 that Congress was now in a position to pass significant legislation on military spending since the courts had held appropriations bills the legal equivalent of declarations of war.

A Massachusetts antiwar suit against Defense Secretary Melvin Laird had been dismissed June 1 by Judge Charles E. Wyzanski Jr. Wyzanski ruled earlier cases had decided that Congress had the power to determine whether armed forces should be used and had "the means to make that power effective." A Massachusetts suit filed directly with the Supreme Court had already been rejected. The U.S. Court of Appeals in Boston ruled Oct. 21 that the war was not illegal, upholding the U.S. district court dismissal of the Massachusetts state suit; Judge Frank M. Coffin, in a decision joined by the other two judges, ruled that the President had acted constitutionally "in the situation of prolonged and undeclared hostilities" and "with steady Congressional support."

A suit against President Nixon and his key military advisers had been filed in U.S. district court in Washington April 7 by Reps. Parren J. Mitchell (D, Md.), Michael J. Harrington (D, Mass.) and Benjamin S. Rosenthal (D, N.Y.). Seeking a legal judgment that the U.S. fighting in Indochina was illegal, the suit contended the Administration should be required to stop "carrying on the war in violation of the U.S. Constitution" and Congress should be given 60 days to explicitly authorize continuation of the war if it so desired.

A group that included state officials, civil rights lawyers and antiwar activists held a conference at the Northwestern University Law School (Evanston, Ill.) in August and agreed to challenge in court what was called President Nixon's "unlimited usurpation of legislative power" in prosecuting the Vietnam war. At a press conference Aug. 20, they said they would seek state bills, such as passed in Massachusetts and Minnesota, challenging the constitutionality of the war. At the news conference, two assistant attorneys general, representing Minnesota and Massachusetts, agreed that the laws in their states had little direct legal impact but said they were politically significant in putting the states on record against the war. The Massachusetts bill had been passed in 1970, and the Minnesota measure cleared the state legislature April 13.

The National Emergency Civil Liberties Committee filed suit in U.S. District Court in Washington Aug. 24 challenging the Vietnam war on behalf of numerous taxpayers. The suit, naming President Nixon and Laird, sought a permanent injunction against further war expenditures and a judgment that the war violated the U.S. Constitution and the U.N. Charter.

The Berrigans & their backers. The Rev. Philip F. Berrigan and five others were indicted Jan. 12 on charges of conspiring to kidnap Henry A. Kissinger, assistant to the President for national security affairs, and for plotting to blow up the heating systems of federal buildings in Washington.

The alleged plot had been described by Federal Bureau of Investigation (FBI) Director J. Edgar Hoover in Senate testimony in November 1970. Hoover had charged that the plotters wanted to disrupt government operations and to hold Kissinger to force the Administration to end the war and release all "political prisoners."

The indictment was announced by Attorney General John N. Mitchell and delivered by a federal grand jury in Harrisburg, Pa., near the federal prison at Lewisburg where Berrigan was imprisoned during part of the alleged conspiracy.

Also named as co-conspirators but not indicted were the Rev. Daniel Berrigan and six others. The Berrigan brothers, both Roman Catholic priests, were currently in the federal prison in Danbury, Conn. on charges of destroying draft records.

The indictment stated that "dynamite charges were to be detonated in approximately five locations" in Washington underground tunnels on Washington's Birthday in February. It said that Philip Berrigan and the Rev. Joseph R. Wenderoth, 35, of Baltimore, also indicted, had investigated the city tunnel system as part of the plot. The indictment said the conspirators planned to kidnap Kissinger the next day.

Besides Berrigan and Wenderoth, the four others indicted were the Rev. Neil R. McLaughlin, 30, of Baltimore; Anthony Scoblick, 30, of Baltimore, a former priest; Eqbal Ahmad, 40, a fellow at the Adlai Stevenson Institute of Public Affairs in Chicago; and Sister Elizabeth McAlister, 31, of Marymount College (Tarrytown, N.Y.). Wenderoth and the other four were arrested Jan. 12 by FBI agents. They and Berrigan were charged with conspiring to maliciously destroy government property; possessing and transporting explosives across state lines; and plotting to kidnap a person across state lines.

Along with Daniel Berrigan, the following persons were named co-conspirators: Sisters Beverly Bell, 43, and Marjorie A. Schuman, 47, both of Washington; William Davidon, 43, a professor at Haverford (Pa.) College; Thomas Davidson, 25, of Washington; Paul Mayer, 39, of Edgewater, N.J., a former priest; and Sister Joques Egan, 52, reported to be a member of the Religious Order of the Sacred Heart of Mary in New York.

Through their attorney, William Kunstler, the Berrigans released a statement Jan. 12 saying that the objective of the indictments "is a simple but deadly one—to destroy the peace movement by creating caricatures of those who oppose the war in Southeast Asia." They said the government "has embarked on a tragic and outrageous course—to stigmatize millions of morally dedicated opponents of our military involvement in Indochina as violent and deranged people."

Two of the six defendants were released on bail Jan. 13. Sister Elizabeth McAlister of New York was released on $5,000 cash bond, and Eqbal Ahmad was released in Chicago on $60,000 bail. Three other defendants —the Revs. Joseph R. Wenderoth and Neil R. McLaughlin, and Anthony Scoblick, a former priest—were freed Jan. 18 on $25,000 bail in the custody of Lawrence Cardinal Shehan, Roman Catholic archbishop of Baltimore.

Sister Jogues Egan, an alleged co-conspirator who had been jailed for refusing to answer grand jury questions, was released Jan. 29 pending appeal of her contempt citation in a ruling by the U.S. Court of Appeals for the 3rd Circuit.

In a speech in Louisville, Ky. Jan. 24 before the governing board of the National Council of Churches, Rep. William R. Anderson (D, Tenn.) said the "issue of political repression is inherent" in the conspiracy prosecution, which he called "the climactic point of all dissent in America." Referring to the Berrigans' imprisonment for destroying draft records, Anderson declared: "Their

act was the frustrating finale of years of prodding an unreceptive society to the needs of justice and peace. They are peacemongers, waging a peace campaign as their nation wages war."

Philip Berrigan and his five co-defendants in the Harrisburg indictment —those indicted were already known as "the Harrisburg Six"—pleaded innocent to the charges at their arraignment Feb. 8 before U.S. District Court Judge R. Dixon Herman in Harrisburg, Pa. The government had charged that the plot was devised to bring pressure to end the war in Indochina.

Berrigan had been brought to Harrisburg for the arraignment from Danbury, Conn., where he was serving a 3½-year sentence in federal prison for destroying draft records at Catonsville, Md. in 1968. After the arraignment, the judge partially lifted travel restrictions on the other five defendants, who had been granted bail.

The defendants and alleged co-conspirators, with Philip Berrigan and his brother Daniel absent, met with newsmen after the arraignment. They issued a prepared statement, which read in part:

"We are 13 men and women who state with clear conscience that we are neither conspirators, nor bombers, nor kidnapers. In principle and in fact we have rejected all acts such as those of which we have been accused.... Our anguish for the victims of the brutal war has led all of us to nonviolent resistance, some of us to the destruction of draft records. But, unlike our accuser, the government of the United States, we have not advocated or engaged in violence against human beings."

The National Federation of Priests' Councils, at its annual meeting in Baltimore March 17, adopted a resolution praising the defendants and attacking Federal Bureau of Investigation Director J. Edgar Hoover for what were called "premature and unfortunate" allegations in the case. The organization, which represented a majority of American priests, lauded "the nonviolent witness of persons in the peace movement as a true form of prophetic ministry." In a separate resolution, the group denounced U.S. involvement in the Indochina war.

A federal grand jury in Harrisburg issued a new indictment April 30 against Philip Berrigan and seven others on charges of plotting to kidnap Kissinger and to blow up heating tunnels in government buildings. The indictment superseded the one returned Jan. 12 against six defendants.

The new indictment named two additional defendants and broadened the charges to include a series of draft board raids. Attached to the indictment were two letters, allegedly exchanged by Berrigan and Sister Elizabeth McAlister, a nun who was also indicted. The letter attributed to Sister Elizabeth described a plan "to kidnap—in our terminology make a citizen's arrest of—someone like Henry Kissinger." Berrigan's alleged reply contained criticisms of the idea but added, "Nonetheless, I like the plan."

The indictment charged that Sister Elizabeth transmitted the letter in August 1970 to Berrigan in the federal prison in Lewisburg, Pa. The letter said that after the kidnaping was accomplished, the group would "issue a set of demands," including a halt to U.S. use of B-52 bombers over North Vietnam, Cambodia and Laos and "release of political prisoners."

The letter said Kissinger would be held "for about a week" during which he would be tried and the trial filmed for the news media. The letter said, "There is no pretense of these demands being met and he would be released after this time with a word that we're nonviolent as opposed to you who would let a man be killed . . . so that you can go on killing."

The reply attributed to Berrigan objected that the plan was too "grandiose" and suggested ways to "weave elements of modesty into it." It also warned of the precedent of a kidnaping: "the first time opens the door to murder—the Tupamaros [guerrillas] are finding that out in Uruguay."

The two new defendants in the indictment were John Theodore Glick, 21, currently serving an 18-month sentence in federal prison (Ashland, Ky.) for a 1970 raid on federal offices in Rochester, N.Y., and Mary Cain Scoblick, 32, of Baltimore, a former nun. In addition to Berrigan and Sister Elizabeth, the other four original defendants, also charged in the new indictment, were: the Rev. Joseph Reese Wenderoth, 35, of Baltimore; the Rev. Neil Raymond McLaughlin, 30, of Baltimore; Anthony Scoblick, 30, a former priest and husband of Mary Cain Scoblick; and Eqbal Ahmad, 40.

Three persons, listed as unindicted co-conspirators in the original indictment, were not named in the new document. Those dropped were the Rev. Daniel Berrigan, Thomas Davidson and Paul Mayer. Still named as unindicted co-conspirators were Sisters Beverly Bell, Marjorie A. Schuman and Jogues Egan and William Davidon.

Attorneys representing the defendants filed a motion in federal district court in Scranton, Pa. May 4 charging the government with violating their clients' rights by releasing the letters allegedly writted by Berrigan and Sister Elizabeth. Asking for a contempt of court citation against William S. Lynch, the chief prosecuting attorney, and U.S. Attorney S. John Cottone, the defense lawyers said the letters were prejudicial and might not be admitted as evidence in a trial.

An affidavit filed by defense attorney Leonard Boudin said the letters had previously been offered to Time and Life magazines but that the magazines had refused to publish them because of a question of their authenticity. Boudin called the inclusion of the letters "extraordinary," but a Justice Department spokesman said, "it is not an uncommon practice for such information to be attached to an indictment."

FBI seizes draft raiders. Federal Bureau of Investigation (FBI) agents and local police foiled Selective Service office raids in federal buildings in Buffalo, N.Y. and Camden, N.J. with arrests of 25 persons late Aug. 21 and early Aug. 22. Both groups were associated with the Catholic Left. However, FBI officials, in announcing the arrests Aug. 22, made no direct connection between the five arrested in Buffalo and the Camden defendants.

Officials in Buffalo said the five young men and women had ransacked files in both the draft and U.S. Army Intelligence offices in the federal building. It was said that FBI agents had been on the scene "checking the security of the building."

A statement by the Buffalo defendants made public through a New York City antiwar group Aug. 23 indicated their aim was to confiscate military intelligence and draft records. The statement said it was "our duty before God and man" to act against "these records that help make the Vietnam war possible."

A U.S. magistrate in Buffalo ordered the five held for a grand jury Aug. 31. One of the defendants, Charles Lee Darst, 22, was the brother of David Darst, a Catonsville (Md.) Nine draft raid defendant who had died in an automobile accident while appealing his sentence. The other four were Jeremiah D. Horrigan, 21; James Martin, 25; Ann Masters, 26; and Maureen C. Considine, 21.

Forty FBI agents were stationed at the Camden Post Office Building for hours preceding the 4 a.m. arrests Aug. 22. Attorney General John N. Mitchell and FBI Director J. Edgar Hoover announced the arrests in Washington, and a Justice Department prosecutor often connected with radical cases, Guy M. Goodwin, had been sent to Camden in advance of the arrests. The government said an informer who had "provided reliable information to the FBI on at least 12 occasions" had infiltrated the group.

Twenty were arrested at the time of the raid, some still on the premises of the federal building, which included offices of the Selective Service board, Army Intelligence and the FBI. The defendants included John Peter Grady, 46, described by the bureau as the "ringleader and mastermind" of the plot. Grady had served as co-chairman of the Catonsville Nine Defense Committee.

Also arrested were two Catholic priests: the Rev. Peter D. Fordi, 34, a New York City Jesuit and member of the East Coast Conspiracy to Save Lives, which had been connected to former draft raids; and the Rev. Michael J. Doyle, 36, assistant pastor of St. Joseph's Pro-Cathedral in Camden. A fourth defendant was the Rev. Milo M. Billman, 39, a Lutheran minister.

Two others, Rosemary Reilly, 22, and Robert Glenn Good, 22, had been involved in a recent draft protest in the office of Selective Service Director Curtis Tarr. In addition, two defendants had been charged with contempt in the Harrisburg grand jury investigation of the alleged conspiracy to kidnap Kissinger: Paul Bernard Couming, 23, and John Swinglish, 27.

The others arrested Aug. 22 were Michael John Giocondo, 42; Joan Reilly, 23; Kathleen Mary Ridolfi, 22; Robert W. Williamson, 21; Terry Edward Buckalew, 20; Anne Cunham, 23, Lianne Moccia, 21; Francis Mel Madden, 32; Barry James Mussi, 22; Sarah Jane Tosi, 19; Margaret Mary Inness, 26; and Keith William Forsyth, 21. A 21th defendant, Dr. William A. Anderson, 36, an osteopath, surrendered Aug. 23. The government complaint alleged that the conspirators had met at his home.

The Rev. Joseph O'Rourke, 33, a New York City Jesuit involved in raising bond for the defendants, said Aug. 23 that "well over one million" files had been destroyed in antidraft activity in the country. A Selective Service spokesman said it would be "hard to discount" that figure but it was "immaterial" since the records could be replaced. The official said there had been "five or more" raids each month in 1971, down from 168 raids in 1970. He said such raids had cost the government $1.16 million in the fiscal year 1969–70.

Robert William Hardy, 32, reported to be the informer in the Camden raid, testified before a grand jury Aug. 26.

Twenty-eight persons were indicted by the grand jury in Camden Aug. 27. Bench warrants were arrested for the seven not already arrested, including two Catholic priests, the Rev. Edward J. Murphy, 34, and the Rev. Edward J. McGowan, 36. The others were Martha Shemeley; Anita Ricci, 22; Eugene F. Dixon, 37; Frank Pommersheim, 27; and a woman only identified as "Jamette" or Jane Doe.

All the defendants were charged with conspiracy to burglarize a government office, steal public records and interfere with the Selective Service System. Twenty-one of the group were also charged in counts involving actually breaking into the building.

GIs indicted in camp bombing. A federal grand jury in Madison, Wis. indicted three Army enlisted men Feb. 11 on charges of blowing up a telephone exchange, an electric substation and a water works at Camp McCoy, Wis. in July 1970. The three soldiers, currently stationed at Fort Carson, Colo., were arrested Feb. 11 by Federal Bureau of Investigation agents.

Named in the indictments, believed to be the first charging soldiers in recent bombings, were Spec. 4 Stephen G. Geden, 21; Spec. 4 Thomas M. Chase, 21; and Spec. 4 Dannie E. Kreps, 21. They had been on temporary duty at Camp McCoy in support of a National Guard summer training program. A fourth man, William B. Powers, was alleged to have been a co-conspirator.

Geden, a Vietnam veteran, and Chase were under general court-martial charges at Fort Carson for participating in an unauthorized demonstration while in uniform. They were said to have distributed antiwar pamphlets during a small demonstration near the gates of the fort.

West Point grad wins CO discharge. The American Civil Liberties Union said Feb. 13 that a West Point graduate had won an honorable discharge on the ground that he was a conscientious objector. The ACLU said the favorable action on the discharge application of Cornelius McNeil Cooper Jr. marked the first time a graduate of the academy had been released as a CO.

In his application filed in October 1970, Cooper said he believed "service in the armed forces is an immoral action." He said he opposed violence and killing and that as a black man, "I am caused to be more than usually sensitive to the fact of violence in life and the effect of violence on men's lives."

Cooper, whose father was a lieutenant in World War II and whose uncle was a lieutenant colonel and a chaplain, said he had first looked favorably on military service but had become a conscientious objector while at West Point.

(1st Lt. Louis P. Font, 24, a West Point graduate publicly opposed to the war in Vietnam, said March 9 he had submitted his resignation at the Army's request. Font said the commander at Ft. Meade, Md. had asked for his resignation declaring that he showed "unwillingness to expend any effort in the performance of duties." Font said his antiwar activities and pending Army charges against him were not mentioned.

Antiwar troupe formed. A group of entertainers announced plans Feb. 16 to tour military bases across the country with an antiwar stage show. At a news conference in New York, actress Jane Fonda said, "It's been very disconcerting for many of us in Hollywood to see that Bob Hope, Martha Raye and other companies of their political ilk have cornered the market and are the only entertainers allowed to speak to soldiers in this country and Vietnam."

She said people with different points of view "have decided the time has come to speak to the forgotten soldiers. They are the majority . . . they want peace and freedom, but they are isolated in the military and they need our support." The group—which also included director Mike Nichols, actor Elliott Gould, comedian Dick Gregory and writer and cartoonist Jules Feiffer—had contingency plans to play at a coffeehouse in Fayetteville, N.C. if authorities at nearby Fort Bragg refused them permission to perform.

About 500 GIs attended the show's debut March 14 at the Haymarket Square Coffee House in Fayetteville, near Ft. Bragg, N.C. The troupe had been denied permission to perform at Ft. Bragg.

The performers had won a federal court injunction March 13 making available a public auditorium seating 4,000, but the group could not raise money for insurance and other expenses.

The show also featured actors Peter Boyle and Donald Sutherland, folk singer Barbara Dane and the Swamp Dogg, a rock band. The show was written by Jules Feiffer.

At a news conference March 15, Boyle and Miss Fonda said the group would file suit to force the armed services to permit the show to be performed at U.S. military bases and to support the show financially.

Among other developments:

■ A federal judge in New York City ordered the Army Feb. 9 to return to duty at Fort Wadsworth a member of an Army band who had been transferred to Fort Bliss, Tex. after he had engaged in antiwar activity. During hearings on the case, Maj. Gen. Richard Ciccollela admitted that he had ordered the transfer of Spec. 4 David B. Cortright because of his antiwar actions, which included an advertisement in the New York Times signed by 38 members of the band. Judge Jack B. Weinstein held that the transfer was a violation of the soldier's constitutional right of freedom of speech, which federal courts had the right to protect.

■ The U.S. Navy Court of Military Review, in an action disclosed Feb. 11, reversed the court-martial conviction of Seaman Roger L. Priest, an editor of an antiwar newsletter charged with disloyalty and promoting disaffection among servicemen. The court overturned the conviction on a technicality, holding that the trial judge had erred by ruling that "disloyalty to an authority of the United States is equivalent to disloyalty to the United States."

Viet Cong urge GIs to desert. A five-point "Order of the Day" issued to Viet Cong troops April 26 appealed to U.S. soldiers in Vietnam to stop fighting or desert. The document was made public in Paris by Duong Donh Thao, a spokesman for the Viet Cong delegation to the Vietnam peace talks.

Thao also disclosed that a "limited" number of "American soldiers were fighting in the ranks of the liberation army" in Vietnam. He said a greater number of U.S. soldiers had deserted and were hiding in South Vietnam "protected by the South Vietnamese population."

The Communist document urged Viet Cong forces: "not to attack those anti-U.S. servicemen . . . who demand repatriation, oppose orders of the U.S. commanders and abstain from hostile action" against the Viet Cong; "to give proper treatment to those U.S. servicemen . . . who carry antiwar literature"; "to stand ready to extend aid and protection to those antiwar U.S. servicemen who have to run away for their opposition to orders of operations. . . ."; "to welcome and give good treatment to those U.S. servicemen who cross over to the South Vietnamese people" and the Viet Cong; and "to

welcome and grant appropriate rewards to those U.S. servicemen . . . who support" the Viet Cong.

The U.S. defense Department in Washington said "there have been repeated rumors" of American deserters fighting with the Viet Cong, "but there is no proof."

Ft. Bragg officers protest war. A spokesman at Fort Bragg, N.C. said May 24 that no action would be taken against 29 officers from the post and the nearby Pope Air Force Base who signed an Armed Forces Day antiwar advertisment in the Fayetteville (N.C.) Observer. The ad and attendance at a Fayetteville antiwar rally had been organized by the Concerned Officers Movement (COM).

It had been reported the day before that the Ft. Bragg officers had been interviewed about their views, and individual unit commanders had suggested to seven of the signers that they might resign from the Army. In a statement May 23, a spokesman for the antiwar officers said, "The Concerned Officers Movement . . . affirms the right of all servicemen to express their views on the war and other issues. Ft. Bragg's COM further asks the armed forces to allow all other servicemen and servicewomen who oppose the war the same right to resign under honorable conditions."

U.S. officer asks Swedish asylum. 1st Lt. John R. Vequist, 24, a West Point graduate who was scheduled to go to Vietnam in November, asked for political asylum in Sweden to protest the Indochina war, according to Swedish police sources June 9. A U.S. Army spokesman in Heidelberg, Germany confirmed that Vequist had been missing from his unit in West Germany since May 20.

Vequist was the first U.S. military officer to ask asylum in Sweden. An estimated 500 American war resisters and deserters were in the country. Pentagon officials also believed Vequist was the first West Point graduate to go absent without leave or desert since the beginning of U.S. involvement in Vietnam.

Swedish officials announced July 8 that Vequist, his wife and daughter had been given a residence permit to stay in the country. The Army had listed Vequist as a deserter.

Antiwar officer court-martialed. A U.S. Air Force court-martial at a base near London found Capt. Thomas S. Culver, 32, guilty July 13 of organizing and taking part in an antiwar demonstration in violation of military regulations. Culver was sentenced to a reprimand and a $1,000 fine July 14. The charges carried a maximum penalty of four years imprisonment, a dishonorable discharge and forfeiture of pay.

The charges involved a protest May 31 by some 300 off-duty U.S. servicemen in civilian clothes. After gathering at the Speakers' Corner in London's Hyde Park, the men walked to the U.S. embassy to present petitions bearing 1,000 signatures of Air Force and Navy personnel protesting the "American war in Indochina."

Culver was charged with violating military regulations by participating in a demonstration in a foreign country and soliciting other servicemen to demonstrate. The defense at the court-martial argued that the protest was not a demonstration and that it was legal under military regulations to petition or present grievances to members of Congress without fear of reprisal.

Following the sentencing, Culver, a member of the Staff Judge Advocate's Office at Lakenheath Air Force Base, said he was "pleased" and "surprised." He said "a reprimand is just about the lightest thing that they can do. It emphasized that the court didn't think this was a serious matter or that my conduct was reprehensible." Culver said, however, the case would be appealed to test the constitutionality of regulations forbidding demonstrations by servicemen overseas. "This is a test case and we're still going to take this through the courts," he said.

About 100 U.S. servicemen and civilians carried petitions against the regulations on demonstrations abroad to the U.S. embassy in London Aug. 1. Many of the servicemen wore disguises to make identification difficult.

Carrier sails despite protests. The carrier USS Constellation and its 80-plane

bomber wing sailed from San Diego for Vietnam Oct. 1 after a six-month "Connie, Stay Home for Peace" campaign launched by a coalition of antiwar groups. The protest culminated in a five-day straw ballot Sept. 17–21 in which more than 54,000 San Diego citizens and military personnel voted almost 5–1 against the carrier's return to Southeast Asia.

The carrier sailed without nine young sailors who had taken refuge in a Roman Catholic church. In a predawn raid Oct. 2, the sailors were arrested and flown to the Constellation, which was 250 miles at sea, and placed in the ship's brig. Attorneys for Nonviolent Action, a group headed by draft resister David Harris that led the campaign, said they would seek a court order for the release of the sailors.

In other court action, federal Judge Howard B. Turrentine rejected a petition Oct. 1 brought on behalf of four Constellation crew members for an injunction to stop the Constellation's return. The plaintiffs had argued that the carrier was on "an illegal mission, including the murder of civilians" and should be stopped pending a vote by the crew on whether they wished to return to Vietnam.

Other groups involved in the protest were the People's Union of Palo Alto, the local unit of the Concerned Officers Movement and the Radical Action Tribes, a San Diego student group. Singer Joan Baez, Harris's wife, who was chief fundraiser for the campaign. Others active in the protest were Donald Sutherland and Jane Fonda, both part of an antiwar troupe that was barred from performing aboard the carrier in May.

Eight sailors who had protested the war by refusing to sail on the Constellation were given "general discharges under honorable conditions" by the Navy Dec. 6. A ninth protester decided to remain on the ship.

Berkeley offers sanctuary. The Berkeley, Calif. city council voted Nov. 10 to offer sanctuary to military deserters, and ordered city police not to cooperate in arresting AWOL servicemen. The 6–1 vote, in which two conservatives joined four radicals elected in April, was in response to a campaign to prevent the aircraft carrier U.S.S. Coral Sea from sailing from Alameda Naval Station to Vietnam.

Berkeley City Attorney Robert T. Anderson opposed providing a sanctuary facility because "I don't think city funds can be used for illegal services," while a police spokesman said "the oath taken by peace officers" would prevail over the resolution if a conflict occurred.

The Coral Sea sailed as scheduled Nov. 12. Apparently, no sailors took advantage of the sanctuary offer, despite claims by antiwar leaders Oct. 12 that over 1,000 of 4,500 crewmen had signed a petition asking Congress to keep the ship from sailing. Navy spokesmen called the claims exaggerated.

Catholic bishops urge Viet war end. The U.S. National Conference of Catholic Bishops Nov. 19 approved their strongest resolution to date against the war in Indochina. The resolution, adopted by a vote of 158–36 at the end of a five-day meeting in Washington, declared the war "immoral" and called for an end to the conflict "with no further delay."

The key sentence of the resolution stated: "At this point in history it seems clear to us that whatever good we hope to achieve through continued involvement in this war is now outweighed by the destruction of human life and of moral values which it inflicts." The bishops concluded: "It is our firm conviction, therefore, that the speedy ending of this war is a moral imperative of the highest priority."

The meaning of the statement in terms of moral discipline for the individual Catholic was unclear. The Most Rev. Thomas J. Gumbleton, auxiliary bishop of Detroit, said at a news conference that the statement meant that anyone who agreed with the statement of the bishops "may not participate in this war." However, the Most Rev. Philip M. Hannan, archbishop of New Orleans, disagreed with Bishop Gumbleton's statement.

The final resolution, a revision of a stronger statement proposed Nov. 18 by a committee headed by Archbishop Humberto Medeiros of Boston, deleted a section that called for an immediate cease-fire by all U.S. forces, except in self-defense, and for unilateral withdrawal at the earliest possible date.

Atrocities & War Crimes

Calley guilty of Mylai massacre. An Army court-martial jury in Ft. Benning, Ga. March 29 found 1st Lt. William L. Calley Jr. guilty of the premeditated murder of at least 22 South Vietnamese civilians at Mylai 4 March 16, 1968. The military jury of six officers March 31 sentenced Calley to life imprisonment at hard labor and ordered his dismissal from the Army and the forfeiture of his pay and allowance. However, he was to retain his officers' status and continue to draw his pay until the case was automatically reviewed by another command.

Calley's trial had started Nov. 12, 1970, was adjourned Dec. 17, 1970, resumed Jan. 11, recessed Jan. 18 to permit him to undergo psychiatric tests ordered by the court and started again Feb. 16 following completion of an Army sanity board hearing at Walter Reed Hospital in Washington Feb. 6. The board found Calley "normal in every respect."

The Calley jury rendered its verdict after 13 days of deliberation. It convicted him of four specifications of premeditated murder of 22 civilians rather than 102 as charged, because witnesses during the trial had disputed the number of dead at Mylai; some said they had counted fewer than 100 bodies. The first specification charged that Calley killed at least 30 noncombatants at the south end of Mylai. This was reduced by the jury to the murder of "an unknown number, no less than one." The second specification dealt with the slayings of 70 civilians in a ditch outside Mylai. This was reduced to murder of "an unknown number, no less than 20." In the two remaining counts, Calley was found guilty of the premeditated murder of one civilian and of assault with intent to commit the murder of a child. In the case of the child, the original charge was murder, but was not conclusively proven at the trial.

Calley pleaded for understanding in addressing the court March 30. He denied having "wantonly killed a human being in my entire life. If I have committed a crime, the only crime I've committed is in my judgment values." Calley said the Army had never described the enemy "as anything other than communism. They never let me believe it was just a philosophy in a man's mind."

Col. Reid W. Kennedy, the presiding military judge, had recessed the court martial Jan. 18 and ordered the psychiatric tests. He did so after a defense psychiatrist had testified that Calley had acted "like a robot" (when his platoon killed women and children in Mylai) because of a compulsion to obey orders of his "father image," Medina.

Among major developments before the trial was recessed:

Jan. 11-12—Former Pfc. Paul D. Meadlo, who had refused earlier in the trial to take the witness stand, testified that he and Calley had fired 300–400 shots at 100 unarmed civilians at Mylai 4. Meadlo had agreed to testify after the Justice Department granted him immunity Jan. 4, warning him that refusal to take the stand could lead to his arrest. Meadlo, a former soldier in Calley's platoon, said he could not tell how many of those who were shot had been mortally wounded. He said he had shot some babies in their mothers' arms because he was afraid the infants might have been wired with grenades as booby traps.

With Meadlo's testimony concluded, the prosecution rested its case.

Jan. 13—Calley's defense counsel succeeded in entering on the record a report filed by the American commander of the Mylai task force to his brigade commander describing the action at the hamlet as "well planned, well executed and successful." The combat-action report was made by Lt. Col. Frank A. Barker Jr., who was killed in a helicopter crash three months after the Mylai incident. It was dated 12 days after the platoon led by Calley moved into Mylai hamlet 4.

Jan. 14—S. Sgt. Dennis R. Vasquez testified that the officers who participated in the assault against Mylai had been urged on the eve of the alleged massacre to "rush in aggressively, close with the enemy and wipe them out for good." Vasquez, who was an artillery air observer flying in Barker's heliocopter that day, said the exhortation was made by Brigade Commander Col. Oren K. Henderson at the meeting which was attended by Medina.

Calley's lawyers had been attempting to show that the defendant was told by Capt. Medina to kill everything at Mylai. Other defense witnesses—including Meadlo—had said the platoon had been briefed by Medina to kill everything— "women, children, livestock."

Jan. 15—Another defense witness, Robert Van Leer, testified that the American assault force was frightened by the toll already taken by enemy mines and booby traps and embittered over grisly tales of the Viet Cong's mistreatment of U.S. prisoners. Leer had served in the same infantry company with Calley. Three weeks before the Mylai incident, he had stepped on a mine and his leg was amputated.

Leer was called to bolster the defense's contention that the shooting at Mylai was inevitable and a justifiable act of war.

During the trial, the defense had presented 20 witnesses to support Calley's contention that Capt. Ernest L. Medina, commander of the company involved in the Mylai operation, had ordered at a briefing the previous day that every living being be killed when the troops moved into the village. Medina denied issuing the order in testimony March 10.

At the resumption of the court-martial Feb. 16, Calley's defense lawyers said their client acknowledged his participation in the slayings at Mylai. They argued, however, that "he did not feel as if he was killing humans, but rather that they were the enemy with whom one could not speak or reason." Taking the witness stand Feb. 22, Calley told the court that the Army had taught him to treat all Vietnamese, soldiers or civilians, as potential enemies. In further testimony Feb. 23, Calley conceded he had shot a group of civilian prisoners herded into a ditch and that he had ordered a soldier to kill another group of civilians. But he insisted the action was taken because "that was the order of the day" issued by Medina. Calley contended he had no regrets because "they were all enemy. They were all to be destroyed."

The defense rested its case Feb. 24 after Calley reiterated that day under cross-examination that he had never questioned Medina's alleged orders. He called Medina a "fine officer" and said he was "very proud to have served under him." Calley told of another directive issued by Medina, but later rescinded, to spare some of the civilians so they could be forced to walk across an enemy minefield ahead of the American troops.

Refuting Calley's testimony, Medina told the court March 10 that he had told his company on the eve of the move into Mylai: "No, you do not kill women and children. You use common sense. If they have a weapon and they are trying to engage you, then you can shoot back but you must use common sense." Under cross-examination by defense attorney George W. Latimer, Medina corroborated Calley's account of the minefield incident, but he insisted that he had never suggested the killing of "innocent civilians." Medina also confessed to attempting to cover up the Mylai incident, saying he felt it was "a disgrace upon the Army uniform" and that he "realized the repercussions it would have against" the U.S.

The alleged order to kill all civilians at Mylai had been previously denied March 5 by Capt. Eugene Kotouc, the intelligence officer of the unit involved in the operation. Kotouc said that on the contrary, Lt. Col. Frank A. Barker Jr., commander of the Mylai task force, had issued no order to kill women and children and no order not to take prisoners. He did direct the troops, however, to destroy "anything of use to the enemy," Kotouc said. He also said he had not heard Medina order that every human be killed in the village.

Conflicting testimony on Calley's mental capabilities at the time of the alleged massacre was provided by psychiatrists for the defense and prosecution. Dr. David G. Crane testified Feb. 18 that Calley lacked the mental ability to carry out premeditated slayings and that he did not "consciously understand" what was happening at the time of the shootings.

Testifying for the prosecution, Army psychiatrists Maj. Henry E. Edwards and Lt. Col. Franklin D. Jones said Feb. 25 that Calley was sane at Mylai and was no more under mental strain than other soldiers taking part in the operation. The two men expressed the opinion that Calley was "free from any mental disease, defect or derangement." They said they found "no evidence of any . . . confusion or disturbance in his behavior at all."

In final arguments before the case went to the jury March 15, government prosecutor Capt. Aubrey M. Daniel 3rd charged that Calley, by his "slaughter of innocent civilians," "prostituted all the humanitarian principles for which this country stands. The accused failed in his duty to his troops, to his country, to mankind."

Attorney Latimer, arguing for acquittal of his client, asserted that the Army had picked Calley as a scapegoat, that he was the "pigeon—the lowest officer on the totem pole." Calley and Medina were thrown into "a race for death certificates" while everyone else accused in the Mylai incident stood a good chance of escaping with honorable discharges, Latimer said.

Reaction to trial—Public figures and private citizens around the U.S., many of them armed forces veterans, reacted quickly to the Calley verdict and sentence.

The White House said March 31 that it had received about 5,000 telegrams in less than 24 hours after the military jury at Ft. Benning, Ga. convicted Calley. White House Press Secretary Ronald L. Ziegler said the ratio was about "100-to-1 in favor of clemency." He added that the White House had received about 1,500 telephone calls, almost all "against the verdict."

Many congressmen said they were perturbed by the conviction. Sen. Abraham A. Ribicoff (D, Conn.), one of those who appealed to Nixon for clemency, said Calley should not be made "to bear sole responsibility for all wrongdoing" connected with the incident at Mylai. Sen. Frank E. Moss (D, Utah) said he planned to introduce a resolution asking the President to reduce the life sentence. Sen. Herman E. Talmadge (D, Ga.) said March 30 that "as a former combat veteran myself, I am saddened to think that one could fight for his flag and then be court-martialed and convicted for apparently carrying out his orders."

Similar sentiments were expressed by members of the House. Rep. John R. Rarick (D, La.) said veterans had told him "that if they were in Vietnam now, they would lay down their arms and come home." Rep. Don Fuqua (D, Fla.) introduced a resolution March 31 calling for an invitation to Calley to address a joint session of Congress. "We are his accusers," Fuqua said. "Let us invite this American serviceman here to tell his story."

One of the most outspoken denunciations of the verdict came from an official of one of the nation's veterans' associations. Herbert B. Rainwater, commander in chief of the Veterans of Foreign Wars, said, "What kind of justice can be expected when the military appoints the judge, jury and the prosecutor."

The Ft. Benning, Ga. post of the American Legion announced plans March 30 to raise $100,000 for Calley's expected appeal and a drive for 10 million signatures on a petition protesting his conviction.

Gov. George C. Wallace of Alabama, addressing a joint session of the state's legislature March 31 in Montgomery, said he was asking the director of Alabama's Selective Service System to investigate whether Alabama could lawfully suspend the draft in the state.

(Upon learning of Wallace's statement, a Pentagon official said governors had "absolutely no authority to give any instructions to local draft boards.")

Some local draft boards, however, took actions on their own. The Quitman, Ga. draft board wired the White House that it would not induct any more young men. Other local boards in Athens, Ga., Blairsville, Ga. and Elizabethtown, Tenn. resigned.

Campaigns calling for Calley's release were also started by local radio stations. In Roswell, N.M., a local station said it was suspending all public service broadcasts for the Army. The same intentions were announced by stations in Wilmington, N.C. and Reidsville, N.C.

Capt. Ernest L. Medina, Calley's immediate superior at the time of the Mylai incident, said in Boston that the verdict was "harsh and severe." Medina, who himself faced court-martial on two counts of murder in connection with his role at Mylai, said he thought all Americans "must share in Calley's guilt."

Among U.S. GIs in South Vietnam, the outcome of the trial evoked indignation. Many servicemen said Calley was convicted as a "scapegoat" for higher-ranking Army officers. Some said Calley was "just another victim of a war nobody wanted to fight."

(Their view differed from the opinion of Army Chief of Staff Gen. William Westmoreland, who said March 18 that the Army's inquiry into the Mylai incident had raised military morale.)

There was little immediate comment on the trial's outcome from foreign dignitaries. One official who commented, President Nguyen Van Thieu of South Vietnam, said he had been confident that justice would punish those who were responsible for killing civilians at Mylai.

Another comment from a foreign source came from Pravda, the Soviet Communist party newspaper. Pravda charged March 31 that Calley was a "scapegoat" and said his trial had been part of "a whole series of machinations by the Pentagon to save from justice most of those involved in the crime."

A number of governors expressed indignation over the verdict. Indiana Gov. Edgar D. Whitcomb, a decorated World War II veteran, ordered all state flags flown at half-mast to protest the verdict. Gov. Jimmy Carter of Georgia proclaimed April 5 an "American Fighting Man's Day" and urged Georgia motorists to drive all week with their auto headlights on. Gov. Calvin L. Rampton of Utah, an officer in the National Guard, said, "I regard the verdict as inappropriate and the sentence as excessive."

Alabama Gov. George C. Wallace, en route with his wife and eight state legislators to a rally in Columbus, Ga. to protest the verdict, stopped off at Ft. Benning for a 12-minute visit with Calley. Following their conversation, Wallace said he did not criticize the Army for the court-martial but believed that Nixon should grant Calley a full pardon.

Later in the day, he was joined at the rally of more than 3,500 persons by Gov. John Bell Williams of Mississippi and Lt. Gov. Lester G. Maddox of Georgia.

State legislatures began drafting resolutions calling for Calley's release. Arkansas' legislature approved a resolution asking President Nixon to grant Calley executive clemency. The lower house of the Kansas legislature backed a resolution urging that Calley be freed. A similar resolution was passed in the Texas Senate. Others were adopted in New Jersey and South Carolina.

The greatest outpouring of pro-Calley sentiment, however, continued to come from private citizens. A telephone survey conducted by the Gallup Poll found that 79% of those contacted disapproved of the verdict. Nearly 83% of those polled said they supported the President's decision to release Calley from the Ft. Benning stockade while his case was being reviewed.

The White House said that the avalanche of letters, telegrams and phone calls—running at a rate of 100-to-1 in favor of Calley—was continuing to pour in from all across the country. Protest marches were held and dozens more were being organized by veterans' groups and private citizens. Some of the bigger demonstrations took place in Gainesville and Jacksonville, Fla., Los Angeles, Kansas City, Mo. and Dallas.

In Lenoir City, Tenn., radio station WLIL said it had received 1,137 telephone calls in a 2½-hour period after Calley's conviction was announced. All but one, a station spokesman said, criticized the court-martial verdict. Radio station WKIP in Poughkeepsie, N.Y. took a one-hour poll and reported that only 36 of 2,000 calls agreed with the verdict.

A Nashville, Tenn. recording company reported it had sold 202,000 copies of a record, "The Battle Hymn of Lieutenant Calley."

One man hijacked an airliner to Cuba and told a passenger he was doing it to protest the Calley conviction.

Members of Congress, ignoring party lines, split sharply over the case and President Nixon's decision to render a final verdict. Senate Minority Leader Hugh Scott (R, Pa.) praised Nixon's intervention, but Sen. Jacob K. Javits (R, N.Y.) said Americans were wrongly being encouraged to honor Calley. Sen. Adlai E. Stevenson III (D, Ill.) said that if Calley was guilty as the court-martial ruled, he "must pay the penalty." But Rep. Ed Edmondson (D, Okla.) introduced a resolution on the House floor calling on Congress to urge a full pardon for Calley.

(According to a Harris Poll conducted for the American Broadcasting Co., which announced the results April 16, 77% of those interviewed felt Calley was singled out for court-martial and punishment although the Mylai incident involved others, including his superior officers; 81% believed that other incidents such as Mylai had occurred; 55% felt Nixon should have given Calley executive clemency; only 24% agreed with the verdict of guilty against Calley; 77% considered that the men at Mylai were "just following orders from higher-ups"; 88% thought it unfair for the higher-ups not to be tried also; 74% said the President should stop such trials or bring the higher-ups to trial; and 58% considered it morally wrong for the U.S. to be fighting in Vietnam, up from 47% in February.)

Army issues fact sheet—To stem the tide of public opinion running against the Calley verdict, the Army April 2 issued a comprehensive "fact sheet" saying that it had "a moral and legal obligation" to try him. The four-page report was mailed to every U.S. Army unit in the world.

According to the report, which Pentagon officials described as a "white paper," the U.S. was obliged under the Geneva convention on rules of war to try Calley and the others accused of covering up what took place at Mylai. In what was seen as an attempt by the Army to counter the charge that Calley was a "scapegoat," the Army said that in all its proceedings against those involved in the incident "we went as far as we could and as far as the evidence supported." The report noted that, of the 13 original defendants in the Mylai case, two had been found innocent in courts-martial, charges had been dismissed against eight, and that Calley alone had been convicted so far. "In the case of Lieutenant Calley," the report said, "we had an overwhelming body of evidence."

Nixon to review Calley case—President Nixon announced through his chief domestic adviser April 3 that he would review the Calley case "before any final sentence is carried out."

Two days earlier, in an unprecedented move, Nixon had ordered the chairman of the Joint Chiefs of Staff to instruct Army authorities to release Calley from the stockade at Ft. Benning, Ga. and return him to his base apartment while his murder conviction was under review.

Nixon's decision to review the Calley case was announced to newsmen at the Western White House in San Clemente, Calif. by John Ehrlichman, the President's chief domestic adviser.

Ehrlichman said Nixon's decision to make the final determination on Calley's guilt or innocence if he was still in office at that time stemmed from his judgment that the trial, "having captured the attention of the American people to the degree that it has," needed "more than the technical review" provided by ordinary military appeal procedures.

Ehrlichman said the President had the right to review and decide Calley's case as commander in chief of the armed forces. He pointed out that as commander in chief Nixon had the power to convene courts-martial and was therefore, "in a technical sense," the senior convening officer of the armed forces.

Prosecutor criticizes Nixon—Capt. Aubrey M. Daniel 3rd, Army prosecutor in the trial, reacted bitterly to Nixon's intervention, which, he said, seriously "weakened" respect for the U.S. judicial process. Daniel uttered his criticism in a letter sent to the White House April 3 and made public April 6.

"The greatest tragedy of all," he said, "will be if political expediency dictates the compromise of such a fundamental moral principle as the inherent unlawfulness of the murder of innocent persons."

Instead of releasing Calley from the stockade, Daniel told Nixon, he should have commended the six officers who found him guilty. Daniel said the President's order made "the action and the courage" of the six jurors "who served their country so well meaningless."

Daniel indicated his belief that the order to release Calley had been influenced by the public outcry over his conviction and sentence.

"Your decision," he told Nixon, "can only have been prompted by the response of a vocal segment of our population, who—while no doubt acting in good faith—cannot be aware of the evidence which has resulted in Lieutenant Calley's conviction."

Nixon defends his role—In answer to questions from a panel of editors at the annual banquet of the American Society of Newspaper Editors in Washington April 16, Nixon defended his intervention in the Calley case. Referring to the widespread national concern over the matter, Nixon said he had acted because "the national interest required it." "When people all over the nation, their congressmen and their senators, are stirred up about a particular issue," he said, a president had "a responsibility to do what he can within the law to try to quiet those fears, to try to bring some perspective into the whole matter." He pointed out that the "fears" about the case did "subside" after the people knew that Calley would "get a fair review and a final review from the President."

He viewed his intervention as "consistent with the judicial process" inasmuch as the case went beyond "simply the innocence or guilt of this one man." There was the problem of war crimes in general and the public debate over their proper handling, he said, and he felt that a Presidential statement "at the highest level should be made once this case is completed."

At his press conference April 29, Nixon said: He would not comment on the merits of the case now "when it's up for appeal" but would "at an appropriate time in my capacity as the final reviewing officer." He considered his intervention in the case proper. The right of bail was given to people in civil criminal cases and there was "great concern expressed throughout the country as to whether or not this was a case involving as it did so many complex factors in which Captain [Lieutenant] Calley was going to get a fair trial." Nixon's intervention "reassured the country and that's one of the reasons that the country has cooled down on this case."

At Nixon's May 1 press conference, a reporter asked whether there was the possibility "that your repeated expression of sympathy for Lt. Calley and your decision to review the case will inevitably have the consequence of influencing" the military judges who would review the case. Nixon replied he was "not trying to influence the reviewing authorities" and he himself would review the case "fairly."

Calley's sentence reduced—Calley's life imprisonment sentence was reduced to 20 years Aug. 20. The reduced sentence was ordered by Lt. Gen. Albert O. Conner, commanding general of the 3rd Army. A 3rd Army spokesman said that the sentence was deemed "appropriate for the offenses for which he [Calley] was convicted."

Medina cleared on Mylai role. A jury of five officers at Ft. McPherson, Ga. acquitted Capt. Ernest L. Medina Sept. 22 of all charges in connection with the killing of South Vietnamese civilians at Mylai.

The jury cleared Medina after deliberating only 60 minutes. The court-martial had begun Aug. 16.

Medina was found not guilty of premeditated murder in the killing of a Vietnamese woman, of involuntary manslaughter in the killing of "not less than 100" Vietnamese civilians and of two counts of assault upon a prisoner by shooting at him twice with a rifle.

Medina, 35, had originally been charged with the premeditated murder of at least 100 civilians during a search-and-destroy operation by his men through Mylai March 16, 1968. He was also charged with murder in the deaths of a woman and a small boy and with two counts of assault on a prisoner.

Col. Kenneth A. Howard, the presiding judge, Sept. 17 threw out the charge that Medina murdered a small boy at Mylai. At the same time, Howard reduced the murder charge that Medina was responsible for the deaths of 100 civilians to involuntary manslaughter. Howard said he had reduced the charge because the government had failed to prove that Medina had any "intent" to kill civilians.

During the trial's closing days, Medina testified that he never saw the ditch at Mylai where Vietnamese civilians were rounded up and slain by U.S. soldiers. Medina said he was unaware of the enormity of the killing until more than a year after the assault on Mylai by his troops.

Several times during his testimony, Medina expressed a low opinion of Lt. William B. Calley. Medina described Calley as an inept officer who had trouble understanding orders and was disliked by his men. In the defense summation, F. Lee Bailey, Medina's chief counsel, described the defendant as "no filthy felon" but "a disciplined commander who honored and loved the uniform he wore and the company it represented."

The government described Medina in its closing argument as an officer who had abrogated his responsibility and who "like Pontius Pilate cannot wash the blood from his hands."

Henderson acquitted of Mylai charges. The last of the Mylai trials came to an end Dec. 17 as a military jury at Ft. Meade, Md. acquitted Col. Oran K. Henderson of charges that he had covered up the March 1968 massacre of South Vietnamese civilians at Mylai by soldiers in his brigade.

Specifically, he was charged with dereliction of duty, failure to investigate acts "thought to be war crimes" and with false swearing. The maximum penalty was six years in prison, forfeiture of pay and dismissal from the Army.

A jury of two generals and six colonels had deliberated for four hours over a two-day period before acquitting Henderson of all three charges against him. All the charges centered on whether Henderson covered up the Mylai slayings by an inadequate investigation.

Henderson, 50, was the commander of the Americal Division's 11th infantry brigade at the time one of its platoons swept through Mylai.

Henderson was the highest-ranking officer to face court-martial on charges connected with the Mylai incident. Only 1st Lt. William L. Calley Jr., a platoon leader at Mylai, was found guilty in the case.

Of the three officers and two enlisted men tried in the case, only Calley was convicted. Charges against 12 officers and seven enlisted men had been dropped.

Moments after the jury returned to the courtroom, Maj. Gen. Charles M.

Mount, the jury president, told Henderson and the court that it had cleared him "upon secret written ballot" of all "specifications and charges."

Specifically, the jury cleared Henderson of "willful dereliction of duty" in not carrying out a proper investigation of atrocity reports at Mylai, of having failed to report alleged war crimes to his division commander and of lying to a Pentagon investigating board about Mylai.

After the jury announced its verdict, Col. Peter S. Wondolowski, the military judge, cited the jury for its "conscientious work," praised the government prosecutor for his "hard-hitting case" and congratulated the defense on Henderson's acquittal.

The verdict was handed down on the 62nd court day of the case, equaling the length of Calley's trial as the longest court-martial in U.S. military history. During the trial, which opened Aug. 23, 106 witnesses took the stand. In addition, the jurors studied more than 150 documents including transcripts of Henderson's earlier testimony to a Pentagon inquiry board investigating Mylai.

Previous Mylai developments. A U.S. Army court-martial at Ft. McPherson, Ga. Jan. 14 acquitted Sgt. Charles E. Hutto of murder in the slaying of South Vietnamese civilians at Mylai 4 March 16, 1968. Hutto had been charged with assault with intent to murder at least six civilians. Hutto's defense attorneys contended that he had followed orders from superiors when he fired at civilians. The chief prosecuting attorney, Capt. Franklin R. Wurtzel, argued that Hutto had the mental capacity to distinguish a legal order from an illegal one.

A statement made by Hutto to Army investigators Nov. 17, 1969 in which he acknowledged firing at civilians was read to the court Jan. 8. The statement said in part that "orders came down to kill all people, destroy the food and kill all the animals."

Three former soldiers involved in the operation against Mylai had testified Jan. 7 that Capt. Ernest L. Medina, their company commander, had ordered his troops "to kill everything in the village." One of the witnesses, Tommy L. Moss, said that at a briefing the day before the operation, Medina had ordered the shooting of children, as well as adults because the children, according to Medina, were "as much VC as the other people."

The Army Jan. 6 had dismissed charges against four more officers accused of suppressing information dealing with the Songmy massacre. Citing "insufficient evidence," Lt. Gen. Jonathan O. Seaman, 1st Army commander at Ft. Meade, Md., dismissed the charges against Lt. Col. David C. Gavin, Lt. Col. William P. Guinn, Maj. Charles C. Calhoun and Maj. Frederic W. Watke. Fourteen officers originally had been charged. The Army Feb. 26 announced the dropping of charges against another of the 14, Capt. Dennis H. Johnson.

Army Secretary Stanley R. Resor announced May 19 that Maj. Gen. Samuel W. Koster had been demoted one grade in rank to brigadier general for his failure to conduct an adequate investigation into the Mylai slayings. The Army also disciplined Brig. Gen. George H. Young Jr. for the same reason by stripping him of his Distinguished Service Medal and by placing a letter of censure in his personal record. Koster also lost his Distinguished Service Medal and had a letter of censure placed in his record. At the time of Mylai, Koster was the commander of the Americal Division, units of which were involved in the killings. Young was the assistant division commander.

Records tell of '68 war crime. A previously unpublicized incident of American servicemen committing atrocities against Vietnamese civilians came to light July 30 in records of the U.S. Court of Military Appeals in Washington.

According to the court's records, soldiers of the Americal Division raped and tortured two teen-age Vietnamese girls in June 1968. One of the girls was later shot to death by an American lieutenant.

Details of the incident were given in the court-martial record of Capt. Leonard G. Goldman, the company commander. Goldman had been convicted of dereliction of duty for not safeguarding the girls and for failing to report a noncombatant's death. The two girls had been held by the troops as suspected Vietcong nurses.

The records were made public as the military appeals court cleared Goldman of the charge of failing to report the girl's death. The court let stand, however, his conviction for failure to safeguard the girls and the sentence of a reprimand and $1,200 fine.

War crimes probe sought. Four Army officers and a Navy officer, all members of the antiwar Concerned Officers Movement, said Jan. 12 they were asking that military courts of inquiry be convened to investigate alleged war crimes and atrocities by U.S. troops in Vietnam. At a Washington press conference, the officers said they were formally requesting the inquiry, under provisions of military law, in letters to the secretaries of the Army and Navy.

The news conference was sponsored by the National Committee for a Citizens Commission of Inquiry into U.S. War Crimes in Vietnam. The Citizens Commission of Inquiry had held a conference in December 1970 during which 36 Vietnam veterans had given accounts of alleged war crimes.

The officers said the 300-page transcript of the veterans' testimony together with other evidence gave "sufficient cause" to ask courts "to investigate U.S. military behavior in relation to principles set down by the Nuremberg proceedings and the Japanese war crimes trials and other international treaties binding on the U.S. government."

Other evidence cited in the officers' letters included a report issued Dec. 29, 1970 by the American Association for the Advancement of Science and arguments by Telford Taylor, chief U.S. prosecutor at the Nuremberg war crimes trials of Nazi officials. The association report said chemical herbicides used in South Vietnam were disrupting the ecology of the region. Taylor, in his book "Nuremberg and Vietnam: An American Tragedy," had discussed implications of the legal basis of the Nuremberg trials.

(During a television program Jan. 8, Taylor suggested that if the Nuremberg principles were applied today, such men as Gen. William C. Westmoreland, who was commander in Vietnam, "could be found guilty" if they were brought to trial for war crimes.)

The four Army officers who requested the inquiry were stationed at Fort Meade, Md. They were Capt. Robert J. Master, 28, and Capt. Grier Merwin, 28, both doctors; Capt Edward G. Fox, 25, a zoologist in the Army Medical Service Corps; and 1st Lt. Louis Font, 24, a West Point graduate who had requested discharge as a conscientious objector. The Navy officer was Lt. (jg.) Peter Dunkelberger, 25, a management systems analyst at the Pentagon.

Four more officers, at a Los Angeles press conference Jan. 20, called for an investigation "of the responsibility" of U.S. military leaders "for war crimes" in Indochina. The four said they "fully support" five officers who called for boards of inquiry into war crimes Jan. 12.

Military leaders cited by the young officers included Gen. William C. Westmoreland, Adm. Elmo R. Zumwalt and Gen. Creighton W. Abrams. The officers, who were introduced to the press by a representative of the National Committee for a Citizens Commission of Inquiry into U.S. War Crimes in Vietnam, were Lts. (jg) John Kent, Edward Shallcross and James Skelly of the Navy and 2nd Lt. Norman Banks of the Air Force. They said three other officers—Lt. (jg) James Schwertman and Lt. Steven Auer of the Navy and 2nd Lt. Ed Kendig of the Marines—joined in the demand.

Three congressmen asked the Secretary of the Army to investigate the treatment of 1st Lt. Louis P. Font, one of the original five officers to call for war crimes boards of inquiry. According to a Washington Post report Feb. 4, criminal charges had been lodged against Font and he had been restricted to Fort Meade, Md. after the post commander first granted his permission to hold a press conference in Washington. The congressmen who questioned Font's treatment were Reps. Parren J. Mitchell (D, Md.), Bella S. Abzug (D, N.Y.) and Ronald V. Dellums (D, Calif.). A spokesman at Fort Meade said there was no connection between the charges against Font and his restriction to the post and his antiwar activity.

Font filed charges Feb. 17 at Fort Meade, Md. accusing two generals of war crimes. The action was announced at a news conference Feb. 18 in Dellums' Washington office.

Font accused Lt. Gen. Jonathan O. Seaman, 1st Army commander, of listing several Vietnam villages in which "all signs of life within them were to be destroyed" in the planning of military operations in 1967. He accused Maj. Gen. Samuel W. Koster, former commander of the Americal Division in Vietnam, of failing to control troops which "indiscriminately killed Vietnamese civilians in order to increase body count." Font based his charges on testimony made by Vietnam veterans at a December 1970 hearing on atrocities organized by an antiwar group in Washington.

(Font was later permitted to resign from the Army.)

The Army announced June 18 at Fort Monroe, Va. that it had dismissed war crimes charges against Gen. Seaman, who had retired. Gen. Ralph E. Haines Jr., commanding general of the Continental Army, said the charges had been dropped because "they were unfounded."

Congressmen ask war crimes probe. Rep. John Conyers Jr. (D, Mich.), joined by Rep. John F. Seiberling Jr. (D, Ohio) and members of the Vietnam Veterans Against the War, called for a Congressional investigation of alleged U.S. war crimes in Vietnam at a press conference Feb. 5. Conyers and Seiberling called on Congress to probe the "serious" charges presented by 100 veterans in a "Winter Soldier" investigation sponsored by the veterans group in Detroit Jan. 31 to Feb. 2.

Conyers said nine congressmen supported the call for a Congressional investigation and that Rep. Ronald V. Dellums (D, Calif.) had introduced a House resolution calling for a probe Feb. 4. Conyers said the Detroit forum presented testimony about U.S. troops killing unarmed civilians, torturing soldiers to get information, killing soldiers trying to surrender and burning villages. He called the 100 veterans "patriots of the highest order."

John Carey, a former Navy lieutenant who served in Vietnam and was a member of the veterans group, said the name "Winter Soldier" investigation was a reference to Thomas Paine's denouncement of "sunshine patriots" during the American War of Independence. Carey said the antiwar veterans did not feel their return from Vietnam relieved them of responsibility to the U.S.

Carey said the war crimes investigation was not an attempt to "accuse one individual." He said the group was concerned with an overall Asian policy, using GIs as "pawns," that permitted atrocities, not by direct order but "with full knowledge of officers at all levels of command." He said prosecution was not the goal of the Detroit hearings but that the group wanted to educate the public so the military could be brought under civilian control.

The Detroit forum presented testimony of Army, Navy and Marine veterans who had served in Vietnam. Actress Jane Fonda was reported to have raised money for the forum through lectures. Also listed as a major contributor was author Mark Lane.

Ex-Green Beret admits 1969 slaying. Robert F. Marasco, a former captain in the U.S. Special Forces who was charged but never tried in the 1969 slaying of a suspected South Vietnamese double agent, said April 2 that he had shot and killed him on orders from the Central Intelligence Agency (CIA).

Marasco said he was admitting his complicity in the death of the agent out of a sense of anger over the conviction of 1st Lt. William L. Calley Jr. on charges of murdering 22 civilians at Mylai.

Marasco, who had become a life insurance salesman, was one of eight Green Berets charged with killing Thai Khac Chuyen, whose body was dropped from a boat into the South China Sea and never found.

(There were no trials as CIA Director Richard Helms decided not to permit any CIA personnel to appear as witnesses. President Nixon was also involved in the CIA decision to drop the case against the Green Berets.)

Marasco, 29, said Chuyen was killed on "oblique yet very, very clear orders" from the CIA. He described Chuyen as "my agent" and said it was "my responsibility to eliminate him with extreme prejudice."

According to Marasco, Chuyen's death was approved "up and down our chain of command."

For the most part, Marasco's story corroborated earlier reports on how the agent was murdered. He said Chuyen, whose identity as a double agent was discovered when he was seen in a Vietcong photograph, was drugged with morphine on a boat before he was shot. Marasco said he killed Chuyen with two shots to the head. His body was then tossed overboard in a weighted mail sack by three officers in the boat.

Because Marasco was no longer in the Army, he was not subject to court-martial. He had never before admitted direct participation in the killing.

8 airmen cleared. The U.S. Army command in Saigon cleared eight helicopter crewmen June 4 of murder charges in connection with the alleged strafing of Vietnamese civilians from their gunships in September 1970. The Army said the charges had been dropped because of insufficient evidence. Maj. Gen. Charles Gettys, Army chief of staff in Vietnam, ordered the charges dropped on recommendation of investigating officers.

The charges against the men were initiated in November 1970 but the Army did not file formal charges until May 4. All eight were accused of attempted murder and premeditated murder.

The crewmen had been accused of firing machine guns and grenade launchers at various targets in the Mekong Delta as their gunships were flying westward from Dongtam. One Vietnamese civilian was killed and 16 wounded.

The crewmen were identified as CWO Michael A. Nicholaou, 21; CWO Stephen J. Becker, 23; WO Roland E. Linstad, 21; WO Camille A. Perret, 20; Spec. 5 Dominic Fino, 20; Spec. 5 John N. Enos, 20; Spec. 4 James L. Dunston, 21; and Spec. 4 Charles R. Thompson, 22.

Donaldson cleared of Vietnam murders. Brig. Gen. John W. Donaldson, 47, was exonerated by the Army Dec. 9 of murder and assault charges accusing him of killing six South Vietnamese civilians while he was a brigade commander in Vietnam.

Lt. Gen. Claire E. Hutchin Jr., commander of the 1st Army at Ft. Meade, Md., where Donaldson was assigned, announced the Army's decision to drop charges. In a brief statement, Hutchin said "evidence established that no offenses were committed by Gen. Donaldson, then a colonel." It was Hutchin's decision as the 1st Army commander to drop the charges.

Donaldson was the highest-ranking officer accused of war crimes in the Vietnam war. He was also the first American general officer to face such charges since Brig. Gen. Jacob H. Smith was charged with war crimes in 1901.

The Donaldson case, involving alleged events occurring in Quangngai province between November 1968 and January 1969, reportedly originated with a report by a helicopter pilot about "potshot" firings from a helicopter at civilians. Donaldson had then been a colonel in command of the Americal Division's 11th Infantry Brigade.

Barnes cleared of cover-up role. The Army cleared Maj. Gen. John Barnes Oct. 15 of charges initiated by an officer in his Vietnam command that he failed to report alleged war crimes by American and allied servicemen in 1969.

The Army said it was dropping the charges after a six-month official inquiry failed to turn up any evidence of guilt.

Barnes and his second-in-command at the time of the alleged war crimes, Col. J. Ross Franklin, were accused by Lt. Col. Anthony B. Herbert of dereliction of duty by failing to report the alleged incidents by U.S. soldiers against prisoners of war and Vietnamese civilians. Herbert had been a battalion commander in the 173d Airborne Brigade, which was under Barnes' command.

In July, the Army had dropped charges against Franklin.

Barnes maintained that Herbert's charges were unfounded and that no reports of atrocities were made to him by Herbert.

Politics, Drugs & Other Developments

Thieu reelected president. Nguyen Van Thieu was re-elected to another four-year term as president of South Vietnam in a controversial uncontested election Oct. 3.

The government's Election Information Center announced Oct. 4 that Thieu had received 91.5% of the 6,311,853 votes cast and that 353,000, or 5.5%, had handed in invalid ballots. Three per cent of the vote was unaccounted for and government officials said they were investigating. Thieu had said during his campaign that he would consider 50% of the vote an expression of confidence in his rule.

A total of 87.7% of the more than seven million eligible voters went to the polls, making it the largest voter turnout in recent Vietnamese history.

Although South Vietnamese government spokesmen insisted that their figures on the results were accurate, the anti-Thieu opposition and foreign diplomats and observers expressed skepticism. In cities such as Saigon, Danang and Hué, where Thieu's strength was considered to be weakest, the president had piled up a huge number of votes, which one diplomat described as "fantastic." Thieu obtained 83% of the vote in Saigon.

Vice President Nguyen Cao Ky Oct. 4 assailed the voting results as rigged. In a statement issued on behalf of the People's Front Against Dictatorship, the newly-formed anti-Thieu group, Ky accused the president of "treading underfoot all the righteous aspirations of the people." He called the results "prefabricated by Mr. Thieu himself and for himself." Ky urged the South Vietnamese Senate "not to recognize the faked results" and called on the Supreme Court to "nullify the uncontested farce." The militant An Quang Buddhist faction charged that Thieu had "killed democracy and given birth to dictatorship."

Thieu Oct. 4 lauded his victory as an expression of the people's fulfilment of "their civil rights in a free and democratic nation." He praised the "political consciousness of the people."

U.S. officials in Washington Oct. 4 reiterated their misgivings about holding an election without rival candidates.

In an election eve broadcast Sept. 30, Thieu had appealed for a 50% vote of confidence in himself and his vice presidential running mate, Tran Van Huong. He said such a turnout would be "an expression of our anti-Communist determination." Thieu avoided the term "presidential" in referring to the election and called the balloting a "national election."

Thieu's victory was achieved despite widespread calls by his opposition for a boycott of the balloting and scattered anti-government demonstrations. In Saigon, a gathering of 300 persons in the

An Quang Pagoda was broken up Oct. 2 as police hurled tear gas into the building. Vice President Ky the same day addressed an anti-government rally of the People's Front Against Dictatorship in Saigon.

Scores of anti-government demonstrations were held in various parts of South Vietnam Oct. 2. The largest rally was held in Hue where 3,000 students attacked police with fire bombs. Police dispersed the demonstrators with tear gas and closed the University of Hue for the remainder of the day to prevent the students from regrouping.

A pro-government group, apparently sponsored by the Thieu administration, had been formed Sept. 28. It launched a campaign to solicit votes for him in various cities with parades and rallies. The organization, called the Anti-Communist People's Movement for Election Participation, was announced in a government press agency release. The group issued a statement "condemning the Communists' dark schemes aimed at sabotaging the Oct. 3 presidential elections."

(The Supreme Court Oct. 2 announced that it had called on Thieu to dismiss three of his appointed province chiefs for interfering with provincial courts investigating alleged irregularities in the Aug. 29 National Assembly elections. Anti-government candidates had lost in all of the three provinces of Binhthuan, Vinhbinh and Baclieu. The decision was not binding on Thieu.)

Among developments preceding the voting:

Ky charges corruption—Vice President Nguyen Cao Ky April 19 had assailed the leadership of President Thieu and had accused the Saigon government of curruption. Ky made the statement a day after he had announced that there was a "good possibility" that he might run for the presidency against Thieu.

Speaking in Saigon, Ky said: "The people have lost all faith in the government. South Vietnam is like a sinking boat with a deceptively good coat of paint, and the man who steers the boat [Thieu] is an unfaithful, disloyal, dishonest fellow." He said corruption in government was "an incurable disease." The only way to eliminate it and achieve social justice in the country was to make sure that "the president and especially his wife, the vice president and his wife, the premier and his wife, cannot be bought," Ky asserted.

The vice president scoffed at a military parade and celebration held in Hué April 17 marking the "southern Laos victory" and attended by Thieu. Ky indicated he did not believe the Laos operation was a victory.

Ky said South Vietnam must "find ways to stop the fighting . . . let's not talk about a military solution to the war." He pointed out that he did not advocate that Saigon should "end the war unilaterally. I mean that we should be strong militarily, economically and socially, so as to work toward a political solution."

In his remarks April 18, Ky had said Vietnamization would be a long-term process, that it would take his country 15–20 years before it was capable of defending itself. However, he termed the current pace of American troop withdrawals as "reasonable." Ky complained that American aircraft supplied to South Vietnam were obsolete and were no match for North Vietnam's MiG-21s.

Ky assailed U.S. war critic Sen. George McGovern (D, S.D.), who had sought information about charges that Ky was involved in opium smuggling. "The day he comes here I will kick him out personally," Ky said.

Election law could bar opposition— The House of Representatives, the lower chamber of the South Vietnamese National Assembly, approved a controversial bill June 3 that could eliminate any serious opposition to President Thieu in the presidential election. The measure was submitted to Thieu for either amendment or approval.

The House passed the bill by a 101–21 vote. It had adopted the measure previously, but it was rejected by the Senate. In order to revive the legislation, the lower chamber had to approve it for a second time with a two-thirds majority.

The measure, an amendment to the nominating clause of the electoral law endorsed by Thieu, required a presidential candidate to have his nomination paper signed by 40 deputies and senators or by 100 members of the elected provincial councils. Political observers were said to believe that these restrictions would make it difficult if not impossible for virtually all potential candidates, including Vice President Nguyen Cao Ky, to qualify. It was felt that only one possible presidential contender, Brig. Gen. Duong Van Minh, could get the required signatures. President Thieu, who controlled a majority of the Assembly legislators and of the provincial councils, would have no trouble in meeting the petition requirements.

Gen. Minh criticized the new election law as unconstitutional June 6. He added: "As far as it personally concerns me, it is insignificant. What is important is the way the Vietnamese people are treated. And the Vietnamese people can count on me."

Minh spoke to a small gathering of Vietnamese in Saigon to mark the second anniversary of the National Progressive Force, a small antigovernment, antiwar movement. The leader of the group, Tran Ngoc Lieng, issued a statement denouncing the new election law. He charged that "the ruling people are again attempting to put a new paint of false democracy on this dictatorial regime, in the form of the coming elections."

The election law was denounced June 7 by Deputy Ngo Cong Duc as a government effort in "preparing a fraudulent election." Duc told a news conference in Saigon that Thieu "will oppress opposition strongly and will ignore laws and the constitution. The brutal government will rig the forthcoming elections openly and will use violence and bad means to remain in power."

Duc had been jailed May 31 on a charge of attempted murder following a fist fight the previous day in the Mekong Delta with Vinhbinh Council President Pham Huu Gia, a supporter of the Thieu government. The incident grew out of a political argument. Duc was released from prison June 4 after a resolution passed by the House June 3 called on the government to set him free. Gia's charges against Duc were "indefinitely postponed," but not dropped.

President Thieu June 9 discounted opposition arguments that the new election law would eliminate all potential rivals from the presidential elections. He predicted that Ky, Minh and an unnamed third candidate would be running against him. Thieu held that the bill was necessary to limit the number of candidates in order to get a clear-cut result in the elections. He had received only 35% of the vote in the 1967 elections.

Thieu & Minh enter race—President Thieu and Gen. Duong Van Minh formally declared their candidacies for the presidential elections.

Thieu said in his announcement July 24 that he had decided to run for another four-year term, "realizing that I still have the responsibility toward the fatherland and the people." Thieu chose Sen. Tran Van Huong, a former premier, as his vice presidential running mate. Under the new election law, Thieu also selected an alternate running mate—Premier Tran Thien Khiem.

In announcing his decision to run against Thieu, Gen. Minh warned July 26 that he would withdraw from the contest if he felt the president was rigging the election. Minh selected Dr. Ho Van Minh, 34, deputy speaker of the House of Representatives, the lower chamber of the National Assembly, as his vice presidential running mate. He picked Sen. Hong Son as his alternate.

Vice President Nguyen Cao Ky reportedly had urged Minh to announce his candidacy at a private meeting held by the two men July 25. Ky hinted in a public statement made later in the day that he might withdraw from the race and throw his support to Minh. The vice president said he had received 114 endorsements of provincial council members to qualify as a candidate, but that only 29 had been validated by the countersignatures of provincial chiefs. Ky charged that Thieu, who appointed the province chiefs, had "given orders" to them not to countersign Ky's endorsements in order to prevent his certification as a candidate.

Ky and Minh had accused Thieu of rigging the election in previous statements July 14 and 15.

In an open letter to Thieu, Ky charged July 14 that the president was attempting to rig the election by pressuring legislators and local councillors "to prevent them from sponsoring the candidates whom you fear." He also accused Thieu of suppressing the news media and of failing "to resolve the war" and to enact promised social reforms.

Gen. Minh charged July 15 that U.S. support for Thieu could prevent an honest election. Minh said his American friends had told him that "a free and honest election will be very difficult with the presence" of U.S. Ambassador Ellsworth Bunker in Saigon. Minh said the Americans wanted him to run so that if Thieu "is elected by only a small margin, it will look like he won in a fair election." Bunker was "a great specialist in elections of this type," Minh asserted.

(U.S. President Richard M. Nixon said at his Aug. 4 press conference: The forthcoming election had some bearing on the pace of the Paris negotiations as far as the North Vietnamese were concerned, since "they feel that unless that election comes out in a way that a candidate they can support, or at least that they are not as much against as they are [South Vietnamese] President Thieu, . . . it will be very difficult for them to have a negotiated settlement." The U.S. position was "one of complete neutrality" concerning the election. "We will accept the verdict of the people of South Vietnam.")

Minh also had charged in a series of previous interviews that Thieu was responsible for the assassination of President Ngo Dinh Diem and his brother Ngo Dinh Nhu in the 1963 coup that overthrew Diem. Minh said Thieu, then a colonel who had participated in the coup, had failed to bring his troops to the presidential palace in time to prevent Diem from escaping. Minh held that if Diem and his brother had been taken into custody at the palace they would not have been murdered.

Thieu denied July 20 that he was rigging the elections. He insisted the balloting would be fair and invited foreign observers to "go anywhere they want in the country." Thieu called Minh a "coward and liar" for linking him to the Diem assassination. Minh had led the coup that deposed Diem. Thieu said at the time he had been informed by Gen. Tran Thien Khiem, now premier, that Minh had told him the "coup was so compli-

cated and difficult that the easiest way is to assassinate Diem."

In response to Thieu's countercharge, Minh July 21 acknowledged responsibility for Diem's death. But he reiterated that the plan was to capture Diem alive and that if Thieu had followed orders to occupy the palace on time "Nhu and Diem would not have escaped and would not have died."

Minh & Ky quit race—Gen. Minh and Vice President Ky withdrew from the presidential race Aug. 20 and 23. Their action left President Thieu as the sole candidate.

Minh and Ky based their decision to withdraw on the ground that Thieu was rigging the election. The two men resisted American pressure to stay in the race. Minh said in his formal statement Aug. 20, "I decided to withdraw because I cannot lend a hand to a dirty farce which would only make the people more desperate and disillusioned with the democratic system." He expressed hope that his action "would arouse the conscience of the responsible authorities."

Minh's formal withdrawal application submitted to the Supreme Court was coupled with several documents, which he claimed proved that the government was manipulating the election. According to the papers, the Saigon regime was engaging in a countrywide campaign to employ "schemes, ruses and maneuvers directed at political parites" and other groups "in order to persuade wavering people and to manipulate and paralyze opposition blocs."

The documents charged that government agents were directed to "infiltrate opposition blocs to sow confusion, buy off their leadership . . . to tail key cadre of the opposition, . . . so that they do not have favorable conditions to work." Minh had turned over the documents to U.S. Deputy Ambassador Samuel D. Berger Aug. 12. Their contents were cabled to Washington where Ambassador Ellsworth Bunker was meeting with President Nixon and other top Administration officials on the Vietnamese elections.

(Minh's press representatives Aug. 14 had made public what they contended to be multiple voting cards to be issued to pro-government voters instructing them to cast ballots more than once.)

Bunker had returned to Saigon Aug. 19 and met with Minh in an apparently unsuccessful last-ditch effort to persuade him to remain a presidential candidate. Bunker was said to have told Minh that he and President Nixon believed that Minh's presence on the ballot would be "good for South Vietnam."

Bunker also discussed the political situation with Thieu Aug. 20. The ambassador was accompanied at the start of the talks by Sen. Robert Dole (Kan.), chairman of the Republican National Committee. Dole later warned that if Thieu remained the only candidate "there will be some very critical reaction [in the U.S.] to a one-man race."

The U.S. State Department Aug. 20 expressed regret that Minh had decided not to participate in the elections. "We favor a fair, honest, and contested election—one that would lead to a choice for the South Vietnamese people," the statement said.

A White House spokesman said Aug. 20 that the Nixon Administration was "assessing the matter and the situation is somewhat fluid."

In his Aug. 23 statement withdrawing from the race, Vice President Ky said "legal irregularities" precluded his remaining a candidate. He accused Thieu of "an indescribable conspiracy to rig the election and use it as a tool for personal gain." Ky's action followed a Supreme Court decision Aug. 21 reinstating him on the ballot. The ruling reversed the court's previous decision Aug. 5 which declared Ky's candidacy invalid. Commenting on the court's first ruling, Ky had said Aug. 12 that the tribunal's decision was illegal and that he still considered himself a candidate.

In one incident, a Vietnamese war veteran had burned himself to death in Saigon Aug. 16 to protest Ky's disqualification from the presidential election and the government's election policies. Ky participated in a mass funeral ceremony Aug. 20.

Ky proposed in his Aug. 23 statement that he and Thieu resign to permit the president of the South Vietnamese Senate to form a transition government that would organize new elections. The vice president said he would run in such new elections provided that all province chiefs and other subordinates appointed by Thieu were removed to insure fair balloting.

Commenting on the Supreme Court's reversal on his candidacy. Ky told a news conference Aug. 23 that "once again the law has been bent to service the political needs of one individual. It has become evident that the forthcoming October elections will simply be conducted within the predetermined limits of a dark effort." Ky called the elections a "farce" with President Thieu "the principal actor in the farce."

The Nixon Administration expressed regret Aug. 23 that Ky had withdrawn. The State Department said "our interest was and is in seeing an honest election." The Administration also defended Ambassador Bunker's efforts to get Ky and Minh to stay in the race as "completely consistent" with the American policy of noninvolvement in the elections. Bunker "could do nothing less than urge that there be a fair and contested election," the State Department said.

Thieu discussed the crisis with his advisers Aug. 23. One of his aides later said: "The president was firm. He considers that nothing has been changed in the elections, which will be organized as scheduled. He noted that Mr. Ky has purposely created the crisis." Another aide said Thieu rejected Ky's proposal that both officials resign to pave the way for the organization of new elections. "It is absolutely out of the question that he should embark on that political adventure, especially at this moment of crisis," the aide said. Bunker met with Thieu later Aug. 23.

Thieu officially uncontested—The government announced officially Sept. 1 that President Thieu would be the only candidate in the Oct. 3 presidential elections. It acted after the Supreme Court had formally removed Vice President Ky from the ballot. Although Ky had announced Aug. 23 that he would not run, technically he remained a candidate until his name was taken off the slate. Ky had asked the tribunal Aug. 26 to take that action.

The court's ruling specifically said the election would be held as scheduled, with Thieu as the sole candidate on the ballot. A government broadcast Sept. 1 said all government agencies were ordered to make "all necessary preparations" for election day.

U.S. Ambassador Ellsworth Bunker, who had been holding talks with Thieu, Ky and Gen. Duong Van Minh on the election crisis, was accused by Minh Sept. 1 of interfering in the elections. The general accused Bunker of using background interviews with the press to spread distorted versions of his talks with Minh. Minh insisted that he had not met with any officials of the American embassy since his withdrawal from the presidential race Aug. 20. He denied an Aug. 29 United Press International report that Minh "had requested the U.S. to take charge of the organization of the presidential elections in South Vietnam" and that Minh had "expressed his wish that the United States could make arrangements to enable him to run in the elections." The statement said an Agence France-Presse story of Aug. 29 had reported that Bunker had circulated the alleged remarks of Minh.

Charges that Thieu was engaged in fraud to insure his re-election were repeated by Ky in a letter he had sent Bunker Aug. 23 in which he explained the reasons for his withdrawal from the presidential race. The message, made public by Ky Aug. 25, said he had come to "the conclusion that the significance of this election has been damaged beyond remedy by the manipulations of the government."

Election rigging cited—Specific cases of government rigging were cited in an interim report released by the National Assembly's Committee on Election Fraud Aug. 27. The committee, composed of 22 anti-government senators and deputies, said it was in possession of proof of irregularities in the Aug. 29 assembly elections and the presidential elections. The panel said that several candidates for the lower house had been arrested without charges and that most were released after a committee protest to the government.

(Local committees July 17 had disqualified about 400 candidates for the assembly elections. Among those barred was Ngo Cong Duc, a strong supporter of Gen. Minh. Duc, heading a group of 18 opposition deputies called the "social bloc," had his candidacy declared invalid under a clause disqualifying "persons working for communism or pro-Communist neutralism.")

Sen. Vu Van Mau, committee chairman, said Thieu and his supporters had attempted to monopolize or hoard the endorsements of province chiefs and legislators required by presidential candidates to qualify for the ballot. The report said in one case an army major had advised his men to vote for the incumbent speaker of the lower house in the Aug. 29 balloting. The committee said in another instance five opposition candidates in Danang had been barred from radio campaigning and that another candidate had been assaulted by a captain in the army's political warfare section.

The committee called attention to a controversial document dealing with cases of alleged election frauds made public by Gen. Minh when he withdrew from the presidential race. The abuses outlined in the paper "give us an early glimpse of the probable outcome of the upcoming elections," the committee said. The document said Thieu had given advice to all 44 province chiefs appointed by him and other officials on how to promote his own candidacy and those of pro-government deputies.

These orders were said to have been given by Thieu on means of undermining opposition candidates: "If they are civil servants, they can be transferred out of their districts. If they are elected village or hamlet chiefs, they should be attacked and discredited by other village council members and officials. In general, their dossiers should be checked to see if there are any instances of improper behavior in their past, so that we can use this evidence to persuade them to work for us, or, if they refuse, to arrest them."

Anti-government, anti-U.S. protests—The alleged election abuses perpetrated by President Thieu precipitated a series of street protests against the South Vietnamese and U.S. governments in Saigon and elsewhere. In Danang, a war veteran burned himself to death Aug. 24, saying he wanted to "defend democracy and freedom" in his country.

Supporters of an anti-American candidate in the National Assembly elections attempted to stage a demonstration in front of the assembly building Aug. 26, but the rally was broken up before it started. The candidate—Tran Tuan Nham—was arrested with four of six demonstrators.

Saigon police Sept. 1 fought with two separate groups of students, numbering 1,000 each, who were staging protests against the government, the U.S. and the war.

National Assembly elections—Opposition candidates scored gains but President Thieu retained a comfortable majority as a result of elections held Aug. 29 for the House of Representatives, the lower chamber of South Vietnam's National Assembly. North Vietnamese and Viet Cong troops stepped up attacks throughout the country in an unsuccessful effort to disrupt the balloting.

Preliminary results released Aug. 31 showed that 50–60 of the house's 159 seats would probably go to opposition candidates. Of the 1,240 nominees, 118 were incumbents. Only about 30 of them were re-elected. Many pro-government incumbents were defeated but in most cases they were replaced by other Thieu-supported candidates. The An Quang Buddhist faction, which opposed the government and the war, appeared to have gained 30 seats, 20 more than it had held in the previous house. About 78% of the eligible voters cast ballots.

The White House expressed pleasure Aug. 30 that the election "appears to have gone smoothly."

The state of alert imposed Aug. 24 for American troops in South Vietnam was lifted Aug. 31. The 9,000 American servicemen in the Saigon area were permitted to leave their barracks for the first time in a week.

Thieu calls vote a referendum—President Thieu declared Sept. 2 that since he was the only candidate in the presidential election, he regarded the outcome as a test of popular support of his policies.

In a radio and television address, Thieu said "if I see the results of the voting confirming the confidence of the people in me, I will continue with another four-year term. But if the results show clearly that the people do not have confidence in me, I will not accept another four-year term and will step down." Thieu did not specify what would constitute a satisfactory result.

Thieu said the fact that he had no other rivals in the race was "no firm legal basis for postponing the election." He deplored the absence of other nominees but blamed the two withdrawn candidates—Vice President Nguyen Cao Ky and Gen. Duong Van Minh—for precipitating the crisis. He accused the two men of "slandering and insulting all national institutes and even myself." Thieu denied their charges of rigging to insure his re-election, asserting that Minh and Ky had "presented a view of the situation in a way that is most profitable to them."

U.S. reaction—The White House said Sept. 2 that Thieu's declaration that the balloting would be tantamount to a vote of confidence "suggests he is obviously attempting to introduce an element of popular choice to the election."

Secretary of State William P. Rogers told a news conference in Washington Sept. 3 that the U.S. accepted Thieu's decision to run unopposed. The secretary said he was "disappointed" that Ky and Minh had withdrawn from the race. But he expressed hope that "the democratic process will continue in South Vietnam." Rogers conceded that the U.S. had failed in its efforts to achieve a contested election, but he said it was preferable to conduct it under Thieu's terms rather than suspend the electoral process entirely. Despite the crisis, the U.S. intended to continue its support of the Saigon government, Rogers said.

Rogers called the Aug. 29 National Assembly elections "a demonstration of democracy." But he said "obviously the elections in a country like Vietnam are not pristine and pure, but neither are ours, for that matter."

Ky denies threat of coup—Vice President Ky was quoted as saying Sept. 3 that he would "destroy" President Thieu and stage a coup to oust him unless the presidential election were postponed. A series of confusing statements issued later by Ky and his office denied that such a threat had been made.

Ky's views were delivered at a background briefing to a group of 10 Western newsmen. They were given with the stipulation that the statements not be attributed directly to Ky but to "sources close to the vice president."

Speaking at Tansonnhut airport in the outskirts of Saigon, Ky was quoted as saying: "I'm going to destroy Thieu and all his clique. If I were to give my life by destroying Thieu, I will do it. When I decide to do it, neither Ambassador Bunker nor the whole American government will be able to stop me. In a political fight I'm not smart, but in a military confrontation I'm a specialist. I told Bunker in 1967 and 1968 that I was the only man in Vietnam who could make a coup, but I told him I had no intention of it, . . . I told him before I do anything I will let him know five minutes in advance. You will see I'll keep my word."

Asked when he planned to carry out his threat, Ky was reported to have said: "It's up to Thieu now, to accept or not to accept a confrontation. He has only one or two weeks. If his one-man show continues, he will establish a dictatorial regime that nobody can accept." Ky warned: "The unrest of the people and the armed forces is greater now than it has ever been. The powder keg is bigger now than it was even in 1963 [when President Ngo Dinh Diem was overthrown in a coup], but we don't have the fuse—yet."

The substance of Ky's statement was contained in a private message of the vice president submitted to the U.S. State Department Sept. 2. It was delivered by Dong Duc Khoi, an adviser to Ky. Khoi had arrived in Washington Sept. 1 and also met with Defense Department officials.

The denial issued by Ky's office Sept. 4 said "nobody may act in the name of 'sources close to the vice president' in order to make public information concerning the vice president."

Ky acknowledged Sept. 5 that he was the source of the Sept. 3 remarks attributed to him but he assailed the quoted statements as "completely untrue." He also dismissed the meeting with the foreign newsmen as "neither a press conference nor an interview," but "an informal talk."

Saigon newspapers reported Sept. 9 that Ky had proposed that Thieu resign and that Ky replace him as provisional president, organizing new elections within two or three months. Ky said he would not be a candidate in those elections.

Generals divided on Thieu—A U.S. intelligence report submitted to Nixon Administration officials Sept. 1 said that South Vietnam's military officers were "less than unanimous" in supporting President Thieu in his decision to run unopposed in the presidential elections. The report said Thieu had met senior army generals and that although most had given him support, some were "noncommittal."

According to the intelligence assessment, the generals had told Thieu that they regarded as unfair the circumstances leading to Vice President Ky's withdrawal from the race. One of the men who met with Thieu, Gen. Hoang Xuan Lam, commander of Military Region I, was quoted as telling the president that the country's senior military officers "should be allowed to meet with Ky." The officers were said to have warned that growing unrest among students and war veterans might accrue to Ky's advantage.

The report also related a recent meeting between Ky and Gen. Can Van Vien, chief of the South Vietnamese Joint General Staff. The account said that although Ky "has shown a tendency to overrate his support in the past" the vice president's meeting with Vien led him to feel "optimistic that Vien would support him in any future political moves." Ky "might be encouraged to oppose Thieu more vigorously if he saw cracks in the president's military support," the report stated.

In a move aimed at neutralizing military and police opposition to his uncontested election, Thieu Sept. 4 promoted 28 generals and appointed a new head of the Vietnamese Intelligence Organization. The action was disclosed Sept. 11. Among those promoted was Gen. Ngo Dzu, commander of Military Region II, raised to the rank of lieutenant general.

Col. Nguyen Khac Binh replaced Maj. Gen. Tran Tranh Phong as national police chief. Both men had close ties with Thieu.

Minh rejected Bunker money offer—An aide to Gen. Duong Van Minh disclosed Sept. 3 that the general rejected an offer of an undisclosed amount of money from U.S. Ambassador Ellsworth Bunker to remain a candidate in the presidential elections. The aide said that at a meeting Aug. 19 Bunker had offered to finance Minh's campaign. The bid made Minh "furious" and as a result he announced his withdrawal from the race the following day, the aide said.

The general's associate said Vice President Nguyen Cao Ky, another withdrawn candidate, had received a similar offer from Bunker totaling about $2 million. The U.S. embassy in Saigon had denied that Bunker had made any offer of money to Minh or Ky.

U.S. senators criticize election—Three U.S. senators made speeches to the Senate Sept. 10 decrying the handling of the South Vietnamese elections.

Sens. Edward W. Brooke (R, Mass.) and Adlai E. Stevenson 3rd (D, Ill.), said there was no longer any reason, in view of the handling of the parliamentary and presidential elections, for the U.S. to continue its military commitment to South Vietnam.

The speech by Sen. Henry M. Jackson (Wash.) drew attention because of his status as a possible Democratic presidential contender and because of his surprising stand that if a "competitive" and "genuine" South Vietnamese presidential election was not arranged, he would "reserve" his position regarding future U.S. military and economic aid to Saigon. Although a supporter of U.S. policy in Vietnam in the past, Jackson said the Nixon Administration had "not only allowed the election situation to deteriorate, it has contributed to the deterioration." The Administration "should stop pretending to be helpless" in the situation, he said, because the U.S. "still has sufficient influence in Vietnam to see that a pointless referendum is transformed into a meaningful political contest, if necessary at a later date."

Sen. George S. McGovern (S.D.), a declared Democratic presidential con-

tender in South Vietnam on a three-day visit as part of a 12-day world tour, said in Saigon Sept. 16 Congress should "seize" on the one-man candidacy of President Thieu "as the final justification for ending our military operations here." The opportunity promised by President Nixon for the South Vietnamese "to decide their own future," McGovern said, "now turns out to be a tightly controlled one-man charade." He called Nixon's Vietnamization policy a "glaring failure" and advocated ending U.S. military support for the Thieu government. McGovern had met with Thieu Sept. 15.

Election protests continue—Two disabled South Vietnamese war veterans attempted to burn themselves to death in protest against Thieu's decision to run unopposed. One incident occurred Sept. 4 at Nhatrang and the other Sept. 6 at the Mekong Delta town of Soctrang. Ky was visiting Nhatrang at the time and arrived at a park where the victim was aflame.

Another war veteran tried to burn himself to death in a protest rally Sept. 9 in the Mekong Delta town of Rachgia. About 1,000 war veterans, demanding the resignation of Thieu, clashed with police.

A resolution adopted by a special session of the South Vietnamese Senate Sept. 22 urged that Thieu postpone the elections and organize new ones "in accordance with democratic procedures." The resolution stated that the appearance of only one candidate in the race exacerbated internal unrest, threatened the survival of the country and ignored the wishes of the people. Twenty-eight of 31 senators present voted for the resolution. Three abstained.

Sen. Huynh Van Cao, a backer of Thieu's re-election who said he was withdrawing his support, asserted that "President Nixon can support President Thieu, but President Nixon cannot force the Vietnamese people to support President Thieu."

The militant anti-government An Quang Buddhist faction Sept. 16 appealed to its followers and others to boycott the presidential elections. A statement issued by the An Quang Pagoda in Saigon charged that the "elections were established by unconstitutional and antidemocratic laws, and have brought about the noncooperation of worthy men and the ever-deepening protest of people from . . . inside and outside the country. . . ." The "worthy men" referred to Vice President Nguyen Cao Ky and Gen. Duong Van Minh, who had withdrawn from the race.

Another Buddhist faction in South Vietnam, the Cambodian Buddhist church, denounced Thieu's candidacy Sept. 19 and urged its two million followers in the country to boycott the elections.

Anti-government riots—A series of demonstrations in Saigon protesting the sole candidacy of President Thieu was marked by violence. Police Sept. 16 broke up a rally of an opposition group near the An Quang Pagoda with tear gas after 10 protesters burned their voter registration cards.

Four separate violent protests were staged in Saigon Sept. 18 with demonstrators hurling stones and Molotov cocktails and police responding with tear gas. One rally was conducted by 18 anti-Thieu deputies of the lower house of the National Assembly. Most of the participants in the three other demonstrations were Buddhist students.

U.S. military servicemen and their vehicles were being subjected to attacks by South Vietnamese protesters, but these assaults were believed connected with objection to the American military presence, rather than with the election crisis itself.

Leaders of one protesting group, the Movement Struggling for the People's Right to Live, said Sept. 15 that their objective was to force all Americans to leave Vietnam immediately. The leaders said that since Aug. 24 more than 1,500 of their followers had burned 32 American Army vehicles.

Thieu sets majority as goal—President Thieu officially opened his uncontested election campaign Sept. 11, declaring he would resign if he did not receive 50% of the vote in the balloting.

Thieu said in a television-radio address that voters wishing to oppose him could cast "an irregular ballot as a ballot expressing nonconfidence." He did not explain what would constitute an invalidated ballot. Thieu appealed for a large vote to provide him with "enough prestige to talk to the world, face the Communists and fight for and preserve the peace platform of the whole country."

Saigon sources had reported Sept. 10 that ballots could only be invalidated by mutilating them or throwing them away. Thieu was said to have rejected as illegal any other proposal, including blank ballots and ones that would permit voters to have a choice of "Yes" or "No."

The U.S. Sept. 13 publicly called on Thieu to explain how ballots could be cast against him. The State Department said "there would have to be some clarification on the way in which the votes cast in the negative in this referendum would by physically expressed."

Thieu confirmed Sept. 20 that a "no confidence" vote could be cast against him in the presidential elections by tearing the ballot, marking it in a way that would invalidate it or leaving it blank. Thieu's remarks were contained in the second speech of his re-election campaign in which he reiterated his hard-line stand against concessions to the Communists. He repeated his opposition to a coalition government with the National Liberation Front, saying it would only be "a step toward the total take-over of power" by the enemy.

Thieu had told a group of 12 foreign correspondents Sept. 16 that he favored keeping a residual force of at least 50,000 American troops in South Vietnam through 1973. The president said a continued U.S. military presence was necessary because he expected the Communists to launch a major offensive in the northern provinces of South Vietnam, either in 1972 or 1973.

Nixon vs. U.S. political role—At an unscheduled press conference Sept. 16, President Nixon said the U.S. should continue to pursue its main objective—to end American involvement when South Vietnam was able to defend itself and the release of American POWs was attained. Regarding proposals to cut off aid to South Vietnam unless a "contested election" took place, Nixon said the U.S. provided aid to 91 countries, only 30 of which had leaders "who are there as a result of a contested election by any standard that we would consider fair. In fact we would have to cut off aid to two-thirds of the nations of the world . . . , to whom we are presently giving aid, if we apply the standards that some suggest we apply to South Vietnam."

If the suggestion was that the U.S. "should use its leverage now to overthrow [South Vietnamese President] Thieu, I would remind all concerned that the way we got into Vietnam was through overthrowing [Ngo Dinh] Diem and the complicity in the murder of Diem, and the way to get out of Vietnam, . . . is not to overthrow Thieu, with the inevitable consequence of the greatly increased danger . . . of that being followed by coup after coup on the dreary road to a Communist takeover."

Nixon said the objective of achieving a democratic process in Vietnam "will not be met perhaps for several generations. But at least we will be on the road. . . . You cannot expect that American-style democracy, meeting our standards, will apply in other parts of the world. We cannot expect that it will come in a country like South Vietnam, which has no tradition whatever, without great difficulty. But we have made progress."

Anti-Thieu group formed—An opposition group, led by Vice President Nguyen Cao Ky, was formed Sept. 26 to promote a boycott of the Oct. 3 presidential elections and to force the ouster of President Nguyen Van Thieu.

The organization was established at a meeting in Saigon of 43 supporters of Ky and Gen. Duong Van Minh and representatives of students, anti-government Buddhists and war veterans. They signed a resolution to form a "People's Coordinating Committee Against Dictatorship." Ky presided over the meeting but did not sign the resolution. Minh was invited but did not attend. The resolution stated that the Coordinating Committee would "urgently invite all other sections of the population who are against the dictatorial rule of Nguyen Van Thieu to join the committee and at the same time to fix a joint program of action."

A radical student-based organization, the Committee to Unify All Activities Against the Nguyen Van Thieu Dictator-

ship, joined the Coordinating Committee Sept. 27. In a statement issued the previous day, the student group had called for a boycott of the election and urged the people "to rise up as one man to destroy Nguyen Van Thieu by all means, including violent means."

The Coordinating Committee Sept. 29 elicited a statement from Gen. Minh in which he asserted that if the election was held "in the existing conditions, the regime of South Vietnam will cease to have a democratic and legal basis, will lose all credit in the eyes of the world, and will be completely alienated from the people."

A government communique Sept. 23 had reaffirmed that the elections would be held as scheduled. It said the balloting could only be stopped by the National Assembly and only by an amendment to the constitution.

Meanwhile, violent street demonstrations continued in Saigon protesting Thieu's uncontested candidacy. In one clash Sept. 23, three U.S. military vehicles were among targets fire-bombed by students and disabled war veterans.

The increasing disturbances prompted Thieu Sept. 29 to order the national police to "shoot down anyone who attempts to burn vehicles in the streets." Addressing a convention of national policemen in Saigon, Thieu said "we cannot tolerate a minority that sows confusion and creates disturbances."

A "gray" alert issued by the U.S. command Sept. 23 ordered the 215,000 American servicemen in South Vietnam confined to their barracks and places of work until three days after the presidential election. The order, which went into effect Sept. 24, referred only to "a possible increase in enemy activity" but the command's action was believed based on fear that American servicemen might be caught in a crossfire between the followers of Thieu and his non-Communist opponents.

American sources in Saigon reported Sept. 23 that the U.S. had warned South Vietnamese generals that any coup carried out against Thieu in the election crisis would bring an end to American support for the Saigon government.

According to the American sources, Saigon's generals "have been told off and on, even before the present crisis, that the United States would not stand still for a coup . . . that such a coup would mean the finish of the American role here." The report added: The South Vietnamese military leaders "have now been reminded that they cannot mess around in politics and expect to remain strong . . . and that their recent decision to stand above the present political troubles is the right course."

The reported warning paralleled a report of separate meetings in Saigon Sept. 23 of Brig. Gen. Alexander M. Haig Jr., President Nixon's deputy assistant for national security affairs, with President Thieu and Vice President Ky.

An aide to Ky said Sept. 24 that Gen. Haig had told the vice president that any violent change in the Saigon government would be contrary to the American purpose of supporting a viable regime. According to the aide, Ky replied that the South Vietnamese people "had the impression that the Americans were responsible for this terrible election situation." Ky was further quoted as saying "it was now up to the Americans to take appropriate action."

Ambassador Ellsworth Bunker had joined the talks with Haig and Thieu.

Thieu re-election upheld. The South Vietnamese Supreme Court, by an 8–1 vote Oct. 22, ruled that the Oct. 3 re-election of President Nguyen Van Thieu was legally valid. The ruling rejected a suit filed Oct. 6 urging the justices to declare the balloting unconstitutional and to nullify the results. The complaint was signed by Trinh Quoc Khanh, leader of the People's Force Against Dictatorship, the anti-Thieu group formed during the election campaign.

Final tallies released by the Supreme Court Oct. 10 had shown that Thieu had received 5,975,018 of 6,331,918 votes cast, or 94.3%.

The South Vietnamese Senate Oct. 19 rejected by a 19–8 vote an opposition motion to investigate charges that the presidential election was rigged. The proposal had been introduced by Sen. Van Mau, head of the militant An Quang Buddhist faction in the Senate.

Thieu inaugurated. Nguyen Van Thieu was inaugurated for his second four-year term as president of South Vietnam Oct. 31. The ceremonies in Saigon were attended by representatives of nearly 30 countries, including the U.S., whose delegation was headed by Treasury Secretary John B. Connally.

As a security precaution, about 30,000 government troops and security forces were deployed in and around Saigon to cope with a possible Communist effort to disrupt the inauguration. American soldiers, placed on the alert, were permitted to enter South Vietnam's cities and towns only on official business and their trips outside military installations were restricted.

In his inaugural address, Thieu proposed to "create favorable conditions for the reunification" of Vietnam, once the fighting stopped, by exchanging mail and visitors with North Vietnam.

Nguyen Cao Ky, the outgoing vice president, reiterated his charge in a farewell television address Oct. 31 that the sole candidacy of Thieu in the Oct. 3 presidential elections left South Vietnam with a weak government that could not stand up to "international pressures." Ky said he would return to his duties in the air force "to share with the combatants the dangers and miseries of the battlefield."

Saigon politician assassinated. A bomb attributed to the Viet Cong Nov. 10 exploded and killed Nguyen Van Bong, 42, founder and leader of the Progressive Nationalist party, a non-Communist political group opposed to the Thieu government. The explosion took place in Bong's car as he drove away from his office in Saigon. Two passengers in the vehicle also were killed.

Bong's movement had been formed April 20, 1969 in opposition to communism and Thieu's government.

Lon Nol visits Saigon. Cambodian Premier Lon Nol conferred with South Vietnamese officials in Saigon Jan. 20–21 and announced agreements to expand relations and reduce tensions between the two countries.

Lon Nol said both sides had agreed to recognize a common border and expand telecommunications, transport and tourism and the joint use of the Mekong River. A mixed commission would be established to inspect the treatment by each nation of the other's nationals. This accord grew out of allegations that Cambodians had massacred Vietnamese, and South Vietnamese troops had mistreated Cambodians during military operations in Cambodia in 1970.

The bilateral conference, however, failed to resolve the dispute over South Vietnamese demands that Cambodia finance the cost of South Vietnamese military operations in Cambodia and Pnompenh's insistence that Saigon pay debts dating to the end of the French colonial occupation in 1954. These matters were to be taken up later at a ministerial level.

Allies to keep support forces. The U.S. and four other countries with troops in South Vietnam agreed April 23 to maintain support forces in the country as their combat soldiers were withdrawn.

The decision was reached at a ministerial-level meeting attended by U.S. Secretary of State William P. Rogers, the foreign ministers of Australia, South Korea and South Vietnam and the New Zealand ambassador to the U.S.

A statement issued by the conferees said as the allies pulled out their combat troops they "should strive to provide for a further period of military support forces capable of providing training, engineer construction, medical, advisory, and other forms of assistance." The statement also noted that the steady progress of Vietnamization had made possible the withdrawals of some of the allied forces.

Australia and New Zealand announced Aug. 18 they would withdraw their combat forces from South Vietnam by the end of 1971. Small training forces of both countries would remain.

Australian Prime Minister William McMahon said the majority of his country's 6,000 troops would be home by Christmas. New Zealand Prime Minister Sir Keith Holyoake said New Zealand's small combat force of 264 men would be pulled out by "about the end of this year."

McMahon said the South Vietnamese were now "in a position to take over"

Australia's responsibility for the security of Phuoctuy Province, a costal area southeast of Saigon. The prime minister said Australia would provide Saigon with $28 million in economic aid over the next three years for civilian projects.

The U.S. government said Aug. 18 the decision of Australia and New Zealand to withdraw their troops from South Vietnam was in accord with the American program of troop withdrawal and Vietnamization.

Australian Defense Minister David Fairbairn said Aug. 20 that Australian losses in South Vietnam since 1965 totaled 473 men killed and 2,202 wounded. The military cost to the Canberra government totaled $182 million while another $16 million was spent on civilian assistance to the South Vietnamese, Fairbairn said.

Australia officially ended its combat role in South Vietnam Nov. 7 by turning over to South Vietnamese forces its main base at Nuidat. A 1,100-man Australian battalion withdrew from the base in preparation for returning home in December.

South Korean Defense Minister Yoo Jae Heung announced Sept. 9 that the withdrawal of part of South Korea's 48,000-man force in South Vietnam had been scheduled to start in December and to be completed by June 1972. The agreement reached by the South Korean and South Vietnamese governments did not specify the number of ROK troops to be removed, but merely said brigade-sized elements of Seoul's force would be withdrawn.

Thieu proposes economic reforms. President Nguyen Van Thieu Nov. 15 proposed a program of sweeping economic reforms aimed at combating inflation and reducing South Vietnam's reliance on American economic assistance.

In a State of the Nation broadcast, Thieu said a number of bills to be introduced in the National Assembly would call for the drastic devaluation of the piaster, modernization of income tax laws, simplification and reduction of export and import taxes and abolition of the "austerity tax" on imports.

Thieu said the purpose of his program was to create a "free exchange system" that would permit the piaster to float on the international money market. "Control of the exchange system will still be maintained to stop all illegal transactions and abuses," he said, "but as a fundamental principle we will gradually move toward a liberal exchange system."

Thieu added: "We must continue development to reduce our dependence on foreign aid, to keep our increasing income and assure our abundant and prosperous life for our people."

The piaster was devalued from 275 to the dollar to over 400.

Vietnamese refugees increase. The start of new allied operations in Indochina in late 1970 had resulted in a sharp increase in the number of war refugees in South Vietnam, according to U.S. Congressional sources quoted by the New York Times March 12.

The report said the U.S. mission in Saigon had informed a number of senators that the monthly number of new refugees between October 1970 and February 1971 had increased more than five times. More than 500,000 refugees were estimated to have been in camps or on relief prior to that period. The greatest upsurge was recorded between November 1970 with the advent of the dry season and February as the allies began preparing the current drives into Cambodia and Laos. The rate was estimated at 27,000 a month.

The new refugees either had been forcibly relocated to other villages by South Vietnamese troops clearing the area for impending military operations or they had been forced to abandon their homes because of U.S. bombings or ground fighting. In one instance, U.S. B-52 bombing raids and South Vietnamese troop operations in the U Minh Forest of the Mekong Delta had resulted in evacuation of about 38,000 new refugees from the area between mid-December 1970 and the last week of February 1971.

The U.S.-run Civil Operations and Rural Development Support Organization had reported that as of May 1970, there were nearly 230,000 refugees in camps in Military Region I in the north and that "most of them do not have adequate opportunities for self-support."

American officials in Saigon reported March 11 that the South Vietnamese government had abandoned plans to shift refugees from the northern to the southern part of the country because the overwhelming majority opposed being moved. Instead, the refugees were to be resettled in safer districts within their provinces. U.S. experts estimated that the number of civilians involved in the proposed move totaled hundreds of thousands.

U.S. and Saigon authorities considered the northernmost section of the country to be hardest hit by the refugee problem. Because of the devastation wrought by the severe fighting in that sector, about one million Vietnamese were said to be living in a state of deprivation.

Pacification drive disclosed. A new pacification program aimed at exerting greater effort in an attempt to smash the Viet Cong political apparatus in South Vietnam was instituted March 1 and endorsed by the U.S. and South Vietnamese commands, it was disclosed April 6.

A copy of the program, called the 1971 Community Defense and Local Development Plan, was made available to the New York Times. Its authenticity was confirmed by Administration sources. Because of its increased scope, the plan was said to be the most expensive one to date, costing the U.S. more than $1 billion and Saigon an undisclosed sum.

The program provided for:

■ Expansion of the People's Self-Defense Force from the current 500,000 to four million. Women would be enlisted in combat units and children over the age of seven would be placed in supporting units. The force was made up entirely of civilians operating in rural areas.

■ The slaying or capture of 14,400 Viet Cong agents under expansion of Operation Phoenix, an intelligence-gathering operation supported by U.S. military.

■ The setting up of a complex "people's intelligence network" to spy on the Communists.

The plan had been transmitted to Washington in January by Gen. Creighton W. Abrams, commander of U.S. forces in South Vietnam. In a covering memorandum, Abrams said that while it was a document of the South Vietnamese government, "it has been thoroughly co-ordinated" with the American command.

The expansion of the pacification program followed confirmed reports that the Viet Cong apparatus remained a major problem in eight South Vietnamese provinces, including four in the Mekong Delta, which supposedly had been pacified. The report also said South Vietnamese forces often preferred to "accommodate, rather than resist, the enemy."

(William E. Colby, head of the American pacification program in South Vietnam since February 1969, resigned June 30 and returned to Washington because of illness of a daughter. George Jacobson, Colby's deputy, was named acting chief of pacification.)

U.S. reports Communist gains. A survey conducted by the American embassy in Saigon told of growing Communist strength in South Vietnam and a threat to the pacification areas evacuated by American troops and in parts of the Mekong Delta, according to the New York Times July 21.

The survey covered the May 1–June 26 period and its findings were transmitted to Washington earlier in July. Nixon Administration officials who had seen the report were quoted as saying that it depicted "deterioration" in security in many areas of the country, an increase in terrorism and assassination and a sharp drop in the number of Communist defections to the Saigon government. The report concluded that "the enemy continues to affect adversely internal security in selected areas" although "the national picture reflects gradual internal security improvement."

Highlights of the U.S. embassy survey:

■ In the Mekong Delta's Military Region IV, there were "sharp enemy reactions against pacification in Kienphong Province by the North Vietnamese army and the Viet Cong"; "enemy activity was increasing in Dinhtuong Province" to the east. "Viet Cong in Vinhbinh and Vinhlong Provinces appear to be building up for an unknown major effort—possibly disruption" of the National Assembly and presidential elections.

■ In Military Region II, in the Central Highlands, there was a "serious control problem" in Binhdinh Province, which represented the "keystone of their [the Communists] attempts to cut the country in two." "The crux of the problem appears to be a leadership failure on the part of the government of South Vietnam."

■ "Enemy activity was strong" in northern Quangngai, Quangnam and Quangtri Provinces.

■ Pacification progress had been achieved in Military Region III, which encompassed Saigon, "but security deteriorated in several areas."

U.S. civilian gets top post. The U.S. command announced May 15 the appointment of John Paul Vann, 46, as director of the Second Regional Assistance Group in Military Region II in central South Vietnam. He was the first civilian to have overall supervision of American military and civilian activities in one of the country's four military regions. Operational control of the 67,000 American troops in Military Region II would remain under the U.S. Military Assistance Command.

For the past five years Vann had headed the U.S. pacification program in the Mekong Delta.

Con Son jail to be rebuilt. The U.S. mission in Saigon announced Feb. 20 that the U.S. would provide $400,000 to build 288 isolation cells to replace the notorious disciplinary Tiger Cage cells at the South Vietnamese prison on Con Son island, a detention center for political dissidents. The mission said a private American construction firm would build the project. The State Department had said Feb. 19 that all prisoners had been removed from Con Son and that the new cells would house only ordinary criminals.

U.S. journalist Don Luce, who had exposed the tiger cage prison cells in 1970, left South Vietnam May 9 after being ordered to leave. In disclosing the ouster order April 28, Luce said he was told that "for special reasons" his visa would not be renewed after it expired May 15. He attributed his expulsion to "the Con Son tiger cage story last summer and because I have continued to speak out against the prison system in Vietnam."

Pentagon disputes defoliation study.
The Defense Department Jan. 8 challenged a scientific study that charged the Army's defoliation operations in South Vietnam with laying waste to nearly 250,000 acres of mangrove forest. Furthermore, a Pentagon spokesman said, the defoliation might have benefited some parts of South Vietnam's economy, notably small farmers and the lumber industry.

The study, made under the auspices of Dr. Matthew S. Meselson, professor of biology at Harvard University, was made public Dec. 29, 1970 at a meeting of the American Association for the Advancement of Science in Chicago. The study asserted that at least a fifth of 1.2 million acres of mangrove forest in South Vietnam had been "utterly destroyed." It added that some unknown factor had prevented vegetation from returning to the ravaged areas.

Defense Department spokesman Jerry W. Friedheim said Meselson could not offer conclusive evidence from his study that the forest would not sustain new vegetation. Friedheim, citing what he described as expert information available to the Pentagon, said there was no certainty that the forest would not re-establish itself.

Friedheim said it was possible that the defoliation might have benefited the small Vietnamese farmers and the forest industry. Friedheim said defoliation "permits easier access, so crews can go in and bring out the wood."

Small farmers, he said, would also benefit because without the heavy jungle foliage they could find "room to grow garden crops right at the edge of the road, where they have easy access to the city."

Friedheim said careful ground observation would be needed to determine whether regeneration of the mangrove forests were possible. He said this could not be determined by observation from a helicopter at 2,000–4,000 feet at which he said he understood Meselson and his group shot aerial photographs of the mangrove swamps.

U.S. Army drug problem in 'Nam. As U.S. newsmen and political leaders warned that drug addiction was reaching

epidemic proportions among U.S. military personnel in Vietnam, the U.S. military command in Saigon Jan. 6 made public plans for a program to combat the spread of drug abuse among American GIs there. The drive was ordered by Gen. Creighton W. Abrams, commander of U.S. forces in Vietnam.

The program was unveiled three days after a Defense Department task force reported that a policy of "permissiveness" with respect to narcotics had led to a breakdown in leadership and discipline mainly at or below the company command levels. The six-man team that toured American military installations in Vietnam and the Far East said drug abuse had become a "military problem" for which the authorities had found no effective curb.

Abrams' directive ordered commanders throughout Vietnam to make ground and air search operations to locate fields where marijuana was being grown. The commanders were ordered to "utilize their resources, equipment and personnel in assisting the South Vietnamese government in eradicating the unlawful growing of marijuana." According to the directive, "under no circumstances will such fields, once discovered, be destroyed by United States forces."

The order also instructed U.S. field commanders to set up programs to curb drug abuse including "identification and reduction of morale and welfare factors such as idleness, loneliness, anxiety and frustration." Councils were to be created to monitor all aspects of any drug problems within a command. In addition, the Army ordered its commanders to step up education programs to better acquaint GIs with the dangers of drug abuse.

The directive also said programs of amnesty and rehabilitation presently under way in some commands would be extended to those "who demonstrate a sincere desire to reform."

The 64-page directive from Abrams estimated that more than 65,000 GIs were involved in drug abuse during 1970. More than 11,000, the directive said, were apprehended or investigated.

The military command in Saigon said there were 9,253 recorded drug violations by American forces in the first 10 months of 1970. Of these, 7,065 were charged with use or possession of marijuana, 1,-

452 with use or possession of such drugs as amphetamines, barbiturates or LSD, and 736 with use or possession of narcotics, usually heroin or opium'.

Gen. John D. Ryan, Air Force chief of staff, announced March 8 a drug amnesty program for those U.S. airmen who voluntarily admitted using drugs and sought medical help. Ryan said amnesty would be given to those servicemen would sought help before they were arrested or came under investigation in connection with drug use. Airmen who turned themselves in would not be punished for using or possessing drugs. They could, however, be subject to administrative action such as being taken off flying assignment status, reassignment or administrative discharge.

South Vietnam acts to curb drug flow— Responding to threats of economic sanctions, the South Vietnamese government reassured U.S. officials that it would take on more of the responsibility of curbing the supply of drugs to American GIs. Vietnamese officials tacitly admitted April 31 that drug abuse in Vietnam was no longer solely an American problem.

The South Vietnamese promised to begin an anti-drug drive after they were warned that continued apathy in dealing with the drug traffic could imperil requests for increased U.S. aid.

In one of the first steps to stop drug smuggling, Premier Tran Thien Khiem May 7 issued an order to have all customs and police officials suspected of corruption transferred or dismissed from the Tansonnhut Airport near Saigon. Within days a number of top police officials were replaced. Among the first were the airport police chief, Mai Van Phu, and his deputy. According to a London Times report, nearly 300 customs and police inspectors had been dismissed from their Tansonnhut posts by May 23.

Saigon police authorities were reported to have admitted that Tansonnhut had been the main point of entry for narcotics smuggled into Vietnam. They were optimistic that the reshuffling of the airport customs staff held some promise for a break in the drug traffic.

Police in Saigon were ordered to step up their arrests of narcotics peddlers.

Authorities said they had arrested "dozens" of Americans for selling or possessing heroin. Two Americans were arrested after they tried to smuggle 3,500 LSD pills into the country.

High level meetings between U.S. and South Vietnamese officials were held throughout May to discuss new ways to combat the drug problem. U.S. Ambassador Ellsworth Bunker conferred several times with President Thieu, while John E. Ingersoll, director of the U.S. Bureau of Narcotics and Dangerous Drugs, was in Saigon to meet with American and local officials.

Bunker gave Thieu a list of recommendations which the President had requested on measures to tighten customs operations and prevent narcotics from being smuggled into Vietnam from Laos, Thailand, Burma and Hong Kong.

Premier Khiem said May 26 that the South Vietnamese government and Cambodia were about to conclude an agreement aimed at controlling the drug traffic between the two countries. Khiem told newsmen that officials of both countries had been working on the anti-smuggling accord for several months.

Another top Vietnamese official, Justice Minister Le Van Thu, said May 28 that the government's anti-drug drive was showing "encouraging results." He said the effort had led to the seizure of 15 pounds of heroin, 6.4 pounds of opium and 1,716 pounds of marijuana. Since Jan. 1, Thu said 1,040 persons had been arrested on drug charges.

South Vietnamese leaders accused—Maj. Gen. Ngo Dzu, commander of South Vietnam's Military Region II, was accused by a U.S. congressman July 7 of being one of the chief heroin traffickers in Southeast Asia.

Dzu responded July 10, calling the allegation the "poor invention" of a jealous army rival and indicating that he thought Communists might have played some role in the report. [See below]

The charge was made by Rep. Robert H. Steele (R, Conn.) in testimony before a House Foreign Affairs subcommittee. Steele had recently returned to the U.S. from a congressional fact-finding tour of Indochina, where, he said, widespread corruption among officials had blocked efforts to halt the heroin traffic.

Steele told the subcommittee that since submitting his mission's report on heroin addiction among U.S. soldiers in Southeast Asia, "I have learned that South Vietnamese military officers continue to deal in large quantities of heroin and to transport it around South Vietnam in military aircraft and vehicles."

Dzu's senior American advisor, John Paul Vann, said July 8 that Dzu had asked President Nguyen Van Thieu to protest Steele's accusation. Vann added that "there is no information available to me that in any shape, manner or fashion would substantiate the charges Congressman Steele has made."

Dzu said July 10 that Steele had become an unwitting dupe in a plot to unseat him from his Region II command, which comprised the Central Highlands. Dzu added that a key role in the "campaign" against him was played by an army major who was an admitted former Communist and was presently associated with a rival of Dzu's.

Steele reaffirmed his charges against Dzu July 9, saying they were based on "hard intelligence."

An American TV news correspondent in Saigon reported July 15 that "extremely reliable sources" had accused President Thieu and then-Vice President Nguyen Cao Ky of using funds from the illicit drug traffic to finance their presidential campaigns.

Thieu described the report July 17 as slanderous. Ky July 18 called the accusation "ridiculous."

The accusations were made by Phil Brady, a National Broadcasting Company correspondent. In a filmed report broadcast on the NBC Nightly News program July 15, Brady charged that both Thieu and Ky were profiting from the drug traffic, that the Vietnamese national police were involved in the drug trade and that Lt. Gen. Dang Van Quang, one of Thieu's key advisors, was one of the biggest "pushers" in South Vietnam.

After learning of Thieu's denial, Brady said: "I stand by my story."

In his July 15 report, Brady said that Maj. Gen. Ngo Dzu, previously accused of involvement in the heroin market activities, was being made a "scapegoat" for other South Vietnamese leaders. Brady said that according to one source Dzu was "expendable" because he was not a political ally of either Thieu or Ky.

Congress studies drug problem—The strongest expressions of concern over the problem of drug abuse in the U.S. armed forces came from fact-finding teams in Congress. Although American military officials had acknowledged that the use of narcotics by soldiers was increasing, the extent was not known until a number of Congressional fact-finding teams issued reports.

After an eight-month study of drug abuse, a special House Armed Services subcommittee reported April 28 that "up to 10%" of the GIs in Vietnam may be using hard narcotics. The subcommittee, headed by Rep. G. Elliott Hagan (D, Ga.), said attempts by the South Vietnamese to control drug trafficking were "almost completely ineffective" because of corrupt public officials and ineffective police measures.

(Daniel Z. Henkin, assistant secretary of defense for public affairs, said May 16 that the Pentagon was uncertain of the total number of enlisted men in Vietnam using heroin. Henkin said "it is very difficult to get good statistics, but there's no question that it is a problem of considerable magnitude.")

The subcommittee said a solution to the drug problem would come only with the withdrawal of U.S. troops from South Vietnam.

Hagan and his subcommittee compiled their report following four months of intermittent hearings and a two-week fact-finding tour of Southeast Asia in January.

According to the subcommittee, as many as 20% of the servicemen in South Vietnam were using marijuana regularly. In South Vietnam, the subcommittee reported, drugs were "more plentiful than cigarettes or chewing gum."

The panel said there was no indication of greater use of drugs in the military among blacks, whites or any other ethnic group.

Forty GIs were reported to have died in Vietnam in 1970 of drug-related causes. In all, military sources said 160 drug-related deaths occurred in the armed forces in 1970.

Another Congressional report on drug abuse among GIs was compiled by a study mission that toured Europe, the Middle East and Far East and Indochina. Its findings were made public May 25 in a report to the House Foreign Affairs Committee.

The investigating team said heroin addiction had become so great a problem among military personnel in Vietnam that its only effective solution was to withdraw all U.S. troops from Southeast Asia. Because of bribery and corruption, the report said, there was little hope that the heroin traffic could be effectively halted in the near future.

The report, written principally by Rep. Robert H. Steele (R, Conn.), told of widespread graft, corruption and bribery among high government and military officials of Laos, Thailand and South Vietnam. Steele was assisted in preparing the report by Rep. Morgan F. Murphy (D, Ill.), Dr. John Brady, staff consultant for the House Foreign Affairs Committee, and Fred Flott, a State Department officer who escorted the group during its nine-nation tour.

In a sequel to its May 25 report, Steele's investigating team urged May 27 that the Army be required to identify and rehabilitate before discharge the soaring numbers of servicemen who had become addicted to heroin in Vietnam.

The House team estimated that there were 26,000–39,000 American heroin addicts in South Vietnam.

Nixon pledges action—At a televised White House news conference June 1, President Nixon pledged to undertake a "national offensive" to counter the drug problem. He said he would meet with Pentagon officials to discuss ways in which the government's military and health apparatus could be mobilized to help addicted soldiers.

The President said part of his program would include discussions with the South Vietnamese government, which he said had a "special responsibility to halting the supply of hard drugs."

Nixon said his program would have four major parts—halting the flow of drug traffic at their foreign sources, intensified prosecution of drug traffickers,

initiating a "massive" educational drive in the U.S. and the rehabilitation of addicts. The President said he believed that addicted servicemen should have the opportunity to be treated before being discharged from the military, but he did not say whether that would be required.

He noted that the addiction problem in Vietnam was especially aggravated by the low cost of heroin.

Military moves to counter addiction— Even before President Nixon announced his plans for a "national offensive" against drugs, the Defense Department was taking steps to fight drug addiction among U.S. military personnel in Vietnam.

Defense Secretary Melvin R. Laird asked the South Vietnamese government May 21 to take stronger measures to stop narcotics from reaching American servicemen. Laird said he had personally informed South Vietnamese President Nguyen Van Thieu and other Vietnamese officials that "we expect them to deal with this problem much more effectively than they have." He said the problem was critical because of the low cost and accessibility of hard narcotics.

The U.S. military command in Saigon declared May 25 that all Vietnamese pharmacies were off limits to American military personnel. U.S. officials said the Army's decision was prompted by the availability without prescription of certain drugs that would require prescriptions in the U.S. Barbiturates and amphetamines were the targets of the U.S. ban.

The command also said steps would be taken to place off limits "all known bars, hotels and other business establishments and areas where there is evidence that selling, pushing or trafficking of narcotics or dangerous drugs take place."

There were also continued efforts to have servicemen voluntarily admit their addiction without facing the threat of disciplinary action.

The Navy announced May 30 that it was inaugurating a 30-day amnesty program to rehabilitate drug addicts among Navy personnel stationed in

South Vietnam. A similar program was established by the Air Force March 8.

Details of the Navy program were announced by Adm. Elmo R. Zumwalt, chief of U.S. Naval Operations, at a news conference in Saigon. Zumwalt said the plan, to begin June 1, would enable those sailors who wanted to "kick the habit" to do so without prejudicing their Navy careers.

Everett G. Hopson, a retired Air Force colonel, was named by the Defense Department June 1 to coordinate its increased efforts to curb drug abuse in the armed forces.

GI addiction below estimates—President Nixon's special adviser on narcotics said July 17 that initial tests of U.S. servicemen leaving Vietnam showed that 4.5% of them were using heroin. The percentage reported by Dr. Jerome Jaffe was considerably lower than other estimates that put the figure at 10–20%.

Jaffe reported the figures to President Nixon after returning from a 10-day trip to South Vietnam, Japan and Hong Kong. He met with Nixon July 17 at the Western White House in San Clemente, Calif., and later told newsmen that the President was pleased with recent progress against GI hard-drug use, but he believed "that it remains a major problem."

The 4.5% figure came from testing of 22,000 American GIs departing Vietnam, although, Jaffe said, they did not represent a cross-section of servicemen in Vietnam. He also said that there was no proof that the drug users were addicts.

U.S. officials close to the antidrug drive were reported July 28 to disagree with Jaffe's estimate. The officials said the figures given by Jaffe did not include GIs who had been arrested or those who, in the hope of beating the urinalysis test, stopped using heroin a few days before they were due to be shipped home. The estimates of the number of GI heroin users in Vietnam varied, but most often the figure was put at 10%–15%.

All Vietnam GIs to get heroin test—The Army's Vietnam command in Saigon announced July 28 that it was expanding its drive against narcotics by having virtually all U.S. servicemen in South Vietnam tested for heroin use.

Previously, only soldiers being processed just before they left for the U.S. at the end of their duty tours were being tested.

According to published reports, the command decided to test all servicemen after learning that some GIs were extending their tour of duty to remain in South Vietnam because of their addiction and the ease with which they could obtain heroin.

The U.S. command said it would refuse to extend the tours of duty of those "found to be drug users or drug dependent." Those servicemen, the command said, would be sent to treatment centers and then be returned to the U.S. at the end of their normal duty tour.

Panels probe GI addiction—Senate and House subcommittees opened hearings July 30 and Aug. 2 into the problem.

Dr. Jerome H. Jaffe, President Nixon's special assistant on narcotics and dangerous drugs, told a special subcommittee of the Senate Government Operations Committee July 30 that 5.5% of servicemen in South Vietnam had shown some signs of heroin addiction.

Jaffe told the panel that the 5.5% figure might not actually mirror the true depth of heroin addiction by U.S. military personnel because the drug identification tests were being given mainly to soldiers ending their tours of duty.

The panel's July 30 session was also marked by criticism by Democrats and Republicans on the subcommittee over the Nixon Administration's apparent unwillingness to identify those South Vietnamese officials said to be trafficking in drugs.

Attorney General John N. Mitchell had informed the subcommittee in June that a list of South Vietnamese officials believed to be drug dealers was on file at the U.S. embassy in Saigon and that he saw no objection to providing the subcommittee with the information in executive session. As of July 30, the panel had not received the list.

At hearings opened Aug. 2 by the House's Public Health and Environment subcommittee of the Interstate and Foreign Commerce Committee, Jaffe said servicemen were trying to confuse the results of their drug identification tests.

Jaffe said GIs were "substituting everything from beer to their grandmother's urine in these urinalysis tests."

Jaffe also said that some soldiers were avoiding detection by quitting their heroin habit a week before the drug test.

New GI tests cut addict figures—The Pentagon released new figures on GI drug use in Vietnam Sept. 4 showing that about one-third of those servicemen identified in earlier tests as heroin users were not taking the drug.

According to the Pentagon's first set of figures, 5.3%–5.4% of those GIs tested by urinalysis were found to be heroin users. The tests had begun June 19.

The Pentagon's second set of figures showed however, that, after testing by a secondary urinalysis technique, 3.6% of the 70,621 servicemen screened since the tests began had been positively confirmed as having heroin in their urine at the time of testing.

A Pentagon spokesman said the first testing procedure apparently showed positive results when substances other than heroin were detected. The second testing technique, he said, was more discriminating.

Army drug program lauded—A six-man inspection team representing the White House's office for drug abuse prevention lauded the Army's program for treating addicted GIs Oct. 1 following a two-week stay in Vietnam. The group called the soldiers' chances of breaking their drug habits through the Army program excellent. Five of the six men on the team were former addicts.

Speaking for the group, Dr. Jerome K. Jaffe, head of the new White House unit, said they had found the military drug treatment staffs "receptive" to their recommendations for emphasis on amnesty programs, improving the methods of detecting drug users and extending the length of treatment.

Jaffe told the Special Subcommittee on Drug Abuse in the Armed Services Oct. 12 that the rate of drug abuse among U.S. soldiers in Vietnam seemed to be leveling off at 5.1%. He reported that 103,279 men had been tested in Vietnam in the last three months. Of those tested, 5,214—or 5.1%—showed traces

of opiates in their urinalysis. Most of those were in the Army. Jaffe laid the Army's higher figures to growing boredom and the "easy availability" of drugs near military bases. Jaffe said that Air Force bases and Navy installations tended to be more isolated.

Jaffe said studies showed that only 10% of military addicts were taking heroin intravenously. He added that the studies indicated that drug abuse among U.S. servicemen was not as widespread "as we had been led to expect last March and April." At that time, there were reports that nearly 15% were using drugs regularly.

'Fragging' incidents up. The Pentagon April 20 confirmed reports that more American GIs in Vietnam were using fragmentation grenades against their fellow soldiers. The incidents, known as "fragging," more than doubled in 1970 over the previous year.

The Pentagon said 209 fragging incidents were reported in Vietnam in 1970, up from 96 in 1969. No records were kept for previous years. According to the statistics, 34 men were killed in 1970 fragging incidents and 39 in 1969.

The figures were released by the Pentagon after Sen. Mike Mansfield (D, Mont.) told the Senate April 20 about the murder of a young West Point graduate who was killed in his sleep when an enlisted man rolled a fragmentation grenade into the officer's billet. Mansfield said the young officer, a native of Montana, "was murdered by a serviceman— a fellow GI." Mansfield called fraggings "just another outgrowth of this mistaken, this tragic conflict."

Service club thefts. A military jury of five officers at the Redstone Arsenal near Huntsville, Ala. convicted M. Sgt. William E. Higdon June 10 of stealing funds and taking kickbacks while running Army service clubs in Vietnam.

Higdon was sentenced June 11 to a dishonorable discharge and fined $25,-000.

The military jury convicted Higdon of stealing $7,200 in cigarette promotion funds and taking $723 in kickbacks while operating a club at Long Binh in 1967 and 1968.

Higdon and seven other persons, including the Army's former highest ranking enlisted man, ex-Sgt. Maj. of the Army William O. Wooldridge, had been indicted Feb. 17 by a federal grand jury in Los Angeles on charges of conspiring to defraud noncommissioned officers' clubs in South Vietnam. The indictments were an outgrowth of a Senate investigation that began in September 1969.

Brother of Hanoi aide defects. Saigon authorities disclosed June 5 the capture of the brother of the former North Vietnamese ambassador to France and his subsequent defection to the South Vietnamese side. The defector was Mai Van So, 53, twin brother of Mai Van Bo, who had been recalled to Hanoi from his Paris post in December 1970.

So, a former Viet Cong officer and logistical chief, had been captured by U.S. troops in December 1969 in Haunghia Province, north of Saigon. In presenting So at a news conference June 7, the government announced that his seizure and defection had been kept secret because he had been assigned to "concrete missions" for the government. So said his disillusionment with the Viet Cong and the good treatment by his American captors influenced his decision to defect.

Publisher released. Former newspaper publisher Nguyen Lau was released from a Saigon prison Nov. 11 after serving a sentence of two years and seven months for having contact with a Viet Cong agent. Lau was freed under the South Vietnamese government's Oct. 31 amnesty for nearly 3,000 prisoners of war and Viet Cong suspects.

Peking-Hanoi aid pact. A Communist Chinese-North Vietnamese aid pact for 1972 was signed in Hanoi Sept. 28 at the conclusion of a five-day visit to Hanoi by a Peking economic and military mission headed by Li Hsien-nien, a deputy premier and Politburo member.

Details of the accord were not disclosed, but the special grants included in the latest agreement were expected to bring Peking's assistance to North Vietnam above the $200 million–$250 million it normally provided annually.

China had promised North Vietnam March 10 that it would provide "all-out" assistance "should United States imperialism go down the road of expanding its war of aggression in Indochina."

The statement was contained in a joint communiqué based on meetings Premier Chou En-lai had held with North Vietnamese officials in Hanoi March 5–8. The communiqué, signed by Chou and North Vietnamese Premier Pham Van Dong, said Peking vowed "to give support to the Vietnamese people and all the three peoples of Indochina in their war against United States aggression and for national salvation."

Chou had said on his arrival in Hanoi March 5 that China had "made adequate preparations" to counter the "serious threat" the U.S. was "posing" to his country by "willfully enlarging their aggressive war in the Indochina area." Peking, he warned, "is prepared ideologically and militarily to eliminate any enemy that endangers its territory."

In welcoming Chou, Premier Pham Van Dong said the visit, not announced in advance, was "an event of paramount importance" at a time when the U.S. was "recklessly engaging in new military adventures." Chou told the North Vietnamese: "Don't thank us for our aid . . . It is you who aid us by fighting in the front lines of anti-imperialist struggle."

Chou was accompanied to Hanoi by a delegation of seven government officials, including two military men—Yeh Chien-ying, a deputy chairman of the Central Committee's Military Commission, and Chiu Huit-so, a deputy chief of the General Staff for rear services.

U.S. Secretary of State William P. Rogers said in Washington March 9 that Chou had visited Hanoi "to give some comfort to the North Vietnamese because they have been suffering setbacks" in Laos. Rogers discounted any increased threat of Chinese intervention in the war. The secretary conceded, however, that the presence of "logistics personnel" in the Chinese delegation indicated that Peking "will try to help resupply the North Vietnamese because they have taken some very severe losses in terms of supplies."

China reiterated its support of North Vietnam in a communique made public Nov. 26. The joint statement demanded that the U.S. stop fighting in Vietnam, Cambodia and Laos and withdraw its support of those anti-Communist regimes. The communique was signed by Premier Dong and Premier Chou En-lai.

A North Vietnamese delegation headed by Premier Pham Van Dong conducted high-level talks with Chinese officials in Peking Nov. 21–25.

More than 500,000 persons had turned out in Peking to welcome the arrival of the North Vietnamese delegation Nov. 20. The Hanoi representatives met with Communist Party Chairman Mao Tsetung Nov. 22.

Dong, who returned to Hanoi Nov. 26, was accompanied by Foreign Minister Nguyen Duy Trinh, Deputy Defense Minister Duy Quy Hai, and Li Ban, vice minister of foreign trade.

North Vietnamese elections. North Vietnamese citizens went to the polls April 11 for the first time since 1964 to elect a new National Assembly. A total of 529 candidates contested 420 seats. The term of the current legislature, elected in 1964, had expired in 1968, but remained in office because of the war. Among the deputies elected in the latest balloting were President Ton Duc Thang, Premier Pham Van Dong, Le Duan, first secretary of the ruling Workers (Communist) party, and Truong Chinh, chairman of the National Assembly.

North Vietnamese floods. North Vietnam's war effort was threatened and its food crop and industry suffered heavy damage in floods that began to sweep the northern part of the country in early July. The Communist party newspaper Nhan Dan acknowledged Aug. 30 that the level of the Red River and other streams had risen to an "unprecedented level."

A Hanoi broadcast Sept. 2 said food crops were destroyed, roads washed out and communications disrupted. Premier Pham Van Dong said military and civilian forces had "in the main triumphed over the flood and warded off a big disaster." Dong did not give casualty figures or damage estimates. But he conceded that the flood was "even bigger than that of 1945" in which an estimated one million people died.

South Vietnam Sept. 6 offered North Vietnam $50,000 for the flood victims. Hanoi rejected the money Sept. 8 as "shameless dupery," which it said was aimed at diverting attention from "inhuman war crimes" committed by U.S. forces against the South Vietnamese people. Private relief efforts were reported under way in Saigon Sept. 10 to aid the flood victims.

Viet Cong-Yugoslav accord. A joint communique issued in Belgrade May 22 announced that Yugoslavia and the Viet Cong's Provisional Revolutionary Government of the Republic of South Vietnam (PRG) had decided to establish diplomatic relations at the ambassadorial level. The statement followed the conclusion of official talks between Yugoslav Foreign Minister Mirko Tepavac and PRG Foreign Minister Mrs. Nguyen Thi Binh. Yugoslavia had extended formal recognition to the PRG in June 1969.

Sweden aids Viet Cong. Foreign Minister Torsten Nilsson announced May 27 that Sweden was expanding its assistance to the Viet Cong. He reported an initial donation of $550,000 worth of material, largely comprising medical supplies and hospital equipment. Nilsson said Sweden planned to make similar contributions to the civilian populations of Laos and Cambodia.

Index

Note: This index follows the Western usage in regard to most Vietnamese names. A Vietnamese individual, therefore, would be listed not under his family name but under the last section of his full name. *E.g.,* Mrs. Nguyen Thi Binh would be indexed thus: BINH, Mrs. Nguyen Thi (not NGUYEN Thi Binh, Mrs.). Exceptions are usually the cases of monks or others (*e.g.,* Ho Chi Minh) who use adopted names; such persons are generally listed under the first sections of their names (HO Chi Minh, not MINH, Ho Chi).

A

ABERNATHY, Rev. Ralph D.—177, 182
ABRAMS, Gen. Creighton W.—4, 10, 38, 64, 69, 118, 226
ABZUG, Rep. Bella (D., N.Y.)—43, 130, 207-8. Antiwar protests—173, 177, 180, 184, 188
ACHESON, Dean—137
AERIAL Warfare:
    Defoliation—13-4, 207, 226
    North Vietnam—75-6, 95-6
    U.S. bombings—175; Cambodia—13, 16-7, 35, 59-61, 67, 72-3, 78, 87-8, 91-2, 94; helicopter use—17, 25, 28, 30, 34, 86, 92, 94; involvement survey—87-8; Laos—2, 5, 13-7, 21-2, 25-6, 28, 30-1, 33-7, 39-40, 42, 65, 67, 85-7, 91; North Vietnam & DMZ—5, 13-5, 39, 58, 62, 65, 67-8, 70-2, 79-87, 96-7, 154-6, 160, 164, 166-7; support of South Vietnamese forces—2, 5, 13, 63-5, 70-1, 86-9, 91-2
    Reconnaissance flights—14, 62, 65, 68, 84, 87, 91
AGENCE France-Presse—216
AGENCY for International Development (AID), U.S.—118
AGNEW, Spiro T.—46, 103, 113. Protestors—101, 177-8, 184
AHMAD, Eqbal—191-2
AIKEN, Sen. George (R., Vt.)—44, 103
AIRBASES—See names
AIR Force, U.S.—15, 96, 196, 230. Antiwar protests—See under DISSENT, U.S. Drug problem—See under 'D'
ALBERT, Rep. Carl (D., Okla.)—45, 103
ALIOTO, Joseph A.—179
ALSOP, Joseph—6
AMERICAN Association for the Advancement of Science—207, 226
AMERICAN Bar Association (ABA)—188

AMERICAN Broadcasting Co. (ABC-TV)—27, 105-6, 134, 203
AMERICAN Civil Liberties Union (ACLU)—185-7, 194
AMERICAN Friends (Quakers) Service Committee—48, 181
AMERICAN Society of Newspaper Editors—104
ANDERSON, Robert T.—197
ANDERSON, Dr. William A.—193
ANDERSON, Rep. William R. (D., Tenn.)—191
AN Quang (Buddhist group)—211, 217, 219, 222
ANTHIS, Maj. Gen. Rollen H.—155
ANTI-Communist People's Movement for Election Participation (South Vietnam)—212
ARENDS, Rep. Leslie (R., Ill.)—117
ARIZONA—182
ARIZONA State University—182
ARKANSAS—202
ARMY, U.S.—33, 89
    Casualties— 1-2, 13, 15, 28, 30-2, 34-5, 39-41, 60, 63-71, 80-1, 84-5, 89, 92, 98, 112. Defoliation—13-4, 207, 226. Draft-101, 109, 112, 119. Drug problem—226-31. Fragging incidents—231. Pay increase—101, 109. Scandal—231-2. Troop withdrawals—1, 3, 16, 48, 66-7, 80; build-ups—158-63, 165-6, 169-70; strength—144-5. War crimes—199-209
    Americal Division—15, 40, 84, 175, 205, 209. Green Berets—208-9. Medical Service Corps—207. Security forces (Vietnamization program)—4. 1st Air Cavalry Unit—178. 1st Cavalry Division (Airmobile)—89. 5th Infantry Division—25, 80. 5th Mechanized Division—72. 17th Air Cavalry—27. 82d Airborne Division—169. 173d Airborne Brigade—80, 209

ASHAU Valley, South Vietnam—64-5, 68, 80
ASIAN Scholars, Committee of Concerned—114
ASSOCIATED Press (AP)—17, 41, 46, 125
AUER, Lt. Steven—207
AUSTRALIA—55, 84, 115, 223

B

BACLIEU Province, South Vietnam—212
BADILLO, Rep. Herman (D., N.Y.)—177, 188
BAEZ, Joan—178, 196
BAHO, South Vietnam: Marine outpost—81
BAILEY, F. Lee—205
BAITHUONG, North VIetnam—96
BALL, George W.—124, 133, 156, 161-2
BALLARD, Leonard H.—46
BAMNAL, Cambodia—91
BAN, Li—233
BAN Dong, Laos—40
BAN Houei Sai, Laos—23, 75
BAN Khot, Laos: Government airstrip—95
BANKS, 2d Lt. Norman—207
BAN Na, Laos—36
BAN Nhik, Laos—77
BAO Dai—137
BARAY, Cambodia—93
BARKER Jr., Lt. Col. Frank A.—200
BARNES, Maj. Gen. John—209
BAYH, Sen. Birch (D., Ind.)—107, 188
BEALL Jr., Sen. Glenn (R., Md.)—101
BECKER, CWO Stephen J.—209
BELL, Beverly—191-2
BELSON, Judge James A.—183
BEN Gnik, Laos—85
BENTSEN, Sen. Lloyd (D., Tex.)—111
BERGER, Samuel D.—214
BERRIGAN, Rev. Daniel—191-2
BERRIGAN, Rev. Philip F.—190-2
BHAN Na, Laos—28
BIBLE, Sen. Alan (D., Nev.)—111
BICKEL, Alexander M.—122
BILLMAN, Rev. Milo M.—193
BINGHAM, Rep. Jonathan B. (D., N.Y.)—108, 123, 174
BINH, Col. Nguyen Khac—219
BINH, Mrs. Nguyen Thi—116, 233. Peace efforts—48-9, 53-6
BINHDINH Province, South Vietnam—15, 225
BINHTHUAN Province, South Vietnam—212
BINHTHUY, South Vietnam: U.S. airbase—66
BLACK, Justice Hugo L.—131-3
BLACKMUN, Justice Harry A.—132-3
BOLOVEN Plateau, Laos—2, 21-3, 26, 75-6, 85, 95
BONG, Nguyen Van—222
BON Karai Pass (Laotian-North Vietnamese border)—14
BOSTON Globe (newspaper)—125-6, 131, 142, 170-1
BOTEIN, Justice Bernard—188

BOUAM Long, Laos—76
BOUDIN, Leonard—192
BOYLE, Peter—194
BOYLE, Richard—89
BRADY, Dr. John—229
BRADY, Phil—228
BRAY 3d, Charles W.—90
BRENNAN Jr., Justice William J.—131-2, 189
BROCK, Sen. William E. (R., Tenn.)—101
BROOKE, Sen. Edward W. (R., Mass.)—7, 104, 219
BRUCE, David K. E.—47-50, 53-6
BUCKALEW, Edward—193
BUCKLEY, Sen. James L. (R., N.Y.)—106, 116
BUDDHISTS—211, 217, 219, 221-2
BULGARIA—116
BUNDY, McGeorge—108, 153, 155-7, 159, 161-2
BUNDY, William P.—143, 150
BUNKER, Ellsworth—4, 118, 219, 222. South Vietnamese elections—214-6. Drug problem—227
BURGER, Chief Justice Warren E.—132-3
BURNS, Maj. Gen. James H.—137
BURROWS, Larry—27
BYRD, Sen. Robert C. (D., W.Va.)—9, 102, 105, 111

C

CALHOUN, Maj. Charles C.—206
CALIFORNIA—203. Demonstrations—43, 176, 178-9, 182, 196-7
CALIFORNIA, University of—42. Santa Barbara campus—43
CALLEY Jr., 1st Lt. William L.—2, 183, 199-205, 208
CAMBODIA—55
    Allied military activity—5, 13, 15-7, 20, 59-61, 72-4, 78-9, 88, 92-4; U.S. bombing—13, 16-7, 35, 59-61, 72-3, 88, 91-2; troop withdrawals—16. Arrests—79
    Civilian casualties—21, 60, 79, 88, 91, 93; atrocities—61, 79; evacuation—79. Communist activity—74, 78-9, 88, 90-1, 93-4
    Foreign relations & aid—90, 94; U.S.—90
    Government forces: casualties—18, 21, 60-1, 74, 90-1, 93; military activity—2, 15-9, 21, 59-61, 74, 79, 88, 90-4
    Peace negotiations—74-5. Political & domestic developments—62, 90, 94
    Refugees—93
    Sihanouk—See under 'S'
CAMP McCoy (Wis.)—194
CAMRANH, South Vietnam: U.S. airbase—66
CAMRANH Bay, South Vietnam—68-9. Government base—15. U.S. base—84
CANADA—30, 179
CANHAM, Erwin D.—126
CANNON, Sen. Howard (D., Nev.)—111

CAO, Sen. Huynh Van—219
CAREY, Rep. Hugh L. (D., N.Y.)—45
CAREY, John—208
CARSON, Everett B.—174
CARTER, Gov. Jimmy (D., Ga.)—202
CASE, Sen. Clifford P. (R., N.J.)—104, 108
CATHOLICS, Roman—190-3, 197
CEASEFIRES—See under PEACE Efforts
CENTRAL Intelligence Agency, U.S. (CIA)—23, 54, 118, 125, 134–5, 138, 140–1, 151–2, 160, 167, 208–9. Laos—28, 77, 82–3, 117
CHAMPASSAK, Sissouk Na—22, 77, 95
CHASE, Spc. 4 Thomas M.—194
CHENG Heng—62, 74, 90
CHICAGO Sun-Times (newspaper)—125-6, 138, 142, 147–8
CHIEU Hoi (Open Arms) program—58
CHINA (Communist), People's Republic of— 48, 55, 114, 136–7. Aid to North Vietnam— 232. Laos—28–9, 42, 83. U.S. incursions— 28–9, 87, 97–8
CHINA (Nationalist), Republic of—114, 137
CHINH, Truong—233
CHIU Huit-so—232
CHOMSKY, Noam—43
CHOU En-lai—55, 114, 232-3
CHRAN Changvar, Cambodia: Naval base— 18
CHRISTIAN Science Monitor (newspaper)— 126, 136–7, 149
CHUOP, Hell—62
CHUP, Cambodia—59, 92-4
CHURCH, Sen. Frank (D., Ida.)—20–1, 27, 97, 103
CHURCHILL, Winston—138
CHUYEN, Thai Khac—208-9
CICCOLLELA, Maj. Gen. Richard—195
CITIZENS for Alternatives Now—107
CLARK, Roger A.—127
CLERGY & Laymen Concerned about Vietnam—48
CLIFFORD, Clark M.—97, 169, 171, 187–8
COFFIN, Judge Frank M.—190
COLBY, William E.—107, 225
COLLINS, Judy—48
COLORADO—182
COLUMBIA, District of—See DISTRICT of Columbia
COLUMBIA Broadcasting System (CBS)— 27, 106, 124, 128, 133–4
COLUMBIA University (N.Y.)—43
COMMAGER, Henry Steele—11
COMMITTEE of Concerned Asian Scholars—114
COMMITTEE of Liaison With Families of Servicemen Detained in North Vietnam (U.S. antiwar group)—58
COMMUNITY Defense & Local Development Plan (South Vietnam)—224
CONCERNED Officers Movement (COM)— 195, 207
CONGRESS, U.S.—See under UNITED States

CONNALLY, John B.—222
CONNER, Lt. Gen. Albert O.—205
CONSIDINE, Maureen C.—193
CON Son Island, South Vietnam—225
CONSTELLATION (U.S. aircraft carrier)— 196
CONYERS, Rep. John (D., Mich.)—177
COOK, Sen. Marlow W. (R., Ky.)—111
COOK-Stevens Amendment—111
COOPER Jr., Cornelius McNeil—194
COOPER, Sen. John Sherman (R., Ky.)—20– 1, 27, 103, 115
CORAL Sea (U.S. aircraft carrier)—196-7
CORMAN, Rep. James C. (D., Calif.)—45
CORNELL University (Ithaca, N.Y.)—87-8
CORTRIGHT, Spc. 4 David B.—195
COTTON, Sen. Norris (R., N.H.)—104
COTTONE, S. John—192
COUMING, Paul Bernard—193
CRANE, Dr. David G.—201
CRANSTON, Sen. Alan (D., Calif.)—112
CRONKITE, Walter—128
CRUMB, Spc. 4 Jan—173
CULVER, Capt. Thomas S.—196
CUNHAM, Anne—193
CUSHMAN, Maj. Gen. John H.—69

D

DAGENS Nyheter (Swedish newspaper)—56
DAM Be, Cambodia—94
DAN, Nguyen Trieu—51-2
DANANG, South Vietnam—211, 216. Government base—15. U.S. bases—66, 69, 71, 84, 158-9
DANE, Barbara—194
DANIEL 3d, Capt. Aubrey M.—201, 204
DARST, Charles Lee—193
DARST, David—193
DAVIDON, William—191-2
DAVIDSON, Thomas—191-2
DAVIS, Angela—44
DAVIS, Rennie—43, 107, 180, 189
DEFENSE, Department of (U.S.)—See under UNITED States
DEFOLIATION—13-4, 207, 226
De GAULLE, Charles—147-8
DELLINGER, David—43, 186, 188-9
DELLUMS, Rep. Ronald V. (D., Calif.)—174, 180, 207-8
DEMILITARIZED Zone (DMZ) (North-South Vietnamese buffer area): Aerial warfare—See under 'A.' Other fighting—13, 69– 72, 81-2
DEMOCRATIC Party, U.S.: Dissent & controversy—8-9, 105-7, 111. Policy Council— 44
DEWEY Canyon II, Operation—25
DIEM, Ngo Dinh—125, 138–42, 144, 149, 214, 221. Coup d'état—145-8
DILLON, C. Douglas—140
DINHTUONG Province, South Vietnam— 225

DISSENT, U.S.:
    Arrests & convictions—42-4, 175, 177-87, 189-94, 196; court action—174, 181, 183-5, 187, 189-90, 193, 195
    Congress: arrests—184; Cambodia—19-21; draft extension—101, 109, 112; conscientious objector status—101, 109; foreign aid—118; Laos—26-7, 44-5, 76-7, 83; Pentagon papers—123-4, 130-1 (see also PENTAGON Papers); Presidential war-making powers—11, 20, 107-8; POWs—111-2; pullout-date controversy—1, 8-9, 45, 101-6, 110-2, 117; Vietnam resolutions—7, 20, 106-8, 110-1, 117-8 (see also specific names); war crimes—207-8; Calley trial—201-3; South Vietnamese elections—219
    Demonstrations: antiwar—42-4, 46, 107, 173-82, 194 (see also specific cities); Calley conviction—202-3; campus unrest—42-4, 182; draft records break-in—192-3; nationwide—180, 182, 189; war supporters—183, 186-89
        Government protesters—180
        Labor unions—43, 176. Lobby & political action—181, 188
        Military—173-6, 189, 194-6; desertions—195; draft resistance & prosecutions—196-7
        Presidential war-making powers controversy—11, 107-8, 112-3, 190
        Religious groups—179, 190-2, 197
DISTRICT of Columbia (Washington)—127. Antiwar demonstrations—42-3, 46, 107, 173, 176-83, 189
DIXON, Eugene F.—193
DONALDSON, Brig. Gen. John W.—209
DONG, Maj. Gen. Du—34
DONG, Pham Van—232-3
DONGHA, South Vietnam—35
DONG Hene, Laos—75
DONGHOI, North Vietnam—96. Airbase—87
DOUGLAS, Justice William O.—131-3, 189
DOW, Rep. John G. (D., N.Y.)—130
DOYLE, Rev. Michael J.—193
DRAFT—See under ARMY, U.S. and DISSENT, U.S.
DRINAN, Rep. Robert (D., Mass.)—188
DRUG Problem: GI addiction—226-7; investigations—228-31; rehabilitation drives—229-31; South Vietnamese involvement—227-9
DUAN, Le—233
DUC, Ngo Cong—213, 216
DUCDUC, South Vietnam—63
DUCMY, South Vietnam: Government training center—66
DULLES, John Foster—138, 140-1
DUNKELBERGER, Lt. (jg.) Peter—207
DUNSTON, Spc. 4 James L.—209
DZU, Maj. Gen. Ngo—63, 218, 227-8

E

EAGLETON, Sen. Thomas F. (D., Mo.)—7
EAST Coast Conspiracy to Save Lives—193
EDMONDSON, Rep. Ed (D., Okla.)—203

EDWARDS, Maj. Henry E.—201
EGAN, Joques—191-2
EHRLICHMAN, John—204
EISENHOWER, Dwight D.—138-41
ELLENDER, Sen. Allen J. (D., La.)—130
ELLSBERG, Daniel—128-9, 135
ELLSBERG, Mrs. Patricia—128
ENOS, Spc. 5 John N.—209
EXPRESS Wieczorny (Polish newspaper)—116

F

FACE The Nation (CBS-TV program)—107
FAIRBAIRN, David—223
FALK, Prof. Richard A.—108
FANNIN, Sen. Paul (R., Ariz.)—180
FEDERAL Bureau of Investigation (FBI), U.S.—128, 180, 190, 192-4
FEDERAL Employes for Peace—180
FEIFFER, Jules—194
FELLOWSHIP of Reconciliation—48, 181
FINDLEY, Rep. Paul (R., Ill.)—174
FINO, Spc. 5 Dominic—209
FIRE Base Aloui, Laos—39
FIRE Base Charlie 2, South Vietnam—72
FIRE Base Fuller, South Vietnam—70-1
FIRE Base Lolo—39
FIRE Base Lonely, South Vietnam—64
FIRE Base Sarge, South Vietnam—70, 82
FIRE Base Sophia, Laos—37
FIRST Amendment (U.S. Constitution)—131-3
FISHOOK, Cambodia—59
FLORIDA—203
FLOTT, Fred—229
FLYNT, Rep. John J. (D., Ga.)—101
FONDA, Jane—194, 196, 208
FONT, 1st Lt. Louis P.—194, 207-8
FORD, Rep. Gerald R. (R., Mich.)—32, 45, 117
FORD, Rep. William D. (D., Mich.)—67
FORDI, Rev. Peter D.—193
FORSYTH, Keith William—193
FOX, Capt. Edward G.—207
FRANCE—55, 115, 117, 136-8
FRANCHEZ, David—178
FRANKLIN, Howard Bruce—42
FRANKLIN, Col J. Ross—209
FREEDOM of Information Act (1966)—130, 135
FRIEDHEIM, Jerry W.—17, 19, 32-3, 35-6, 62, 226
FRIEDMAN, Leon—189
FROINES, John—180
FUJII, Dennis—30
FULBRIGHT, Sen. J.W. (D., Ark.)—6-7, 20-1, 97, 101-2, 108, 118. Laos—27, 45, 77, 83. Pentagon papers—122-4, 128
FUQUA, Rep. Don (D., Fla.)—201-2

G

GAI, Brig. Gen. Vu Van—72
GALLUP Poll—9, 46, 106, 203
GAMBRELL, Sen. David (D., Ga.)—111

GAVIN, Lt. Col. David C.—206
GEDEN, Spc. 4 Stephen G.—194
GELB, Leslie H.—135-6
GENEVA Convention (1954)—138-41
GERMANY, West—115, 117, 195
GESELL, Judge Gerhard A.—127, 134-5
GETTYS, Maj. Gen. Charles—209
GEORGE Washington University—42
GEORGIA—202
GIA, Pham Huu—213
GIAI, Brig. Gen. Vu Van—65
GIBBONS, Harold J.—43, 177
GIOCONDO, Michael John—193
GLICK, John Theodore—192
GOLDMAN, Capt. Leonard G.—206-7
GOLDWATER, Sen. Barry (R., Ariz.)—107, 124, 154
GOOD, Robert Glenn—193
GOODELL, Charles E.—46
GOODPASTER, Lt. Gen. Andrew J.—162
GOODWIN, Guy M.—193
GORDON, Jerry—43, 189
GOULD, Elliott—194
GOULDING, Phil—171
GRADY, John Peter—193
GRAVEL, Sen. Mike (D., Alaska)—112, 130-1, 188
GREAT Britain—29, 55, 115, 117, 124, 140, 179, 196
GREENE, Judge Harold H.—181
GREGORY, Dick—194
GRIFFIN, Sen. Robert P. (R., Mich.)—102, 131
GRISWOLD, Erwin N.—127
GROMYKO, Andrei A.—56
GUINN, Lt. Col. William D.—206
GULF of Siam—16-7
GULF of Tonkin—121, 124, 129-30, 151, 153, 155, 189
GUMBLETON, Most Rev. Thomas J.—197
GURFEIN, Judge Murray I.—122-3, 126-7

H

HABIB, Philip C.—57
HAGAN, Rep. G. Elliott (D., Ga.)—228
HAI, Duy Quy—233
HAIG Jr., Brig. Gen. Alexander M.—222
HAINES Jr., Gen. Ralph E.—208
HALLECK, Judge Charles W.—183
HAMNGHI, South Vietnam: Government post—40
HANNAH, Dr. John A.—118
HANNAN, Most Rev. Philip M.—197
HANSEN, Sen. Clifford P. (R., Wyo.)—101, 106
HARDY, Robert William—193
HARLAN, Justice John M.—132-3
HARRIMAN, W. Averell—9, 44, 49, 108, 124
HARRINGTON, Rep. Michael J. (D., Mass.)—7, 190
HARRIS, David—178, 196
HARRIS, Robert—42
HARRIS (Luis) Survey—9, 46, 203
HART Jr., Judge George L.—174

HARTKE, Sen. Vance (D., Ind.)—103, 106, 177-8, 182
HARVARD University—43-4
HATFIELD, Sen. Mark (R., Ore.)—7, 103-4, 106
HATINH Province, North Vietnam—84. Missile base—14
HEBERT, Rep. F. Edward (D., La.)—130
HELMS, Richard—208
HENDERSON, Col. Oren K.—200, 205-6
HENG, Cheng—62, 74, 90
HENKIN, Daniel Z.—228
HERBERT, Lt. Col. Anthony B.—209
HERMAN, Judge R. Dixon—191
HESS, Michael D.—122
HEUNG, Yoo Jae—223
HIEN, Lt. Col. Le Trung—73
HIEU, Maj. Gen. Nguyen Van—73
HIGDON, M. Sgt. William E.—231
HILDEBRAND, Maj. Leland L.—96
HILSMAN, Roger—125, 142, 147-8
HO Chi Minh—134, 136-8
HO Chi Minh Trail—2, 5, 41. U.S. bombing—10, 13-4, 21, 25, 28, 30-3, 35-6, 39-40, 64-5, 67, 79, 87, 96-7
HOFFMAN, Abbie—180, 186
HOLLINGS, Sen. Ernest F. (D., S.C.)—111
HOLYOAKE, Sir Keith—223
HONG Ha Ha, Laos: South Vietnamese artillery base—34
HOOVER, J. Edgar—190, 193
HOPE, Bob—58, 194
HOPSON, Everett G.—230
HORRIGAN, Jeremiah D.—193
HOUEI Kong, Laos—75-6
HOWARD, Col. Kenneth A.—205
HUE, South Vietnam—211-2
HUE, University of—212
HUGHES, Sen. Harold E. (D., Iowa)—45, 103, 105-6
HUIK, Jung Nae—113
HUMPHREY, Sen. Hubert H. (D., Minn.)—44, 105, 115, 124
HUNGARY—116
HUONG, Sen. Tran Van—213
HUTCHIN Jr., Lt. Gen. Claire E.—209
HUTTO, Sgt. Charles E.—206

I

IFSHIN, David—43
ILLINOIS—42, 182
INDIA—30
INGERSOLL, John E.—227
INNESS, Margaret Mary—193
IN Tam, Brig. Gen.—62
INTERNATIONAL Bank for Reconstruction & Development (World Bank)—124
INTERNATIONAL Control Commission (ICC) (Canada, India & Poland)—30, 66, 152
IOWA—42
IRONWORKERS Union: Local 361—183
IRWIN 2d, John N.—77

ITALY—115
IZVESTIA (Soviet government newspaper)—116

J

JACKSON, Sen. Henry M. (D., Wash.)—27, 105, 219
JACKSON State College (Miss.)—180
JACOBS Jr., Rep. Andrew (D., Ind.)—108
JACOBSON, George—225
JAFFE, Dr. Jerome—230-1
JAPAN—116
JAVITS, Sen. Jacob (R., N.Y.)—103, 106, 116, 203
JENMIN Jih Pao (Chinese Communist Party newspaper)—29, 53
JESUITS—193
JOHNSON, Arthur—175
JOHNSON, Capt. Dennis H.—206
JOHNSON, Maj. Kenneth R.—96
JOHNSON, Lyndon Baines—107. Pentagon papers—121, 125, 133, 142, 145, 148, 150, 152-3, 171; troop build-up—158-63, 160, 166-7; U.S. bombing—151, 154-6, 160, 166-7
JONES, Lt. Col. Franklin D.—201
JORDAN, Sen. Len B. (R., Ida.)—111
JULIAN, Anthony—125

K

KANDAL, Cambodia—79
KANDOL Chrum, Cambodia—72
KANSAS—202
KAPLAN, Douglas—189
KATTENBURG, Paul H.—148
KAUFMAN, Judge Irving R.—126
KENDIG, 2d Lt. Ed—207
KENNEDY, Sen. Edward M. (D., Mass.)—57, 89, 112, 116. Laos—44-5, 77. Protesters—173-4, 181, 183-4. Refugees—23, 88, 106-8
KENNEDY, John F.—125, 133, 141-5
KENNEDY, Col. Reid W.—199
KENNEDY, Robert F.—125
KENT, Lt. (jg) John—207
KENT State University (Ohio)—43, 180, 182
KERRY, John F.—107, 113, 173-7
KESSLER, Sgt. Bruce N.—175
KHANH, Gen. Nguyen—124-5, 149
KHANH, Trinh Quoc—222
KHESANH, South Vietnam—39-40. U.S. Marine base—21, 25, 28, 34-5, 37, 68
KHET Kandol, Cambodia—16
KHIEM, Tran Thien—213-4, 227
KHMER Rouge—16
KHOI, Dong Duc—218
KIENPHONG Province, South Vietnam—225
KING, Mrs. Coretta Scott—177
KING Jr., Rev. Dr. Martin Luther—177
KISSINGER, Henry A.—6, 32, 53, 114-5, 190, 193
KLEAH Sanday, Cambodia—93
KLEIN, Herb—6
KNIGHT Newspapers Inc.—126, 168

KNOKSY, Gen. Thongphanh—22, 36, 82
KOMPONG Ampil, Cambodia—74
KOMPONG Cham Province, Cambodia—59
KOMPONG Chamland, Cambodia—74
KOMPONG Seila, Cambodia: Government post—16
KOMPONG Som, Cambodia—59-61. Port—15-6
KOMPONG Thmar, Cambodia—93
KOMPONG Thom, Cambodia—90
KOMPONG Trach, Cambodia—72
KONTUM Province, South Vietnam—37
KOREA, People's Republic of (North)—137
KOREA, Republic of (South)—113, 137, 223
KOSTER, Maj. Gen. Samuel W.—206, 208
KOSYGIN, Aleksei N.—22, 29
KOTOUC, Capt. Eugene—201
KREK, Cambodia—92
KREPS, Spc. 4 Dannie E.—194
KRULAK, Maj. Gen. Victor C.—148
KUNSTLER, William—191
KY, Nguyen Cao—30, 52-3, 116, 149, 228. Elections—211-8, 221
KYES, Roger—139
KYODO (Japanese news agency)—21-2, 26

L

LABOR-University Alliance—43
LAICHAU Province, North Vietnam—87
LAIKHE, South Vietnam: Government airbase—80
LAIRD, Melvin R.—22, 57-8, 91, 122, 129, 189, 229. Cambodia—4, 17-20, 90. Laos—26-7, 36, 39. U.S. bombing—17-8, 97; troop withdrawals—4, 102-4
LAM, Lt. Gen. Hoang Xuan—28, 35, 41, 85, 218
LAM, Pham Dang—49, 51
LAM Son 719, Operation—25, 64
LAM Son 720, Operation—64
LANDING Zone Brown, Laos: Artillery base—37, 39
LANDRUM, Rep. Phil (D., Ga.)—101
LANE, Mark—208
LANGVEI, South Vietnam—40. Government post—35
LANSDALE, Col. Edward G.—140
LAO Theung (Laotian tribesmen)—36
LAOBAO, Laos—37
LAOS—55, 149, 152, 154-6, 158
    Allied military activity—5, 13, 21, 25-8, 30-42, 75-7, 85, 174; U.S. bombing—2, 13-4, 16-7, 21-2, 25-6, 28, 30-42, 65, 67, 76, 85-6, 151, 153; strength—85
    Civilian casualties—37; evacuation—28. Chinese troops—42, 83. Communist terrorist action—25-8, 30-4, 37-8, 41-2, 75-7, 85-6, 95
    Government forces: casualties—23, 36, 75-7, 85, 95; military action—36, 41-2, 85, 95; air force—28, 42, 86
    Invasion—25-42; foreign reaction—29-30; see also DISSENT, U.S.
    POWs—51, 57-8

Refugees—23, 28
Thailand—82-3, 95
U.S. aid—23, 117
LATIMER, George W.—201
LAU, Nguyen—232
LE, Nguyen Thanh—47-9, 51, 53, 56-7
LEDOGAR, Stephen—47, 57
LEER, Robert Van—200
LEGGETT, Rep. Robert L. (D., Calif.)—80
LEMNITZER, Gen. Lyman L.—145
LEWIS, Anthony—53
LEWIS, John Wilson—108
LI Hsien-nien—232
LICHT, Gov. Frank (D., R.I.)—106
LIENG, Tran Ngoc—213
LIFE (magazine)—27
LINSTAD, WO Roland E.—209
LITTAUER, Prof. Raphael—87-8
LOCHNINH, South Vietnam—57
LODGE, Henry Cabot—145-6
LOLO, Laos: Artillery base—35, 37
LONG Binh, South Vietnam—231
LONG Tieng, Laos—27. Government base—36, 95
LON Nol—61-2, 90, 94, 222-3
Los ANGELES Times (newspaper)—126, 148, 158
Los ANGELES Times News Service—125
LOWENSTEIN, Rep. Allard K. (D., N.Y.)—107, 188
LUANG Prabang, Laos—22, 37-8, 41
LUCE Don—225
LYTTLE, Bradford—186

M

MACALESTER College (St. Paul)—182
MADDEN, Francis Mel—193
MADDOX (U.S. destroyer)—151
MADDOX, Gov. Lester G.—183, 202
MALECH, Arnold M.—184
MANDEL, Gov. Marvin—182
MANSFIELD, Sen. Michael J. (D., Mont.)—115, 118. Laos—44-6. Pentagon papers—123, 129-31. U.S. troops—104, 106, 110-2, 117
MANSFIELD Amendment—110-2, 117
MAO Tse-tung—114, 137
MARASCO, Robert F.—208-9
MARDIAN, Robert C.—122
MARINE Corp, U.S.—158-9, 161-2
MARSHALL, Charles C.—107
MARSHALL, Justice Thurgood—131, 133
MARTIN, Maj. George E.—73
MARTIN, James—193
MARYLAND—42
MARYLAND, University of—182
MASSACHUSETTS—43, 175, 182
MASSACHUSETTS Institute of Technology—43
MASTER, Capt. Robert J.—207
MASTERS, Ann—193
MATAK, Lt. Gen. Sisowath Sirik—61-2, 79
MATHIAS, Sen. Charles McC. (D., Md.)—103-4

MATSUNAGA, Rep. Spark (D., Hawaii)—45
MAU, Sen. Vu Van—216, 222
MAYDAY Tribe (U.S. antiwar group)—2, 107, 181
MAYER, Paul—191-2
McALISTER, Elizabeth—191-2
McCARTHY, Eugene J.—44, 175
McCLELLAN, Sen. John L. (D., Ark.)—111
McCLOSKEY Jr., Rep. Paul N. (R., Calif.)—83, 107-8, 116, 123-4, 128, 178, 180, 188
McCLOSKEY, Robert J.—17
McCONE, John A.—160
McCOY, Camp (Wis.)—194
McDONALD, Joe—177
McGILL, Dr. William J.—44
McGOVERN, Sen. George S. (D., S.D.)—4, 7, 44, 46, 103-6, 115, 123, 173-4, 219
McGOVERN-Hatfield Resolution—106-8, 110
McGOWAN, Rev. Edward J.—193
McINTIRE, Rev. Carl—183
McLAUGHLIN, Rev. Neil R.—190-2
McMAHON, William—55, 223
McNAMARA, Robert S.—121, 124-5, 131, 135, 142, 144-5, 148, 151-2, 155-6, 161-5, 167-9
McNAUGHTON, John T.—150, 155-7, 162-4, 166, 168
MEADLO, Pfc. Paul D.—200
MEDEIROS, Archbishop Humberto—197
MEDINA, Capt. Ernest L.—199-202, 205-6
MELMAN, Seymour—43
MENDES-France, Pierre—138
MEO (Laotian tribe)—28, 36, 82, 95
MEREDITH, Judge James H.—126
MERWIN, Capt. Grier—207
MESELSON, Dr. Matthew S.—226
MEXICAN American Political Association—178
MICHIGAN—43
MICHIGAN, University of—42
MIKVA, Rep. Abner (D., Ill.)—177
MILLIGAN, Mike—174
MINH, Brig. Gen. Duong Van—53, 148-9, 213-4, 216, 219
MINH, Dr. Ho Van—213
MINH, Lt. Gen. Nguyen Van—60, 73, 78
MINNESOTA—182
MISSISSIPPI—202
MISSOURI—176, 203
MITCHELL, John N.—122, 190, 230. Antiwar protesters—180-1, 183-5, 193
MITCHELL, Rep. Parren J. (D., Md.)—180, 190, 207
MOCCIA, Lianne—193
MONDALE, Sen. Walter F. (D., Minn.)—7, 174
MOORER, Thomas H.—4, 22
MOORHEAD, Rep. William S. (D., Pa.)—123-4, 130
MORGAN, Rep. Thomas (D., Pa.)—45
MOSS, Sen. Frank E. (D., Utah)—201
MOSS, Rep. John E. (D., Calif.)—130, 135
MOSS, Tommy L.—206
MOUNT, Maj. Gen. Charles M.—205-6

MOVEMENT Struggling for the People's Right to Live (South Vietnam)—220
MUGIA Pass (Laotian-North Vietnamese border area)—3, 13-5, 79
MULLER, Lt. Robert O.—175
MUONG Phalane, Laos—75
MUONG Soui, Laos—22
MURPHY, C. Francis—185
MURPHY, Rev. Edward J.—193
MURPHY Rep. Morgan F. (D., Ill.)—229
MUSKIE, Sen. Edmund S. (D., Me.)—7, 20, 45, 103, 105, 107
MUSSI, Barry James—193
MYLAI Massacre—2, 199-201, 205-6

N

NAN Province, Thailand—82
NATIONAL Action Group (NAG)—181
NATIONAL Broadcasting Co. (NBC)—106. Nightly News (TV-program)—228
NATIONAL Committee for a Citizens Commission of Inquiry into U.S. War Crimes in Vietnam—207-8
NATIONAL Conference of Catholic Bishops—197
NATIONAL Convocation of Lawyers to End the War—188
NATIONAL Emergency Civil Liberties Committee—190
NATIONAL Federation of Priests' Councils—191
NATIONAL Guard—179, 182
NATIONAL League of Families of American Prisoners & Missing in Southeast Asia—51, 57
NATIONAL Liberation Front (NLF)—50, 125. See also VIET Cong
NATIONAL Peace Action Coalition (NPAC)—43, 176-8, 189
NATIONAL Progressive Force (South Vietnam)—213
NATIONAL Student Association (NSA)—43
NATIONAL Welfare Rights Organization (NWRO)—181-2
NAVY, U.S.—65, 96, 197. Drug problem—229-30. 7th Fleet—16-7, 81
NEAK Luong, Cambodia—15-6, 79
NEAK Sam, Brig. Gen.—60
NEDZI, Rep. Lucien N. (D., Mich.)—188
NELSON, Sen. Gaylord P. (D., Wash.)—123
NEW Democratic Party (Canada)—179
NEW Jersey—203
NEWMAN, Edwin—133
NEW Mexico—202
NEW Mobilization Committee to End the War in Vietnam (New Mobe)—43, 178
NEWSWEEK (magazine)—60, 125
NEW York—42, 182, 188
NEW York City Bar Association—188
NEW York Post (newspaper)—46
NEW York Times (newspaper)—10, 46, 50, 54, 76, 90, 104, 178, 187, 195, 224-5. Pentagon papers—121-2, 140-1, 145, 151, 163-5, 168, 170; court action—122-3, 125-7, 129, 131-3

NEW Zealand—115, 223
NGHEAN Province, North Vietnam—96
NGHI, Le Than—29-30
NHA, Hoang Duc—6
NHAM, Tran Tuan—217
NHAN Dan (North Vietnamese Communist party newspaper)—22, 41, 55, 233
NHU, Ngo Dinh—146-9, 214
NICHOLAOU, CWO Michael A.—209
NICHOLS, Mike—194
NILSSON, Torsten—233
NIXON, Richard M.—22, 38
　　　Air war survey—87-8. Antiwar protesters—46, 179, 186
　　　　Calley trial—203-5
　　　　Draft issue—101
　　　　Foreign policy—113-4; China visit—114-5
　　　　Military drug problem—229
　　Peace negotiations—49, 56. Pentagon papers—121-2, 129. Popularity—9. POWs—49, 57, 104-5, 109, 119
　　　　War policy: Cambodia—99, 119-20; Laos—38, 83, 99; pullout-date controversy—49, 99-100, 102, 104, 109-10, 117; troop withdrawals—38, 48, 99, 118-9; U.S. bombing—86
NOL, Lon—61-2, 90, 94, 222-3
NORTH Carolina—202
NORTHWESTERN University Law School (Ill.)—190
NOTLEY, Danny S.—175
NUREMBERG and Vietnam: An American Tragedy (book)—207

O

OHIO—43, 183
O'NEILL, Lt. John—113, 175
O'NEILL Jr., Rep. Thomas P. (D., Mass.)—45
OPERATION Dewey Canyon II—25
OPERATION Lam Son 719—25
OPERATION Lam Son 720—64, 80
OPERATION Lam Son 810—85
OPERATION Phoenix—224
OPERATION Rolling Thunder (1965)—154, 156-7, 159
OPINION Research Corp.—6
ORLANDO, Salvatore—189
O'ROURKE, Rev. Joseph—193
OUANE Rathikoune, Gen.—27

P

PAINE, Thomas—208
PAK Ou, Laos—38
PAKSE, Laos—77
PAKSONG, Laos—76, 85, 95
PAN-Asia Newspaper Alliance—27
PAO, Maj. Gen. Vang—28
PARIS Conference—30. Ceasefire proposals—49-50, 77-8. Communists—33, 47; boycott—48, 87; proposals & conditions—48, 50-5, 77-8; pullout-date—49-50; U.S.

bombing—87. POWs—47, 51, 58. Stalemate—47, 58. U.S.—53-6
PARK, Chung Hee—113
PARROT's Beak, Cambodia—72, 78
PATHET Lao (Patriotic Front of Laos, pro-Communist Laotian forces)—23, 26. Military activity—7-8, 30, 36-8, 40, 42, 95. Peace efforts & proposals—50, 75, 77-8
PAULING, Linus—44
PEACE Efforts: Ceasefires & violations—13, 15, 67, 98. China (Communist)—55. Meetings & proposed meetings—55-7. Pacifists—48. Proposals & reactions—53-6, 74-5. See also PARIS Conference
PEAGLONG, Cambodia—88
PECK, Dr. Sidney—43, 188
PENNSYLVANIA—43
PENNSYLVANIA, University of—7
PENTAGON Papers—121-71. Congress—130-1. Court action—122-3, 125-33. Declassification—134. Ellsberg—128-9. Reactions—121-4, 134-6. Secret study—121. Troop strength—144-5
PEOPLE'S Coalition for Peace & Justice—43, 177-9, 182, 186, 188-9
PEOPLE'S Coordinating Committee Against Dictatorship (South Vietnam)—221
PEOPLE'S Front Against Dictatorship (South Vietnam)—211, 222
PEOPLES Lobby—181
PEOPLE'S Self-Defense Force (South Vietnam)—224
PEOPLE'S Union of Palo Alto (Calif.)—196
PERCY, Sen. Charles (D., Ill.)—103
PERRET, WO Camille A.—209
PHALANE, Laos—22
PHILADELPHIA Resistance—43
PHILADELPHIA Yearly Meeting of the Religious Society of Friends—179
PHOENIX, Operation—224
PHONG, Maj. Gen. Tran Tranh—219
PHOUC, Tran Van—18
PHOU Pha Sai, Laos—76
PHOU So, Laos—22
PHU, Mai Van—227
PHU, Brig. Gen. Pham Van—31, 72
PHU Loc, Laos—30-2
PHULOI, South Vietnam—80
PHUOCTUY Province, South Vietnam—223
PICH Nil, Cambodia—16
PLAINE des Jarres, Laos—2, 22, 76, 82, 95
PLEIKU Province, South Vietnam—15, 156-7. U.S. airbase—66
PLIMPTON, Francis T. P.—188
PNOMPENH, Cambodia—4, 16, 18-9, 21, 59, 74. Fighting—88, 91, 93
POCHENTONG, Cambodia (international airport)—18
POLAND—30, 116
POMMERSHEIM, Frank—193
POPE Air Force Base (N.C.)—195
PORTER, William J.—55, 57-8
POTTER, Kent—27
POVEDA, Capt. Carlos A.—40
POWERS, William B.—194

PRAKHAM, Cambodia—90, 94
PRAVDA (Soviet Communist Party newspaper)—29, 98, 202
PREK Phoneu, Cambodia—18
PRESS—27, 33. Freedom of press controversy—131-3. See also specific newspapers or news service
PREY Bang, Cambodia—74
PREY Khiev, Cambodia—18
PREYVENG, Cambodia—79
PRIEST, Roger L.—195
PRISONERS of War—111-2. Camp raids—17-8. Deaths—57. Lists—47, 57. POW families—51, 57, 176. Release & negotiations—47, 49-51, 56-8. Treatment—49
PUBLIC Opinion Polls—5-6, 9, 46, 106, 203

Q

QUAKERS—177, 179. American Friends Service Committee—48, 181
QUAN Doi Nhan Dan (North Vietnamese army newspaper)—31, 40
QUANG, Lt. Gen. Dang Van—228
QUANGBINH Province, North Vietnam—96
QUANGDINH Province, North Vietnam—84
QUANGLANG, North Vietnam—96. Airfield—87
QUANGNAM Province, South Vietnam—225
QUANGNGAI Province, South Vietnam—209, 225
QUANGTIN Province, South Vietnam—80. U.S. artillery base—63
QUANGTRI Province, South Vietnam—31, 56, 69, 71, 91. Government base—35
QUINHON, South Vietnam—66

R

RADICAL Action Tribes—196
RAINWATER, Herbert B.—108, 176, 202
RAMADIER, Paul—138
RAMPTON, Gov. Calvin L.—202
RAND Corp.—128-9
RANGEL, Rep. Charles B. (D., N.Y.)—180
RARICK, Rep. John R. (D., La.)—183, 201
RATHIKOUNE, Gen. Ouane—27
RAYE, Martha—194
REAGAN, Gov. Ronald (R., Calif.)—46
RED Cross, International—51
REEDY, George E.—108
REFUGEES—23, 28, 88, 93, 106-8, 224
REID, Rep. Ogden R. (R., N.Y.)—130, 135
REILLY, Joan—193
REILLY, Rosemary—186, 193
RENMIN Ribao (Chinese Communist Party newspaper)—See JENMIN Jih Pao
REPUBLICAN Party, U.S.—45-6, 100-1, 106, 111
RESERVE Officers Training Corps, U.S. (ROTC)—43
RESOR, Stanley R.—206
RIBICOFF, Sen. Abraham A. (D., Conn.)—201
RICCI, Anita—193

RIDOLFI, Kathleen Mary—193
ROGERS, William P.—22, 108, 115, 118, 122, 217, 232. U.S. role in war—5-6, 20-1, 26-7, 97, 100, 223
ROLLING Thunder Operation (1965)—154, 156-7, 159
ROSENTHAL, Rep. Benjamin S. (D., N.Y.)—190
ROSTENKOWSKI, Rep. Dan (D., Ill.)—45
ROSTOW, Walt W.—134, 157-8, 162, 164
RUMLONG, Cambodia—90-1
RUSK, Dean: Pentagon papers—124-5, 133-4, 137, 144-5, 148, 153-4, 161, 167
RUSSO Jr., Anthony J.—128, 135
RYAN, Gen. John D.—227

S

SACRED Heart of Mary (religious order)—191
SAIGON, South Vietnam—86, 211, 220
SAIGON Military Mission (SMM)—140-1
St. JOSEPH Pro-Cathedral (N.J.)—193
St. LOUIS Post-Dispatch (newspaper)—126, 128, 131, 165
SAMDECH Yos, Cambodia: Government airfield—59
SAM Thong, Laos—27-8, 36
SARAGANE, Laos—95
SATO, Eisaku—116
SAYABOURY Province, Laos—82-3
SAXBE, Sen. William B. (R., O.)—7, 101, 104, 106
SCANDINAVIAN Airlines System (SAS)—56
SCHMITZ, Rep. John (R., Calif.)—116, 183
SCHUMAN, Marjorie A.—191-2
SCHWEIKER, Sen. Richard S. (D., Pa.)—103
SCHWERTMAN, Lt. (jg) James—207
SCOBLICK, Anthony—190-2
SCOBLICK, Mary Cain—192
SCOTT, Sen. Hugh (R., Pa.)—9, 22, 100, 102-3, 123, 131, 203
SEABORN, J. Blair—152
SEAMAN, Lt. Gen. Jonathan O.—206, 208
SEAMANS Jr., Robert C.—95
SEEGER, Pete—177
SELECTIVE Service System, U.S.—110, 129-30, 192-3; see also 'Draft' under ARMY, U.S., and 'Draft resistance' under DISSENT, U.S.
SENATE, U.S.—See 'Congress' under UNITED States
SEXTON, S. Sgt. John C.—57
SEYMOUR Jr., Whitney N.—127
SHAFFER, Gene—183
SHALLCROSS, Lt. Edward—207
SHARP, Adm. U.S. Grant—153, 164, 168
SHEARES, Dr. Benjamin—113
SHEHAN, Lawrence Cardinal—191
SHEMELEY, Martha—193
SHIMANOTO, Keisaburo—27
SIAM, Gulf of—16-7
SIGLER, Richard—176

SIHANOUK, Prince Norodom (Cambodia)—50, 75
SINAY, Lynda R.—129, 135
SISSOUK Na Champassak—22, 77, 95
SKELLY, Lt. James—207
SMITH, Howard K.—38
SMITH, Brig. Gen. Jacob H.—209
SMITH, Sen. Margaret Chase (R., Me.)—135-6
SMITH, Walter Bedell—138-9
SNOUL, Cambodia—73, 76
SO, Mai Van—232
SOCTRANG, South Vietnam: U.S. airbase—66
SON, Sen. Hong—213
SO Satto, Col.—93
SOUK Vongasak, Prince (Laos)—75
SOUPHANOUVONG, Prince (Laos)—30, 75, 77-8
SOUTH Carolina—203
SOUTHEAST Asia Treaty Organization (SEATO)—143
SOUTHERN Christian Leadership Conference—177, 181-2
SOUVANNA Phouma, Prince (Laos)—22-3, 26, 29, 75, 77-8, 152-3
SPOCK, Dr. Benjamin—179
SPONG Jr., Sen. William B. (D., Va.)—111
SRANG, Cambodia—74
STANFORD University—42
STEELE, Rep. Robert H. (R., Conn.)—227-9
STENNIS, Sen. John C. (D., Miss.)—20, 27, 111
STEVENS, Sen. Ted (D., Alaska)—103, 111
STEVENSON III, Sen. Adlai E. (D., Ill.)—203, 219
STEWART, Justice Potter—131-2
STEWART, Judge William—174
STUDENT & Youth Conference on a People's Peace—43
STUDENTS for a Democratic Society (SDS)—177
STUNG Chhay Pass, Cambodia—16
SULLIVAN, William II.—108
SULLY, Francois—60
SULZBERGER, C. L.—10
SUSSKIND, David—175
SUTHERLAND, Donald—194, 196
SVAYRIENG, Cambodia—79
SWAMP Dogg—194
SWEDEN—49, 56, 195-6, 233
SWINGLISH, John—193
SYMINGTON, Sen. Stuart (D, Mo.)—27, 76-7, 83, 117, 122

T

TAFT Jr., Sen. Robert (R., O.)—100-1, 106
TALMADGE, Sen. Herman E. (D., Ga.)—111, 201
TAM, Brig. Gen. In—62
TANG Krasang, Cambodia—93
TAPIA, Abe—178
TARR, Curtis W.—181-2, 186
TASS (Soviet news agency)—22, 29, 84, 97

TAYLOR, Gen. Maxwell D.: Pentagon papers—124, 142–6, 148–51, 153–7, 159, 162
TAYLOR, Telford—207
TCHEPONE, Laos—32, 35, 37
TEAMSTERS, Chauffeurs, Warehousemen & Helpers of America, International Brotherhood of—43
TENNESSEE—202–3
TEPAVAC, Mirko—233
TET Offensive—131, 168
TEXAS—202–3
THAI, Vu Van—135
THAILAND—4, 22, 36, 82–3, 95, 115
THANG, Ton Duc—233
THANT, U—56, 79
THAO, Duong Dinh—55, 195
THI, Dinh Ba—57
THIEU, Nguyen Van—6, 64, 116, 118, 149, 202. Economy—223–4. Elections—2, 211–7, 220–2; dissention—213, 216–21; laws—212–3. Laos—26, 32, 41
THO, Le Duc—52–3
THOMPSON, Spc. 4 Charles R.—209
THOMPSON, Spec. 4 Randy—40
THU, Le Van—227
THUY, Xuan—6. Peace talks—47, 55, 58; proposals & conditions—48–50
TIMES (London newspaper)—227
TONKIN, Gulf of—121, 124, 129–30, 151, 153, 155. Resolution—189
TOSI, Sarah Jane—193
TOWER, Sen. John G. (R., Tex.)—116, 124
TRANH, Nguyen Van—58
TRAVERS Jr., Herbert F.—126
TRI, Lt. Gen. Do Cao—18, 60
TRINH, Nguyen Duy—233
TRUMAN, Harry S.—136–8
TRUONG, Maj. Gen. Ngo Quang—69
TRUONG Khanh, South Vietnam—175
TUCKNER, Howard—27
TUOL Leap, Cambodia—91
TURRENTINE, Judge Howard B.—196
TUYHOA, South Vietnam: Government base—15

U

U MINH Forest, South Vietnam—69, 78, 86
UNION of Soviet Socialist Republics (USSR)—22, 29, 55–6, 59, 97–8, 116, 137
UNIONS—See specific union
UNITED Automobile Workers (UAW)—43
UNITED Press International (UPI)—125
UNITED States:
Aerial Warfare, Air Force, Army—See under 'A.' Agency for International Development (AID)—23
Bureau of Narcotics & Dangerous Drugs—227
Cambodia—5, 13, 15–9, 59–61, 78–9, 87–8, 90. China visit & developments—114–7. Congress—20, 23, 26–7, 77, 83, 106, 108–9, 118, 123, 130, 136, 173–5, 178, 228–9; Calley trial—201; dissent & controversy—1, 7–9, 11, 19–21, 26–7, 44, 76–7, 83, 97, 101–12, 117–8, 207–8, 219; draft—101, 109, 112;

military drug problem—228–31 (see also DRUG Problem under 'D'); 'Pentagon papers'—123, 130–1
Defense Department—14, 17, 19, 32–3, 35–6, 39, 97, 121, 195, 226; 'Pentagon papers'—see under 'P'; troop withdrawals—see below; see also AIR Force and ARMY under 'A,' NATIONAL Guard and NAVY under 'N.' Dissent—See under 'D'
Foreign aid—118
Justice Department—121–3, 125–7, 135, 174, 177, 180–1, 183, 192, 200
Laos—2, 5, 13–8, 21–3, 27–9, 32–3, 35–6, 38–9, 42, 77, 83, 85–7
Marine Corps—See MARINE Corps.
National Guard—See under 'N.' National Security Council, U.S.—137, 139–41, 143–5, 148, 151–2, 156. Navy—See under 'N'
Peace efforts—See PARIS Conference and PEACE Efforts under 'P.' 'Pentagon papers' and Prisoners—See under 'P'
Refugees—See under 'R'
Selective Service System—110, 129–30, 192–3; see also Draft under ARMY, U.S.; and 'Draft resistance' under DISSENT, U.S. South Vietnam—See VIETNAM, South. State Department—17, 26, 29, 38, 82, 95, 118, 121, 134, 136–7, 139, 147–9, 160–1. Supreme Court—127–8, 131–3, 174, 189; other courts—127, 133, 185–6, 190
Troop withdrawals—1, 3, 16, 48, 66–7, 99, 113, 118–9
War crimes investigations—199–201, 203–9; see also WAR Crimes & Atrocities
UNIVERSITIES—See specific name(s)
UPTON, John—176

V

VANIK, Rep. Charles A. (D., O.)—174
VANN, John Paul—225, 228
VASQUEZ, S. Sgt. Dennis R.—200
VAUGHAN, Lt. Samuel R.—96
VEQUIST, 1st Lt. John R.—195–6
VETERANS of Foreign Wars (VFW)—108, 175, 183, 202
VIEN, Gen. Can Van—218
VIET Cong—116, 142, 195
Military activity: Cambodia—15–8, 21–3, 36, 59–61, 72–4, 78–9, 88, 90–1, 94; casualties—2, 13, 15–6, 18, 21, 28, 32, 34, 37, 40, 59–60, 63–4, 67–8, 70, 73, 78–9, 81–2, 84, 86, 90–1, 94–5; ceasefires—see under PEACE Efforts; prisoners held by South Vietnam—80
Foreign relations—233; Laos—27–8, 36–8, 41–2; South Vietnam—35, 37, 63–71, 80, 84, 86, 91–2, 156, 159, 225
National Liberation Front (NLF)—50, 125
Peace negotiations & proposals—51–3, 56–7. POW release—47–8, 57. Provisional Revolutionary Government (PRG)—233
VIET Minh—55

VIETNAM (North), People's Republic of:
Civilian casualties—62, 87
Military forces activities: Air force—
95-6. Cambodia—15-8, 59-61, 72-4, 78, 88-
94; casualties—2, 13, 15-6, 18, 23, 25, 28,
59-61, 63-4, 66-8, 70-3, 76-9, 81-2, 84-6,
88-92, 94-5; ceasefires—see under PEACE
Efforts; Communist Chinese aid—232; elections—233; Laos—21-3, 27-9, 33-8, 41-2,
75-7, 85-6, 95; 9th Division—59, 94
Peace negotiations—56-7; POW release—50-1, 58
South Vietnam—35, 37, 63-71, 80-2,
84, 86, 91-2
Troop strength—62, 80, 89, 91, 96, 225
U.S. bombing raids—13-5, 39, 58, 62,
65, 67-8, 79, 81, 83-4, 86-7, 96-7, 131, 154-
6, 160, 164
VIETNAM (South), Republic of—55, 113
Amnesty—232. Assassinations—222
Cambodian relations—94. Civilian casualties—15, 63, 66-7, 69-70, 84, 89; atrocities—199-201. Communist terrorist
activity—15, 64, 67, 84, 86, 222
Defoliation—226. Domestic & political
developments: arrests—213, 216-7; Congress—215, 217, 219; demonstrations—213,
216-7, 219-21; elections—2, 211-7, 220-2;
laws—212-3; military opposition—218-9;
pacification program—224-5
Military forces & actions: atrocities—
61; casualties—2, 13, 15, 25-6, 28, 30-5, 37,
39-41, 59-74, 78, 80-2, 84, 86, 89, 91-2, 94;
Cambodia—5, 13, 15-6, 21, 59-74, 78, 88-9,
91-4; Laos—5, 13, 21-2, 25-8, 30-1, 33-4,
37-9, 42, 85; troop strength—31, 35-6, 40,
60, 85, 92; marines—21, 39-40, 65, 68, 70;
1st Infantry Division—31, 34, 65, 72; 5th Division—73-4
POWs—17-8, 57-8
Refugees—88, 224
Supreme Court—212, 215
U.S. troops: drug problem—227-31;
strength—106, 119, 158 63, 165; with-
drawals—1, 3, 16, 48, 66-7, 80, 99, 113, 118-
9, 223
VIETNAM Veterans Against the War—88,
107, 113, 173, 175-6, 208
VIETNAM Veterans For a Just Peace—175
VIHEAR Suor, Cambodia—74, 94
VINHBINH Province, South Vietnam—212,
225
VINHLONG Province, South Vietnam—225
VINSON, Mrs. Joan—51
VOGT Jr., Lt. Gen. John W.—32-3, 35
VONGSAK, Souk—23

W

WALD, George—43
WALLACE, Gov. George C.—183, 202

WALTER Reed Hospital (Washington,
D.C.)—199
WALTERS, Barbara—133
WAR Crimes & Atrocities: Cambodia—61,
79. Mylai massacre—2, 199-201, 205-6.
Trials & convictions—199-201, 203-9;
domestic & foreign reactions—201-2.
Veterans' testimony—174-5
WAR Resisters League—181
WARNKE, Paul C.—9, 169
WASHINGTON, University of (Seattle)—42
WASHINGTON Post (newspaper)—6, 82-3,
137-40, 143, 146, 148, 167-8, 207. Court
action—125, 127-8, 131-3
WATKE, Maj. Frederic W.—206
WEATHER Underground—46
WEICKER Jr., Sen. Lowell P. (R., Conn.)—
100-1, 103
WEINSTEIN, Judge Jack B.—195
WELLS, Lt. Kenneth R.—96
WENDEROTH, Rev. Joseph R.—190-2
WEST Germany—115, 117, 195
WESTMORELAND, Gen. William—162-4,
168, 170-1, 202, 207
WEST Point (N.Y.) Military Academy—194
WHALEN Jr., Rep. Charles W. (R., Ohio)—
117
WHEELER, Gen. Earle—155, 163-4, 169, 171
WHITCOMB, Gov. Edgar D.—202
WHITE, Justice Byron R.—131-2
WHITLAM, Gough—55
WILEY, George—177, 182
WILLIAMS, Hosea—182
WILLIAMSON, Robert W.—193
WILSON, Harold—160-1
WILSON, Jerry V.—176, 179, 181
WISCONSIN—188-9
WISCONSIN, University of—42, 182
WOODCOCK, Leonard—43
WOOLDRIDGE, William O.—232
WONDOLOWSKI, Col. Peter S.—206
WORKERS (Communist) Party (North
Vietnam)—233
WRIGHT, Judge J. Skelly—127
WURTZEL, Capt. Franklin R.—206
WYZANSKI Jr., Charles E.—189-90

Y

YEH Chien-ying—232
YEW, Lee Kuan—113
YUGOSLAVIA—116, 233
YOST, Charles W.—108
YOUNG Jr., Brig. Gen. George H.—206

Z

ZIEGLER, Ronald L.—32, 45, 57, 87, 115,
118, 188, 201. 'Pentagon papers'—121, 129.
Troop withdrawals—100, 102, 110-1, 117
ZION, Sidney—128
ZUMWALT, Adm. Elmo R.—207, 230